DRAMATISTS SOURCEBOOK

2000–2001 EDITION

D1557541

DRAMATISTS SOURCEBOOK

2000–2001 EDITION

Complete opportunities for playwrights, translators, composers, lyricists and librettists

EDITED BY
Kathy Sova
Samantha R. Healy
Jennifer Sokolov

THEATRE COMMUNICATIONS GROUP NEW YORK

Published by Theatre Communications Group, Inc.
355 Lexington Ave., New York, NY 10017-6603.

This publication is made possible in part with public funds from the New York
State Council on the Arts, a State Agency.

TCG books are exclusively distributed to the book trade by Consortium Book Sales
and Distribution, 1045 Westgate Dr., St. Paul, MN 55114.

Manufactured in the United States of America

ISSN 0733-1606
ISBN 1-55936-191-3

CONTENTS

PREFACE

We at TCG are proud to publish our 20th edition of the *Dramatists Sourcebook*.

We are happy you have decided to buy the latest edition of the *Sourcebook*, because every year nearly 75% of its content is revised. We contact each listing, and most organizations make changes—a new contact name, a new mailing or email address, the cancellation or postponement of a program, new guidelines, etc. If a listing's organization doesn't respond (and numerous attempts are made to contact each one), we do not include them. We can safely say that at press time all the listings included here are in existence and that the information is correct.

New and improved. Our Online Resources chapter has been greatly revised. It now lists reference materials and serves as a basic theatre, culture and production/publication resource for playwrights. Please check it out.

Using the *Sourcebook*. Select those listings your work is best suited for and follow the guidelines meticulously. The Special Interests Index is helpful in finding those listings that may be suited to your type of work. When instructed to write for guidelines, do so. This is a good idea in general as sometimes dates and guidelines change after the *Sourcebook* is published. Most important is to ALWAYS ENCLOSE AN SASE with every mailed script if you'd like it returned (unless the entry specifies that scripts will not be returned). If a listing says it accepts scripts, it is always assumed that an SASE must be sent along for return; we do not restate this for every listing. Also, always assume the deadline dates in this book refer to the day materials should arrive, not the postmark date.

Study Tony Kushner's "A Simple Working Guide for Playwrights" (page xi, the Prologue). It's filled with great advice.

You should know that throughout this book, "full-length play" means just that—a full-length, original work for adult audiences, without a score or libretto. One-acts, musicals, adaptations, translations, plays for young audiences, solo pieces, performance art and screenplays are listed separately. "Young audiences" refers to audiences age 18 or younger, "young playwrights" refers to playwrights age 18 or younger, "students" refers to college students or students in an affiliated writing program.

Entries are alphabetized by first word (excluding "the") even if they start with a proper name. So, for example, "Mark Taper Forum" is listed under "M." In the index, you will also find this theatre cross-listed under "T." We also use a word-by-word alphabetizing style, which would place an organization, such as "A. D. Players" before "Academy Theatre." Regardless of the way "theatre" is spelled in an organization's name, we alphabetize it as if it were spelled "re," not "er."

We want to improve the *Sourcebook*. And we rely on your feedback. Because of previous comments we have weeded out some listings that weren't serving you properly, and corrected others to reflect their policies more accurately. So, let us know how we can serve you better. Write/email: ksova@tcg.org; Kathy Sova, *Dramatists Sourcebook* Editor, TCG, 355 Lexington Ave, New York, NY 10017-6603.

I want to thank my excellent coeditors: Samantha R. Healy and Jennifer Sokolov, who, with devotion and good cheer, worked incredibly hard to pursue and edit the listings; Samantha really pulled the whole effort together, and I am grateful. Jennifer, our resident Web site editor at TCG, spent many months researching and rewriting the Online Resources chapter. It is now a really useful and dynamic section of the book. Thanks to Hillary Jackson—she contacted many of the listings in this book, maintained a flawless database and helped prepare the galleys, always happily. Wendy Weiner, an excellent editor, and once coeditor of *Dramatists Sourcebook*, came back this year to proof the volume, and really did a fantastic job of styling the book into shape. Thanks to Kitty Suen, for her beautiful redesign of the *Sourcebook*, and to Warren Nichols, our resident MIS director, who unchained the book from its DOS platform—with wonderful charm he dropped everything to solve glitch after glitch. Without him the upgrade would have been impossible. Putting this book together is a year-long project combining the Herculean effort of these many fine people, and I owe them all an immeasurable amount of thanks.

Most importantly, I thank you, our readers, for putting your trust in the *Sourcebook*. We have done our very best work for you and hope the *Sourcebook* helps you through *your* Herculean efforts. We wish you all good things. I am also grateful to our listing organizations for their willingness to update their information every year. We thank all of you for your patience this year, and for your commitment in the past. Our goal is to help bring you two together—the playwright and the facilitator—and we hope we've helped do just that.

Kathy Sova
July 2000

PROLOGUE

A Simple Working Guide for Playwrights
by Tony Kushner

A) Format: Most playwrights use a format in which character headings are placed centered above the line and capitalized:

LIONEL

I don't possess a mansion, a car, or a string of polo ponies...

Lines should be single-spaced. Stage directions should be indented and single-spaced. If a character's line is interrupted at the end of the page, its continuance on the following page should be marked as such:

LIONEL (CONT'D)

or a string of polo ponies...

There are denser, and thus more economical, formats; since Xeroxing is expensive, and heavy scripts cost more to ship, you may be tempted to use these, but a generously spaced format is much easier to read, and in these matters it doesn't pay to be parsimonious.

B) Typing and reproducing: Scripts should be typed neatly and reproduced clearly. Remember that everyone who reads your script will be reading many others additionally, and it will work to your serious disadvantage if the copy's sloppy, faded, or otherwise unappealing. If you use a computer printer, eschew old-fashioned dot-matrix and other robotic kinds of print.

Also, I think it's best to avoid using incredibly fancy word-processing printing programs with eight different typefaces and decorative borders. Simple typescript, carefully done, is best. Check for typos. A playwright's punctuation may be idiosyncratic for purposes of expressiveness, but not too idiosyncratic, and spelling should be correct.

C) Sending the script:

1) The script should have a title page with the title, your name, address and phone number, or that of your agent or representative. Scripts are now automatically copyrighted at the moment of creation, but simply writing © and the date on the title page can serve as a kind of scarecrow for thievish magpies.

2) Never, never send an unbound script. Loose pages held together by a rubber band don't qualify as bound, nor do pages clamped together with a mega-paperclip. A heavy paper cover will protect the script as it passes from hand to hand.

3) Always, always enclose a self-addressed stamped envelope (SASE) or you will never see your script again. You may enclose a note telling the theatre to dispose of the copy instead of returning it; but you must have the ultimate fate of the script planned for in the eventuality of its not being selected for production. Don't leave this up to the theatre! If you want receipt of the script acknowledged, include a self-addressed, stamped postcard (SASP).

D) Letter of inquiry and synopsis: If a theatre states, in its entry in the *Sourcebook*, that it does not accept unsolicited scripts, believe it. Don't call and ask if there are exceptions; there aren't. A well-written and concise letter of inquiry, however, accompanied by a synopsis possessed of similar virtues can get you an invitation to submit your play. It's prudent, then, to spend time on both letter and synopsis. It is, admittedly, very hard for a writer to sum up his or her work in less than a page, but this kind of boiling-down can be of value beyond its necessity as a tool for marketing; use it to help clarify for yourself what's central and essential about your play. A good synopsis should briefly summarize the basic features of the plot without going into excessive detail; it should evoke both the style and the thematic substance of the play without recourse to clichéd description ("This play is about what happens when people lose their dreams..."); and it should convey essential information, such as cast size, gender breakdown, period, location, or anything else a literary manager deciding whether to send for the play might want to know. Make reference to other productions in your letter, but don't send thick packets of reviews and photos. And don't offer your opinion of the play's worth, which will be inferred as being positive from the fact that you are its parent.

E) Waiting: Theatres almost always take a long time to respond to playwrights about a specific play, frequently far in excess of the time given in their listings in the *Sourcebook*. This is due neither to spite nor indolence. Literary departments are usually understaffed and their workload is fearsome. Then, too, the process of selection invariably involves a host of people and considerations of all kinds. In my opinion you do yourself no good by repeatedly calling after the status of your script; you will become identified as a pest. It's terribly expensive to copy and mail scripts, but you must be prepared to shoulder the expense and keep making copies if they don't get returned. If, after a certain length of time past the deadline, you haven't heard from a theatre, send a letter inquiring politely about the play, reminding the appropriate people that you'd sent an SASE with the script; and then forget about it. In most cases, you will get a response and the script returned eventually.

One way to cut down on the expenses involved is to be selective about venues for submission. Reading *Sourcebook* entries and scrutinizing a copy of *Theatre Profiles* (see Useful Publications) will help you select the theatres most compatible with your work. If you've written a musical celebration of the life of Phyllis Schlafly, for example, you won't want to send it to theatres with an interest in radical feminist dramas. Or you won't necessarily want to send your play about the history of Western imperialism to a theatre that produces an annual season of musical comedy.

F) Produce yourself! In *Endgame*, Clov asks Hamm, "Do you believe in the life to come?" and Hamm responds, "Mine was always that." The condition of endless deferment is one that modern American playwrights share with Beckett's characters and other denizens of the postmodern world. Don't

PROLOGUE

spend your life waiting. You may not be an actor, but that doesn't mean that action is forbidden you. Playwrights can, with very little expense, mount readings of their work; they can band together with other playwrights for readings and discussions; and they can, if they want to, produce their work themselves. Growth as a writer for the stage depends on seeing your work on stage, and if no one else will put it there, the job is up to you. At the very least, and above all else, while waiting, waiting, waiting for responses and offers, keep reading, thinking and writing.

Tony Kushner's plays include *A Bright Room Called Day*, *Angels in America* (Parts One and Two) and *Slavs!*; as well as adaptations of Corneille's *The Illusion*, Ansky's *The Dybbuk*, Brecht's *The Good Person of Szechuan* and Goethe's *Stella*. Current projects include two plays: *Homebody/Kabul* and *Henry Box Brown or The Mirror of Slavery*, and two musical plays: *St. Cecilia or The Power of Music* and *Caroline or Change*. He is collaborating with Maurice Sendak on an American version of the children's opera, *Brundibar*. Mr. Kushner has been awarded a Pulitzer Prize for Drama, two Tony Awards, the Evening Standard Award, an OBIE, the New York Drama Critics Circle Award, an American Academy of Arts and Letters Award, and a Whiting Writers Fellowship, among other awards; recently he received a Lila Wallace/Reader's Digest Fellowship and a medal for Cultural Achievement from the National Foundation for Jewish Culture. He grew up in Lake Charles, Louisiana, and he lives in New York.

PART ONE
SCRIPT OPPORTUNITIES

Production

Prizes

Publication

Development

PRODUCTION

What theatres are included in this section?

The overwhelming majority of the not-for-profit professional theatres throughout the United States is represented here. In order to be included, a theatre must meet professional standards of staffing, programming and budget; most have been operating for at least two years. Commercial and amateur producers are not included.

How should I go about deciding where to submit my play?

Don't send it out indiscriminately. Take time to study the listings and select those theatres most likely to be receptive to your material. Find out all you can about each of the theatres you select. Visit the theatre's Web site. Read *American Theatre* to see what plays the theatres are currently presenting and what their other activities are (see Useful Publications for more information). Whenever possible, go to see the theatre's work.

When I submit my play, what can I do to maximize its chances?

First, read carefully the Simple Working Guide for Playwrights in the Prologue of this *Sourcebook* for good advice on script submission. Then follow each theatre's guidelines meticulously. Pay particular attention to the Special Interests section: If a theatre specifies "gay and lesbian themes only," do not send them your heterosexual romantic comedy, however witty and well written it is. Also, bear in mind the following points about the various submission procedures:

1) "Accepts unsolicited scripts": Don't waste the theatre's time and yours by writing to ask permission to submit your play—just send it. If you want an acknowledgment of receipt, say so and enclose a self-addressed stamped postcard (SASP) for this purpose. **Always enclose a self-addressed stamped envelope (SASE) for the return of a script.**

2) "Synopsis and letter of inquiry": Never send an unsolicited script to these theatres. Prepare a clear, cogent and *brief* synopsis of your play and send it along with any other materials requested in the listing. The letter of inquiry is a cover note asking for permission to submit the script; if there is something about your play or about yourself as a writer that you think may spark the theatre's interest, by all means mention it, but keep the letter brief. We've asked theatres requiring letters and synopses to give us two response times—one for letters and one for scripts should they ask to see one. All response times are approximate, and theatres may take longer to respond than stated. Always enclose an SASP for the theatre's response, unless the theatre specifies that it only responds if it wants to see the script.

3) "Professional recommendation": Send a script (not a letter of inquiry) accompanied by a letter of recommendation from a theatre professional. Wait until you can obtain such a letter before approaching these theatres.

4) "Agent submission": If you do not have an agent yet, do not submit to these theatres. Wait until you have had a production or two and have acquired a representative who can submit your script for you.

5) "Direct solicitation to playwright or agent": Do not submit to these theatres. If they are interested in your work you will hear from them.

6) Do not email your submissions. Email and Web addresses are included for the purpose of general inquiries and, in some cases where stated, to obtain guidelines or applications. Perhaps in the future, producing organizations may open up their email channels to accept brief synopsis submissions, but for now there are very few willing to do so. Respect their submission procedures.

A CONTEMPORARY THEATRE

(Founded 1965)

The Eagles Building, 700 Union St; Seattle, WA 98101–2330;
   (206) 292–7660, FAX 292–7670;
   Web site http://www.acttheatre.org

Gordon Edelstein, *Artistic Director*

Submission procedure: no unsolicited scripts; direct solicitation to playwright or agent; will accept synopsis, 10-page dialogue sample and letter of inquiry from Northwest playwrights only. **Types of material:** full-length plays, translations, adaptations, musicals, solo pieces. **Special interests:** current social, political and psychological issues; plays theatrical in imagination, and storytelling; multicultural themes; not keen on kitchen-sink realism or message plays. **Facilities:** 390 seats, thrust stage; 390 seats, arena stage; 150 seats, cabaret. **Best submission time:** Sep-Apr. **Response time:** 4-6 months letter; 6-12 months script. **Special programs:** new play development workshops. FirstACT: play commissions and workshops. ACT/Hedgebrook Women Playwrights Festival (see Development).

A. D. PLAYERS

(Founded 1967)

2710 West Alabama St; Houston, TX 77098; (713) 526–2721,
   FAX 439–0905; email adplayers@hern.org

Literary Manager

Submission procedure: accepts unsolicited scripts. **Types of material:** full-length plays, one-acts, adaptations, plays for young audiences, musicals. **Special interests:** plays for students pre-kindergarten–grade 6; "plays that uphold family values and support moral decisions that allow for growth of individuals with themselves, others and God"; children's plays which allow for audience participation and have strong role models; no plays about "witchcraft, demons or ghosts." **Facilities:** Grace Theater, 220 seats, proscenium stage; Rotunda Theater, 148 seats, arena stage. **Production considerations:** for Grace Theater: cast limit of 12, prefers less than 10; no more than 2 sets, maximum height 11' 6"; no fly space; minimal lighting. For Rotunda Theater: cast limit of 6; minimal scenery; no wing space; shows no longer than one hour; prefers musicals. **Best submission time:** year-round. **Response time:** 6-10 months. **Special programs:** Theater Arts Academy: includes playwriting classes.

A NOISE WITHIN

(Founded 1991)
3603 Seneca Ave; Los Angeles, CA 90039; (323) 953-7787,
FAX 953-7794
Art Manke, *Artistic Co-Director*
Submission procedure: accepts unsolicited scripts. **Types of material:** translations, adaptations. **Special interests:** translations and adaptations of classical material only. **Facilities:** A Noise Within, 200-300 seats, thrust stage. **Best submission time:** fall. **Response time:** 6-8 months.

ABOUT FACE THEATRE

(Founded 1995)
3212 North Broadway; Chicago, IL 60657; (773) 549-7943,
FAX 935-4483; email faceline1@aol.com;
Web site http://www.aboutface.base.org
Carl Hippensteel, *Literary Manager*
Submission procedure: no unsolicited scripts; synopsis, first 10 pages of script, cast list, resume and letter of inquiry. **Types of material:** full-length plays, one-acts, adaptations, musicals, performance art. **Special interests:** "queer" plays only; prefers lesbian plays; material that challenges moral expectations and ideas about gender and sexuality in historical or contemporary contexts; imaginative scripts of literary caliber that break traditional ideas about dramatic form, structure, presentation and characters. **Facilities:** About Face Theatre, 99 seats, flexible thrust stage. **Production considerations:** no fly space; limited backstage space. **Best submission time:** year-round. **Response time:** 3 months letter; 6 months script. **Special programs:** Face to Face Workshop Series: readings, rough stagings and audience response.

THE ACTING COMPANY

(Founded 1972)
Box 898, Times Square Station; New York, NY 10108;
(212) 944–5517, FAX 944–5524;
email mail@theactingcompany.org;
Web site http://www.theactingcompany.org
Margot Harley, *Producing Director*
Richard Corley, *Associate Producing Director*

Submission procedure: no unsolicited scripts; professional recommendation. **Types of material:** full-length plays, one-acts, translations, adaptations, musicals. **Special interests:** mainly classical repertory but occasionally produces new works suited to acting ensemble of approximately 8 men, 3 women, age range 24–45; prefers works with poetic dimension and heightened language. **Facilities:** no permanent facility; touring company which plays in New York City for 1 or 2 weeks a year. **Production considerations:** productions tour in repertory; simple, transportable proscenium-stage set. **Best submission time:** Nov–Jan. **Response time:** 3 months.

ACTORS & PLAYWRIGHTS' INITIATIVE

(Founded 1989)
359 South Burdick St, Suite 205; The Epic Center;
Kalamazoo, MI 49007; (616) 343–8310, FAX 343–8450
Robert C. Walker, *Artistic Director*

Submission procedure: no unsolicited scripts; professional recommendation. **Types of material:** full-length plays, one-acts, translations, adaptations, plays for young audiences, musicals, solo pieces. **Special interests:** aggressive and provocative social-political plays; plays that explore heterosexual, gay and bisexual relationships. **Facilities:** API Theatre at the Epic Center, 120 seats, black box. **Production considerations:** cast limit of 10; minimal set, costumes, props; minimal fly space. **Best submission time:** Oct–Feb. **Response time:** 6 months. **Special programs:** Firstage Script Development Reader's Theatre: developmental year-round reading series.

ACTOR'S EXPRESS

(Founded 1988)
King Plow Arts Center, J-107; 887 West Marietta St NW;
Atlanta, GA 30318; (404) 875-1606, FAX 875-2791;
email actorsexpress@mindspring.com
Literary Manager
Submission procedure: no unsolicited scripts; 10-page dialogue sample, character breakdown, professional recommendation and letter of inquiry. **Types of material:** full-length plays, translations, adaptations, musicals. **Special interests:** new musicals; socially relevant material; minority and gay themes; works with poetic dimension. **Facilities:** Actor's Express, 150 seats, black box. **Production considerations:** modest production demands; no fly space. **Best submission time:** Nov–Jan. **Response time:** 6 weeks letter; 4-6 months script.

ACTORS' GANG THEATER

(Founded 1981)
6201 Santa Monica Blvd; Hollywood, CA 90038; (323) 465-0566,
FAX 467-1246; email actorsgng1@aol.com
Chris Wells, *Literary Manager*
Submission procedure: no unsolicited scripts; professional recommendation. **Types of material:** full-length plays, plays for young audiences. **Special interests:** highly theatrical political or avant-garde works. **Facilities:** Actors' Gang Theater, 99 seats, flexible stage; Actors' Gang El Centro, 40 seats, flexible stage. **Best submission time:** year-round. **Response time:** 2 months.

ACTORS' GUILD OF LEXINGTON

(Founded 1984)
139 West Short St; Lexington, KY 40507; (859) 233-7330,
FAX 233-3773; email agl@lex.infi.net;
Web site http://www.actorsguildoflexington.org
Deb Shoss, *Producing Director*
Submission procedure: no unsolicited scripts; synopsis and letter of inquiry; prefers email submission. **Types of material:** full-length plays, solo pieces. **Facilities:** Main Stage, 99-120 seats, proscenium stage. **Production considerations:** cast limit of 8; no wing or fly space; prefers single set. **Best submission time:** year-round. **Response time:** 1 month letter; 2-3 months script.

ACTORS' THEATRE
(Founded 1983)
Box 780; Talent, OR 97540; (541) 535-5250; email alzado47@aol.com
Peter Alzado, *Artistic Director*
Submission procedure: no unsolicited scripts; synopsis, dialogue sample and letter of inquiry. **Types of material:** full-length plays, one-acts, translations, adaptations. **Facilities:** Actors' Theatre, 108 seats, thrust stage. **Best submission time:** year-round. **Response time:** 3 months letter; 4 months script.

ACTORS THEATRE OF LOUISVILLE
(Founded 1964)
316 West Main St; Louisville, KY 40202-4218; (502) 584-1265,
    FAX 561-3300
Michael Bigelow Dixon, *Literary Manager*
Amy Wegener, *Assistant Literary Manager*
Submission procedure: direct solicitation to playwright or agent; for Humana Festival (see below): no unsolicited scripts; accepts synopsis and dialogue sample (but prefers professional recommendation or agent submission). **Types of material:** full-length plays, one-acts, translations, adaptations, solo pieces. **Special interests:** plays of ideas; language-oriented plays; plays with passion, humor and experimentation. **Facilities:** Pamela Brown Auditorium, 637 seats, thrust stage; Bingham Theatre, 320 seats, arena stage; Victor Jory Theatre, 159 seats, thrust stage. **Best submission time:** year-round. **Response time:** 6-9 months (most scripts returned in fall). **Special programs:** National Ten-Minute Play Contest (see Prizes); Humana Festival of New American Plays: annual presentation of new work in rotating rep; *deadline:* ongoing; *notification:* fall 2000; *dates:* Feb-Mar 2001.

ADOBE THEATRE COMPANY
(Founded 1991)
453 West 16th St; New York, NY 10011; (212) 352-0441,
    FAX 352-0441 (call first); Web site http://www.adobe.org
Jordan Schildcrout, *Literary Manager*
Submission procedure: no unsolicited scripts; synopsis, dialogue sample and letter of inquiry. **Types of material:** full-length plays, one-acts, adaptations. **Special interests:** comedies that subvert conventional theatrical form and genre. **Facilities:** Ohio Theatre, 75 seats, flexible stage. **Production considerations:** prefers large cast and characters in their thirties. **Best submission time:** year-round. **Response time:** 2 months letter; 4 months script.

ALABAMA SHAKESPEARE FESTIVAL
(Founded 1972)
1 Festival Dr; Montgomery, AL 36117–4605; (334) 271–5300
Kent Thompson, *Artistic Director*
Gwen Orel, *Literary Manager*
Submission procedure: accepts unsolicited scripts with letter of inquiry for Southern Writers' Project only (see below); agent submission for all other plays. **Types of material:** full-length plays, adaptations, plays for young audiences. **Special interests:** new plays with southern or African-American themes. **Facilities:** Festival Stage, 750 seats, modified thrust stage; Octagon, 225 seats, flexible stage. **Best submission time:** year-round. **Response time:** 2 months letter; 12 months script. **Special programs:** Southern Writers' Project: project to commission and develop plays based on southern and/or African-American issues; address submissions to Southern Writers' Project.

ALLEY THEATRE
(Founded 1947)
615 Texas Ave; Houston, TX 77002; (713) 228–9341
Gregory Boyd, *Artistic Director*
Submission procedure: no unsolicited scripts; professional recommendation. **Types of material:** full-length plays, translations, adaptations, musicals. **Facilities:** Main Stage, 800 seats, thrust stage; Arena Stage, 300 seats, arena stage. **Best submission time:** year-round. **Response time:** 2-6 months.

ALLIANCE THEATRE COMPANY
(Founded 1968)
1280 Peachtree St NE; Atlanta, GA 30309; (404) 733–4650,
    FAX 733–4625; Web site http://www.alliancetheatre.org
Literary Department
Submission procedure: no unsolicited scripts; synopsis, maximum 10-page dialogue sample and letter of inquiry. **Types of material:** full-length plays, one-acts, plays for young audiences, musicals. **Special interests:** work that speaks to a culturally diverse community; plays with compelling stories and engaging characters, told in adventurous ways. **Facilities:** Alliance Theatre, 800 seats, proscenium stage; Studio Theatre, 200 seats, flexible stage. **Best submission time:** Mar–Sep. **Response time:** 1-2 months letter; 6 months script.

ALLIED THEATRE GROUP
(Formerly Stage West)
(Founded 1979)
3055 South University Dr; Fort Worth, TX 76109-5608;
(817) 924-9454, FAX 926-8650; email stgwest@ix.netcom.com;
Web site http://www.stagewest.org
Jim Covault, *Artistic Director*
Submission procedure: no unsolicited scripts; synopsis and letter of inquiry.
Types of material: full-length plays, translations, adaptations, solo pieces.
Special interests: Hispanic plays; contemporary issues. **Facilities:** Stage West,
190 seats, arena stage. **Production considerations:** prefers cast limit of 9. **Best
submission time:** Jan-Mar. **Response time:** 1 month letter; 3 months script.

AMAS MUSICAL THEATRE, INC.
(Founded 1968)
450 West 42nd St, Suite 2J; New York, NY 10036; (212) 563-2565,
FAX 268-5501; email amas@westegg.com;
Web site http://www.westegg.com/amas
Donna Trinkoff, *Producing Director*
Submission procedure: accepts unsolicited scripts. **Types of material:**
musicals, cabaret/revues. **Special interests:** multicultural casts and themes.
Facilities: no permanent facility; company performs in various proscenium or
black box venues with 74-99 seats. **Production considerations:** cast limit of 15.
Best submission time: summer, winter. **Response time:** 3-6 months. **Special
programs:** AMAS Six O'Clock Musical Theatre Lab: a reading series for new
musicals open to composers, lyricists and librettists; writer must supply cast and
musical director; AMAS provides theatre and publicity.

AMERICAN CABARET THEATRE
(Founded 1989)
401 East Michigan St; Indianapolis, IN 46204;
(317) 631-0334, FAX 686-5443; email cabaret@indy.net;
Web site http://americancabarettheatre.com
Claude McNeal, *Artistic Director/Founder*
Submission procedure: no unsolicited scripts; synopsis and letter of inquiry;
prefers professional recommendation. **Types of material:** cabaret/revues.
Special interests: cabaret/revues dealing with original American themes.
Facilities: Mainstage, 400 seats, proscenium stage; Second Stage, 150 seats,
proscenium stage. **Production considerations:** cast size of 6-12; limited fly,
wing and storage space. **Best submission time:** Jul-Sep. **Response time:** 1-2
months letter; 2-3 months script.

AMERICAN CONSERVATORY THEATER

(Founded 1965)
30 Grant Ave, 6th Floor; San Francisco, CA 94108–5800;
  (415) 439–2445, FAX 834–3360
Paul Walsh, *Dramaturg*
Submission procedure: no unsolicited scripts; agents and theatre professionals only may send synopsis, maximum 10-page dialogue sample and letter of inquiry. **Types of material:** full-length plays, translations, adaptations. **Facilities:** Geary Theater, 1000 seats, proscenium stage. **Best submission time:** year-round. **Response time:** 6–12 months.

AMERICAN MUSIC THEATER FESTIVAL/ PRINCE MUSIC THEATER

(Founded 1984)
100 South Broad St, Suite 650; Philadelphia, PA 19110;
  (215) 972–1000, FAX 972–1020; Web site http://www.amtf.org
Ben Levit, *Artistic Director*
Submission procedure: no unsolicited scripts; synopsis, cassette and letter of inquiry. **Types of material:** music-theatre works including musical comedy, music drama, opera, experimental works, solo pieces. **Facilities:** Prince Music Theater, 450 seats, proscenium stage. **Best submission time:** year-round. **Response time:** 3 weeks letter; 6 months script.

THE AMERICAN PLACE THEATRE

(Founded 1964)
111 West 46th St; New York, NY 10036; (212) 840–2960
Literary Department
Submission procedure: no unsolicited scripts; agent submission. **Types of material:** full-length plays, adaptations, performance art. **Special interests:** works by American playwrights only, with particular emphasis on plays by ethnic minorities. **Facilities:** Main Stage, 180–299 seats, flexible stage; Cabaret Space, 75 seats, flexible stage; First Floor Theatre, 75 seats, flexible stage. **Best submission time:** Sep–Jun. **Response time:** 3–4 months.

AMERICAN RENEGADE THEATRE COMPANY
(Founded 1991)
11136 Magnolia Blvd; North Hollywood, CA 91601; (818) 763-4430
Barry Thompson, *Literary Manager*
Submission procedure: accepts unsolicited scripts. **Types of material:** full-length plays. **Special interests:** contemporary American plays. **Facilities:** Front Theatre, 99 seats, proscenium stage; Back Theatre, 45 seats, black box. **Best submission time:** year-round. **Response time:** 3-6 months. **Special Programs:** American Renegade Playwriting Contest (see Prizes).

AMERICAN REPERTORY THEATRE
(Founded 1979)
64 Brattle St; Cambridge, MA 02138; (617) 495-2668;
    Web site http://www.amrep.org
Scott Zigler, *Artistic Associate*
Submission procedure: no unsolicited scripts; agent submission. **Types of material:** full-length plays, translations, adaptations, musicals, cabaret/revues. **Special interests:** prefers plays "which lend themselves to poetic use of the stage." **Facilities:** Loeb Drama Center, 556 seats, flexible stage; Holyoke Street Theatre, 350 seats, proscenium stage; Church Street Theatre, 200 seats, black box. **Production considerations:** cast limit of 15. **Best submission time:** year-round. **Response time:** 1-3 months.

AMERICAN STAGE COMPANY
(Founded 1986)
Box 336; Teaneck, NJ 07666
Matthew Parent, *Producing Artistic Director*
Submission procedure: no unsolicited scripts; synopsis, dialogue sample and letter of inquiry. **Types of material:** full-length plays, musicals. **Facilities:** American Stage in Residence at Fairleigh Dickinson University, 290 seats, proscenium stage. **Production considerations:** cast limit of 15; orchestra limit of 6. **Best submission time:** year-round. **Response time:** 1 month letter; 6 months script.

AMERICAN STAGE FESTIVAL

(Founded 1974)
14 Court St; Nashua, NH 03060; (603) 889–2336, FAX 889–2330
Attn: New Scripts, EARLY STAGES
Submission procedure: accepts unsolicited scripts with SASE for response; include cassette of 2–3 songs for musicals. **Types of material:** full-length plays, musicals. **Special interests:** material with strong emotional content that tells a compelling story, including ones that explore what used to be called "The American Dream." **Facilities:** Summer Stage, 492 seats, proscenium stage; Year-Round Stage, 277 seats, thrust stage. **Production considerations:** cast limit of 10 for plays, 15 plus 5 musicians for musicals. **Best submission time:** Sep–Dec. **Response time:** 2–3 months letter; 4–6 months script. **Special Programs:** EARLY STAGES: summer weekly staged reading series with audience response.

AMERICAN THEATER COMPANY

(Founded 1985)
1909 West Byron St; Chicago, IL 60613; (773) 929–5009,
    FAX 929–5171; email atcdir@aol.com
Brian Russell, *Artistic Director*
Submission procedure: no unsolicited scripts; synopsis and letter of inquiry with SASP for response. **Types of material:** full-length plays, translations, adaptations, musicals. **Special interests:** language-oriented plays that utilize heightened theatrical reality; musicals; substantive comedies; social and political themes. **Facilities:** American Theater Company, 137 seats, modified thrust stage. **Production considerations:** prefers cast limit of 15; modest technical demands. **Best submission time:** year-round. **Response time:** 2–4 months letter; 6–12 months script.

AMERICAN THEATRE OF ACTORS, INC.

(Founded 1976)
314 West 54th St; New York, NY 10019; (212) 581–3044
James Jennings, *Artistic Director*
Submission procedure: accepts unsolicited scripts. **Types of material:** full-length plays, one-acts. **Special interests:** realistic plays dealing with contemporary social issues. **Facilities:** Chernuchin Theatre, 140 seats, proscenium stage; Sargent Theatre, 65 seats, proscenium stage; Beckmann Theatre, 35 seats, arena stage. **Production considerations:** cast limit of 8; minimal sets. **Best submission time:** year-round. **Response time:** 2 weeks.

APPLE TREE THEATRE
(Founded 1983)
595 Elm Place, Suite 210; Highland Park, IL 60035; (847) 432–8223,
FAX 432–5214; Web site http://www.appletreetheatre.com
Submission procedure: no unsolicited scripts; direct solicitation to playwright or agent. **Types of material:** full-length plays, adaptations, plays for young audiences, musicals. **Facilities:** Apple Tree Theatre, 177 seats, modified thrust stage. **Production considerations:** cast limit of 9; unit set. **Special programs:** staged readings.

ARDEN THEATRE COMPANY
(Founded 1988)
40 North 2nd St; Philadelphia, PA 19106; (215) 922–8900;
FAX 922–7011; Web site http://www.libertynet.org/~arden
Terrence J. Nolen, *Producing Artistic Director*
Submission procedure: no unsolicited scripts; synopsis and letter of inquiry. **Types of material:** full-length plays, translations, adaptations, musicals. **Special interests:** new adaptations of literary works. **Facilities:** Haas Stage/Mainstage, 400 seats, flexible stage; Arcadia Stage/Studio Theatre, 175 seats, flexible stage. **Best submission time:** year-round. **Response time:** 3 months letter; 6 months script.

ARENA STAGE
(Founded 1950)
1101 6th St SW; Washington, DC 20024; (202) 554–9066,
FAX 488–4056
Cathy Madison, *Literary Manager*
Submission procedure: accepts unsolicited scripts from DC, MD, VA writers only; all other writers send synopsis, bio and letter of inquiry. **Types of material:** full-length plays, translations, adaptations, solo pieces. **Special interests:** unproduced works; plays for a multicultural company; plays by women, writers of color, physically disabled writers and other "nonmainstream" artists. **Facilities:** Fichandler Stage, 827 seats, arena stage; The Kreeger Theater, 514 seats, modified thrust stage; The Old Vat Room, 110 seats, cabaret stage. **Best submission time:** year-round. **Response time:** 1 day letter; 6-12 months script. **Special programs:** Student Playwright's Project Performance: staged reading for 4 writers, grades 3-12.

ARIZONA THEATRE COMPANY

(Founded 1966)
Box 1631; Tucson, AZ 85702–1631; (520) 884–8210
Samantha K. Wyer, *Associate Artistic Director*
Submission procedure: no unsolicited scripts; synopsis, 10-page dialogue sample, production history, resume and letter of inquiry. **Types of material:** full-length plays, translations, adaptations, musicals. **Facilities:** Herberger Theater Center (in Phoenix), 800 seats, proscenium stage; Temple of Music and Art (in Tucson), 600 seats, proscenium stage. **Best submission time:** spring–summer. **Response time:** 1 month letter; 4–6 months script. **Special programs:** New Play Reading Series: rehearsed readings followed by discussion with audience. National Hispanic Playwriting Award (see Prizes).

ARKANSAS REPERTORY THEATRE

(Founded 1976)
Box 110; Little Rock, AR 72203–0110; (501) 378–0445,
    FAX 378–0012
Brad Mooy, *Literary Manager*
Submission procedure: no unsolicited scripts; synopsis and letter of inquiry. **Types of material:** full-length plays, musicals, cabaret/revues, solo pieces. **Facilities:** Arkansas Repertory Theatre, 354 seats, proscenium stage; Second Stage, 99 seats, black box. **Production considerations:** prefers small cast. **Best submission time:** year-round. **Response time:** 3 months letter; 3–6 months script. **Special programs:** New Playreading Series.

ARROW ROCK LYCEUM THEATRE

(Founded 1961)
High St; Arrow Rock, MO 65320; (660) 837–3311, FAX 837–3112;
    Web site http://www.lyceumtheatre.org
Michael Bollinger, *Artistic Producing Director*
Submission procedure: no unsolicited scripts; direct solicitation to playwright or agent. **Types of material:** full-length plays, translations, adaptations, musicals. **Facilities:** Arrow Rock Lyceum Theatre, 408 seats, semithrust stage.

ART STATION

(Founded 1986)
Box 1998; Stone Mountain, GA 30086; (770) 469–1105,
FAX 469–0355; email jon@artstation.org;
Web site http://www.artstation.org
Jon Goldstein, *Literary Manager*

Submission procedure: accepts unsolicited scripts. **Types of material:** full-length plays, adaptations, musicals, solo pieces. **Special interests:** works not produced professionally; plays by southern playwrights, or which describe the southern experience. **Facilities:** ART Station Theatre, 100 seats, proscenium/thrust stage. **Production considerations:** cast limit of 6; single set; no fly space. **Best submission time:** Jun–Dec. **Response time:** 4 months. **Special programs:** ART Station Playwrights Project: year-round playwrights group meets bimonthly to critique and develop new works; presents monthly staged readings.

ARTISTS REPERTORY THEATRE

(Founded 1981)
1516 Southwest Alder St; Portland, OR 97205; (503) 241–9807,
FAX 241–8268; email allen@artistsrep.org;
Web site http://www.artistsrep.org
Allen Nause, *Artistic Director*

Submission procedure: no unsolicited scripts; synopsis and letter of inquiry. **Types of material:** full-length plays, adaptations. **Facilities:** Reiersgaard Theatre, 170 seats, flexible black box. **Production considerations:** cast limit of 13; 1 set or unit set. **Best submission time:** year-round. **Response time:** 1 month letter; 6 months script. **Special programs:** Play Lab: staged reading series.

ARTS AT ST. ANN'S

(Founded 1979)
157 Montague St; Brooklyn, NY 11201; (718) 834–8794,
FAX 522–2470
Susan Feldman, *Artistic Director*

Submission procedure: no unsolicited scripts; synopsis and letter of inquiry. **Types of material:** full-length plays, musicals. **Special interests:** musical-theatre works. **Facilities:** Church of St. Ann and Holy Trinity, 652 seats, flexible stage; Parish Hall, 100 seats, flexible stage. **Best submission time:** Jan–Feb; Jul–Aug. **Response time:** 2 months letter; 3 months script.

ARVADA CENTER FOR THE ARTS & HUMANITIES
(Founded 1976)
6901 Wadsworth Blvd; Arvada, CO 80003; (303) 431-3080,
    FAX 431-3083
Kathy Kuehn, *Performing Arts Director*
Submission procedure: no unsolicited scripts; synopsis and letter of inquiry.
Types of material: plays for young audiences only. **Special interests**: plays for
preschool-grade 6. **Facilities:** Arvada Center Amphitheater, 1200 seats,
proscenium stage; Arvada Center Main Stage, 498 seats, thrust stage. **Production
considerations:** cast limit of 6-9; minimal set. **Best submission time:** Sep-Mar.
Response time: 3-5 months letter; 5-8 months script.

ASIAN AMERICAN THEATER COMPANY
(Founded 1973)
1840 Sutter St, Suite 207; San Francisco, CA 94115;
    (415) 440-5545, FAX 440-5597; email aatc@wenet.net
Pamela A. Wu, *Producing Director*
Submission procedure: accepts unsolicited scripts with synopsis, character
breakdown, resume and letter of inquiry. **Types of material:** full-length plays,
adaptations, plays for young audiences. **Special interests:** plays that explore
diversity of the Asian-Pacific-American experience. **Facilities:** no permanent
facility. **Best submission time:** year-round. **Response time:** 3-6 months.

ASOLO THEATRE COMPANY
(Founded 1960)
5555 North Tamiami Trail; Sarasota, FL 34243; (941) 351-9010,
    FAX 351-5796; email bruce_rodgers@asolo.org;
    Web site http://www.asolo.org
Bruce E. Rodgers, *Associate Artistic Director*
Submission procedure: no unsolicited scripts; 1-page synopsis and letter of
inquiry with SASE for response. **Types of material:** full-length plays, translations,
adaptations, solo pieces. **Special interests:** adaptations of great literature.
Facilities: The Mertz Theatre, 499 seats, proscenium stage; The Cook Theatre,
161 seats, proscenium stage. **Best submission time:** Jun-Aug. **Response time:**
2 months letter; 6 months script.

ATLANTIC THEATER COMPANY

(Founded 1984)
453 West 16th St; New York, NY 10011; (212) 691–5919,
FAX 691–6280
Toni Amicarella, *Literary Manager*
Submission procedure: no unsolicited scripts; agent submission. **Types of material:** full-length plays, adaptations. **Facilities:** Atlantic Theater Mainstage, 160 seats, proscenium stage; Black Box, 70 seats, proscenium stage. **Best submission time:** fall–winter. **Response time:** 3-6 months. **Special programs:** Atlantic 453: year-round play readings, workshops and productions in Black Box.

ATTIC THEATRE CENTRE

(Founded 1987)
6562 1/2 Santa Monica Blvd; Hollywood, CA 90038;
   (323) 469–3786, FAX 463–9571
James Carey, *Producing Artistic Director*
Submission procedure: no unsolicited scripts; synopsis, dialogue sample and letter of inquiry with SASE for response. **Types of material:** full-length plays, one-acts, solo pieces. **Facilities:** Mainstage, 53 seats, black box; Attic 2, 43 seats, black box. **Production considerations:** simple sets; no fly or wing space. **Best submission time:** year-round. **Response time:** 1 month letter; 3-6 months script. **Special programs:** play reading series; developmental workshops; Attic Theatre Ensemble's One-Act Marathon (see Prizes).

AULIS COLLECTIVE FOR THEATER AND MEDIA, INC.

(Founded 1996)
Box 673, Prince St Station; New York, NY 10012
Literary Manager
Submission procedure: no unsolicited scripts; synopsis, resume and letter of inquiry with SASE for response. **Types of material:** full-length plays, one-acts, solo pieces, performance art. **Special interests:** works that explore the connections between domestic violence against children and global violence; plays with music. **Facilities:** no permanent space; various black box theatres under 99 seats. **Best submission time:** year-round. **Response time:** 6 months letter; 12 months script.

AURORA THEATRE COMPANY

general @ auroratheatre.org
Ms. Nancy Carlin

(Founded 1992)
2315 Durant Ave; Berkeley, CA 94704; (510) 843-4822,
    FAX 843-4826; Web site http://auroratheatre.org
Literary Manager
Submission procedure: no unsolicited scripts; synopsis and letter of inquiry.
Types of material: full-length plays, adaptations. **Special interests:** plays
emphasizing language and ideas. **Facilities:** Aurora Theatre, 67 seats, arena stage.
Production considerations: cast limit of 8; minimal production demands. **Best
submission time:** year-round. **Response time:** 6 months letter; 6 months script.

AXIS THEATRE

(Founded 1992)
3600 Clipper Mill Rd, #114; Baltimore, MD 21211;
    (410) 243-5237, FAX 243-1294;
    Web site http://www.axistheatre.org
Brian Klaas, *Artistic Director*
Submission procedure: accepts unsolicited scripts; include cassette or CD for
musicals. **Types of material:** full-length plays, musicals. **Special interests:**
nonrealistic plays. **Facilities:** Axis Theatre, 68 seats, proscenium stage.
Production considerations: cast limit of 10; small space. **Best submission time:**
Jun-Oct. **Response time:** 3-5 months script.

THE B STREET THEATRE

(Founded 1991)
2711 B St; Sacramento, CA 95816; (916) 443-5391,
    FAX 443-0874; email bstreetfac@aol.com
Buck Busfield, *Producing Director*
Submission procedure: no unsolicited scripts; agent submission. **Types of
material:** full-length plays. **Special interests:** contemporary comedies and
dramas. **Facilities:** The B Street Theatre, 150 seats, black box. **Production
considerations:** cast limit of 6; no fly space; modest production demands. **Best
submission time:** year-round. **Response time:** 3-6 months.

BAILIWICK REPERTORY

(Founded 1982)
Bailiwick Arts Center; 1229 West Belmont; Chicago, IL 60657–3205;
   (773) 883–1090; email bailiwickr@aol.com
   Web site http://bailiwick.org
David Zak, *Artistic Director*
Submission procedure: submission guidelines available on Web. **Types of material:** full-length plays, translations, adaptations, musicals, solo pieces. **Special interests:** translations and adaptations; theatrically inventive and/or politically intriguing works; work appropriate for Deaf Bailiwick Artists, especially work by deaf or hard-of-hearing writers. **Facilities:** Mainstage, 150 seats, flexible/thrust stage; cabaret/studio, 100 seats, flexible stage. **Best submission time:** year-round. **Response time:** 8-12 months. **Special programs:** Pride Performance Series: year-round exploration of works of interest to the lesbian and gay communities, culminating in summer festival. Director's Festival: annual directors' showcase of 48 plays, 10-50 minutes long, staged in black-box setting. Studio Series: workshops and readings of plays, performance pieces and musicals. Submission guidelines for special programs available on Web.

BARKSDALE THEATRE

(Founded 1953)
1601 Willow Lawn Dr, Suite 301E; Richmond, VA 23230;
   (804) 282–9440, FAX 288–6470; email barksdalev@aol.com
Randy Strawderman, *Artistic Director*
Submission procedure: no unsolicited scripts; synopsis and letter of inquiry. **Types of material:** full-length plays, one-acts, translations, adaptations, plays for young audiences, musicals, cabaret/revues, solo pieces. **Facilities:** Mainstage, 214 seats, arena stage. **Production considerations:** small cast, minimal production demands; no fly or wing space. **Best submission time:** summer. **Response time:** 6 months letter; 12 months script.

THE BARROW GROUP

(Founded 1986)
Box 5112; New York, NY 10185; (212) 253–2001, FAX 253–1909
Literary Manager
Submission procedure: no unsolicited scripts; professional recommendation. **Types of material:** full-length plays, translations, adaptations. **Facilities:** no permanent facility. **Production considerations:** cast limit of 12; minimal sets. **Best submission time:** year-round. **Response time:** 1-6 months.

BARTER THEATRE
(Founded 1933)
Box 867; Abingdon, VA 24212-0867; (540) 628-2281,
   FAX 628-4551; email barter@naxs.com;
   Web site http://www.bartertheatre.com
Richard Rose, *Producing Artistic Director*
Submission procedure: no unsolicited scripts; synopsis, dialogue sample and letter of inquiry; include cassette for musicals. **Types of material:** full-length plays, translations, adaptations, plays for young audiences, musicals. **Special interests:** social issues and current events; works that expand theatrical form; nonurban-oriented material. **Facilities:** Barter Theatre, 508 seats, proscenium stage; Barter's Stage II, 140 seats, flexible stage. **Production considerations:** cast of 4-10. **Best submission time:** Mar, Sep. **Response time:** 9 months letter; 12 months script. **Special programs:** Barter's Early Stages: script development program.

BAY STREET THEATRE
(Founded 1991)
Box 810; Sag Harbor, NY 11963; (631) 725-0818,
   FAX 725-0906; Web site http://www.baystreet.org
Mia Emlen Grosjean, *Literary Manager*
Submission procedure: no unsolicited scripts; agent submission. **Types of material:** full-length plays, musicals, solo pieces. **Special interests:** plays that challenge as well as entertain; plays that "address the heart of our community and champion the human spirit." **Facilities:** Mainstage, 299 seats, thrust stage. **Production considerations:** cast limit of 8-9; prefers unit set; no fly or wing space; small-scale musicals only. **Best submission time:** year-round. **Response time:** 3-6 months. **Special programs:** reading series: readings of 3 new plays each fall and spring; playwright receives $50 honorarium and travel from New York City; scripts for special programs selected through theatre's normal submission procedure.

THE BELMONT PLAYHOUSE

(Founded 1991)
2385 Arthur Ave; Bronx, NY 10458; (718) 364–4700,
FAX 563–5053; email thebelmont@hotmail.com
Dante Albertie, *Artistic Director*
Submission procedure: accepts unsolicited scripts. **Types of material:** full-length plays, translations, adaptations. **Special interests:** plays with Italian-American or urban themes. **Facilities:** Belmont Playhouse, 75 seats, black box; Performance Space, 25-100 seats, platform. **Production considerations:** cast limit of 6; one set; no fly space. **Best submission time:** year-round. **Response time:** 3-5 months.

BERKELEY REPERTORY THEATRE

(Founded 1968)
2025 Addison St; Berkeley, CA 94704; (510) 204–8901,
FAX 841–7711; email turg@berkeleyrep.org
Dramaturg
Submission procedure: no unsolicited scripts; direct solicitation to playwright or agent. **Types of material:** full-length plays, translations, adaptations. **Facilities:** 600-seat proscenium stage opening Mar 2001; Mark Taper stage, 400 seats, thrust stage. **Special programs:** Parallel Season: productions of 2-3 new plays each season. Commissioning program. In-house readings and workshops.

BERKSHIRE THEATRE FESTIVAL

(Founded 1928)
Box 797; Stockbridge, MA 01262; (413) 298–5536, FAX 298–3368;
email info@berkshiretheatre.org;
Web site http://www.berkshiretheatre.org
Kate Maguire, *Producing Director*
Submission procedure: no unsolicited scripts; agent submission. **Types of material:** full-length plays, musicals, solo pieces. **Facilities:** Playhouse, 415 seats, proscenium stage; Unicorn Theatre, 122 seats, thrust stage. **Production considerations:** cast limit of 8 for plays; small orchestra for musicals. **Best submission time:** Oct-Dec. **Response time:** 12 months.

BILINGUAL FOUNDATION OF THE ARTS

(Founded 1973)
421 North Ave 19; Los Angeles, CA 90031; (323) 225-4044,
    FAX 225-1250
Agustin Coppola, *Dramaturg*

Submission procedure: accepts unsolicited scripts. **Types of material:** full-length plays, translations, adaptations, plays for young audiences. **Special interests:** plays with Hispanic themes or by Hispanic playwrights only. **Facilities:** BFA's Little Theatre, 99 seats, thrust stage; uses theatres at Los Angeles Center for the Arts for some mainstage productions. **Production considerations:** cast limit of 10; simple set. **Best submission time:** year-round. **Response time:** 3-6 months.

BIRMINGHAM CHILDREN'S THEATRE

(Founded 1947)
Box 1362; Birmingham, AL 35201; (205) 458-8181, FAX 458-8895;
    Web site http://www.bct123.org
Burt Brosowsky, *Executive Director*

Submission procedure: accepts unsolicited scripts; prefers synopsis and letter of inquiry. **Types of material:** plays for young audiences. **Special interests:** interactive plays for preschool-grade 2; presentational plays for K-6. **Facilities:** Birmingham-Jefferson Civic Center Theatre, 1073 seats, thrust stage; Studio Theatre, up to 250 seats, lab space. **Production considerations:** prefers cast of 4-6. **Best submission time:** Sep-Dec. **Response time:** 2 weeks letter; 2-6 months script.

BLOOMSBURG THEATRE ENSEMBLE

(Founded 1978)
226 Center St; Bloomsburg, PA 17815; (570) 784-5530,
    FAX 784-4912; Web site http://www.bte.org
Tom Byrn, *Play Selection Chair*

Submission procedure: no unsolicited scripts; synopsis, dialogue sample, professional recommendation and letter of inquiry. **Types of material:** full-length plays, translations, adaptations. **Special interests:** new translations of classics; rural themes; plays suitable for small acting ensemble. **Facilities:** Alvina Krause Theatre, 350 seats, proscenium stage. **Production considerations:** small to mid-sized cast; 1 set or unit set. **Best submission time:** summer. **Response time:** 3 months letter; 6 months script.

BoarsHead Theater
(Founded 1966)
425 South Grand Ave; Lansing, MI 48933; (517) 484-7800,
FAX 484-2564
John Peakes, *Artistic Director*
Submission procedure: no unsolicited scripts; synopsis, character breakdown, 6–10-page dialogue sample and letter of inquiry with SASP for response. **Types of material:** full-length plays, plays for young audiences. **Special interests:** one-act plays for young audiences only; plays that make use of theatrical conventions or create new ones; social issues; comedies; no musicals. **Facilities:** Center for the Arts, 249 seats, thrust stage. **Production considerations:** cast limit of 4-6 for children's shows. **Best submission time:** year-round. **Response time:** 1 month letter; 3-6 months script. **Special programs:** staged readings of 5 new plays a year.

Borderlands Theater
(Founded 1986)
Box 2791; Tucson, AZ 85702; (520) 882-8607,
FAX 882-7406 (call first); email bltheater@aol.com
Submission procedure: no unsolicited scripts; synopsis and letter of inquiry. **Types of material:** full-length plays, translations, adaptations. **Special interests:** cultural diversity; race relations; "border" issues, including concerns of the geographical border region as well as the metaphorical borders of gender, class and race. **Facilities:** Pima Community College Center for the Arts: 1st theatre, 400 seats, proscenium stage; 2nd theatre, 160 seats, black box. **Production considerations:** cast limit of 12; minimal set. **Best submission time:** year-round. **Response time:** 1 month letter; 3-6 months script.

Brava! For Women in the Arts
(Founded 1986)
2781 24th St; San Francisco, CA 94110; (415) 641-7657,
FAX 641-7684; email ellen@brava.org;
Web site http://www.brava.org
Ellen Gavin, *Artistic/Executive Director*
Submission procedure: no unsolicited scripts; synopsis, dialogue sample and letter of inquiry. **Types of material:** full-length plays, one-acts, plays for young audiences. **Special interests:** premieres by women of color; lesbian playwrights. **Facilities:** Brava Theater Center, 375 seats, thrust stage; Barbie Stein Youth Theater, 100 seats, black box. **Best submission time:** year-round. **Response time:** 6 months letter; 8 months script. **Special programs:** Teatro Armonia: year-round playwriting and performance classes for young artists. Adult playwriting workshops.

BRISTOL RIVERSIDE THEATRE

(Founded 1986)
Box 1250; Bristol, PA 19007; (215) 785-6664, FAX 785-2762;
    email brtboss@aol.com; Web site http://www.brtstage.org
David J. Abers, *Assistant to Artistic Director*
Submission procedure: accepts unsolicited scripts. **Types of material:** full-length plays, one-acts, translations, adaptations, musicals, solo pieces. **Special interests:** cutting-edge works; plays that experiment with form; translations; musicals. **Facilities:** Bristol Riverside Theatre, 302 seats, flexible stage. **Production considerations:** cast limit of 10 for plays, 18 for musicals, 9 for orchestra; minimal production demands. **Best submission time:** spring. **Response time:** 12-18 months. **Special programs:** year-round reading series.

CALIFORNIA REPERTORY COMPANY

(Founded 1989)
1250 Bellflower Blvd; Long Beach, CA 90840-2701;
    (562) 985-5357, FAX 985-2263
Howard Burman, *Artistic Producing Director*
Paul Stuart Graham, *Managing Director*
Submission procedure: no unsolicited scripts; direct solicitation to playwright or agent. **Types of material:** full-length plays, translations, adaptations. **Special interests:** international works. **Facilities:** UT Theatre, 400 seats, proscenium stage; Studio Theatre, 225 seats, flexible stage; Edison Theatre, 99 seats, flexible stage; Players Theatre, 90 seats, proscenium stage. **Production considerations:** cast of 8-18.

CALIFORNIA SHAKESPEARE FESTIVAL

(Founded 1973)
701 Heinz Ave; Berkeley, CA 94710; (510) 548-3422,
    FAX 843-9921; email letters@calshakes.org;
    Web site http://www.calshakes.org
Artistic Associate
Submission procedure: no unsolicited scripts; synopis and letter of inquiry. **Types of material:** translations, adaptations. **Special interests:** new translations and adaptations of classical plays suitable for large-scale, outdoor production only. **Facilities:** Bruns Amphitheatre, 521 seats, outdoor proscenium. **Best submission time:** fall. **Response time:** 6 months letter; 6 months script.

CALIFORNIA THEATRE CENTER

(Founded 1976)
Box 2007; Sunnyvale, CA 94087; (408) 245-2979, FAX 245-0235;
    email ctc@ctcinc.org
Will Huddleston, *Resident Director*

Submission procedure: accepts unsolicited scripts; prefers synopsis and letter of inquiry. **Types of material:** plays for young audiences. **Special interests:** classics adapted for young audiences; adaptations of literature; historical material. **Facilities:** company primarily tours to large proscenium-stage theatres; Sunnyvale Performing Arts Center (home theatre), 200 seats, proscenium stage. **Production considerations:** cast limit of 8 for professional touring productions; minimum cast of 15 for conservatory productions; modest production demands. **Best submission time:** year-round. **Response time:** 1 month letter; 4-6 months script.

CAPITAL REPERTORY COMPANY

(Founded 1981)
111 North Pearl St; Albany, NY 12207; (562) 462-4531, ext 293,
    FAX 462-4531
Margaret Mancinelli-Cahill, *Producing Artistic Director*

Submission procedure: no unsolicited scripts; synopsis and 10-page dialogue sample. **Types of material:** full-length plays, translations, adaptations, music-theatre works. **Facilities:** Capital Repertory Theatre, 299 seats, thrust stage. **Best submission time:** late spring. **Response time:** 6 months.

THE CAST THEATRE

(Founded 1976)
804 North El Centro Ave; Hollywood, CA 90038; (323) 462-0265
Literary Manager

Submission procedure: accepts unsolicited scripts. **Types of material:** full-length plays. **Special interests:** previously unproduced works. **Facilities:** Cast at the Circle, 99 seats, proscenium stage; Cast, 65 seats, proscenium stage. **Best submission time:** year-round. **Response time:** 6 months.

CASTILLO THEATRE

(Founded 1983)
500 Greenwich St, Suite 201; New York, NY 10013;
(212) 941-5800, FAX 941-8340; email castilloth@aol.com;
Web site http://www.castillo.org
Diane Stiles, *Managing Director*
Submission procedure: no unsolicited scripts; direct solicitation to playwright or agent only. **Types of material:** full-length plays, one-acts. **Special interests:** plays that address social, cultural and political concerns and challenge theatrical and social convention; multiracial/multicultural issues. **Facilities:** Castillo Theatre, 71 seats, thrust stage.

CELEBRATION THEATRE

(Founded 1982)
7985 Santa Monica Blvd; Los Angeles, CA 90046; (323) 957-1884,
FAX 957-1826; Web site http://www.celebrationtheatre.com
Tom Jacobson, *Literary Manager*
Submission procedure: accepts unsolicited scripts. **Types of material:** full-length plays, one-acts, adaptations, musicals, cabaret/revues. **Special interests:** plays not previously produced on the West Coast with gay and lesbian themes. **Facilities:** Celebration Theatre, 65 seats, thrust stage. **Production considerations:** cast limit of 12; single set. **Best submission time:** year-round. **Response time:** 6 months.

CENTER STAGE

(Founded 1963)
700 North Calvert St; Baltimore, MD 21202-3686; (410) 685-3200,
FAX 539-3912; email cstoudt@centerstage.org
Charlotte Stoudt, *Resident Dramaturg*
Submission procedure: no unsolicited scripts; synopsis, sample pages and letter of inquiry. **Types of material:** full-length plays, translations, adaptations, music-theatre works, solo pieces. **Special interests:** plays with no previous mainstage production; plays about the African-American experience. **Facilities:** Pearlstone Theater, 541 seats, modified thrust stage; Head Theater, 100-400 seats, flexible space. **Best submission time:** year-round. **Response time:** 5-7 weeks letter; 4-6 months script.

CENTRE STAGE–SOUTH CAROLINA!

(Founded 1983)
Box 8451; Greenville, SC 29604–8451; (864) 233–6733,
    FAX 233–3901; email cbla@infoave.net
Claude W. Blakely, *Administrative Director*

Submission procedure: accepts unsolicited scripts. **Types of material:** full-length plays, one-acts, plays for young audiences, musicals, cabaret/revues. **Special interests:** plays for young audiences; issues of interest to senior citizens and minorities; musical revues. **Facilities:** Mainstage, 292 seats, thrust stage. **Production considerations:** 2 sets; no fly space; limited wing space. **Best submission time:** year-round. **Response time:** 2 months. **Special programs:** Sunday Evenings Readers Theatre: regularly scheduled rehearsed readings presented for public followed by audience discussion.

CENTER THEATER ENSEMBLE

(Founded 1985)
1346 West Devon Ave; Chicago, IL 60660; (773) 508–0200
Dale Calandra, *Literary Manager*

Submission procedure: no unsolicited scripts; synopsis, resume and letter of inquiry with SASE for response. **Types of material:** full-length plays, translations, adaptations, musicals, solo pieces. **Special interests:** comedies; plays creating a heightened reality; language-oriented plays; dramas of substance; original musicals only. **Facilities:** Mainstage, 75 seats, modified thrust stage; Studio, 35 seats, black box. **Production considerations:** cast limit of approximately 12; limited wing space, no fly space. **Best submission time:** year-round. **Response time:** 3 months letter; 3 months script. **Special programs:** Playwrights Workshop Series: participation by invitation only. Actor/Director/Playwright Unit: participants meet monthly to work on scripts; some scripts given staged reading, possibly leading to 2-week developmental workshop and performances and/or full production; participants selected through personal interview; Chicago-area playwrights contact Dale Calandra, Workshop Coordinator, for appointment.

CHARLOTTE REPERTORY THEATRE

(Founded 1976)
129 West Trade St; Charlotte, NC 28202; (704) 333–8587,
    FAX 333–0224
Claudia Carter Covington, *Literary Manager*
Submission procedure: accepts unsolicited scripts. **Types of material:** full-length plays. **Special interests:** professionally unproduced work; no children's works. **Facilities:** Booth Theatre at North Carolina Blumenthal Performing Arts Center, 450 seats, flexible stage. **Best submission time:** year-round. **Response time:** 3-6 months. **Special programs:** Festival of New American Plays: annual festival of staged readings; stipend, transportation and housing provided.

CHICAGO DRAMATISTS

See Membership and Service Organizations.

THE CHILDREN'S THEATRE COMPANY

(Founded 1965)
2400 Third Ave S; Minneapolis, MN 55404–3597; (612) 874–0500,
    FAX 874–8119
Elissa Adams, *Director of New Play Development*
Submission procedure: no unsolicited scripts; synopsis, first 20 pages of script, resume and letter of inquiry. **Types of material:** full-length plays, one-acts, translations, adaptations, plays for young audiences, musicals. **Special interests:** adaptations or original plays for young audiences; work samples from writers with no previous experience writing for children's theatre. **Facilities:** Children's Theatre Company, 745 seats, proscenium stage. **Best submission time:** Jul-Feb. **Response time:** 1 month letter; 6 months script. **Special programs:** Threshold: 1-4 works for young audiences commissioned each year for developmental laboratory.

CHILDSPLAY

(Founded 1977)
Box 517; Tempe, AZ 85280; (480) 350-8101, FAX 350-8584
David Saar, *Artistic Director*

Submission procedure: no unsolicited scripts; synopsis, 10-page dialogue sample and letter of inquiry. **Types of material:** plays for young audiences including full-length plays, adaptations, musicals, performance art. **Special interests:** nontraditional plays; material that entertains and challenges both performers and audiences; 2nd and 3rd productions of unpublished work. **Facilities:** Herberger Theater Center Stage, 800 seats, proscenium stage; Scottsdale Center for the Arts, 800 seats, proscenium stage; Stage West, 350 seats, proscenium stage; Tempe Performing Arts Center, 175 seats, black box; also performs in Tucson (no permanent space). **Production considerations:** some van-sized touring productions. **Best submission time:** Jun–Oct. **Response time:** 1 month letter; 3 months script. **Special programs:** commissioning program.

CINCINNATI PLAYHOUSE IN THE PARK

(Founded 1960)
Box 6537; Cincinnati, OH 45206-0537; (513) 345-2242
Edward Stern, *Producing Artistic Director*

Submission procedure: no unsolicited scripts; agent submission. **Types of material:** full-length plays, translations, adaptations, musicals. **Facilities:** Robert S. Marx Theatre, 626 seats, thrust stage; Thompson Shelterhouse, 225 seats, thrust stage. **Best submission time:** year-round. **Response time:** 6–8 months. **Special programs:** Lois and Richard Rosenthal New Play Prize (see Prizes).

CITY THEATRE COMPANY
(Founded 1974)
57 South 13th St; Pittsburgh, PA 15203; (412) 431–4400,
   FAX 431–5535; email caquiline@citytheatre-pgh.org;
   Web site http://www.citytheatre-pgh.org
Carlyn Aquiline, *Literary Manager/Dramaturg*
Submission procedure: no unsolicited scripts; synopsis, 15-20-page dialogue sample, character breakdown, resume, list of previous productions and letter of inquiry with SASE for response; include cassette for musicals. **Types of material:** full-length plays, translations, adaptations, musicals, solo pieces. **Special interests:** "new, innovative, theatrical plays of substance and ideas"; plays not yet produced; unconventional form, content and/or use of language; plays by underrepresented voices (e.g., women, writers of color, disabled writers). **Facilities:** Mainstage, 272 seats, flexible stage; HamburgStudio, 99 seats, black box. **Production considerations:** prefers cast limit of 10. **Best submission time:** year-round. **Response time:** 2 months letter; 6-8 months script. **Special Programs:** New Works On Stage: play commissioning and development program; Young Playwrights Festival: contest with workshop productions for 7th-12th graders in Western Pennsylvania (call for spring deadline).

CLARENCE BROWN THEATRE COMPANY
(Founded 1974)
206 McClung Tower; Knoxville, TN 37996; (423) 974–6011,
   FAX 974–4867; email cbt@utk.edu;
   Web site http://web.utk.edu/~cbt/
Bill Black, *Acting Producing Artistic Director*
Submission procedure: no unsolicited scripts; synopsis, character breakdown, 1-2 pages of dialogue and letter of inquiry. **Types of material:** full-length plays. **Special interests:** contemporary American plays. **Facilities:** Clarence Brown Theatre, 600 seats, proscenium stage; Carousel Theatre, 250 seats, arena stage. **Best submission time:** year-round. **Response time:** 1 month letter; 1 month script.

CLASSIC STAGE COMPANY
(Founded 1969)
136 East 13th St; New York, NY 10003; (212) 677–4210, FAX 477–7504
Literary Associate
Submission procedure: no unsolicited scripts; synopsis, dialogue sample and letter of inquiry. **Types of material:** translations and adaptations of "classic literature and themes only." **Special interests:** translations and adaptations of classic plays; adaptations of major nondramatic classics; prefers highly theatrical work. **Facilities:** Classic Stage Company, 180 seats, flexible stage. **Best submission time:** year-round. **Response time:** 2 months letter; 3 months script.

THE CLEVELAND PLAY HOUSE
(Founded 1916)
8500 Euclid Ave; Cleveland, OH 44106–0189; (216) 795–7000,
    FAX 795–7007
Scott Kanoff, *Literary Manager/Resident Director*
Submission procedure: no unsolicited scripts; resume and letter of inquiry with SASE for response. **Types of material:** full-length plays, adaptations, musicals. **Facilities:** Kenyon C. Bolton Theatre, 548 seats, proscenium stage; Francis E. Drury Theatre, 504 seats, proscenium stage. **Best submission time:** year-round. **Response time:** 1-2 months letter; 1-3 months script. **Special programs:** The Next Stage (see Development).

CLEVELAND PUBLIC THEATRE
(Founded 1981)
6415 Detroit Ave; Cleveland, OH 44102–3011; (216) 631–2727,
    FAX 631–2575; email cpt@en.com;
    Web site http://www.clevelandartists.net/cpt
James A. Levin, *Artistic Director*
Submission procedure: no unsolicited scripts; synopsis, 5-page dialogue sample and letter of inquiry. **Types of material:** full-length plays, one-acts, solo pieces. **Special interests:** experimental, poetic, politically, intellectually and spiritually challenging works; voices not heard in the mainstream (people of color, women, gays and lesbians, seniors, youth under 18); no standard commercial fare or "anything you might see on TV." **Facilities:** Gordon Square Theatre, 550 seats, flexible thrust; Cleveland Public Theatre, 150-175 seats, flexible stage (arena/proscenium); Down Stage, 60 seats, black box. **Production considerations:** cast limit of 10; simple set. **Best submission time:** year-round. **Response time:** 6 weeks letter; 9 months script. **Special programs:** New Plays Festival: 2-week developmental workshops of 6 plays culminating in stage readings; scripts selected through theatre's normal submission procedure; *deadline:* 1 Aug 2001; *notification:* Dec 2001; *dates:* Jan-Mar 2002.

COCONUT GROVE PLAYHOUSE
(Founded 1954)
3500 Main Highway; Miami, FL 33133; (305) 442-2662,
FAX 444-6437
Arnold Mittelman, *Producing Artistic Director*
Submission procedure: no unsolicited scripts; synopsis and letter of inquiry.
Types of material: full-length plays, translations, musicals, cabaret/revues.
Special interests: dramas, musicals. **Facilities:** Mainstage, 1100 seats,
proscenium stage; Encore Room, 150 seats, cabaret. **Best submission time:** year-
round. **Response time:** 1 week letter; 2 months script.

THE COLONY THEATRE COMPANY
(Formerly The Colony Studio Theatre)
(Founded 1975)
555 North Third St; Burbank, CA 91501; (818) 558-7000,
FAX 558-7110; email wayneliebman@colonytheatre.org;
Web site http://www.colonytheatre.org
Wayne Liebman, *Literary Manager*
Submission procedure: no unsolicited scripts; professional recommendation
with 1-page synopsis, first 10 pages of play, cast breakdown, production history,
resume and SASE for response. **Types of material:** full-length plays, adaptations,
musicals. **Special interests:** comedies, dramas; well-crafted plays of theatrical
imagination and emotional resonance which address universal themes; plays by
women. **Facilities:** Burbank Center Stage, 276 seats, thrust stage. **Production
considerations:** cast of 3-12; plays cast from resident company; 1 set. **Best
submission time:** Feb-Nov. **Response time:** 2 months letter; 6 months script

COMMONWEAL THEATRE COMPANY
(Founded 1989)
Box 15; Lanesboro, MN 55949; (507) 467-2905, FAX 467-2468;
email cmmnweal@means.net
Hal Cropp, *Core Artist*
Submission procedure: no unsolicited scripts; professional recommendation.
Types of material: full-length plays, translations, adaptations. **Facilities:** St.
Mane Theatre, 126 seats, proscenium stage. **Production considerations:** prefers
cast limit of 9; 1 set; no wing space. **Best submission time:** Oct-Dec. **Response
time:** 1 month. **Special programs:** Commonweal New Play Workshop: annual 2-
week developmental workshop for 1 script chosen from regular submissions; play
receives rehearsals culminating in staged reading for invited audience; playwright
receives housing during workshop.

COMPANY OF FOOLS

(Founded 1992)
Box 329; Hailey ID 83333; (208) 788-1051, FAX 788-6152;
   email fools@svidaho.net;
   Web site http://www.companyoffools.org
Denise Simone, *Managing Director*

Submission procedure: no unsolicited scripts; synopsis and letter of inquiry.
Types of material: full-length plays, one-acts, translations, adaptations, plays for
young audiences. **Special interests:** plays with focus on American themes; stories
of "the human heart in conflict with itself." **Facilities:** Liberty, 240 seats,
proscenium stage; Mint, 30-90 seats, flexible stage. **Production considerations:**
cast limit of 13. **Best submission time:** year-round. **Response time:** 3 months
letter; 4 months script.

CONEY ISLAND, USA

(Founded 1980)
1208 Surf Ave; Coney Island, NY 11224; (718) 372-5159,
   FAX 372-5101; email dzigun@echonyc.com;
   Web site http://www.coneyisland.com
Dick D. Zigun, *Artistic Director*

Submission procedure: no unsolicited scripts; synopsis, resume, reviews of prior
work and letter of inquiry. **Types of material:** company books already existing
productions of plays and performance art. **Special interests:** new and old
vaudeville; pop music; pop culture; Americana bizarro. **Facilities:** Sideshows by
the Seashore, 99 seats, arena stage; Coney Island Museum, 74 seats, cabaret stage;
also open-air performances on streets. **Best submission time:** year-round.
Response time: 1 month letter; 6 months script.

CONTEMPORARY AMERICAN THEATER FESTIVAL

(Founded 1991)
Box 429; Shepherdstown, WV 25443; (304) 876-3473,
   FAX 876-0955; Web site http://www.catf.org
Ed Herendeen, *Producing Director*
Catherine Irwin, *Managing Director*

Submission procedure: no unsolicited scripts; synopsis and letter of inquiry.
Types of material: full-length plays. **Special interests:** new American plays;
contemporary issues. **Facilities:** Main Stage, 350 seats, proscenium stage; Studio
Theater, 99 seats, black box. **Best submission time:** fall. **Response time:** 1
month letter; 3-6 months script.

CORNERSTONE THEATER COMPANY

(Founded 1986)
708 Traction Ave; Los Angeles, CA 90013; (213) 613–1700,
    FAX 613–1714; email tparran@cornerstonetheater.org
Teeko Parran, *Program Associate*
Submission procedure: no unsolicited scripts; letter of inquiry only. **Types of material:** full-length plays, adaptations, musicals. **Special interests:** company primarily interested in collaborating with playwrights to develop new works or contemporary adaptations of classics, focusing on specific communities. **Facilities:** no permanent facility. **Best submission time:** year-round. **Response time:** 2 months.

THE COTERIE THEATRE

(Founded 1979)
2450 Grand Ave; Kansas City, MO 64108–2520; (816) 474–6785,
    FAX 474–7112; email jefchurch@aol.com;
    Web site http://www.thecoterie.com
Jeff Church, *Producing Artistic Director*
Submission procedure: no unsolicited scripts; synopsis, resume and letter of inquiry with SASE for response. **Types of material:** works for young and family audiences, including adaptations, musicals and solo pieces. **Special interests:** ground-breaking works only; plays with culturally diverse casts or themes; social issues; adaptations of classic or contemporary literature; musicals. **Facilities:** The Coterie Theatre, 240 seats, flexible stage. **Production considerations:** cast limit of 12, prefers 5–7; no fly or wing space. **Best submission time:** year-round. **Response time:** 6–8 months letter; 6–8 months script.

COURT THEATRE

(Founded 1955)
5535 South Ellis Ave; Chicago, IL 60637; (773) 702–7005,
    FAX 834–1897
Resident Dramaturg
Submission procedure: no unsolicited scripts; synopsis, dialogue sample and letter of inquiry with email address for response. **Types of material:** translations and adaptations of classic texts only. **Special interests:** infrequently produced or "undiscovered" material. **Facilities:** Abelson Auditorium, 253 seats, thrust stage. **Production considerations:** limited fly space. **Best submission time:** summer. **Response time:** 6 weeks letter; 1–6 months script.

CROSSROADS THEATRE COMPANY

(Founded 1978)
7 Livingston Ave; New Brunswick, NJ 08901; (732) 249–5581,
FAX 249–1861
Literary Department
Submission procedure: no unsolicited scripts; synopsis, 10-page dialogue sample, bio and/or resume and letter of inquiry. **Types of material:** full-length plays, one-acts, translations, adaptations, musicals, cabaret/revues, performance art. **Special interests:** African-American, African and West Indian issue-oriented, experimental plays that examine the complexity of the human experience. **Facilities:** Crossroads Theatre, 300 seats, thrust stage. **Best submission time:** year-round. **Response time:** 6-8 months letter; 12 months script. **Special programs:** The Genesis Festival: A Celebration of New Voices in African-American Theatre: spring series of public readings and special events for the purpose of developing new plays; scripts selected through theatre's normal submission procedure.

CUMBERLAND COUNTY PLAYHOUSE

(Founded 1965)
Box 830; Crossville, TN 38557; (931) 484–4324, FAX 484–6299
Jim Crabtree, *Producing Director*
Submission procedure: no unsolicited scripts; synopsis and letter of inquiry. **Types of material:** full-length plays, adaptations, plays for young audiences, musicals. **Special interests:** works for family audiences; works with southern or rural background; works about Tennessee history or culture. **Facilities:** Cumberland County Playhouse, 490 seats, proscenium stage; Theater-in-the-Woods, 200 seats, outdoor arena; Adventure Theater, 180-220 seats, flexible black box. **Best submission time:** Aug–Dec. **Response time:** 2 weeks letter (if interested); 6-12 months script.

DALLAS CHILDREN'S THEATER

(Founded 1984)
2215 Cedar Springs; Dallas, TX 75201; Web site http://www.dct.org
Artie Olaisen, *Administrative Artist*
Submission procedure: no unsolicited scripts; synopsis, character/set breakdown and letter of inquiry. **Types of material:** full-length plays, adaptations, plays for young audiences. **Special interests:** works for family audiences; adaptations of classics; historical plays; socially relevant works. **Facilities:** El Centro Theater, 500 seats, proscenium stage; Crescent Theater, 180 seats, flexible stage. **Best submission time:** year-round. **Response time:** 3 months letter; 6 months script.

DALLAS THEATER CENTER
(Founded 1959)
3636 Turtle Creek Blvd; Dallas, TX 75219-5598; (214) 526-8210,
   FAX 521-7666
Preston Lane, *Literary Office*
Submission procedure: no unsolicited scripts; professional recommendation.
Types of material: full-length plays, adaptations, translations, solo pieces.
Special interests: plays that explore language or form; material relating to the
African-American or Hispanic experience. **Facilities:** Arts District Theater, 530
seats, flexible stage; Kalita Humphreys Theater, 466 seats, thrust stage. **Best
submission time:** year-round. **Response time:** 9-12 months.

DELAWARE THEATRE COMPANY
(Founded 1978)
200 Water St; Wilmington, DE 19801-5030; (302) 594-1104,
   FAX 594-1107
Fontaine Syer, *Artistic Director*
Submission procedure: no unsolicited scripts; synopsis and letter of inquiry
from DE, MD and PA playwrights only. **Types of material:** full-length plays,
translations, adaptations. **Facilities:** Delaware Theatre Company, 390 seats, thrust
stage. **Production considerations:** cast limit of 10. **Best submission time:** Feb-
May. **Response time:** 1 month letter; 3 months script.

DELL'ARTE PLAYERS COMPANY
(Founded 1971)
Box 816; Blue Lake, CA 95525; (707) 668-5663, FAX 668-5665;
   email dellarte@aol.com; Web site http://www.dellarte.com
Michael Fields, *Managing Artistic Director*
Submission procedure: no unsolicited scripts; synopsis and letter of inquiry.
Types of material: full-length plays, translations, adaptations, plays for young
audiences, solo pieces. **Special interests:** comedies; issue-oriented works in
commedia dell'arte style; Christmas plays for young audiences. **Facilities:**
Dell'Arte Players, 100 seats, flexible stage. **Production considerations:** company
of 3-4 actors; production demands adaptable to touring. **Best submission time:**
Jan-Mar. **Response time:** 3 weeks letter; 6 weeks script.

DENVER CENTER THEATRE COMPANY

(Founded 1979)
1050 13th St; Denver, CO 80204;
Bruce K. Sevy, *Associate Artistic Director/New Play Development*
Submission procedure: accepts unsolicited scripts; write for guidelines with
SASE for response. **Types of material:** full-length plays. **Special interests:** work
not produced professionally. **Facilities:** The Stage, 642 seats, thrust stage; The
Space, 450 seats, arena stage; The Ricketson, 250 seats, proscenium stage; The
Source, 200 seats, thrust stage. **Best submission time:** year-round. **Response
time:** 4-6 weeks letter; 4-6 months script. **Special programs:** Denver Center
Theatre Company U S WEST Theatre Fest (see Development); Francesca Primus
Prize (see Prizes).

DETROIT REPERTORY THEATRE

(Founded 1957)
13103 Woodrow Wilson Ave; Detroit, MI 48238; (313) 868-1347,
    FAX 868-1705
Barbara Busby, *Literary Manager*
Submission procedure: accepts unsolicited scripts. **Types of material:** full-
length plays. **Special interests:** issue-oriented plays. **Facilities:** Detroit Repertory
Theatre, 194 seats, proscenium stage. **Production considerations:** prefers cast
limit of 8. **Best submission time:** Sep-Feb. **Response time:** 3-6 months.

DIXON PLACE

(Founded 1986)
258 Bowery; New York, NY 10012; (212) 219-3088, FAX 274-9114
Andrew J. Mellen and Micah Schraft, *Curators of New Play
    Reading Series*
Submission procedure: no unsolicited scripts; direct solicitation to playwright
or agent. **Types of material:** full-length plays, one-acts, musicals. **Special
interests:** works by New York City-based writers only; works by women; writers
of color; "adventurous settings"; no "kitchen-sink soap operas." **Facilities:** Dixon
Place, 70 seats, thrust stage. **Production considerations:** readings only; small
stage; no sets; minimal lighting.

DO GOODER PRODUCTIONS, INC.

(Founded 1994)
359 West 54th St, Suite 4FS; New York, NY 10019; (212) 581–8852,
FAX 541–7928; email dogooder@panix.com;
Web site http://www.panix.com/~dogooder
Mark Robert Gordon, *Founding Artistic Director*

Submission procedure: no unsolicited scripts; direct solicitation to playwright or agent. **Types of material:** full-length plays, one-acts, solo pieces. **Facilities:** no permanent facility; performs in various 99-150-seat venues.

DOBAMA THEATRE

(Founded 1960)
1846 Coventry Rd; Cleveland Heights, OH 44118; (216) 932–6838,
FAX 932–3259

Submission procedure: accepts unsolicited scripts from OH playwrights only; others send synopsis, sample pages and letter of inquiry. **Types of material:** full-length plays, solo pieces. **Special interests:** plays with opportunities for ethnically diverse casting; plays that make a statement about contemporary life. **Facilities:** Dobama Theatre, 200 seats, thrust stage. **Production considerations:** prefers cast limit of 9; limited production demands; no fly space. **Best submission time:** year-round. **Response time:** 9 months letter; 9-12 months script. **Special programs:** one world premiere: production of 1 new play included in mainstage season each year; preference given to members of Cleveland Play House Playwrights' Unit; Owen Kelly Adopt-a-Playwright Program: 2 full-length plays by OH residents each given developmental work with director, dramaturg and cast, culminating in readings; playwright must be available to participate; to apply, submit script to the attention of the program; *deadline:* 1 Feb 2001; *notification:* 15 May 2001; *dates:* Jun 2001. Marilyn Bianchi Kids' Playwriting Festival: annual short-play competition open to students attending Cuyahoga County schools, grades 1-12; winners receive savings bonds, publication and/or full production; write for application starting Sep 2000; *deadline:* Feb 2001; exact date TBA.

DORSET THEATRE FESTIVAL

(Founded 1976)
Box 510; Dorset, VT 05251; (802) 867-2223, FAX 867-0144;
  email theatre@sover.net;
  Web site http://www.theatredirectories.com
Jill Charles, *Artistic Director*

Submission procedure: no unsolicited scripts; synopsis, 10-page dialogue sample, character/set breakdown and letter of inquiry with SASP for response; include production history of readings in New York City-New England area if available. **Types of material:** full-length plays. **Special interests:** plays with broad commercial appeal. **Facilities:** Dorset Playhouse, 218 seats, proscenium stage. **Production considerations:** cast limit of 8; prefers 1 set or unit set. **Best submission time:** Sep-Dec. **Response time:** 3 months letter; 6-12 months script. **Special programs:** Dorset Colony for Writers (see Colonies).

DOUBLE EDGE THEATRE

(Founded 1982)
948 Conway Rd, Ashfield, MA 01330; (413) 628-0277,
  FAX 628-0026; email DETfarm@aol.com
Carlos Uriona, *Associate Director*

Submission procedure: no unsolicited scripts; accepts video of original performance only. **Types of material:** solo pieces, performance art. **Special interests:** artists who create their own work. **Facilities:** DET Performance Space, 100 seats, flexible stage; DET Pavillion, 75 seats, flexible stage. **Best submission time:** year-round. **Response time:** 6 months. **Special programs:** Artists-in-Residence: 1-3-month program in which artists create original performance work at DET, housing and rehearsal space provided. Residency program, 2 day-2 weeks long, in which artists conduct necessary research.

DRAMA DEPT., INCORPORATED

(Founded 1995)
27 Barrow St; New York, NY 10014; (212) 633-9108;
  email dramadept@aol.com; Web site http://www.dramadept.com
Michael S. Rosenberg, *Managing Director*

Submission procedure: no unsolicited scripts; all projects initiated by company members. **Types of material:** full-length plays, one-acts, translations, adaptations, musicals, cabaret/revues. **Special interests:** neglected classics. **Facilities:** no permanent facility.

DUDLEY RIGGS INSTANT THEATRE COMPANY
(Founded 1954)
1586 Burton St; St. Paul, MN 55108; (612) 647-6748,
FAX 647-5637
Dudley Riggs, *Producing Director*
Submission procedure: accepts unsolicited scripts with synopsis and letter of inquiry; include cassette for musicals. **Types of material:** capsule musicals/songs, cabaret/revues, solo pieces. **Special interests:** prefers work with no previous mainstage productions; comedies; satiric comedies about contemporary issues such as intergenerational relationships, aging, retirement, loss and recovery. **Facilities:** Dudley Riggs Theatre, 260 seats, modified thrust stage. **Production considerations:** cast limit of 3-7. **Best submission time:** year-round. **Response time:** 8 months.

EAST WEST PLAYERS
(Founded 1965)
244 South San Pedro St, Suite 301; Los Angeles, CA 90012;
(213) 625-7000, FAX 625-7111;
email info@eastwestplayers.org;
Web site http://eastwestplayers.org
Ken Narasaki, *Literary Manager*
Submission procedure: accepts unsolicited scripts with SASE for response. **Types of material:** full-length plays, translations, adaptations, plays for young audiences, musicals. **Special interests:** plays by or about Asian-Pacific-Americans. **Facilities:** The David Henry Hwang Theatre at Union Center for the Arts, 265 seats, proscenium stage. **Production considerations:** minimal production demands. **Best submission time:** year-round. **Response time:** 3-8 months. (See Prizes and David Henry Hwang Writers Institute in Development.)

ECCENTRIC THEATRE COMPANY
(Founded 1992)
413 D St; Anchorage, AK 99501; (907) 274-2599,
FAX 277-4698; email cyrano@ak.net;
Web site http://www.cyrano.org
Sandy Harper, *Producer*
Submission procedure: no unsolicited scripts; professional recommendation. **Types of material:** full-length plays, one-acts, adaptations, solo pieces. **Facilities:** Cyrano's Off Center Playhouse, 86 seats, black box. **Best submission time:** year-round. **Response time:** 8 months.

EDYVEAN REPERTORY THEATRE

(Founded 1967)
Box 47509; Indianapolis, IN 46227–7509; (317) 788–2075,
    FAX 788–2079; email ert@indy.net;
    Web site http://www.edyvean.org
Frederick Marshall, *Administrative Director*

Submission procedure: no unsolicited scripts; synopsis and letter of inquiry. **Types of material:** full-length plays, one-acts, musicals. **Facilities:** Mainstage, 750 seats, proscenium stage. **Best submission time:** summer. **Response time:** 6 months letter; 9 months script.

EL PORTAL CENTER FOR THE ARTS

(Formerly Actors Alley)
(Founded 1971)
El Portal Center for the Arts; 5269 Lankershim Blvd;
    North Hollywood, CA 91601; (818) 508–4234, FAX 508–5113;
Jeremiah Morris, *Artistic Director*

Submission procedure: no unsolicited scripts; agent submission. **Types of material:** full-length plays, translations, adaptations, plays for young audiences. **Special interests:** works by southern CA-based writers. **Facilities:** Pavilion, 350 seats, proscenium/thrust stage; Circle Forum, 99 seats, flexible stage; Store Front Theatre, 42 seats, proscenium stage. **Production considerations:** small cast for Store Front. **Best submission time:** Nov. **Response time:** 12 months. **Special programs:** year-round reading series.

THE EMELIN THEATRE FOR THE PERFORMING ARTS

(Founded 1973)
Library Lane; Mamaroneck, NY 10543; (914) 698–3045,
    FAX 698–1404; email emelin98@aol.com;
    Web site http://www.emelin.org
John Raymond, *Managing Director*

Submission procedure: accepts unsolicited scripts with professional recommendation only; include video for solo pieces. **Types of material:** full-length plays, chamber musicals, cabaret/revues, solo pieces. **Facilities:** The Emelin Theatre, 280 seats, proscenium stage. **Production considerations:** small cast; no fly space. **Best submission time:** year-round. **Response time:** 2 months.

THE EMPTY SPACE THEATRE
(Founded 1970)
3509 Fremont Ave N; Seattle, WA 98103–8813; (206) 547–7633,
   FAX 547–7635; Web site http://emptyspace.com
Eddie Levi Lee, *Artistic Director*
Submission procedure: accepts unsolicited scripts with SASE for response from Puget Sound region playwrights only; others send synopsis, 10-page dialogue sample and letter of inquiry with SASP for response. **Types of material:** full-length plays, translations, adaptations, musicals, solo pieces. **Special interests:** "plays unique to the event of live theatre." **Facilities:** The Empty Space Theatre at the Fremont Palace, 150 seats, endstage. **Production considerations:** prefers small casts. **Best submission time:** year-round. **Response time:** 1–2 months.

ENSEMBLE STUDIO THEATRE
(Founded 1972)
549 West 52nd St; New York, NY 10019; (212) 247–4982,
   FAX 664–0041
Jamie Richards, *Executive Producer*
Submission procedure: accepts unsolicited scripts. **Types of material:** full-length plays, one-acts. **Facilities:** Mainstage, 99 seats, black box; Studio, 60 seats, proscenium stage. **Best submission time:** year-round. **Response time:** 6 months. **Special programs:** summer reading series and playwriting workshops. First Look: reading series of full-length plays. Going to the River: annual festival and ongoing monthly reading series celebrating African-American women playwrights. First Light: festival of new works exploring the worlds of science and technology. Annual Marathon of One-Act Plays: one-act play festival; *deadline:* 1 Dec 2000; *dates:* May–Jun 2001.

ENSEMBLE THEATRE OF CINCINNATI
(Founded 1986)
1127 Vine St; Cincinnati, OH 45210; (513) 421–3555,
   FAX 562–4104
D. Lynn Meyers, *Producing Artistic Director*
Submission procedure: no unsolicited scripts; synopsis, dialogue sample, resume and letter of inquiry. **Types of material:** full-length plays, adaptations, plays for young audiences. **Facilities:** Ensemble Theatre of Cincinnati, 202 seats, thrust stage. **Production considerations:** cast limit of 6; simple set. **Best submission time:** Sep. **Response time:** 1 month letter; 4 months script.

ESSENTIAL THEATRE
(Founded 1987)
995 Greenwood Ave, #6; Atlanta, GA 30306; (404) 876-8471
Peter Hardy, *Producing Artistic Director*
Submission procedure: accepts unsolicited scripts. **Types of material:** full-length plays. **Special interests:** work not produced professionally; will also consider second or third production. **Facilities:** no permanent facility. **Best submission time:** spring. **Response time:** 6 months.

EUREKA THEATRE COMPANY
(Founded 1972)
555 Howard St, Suite 201A; San Francisco, CA 94105;
    (415) 243-9899, FAX 243-0789
Dawson Moore, *Literary Manager*
Submission procedure: no unsolicited scripts; 5-10-page dialogue sample, character list and letter of inquiry. **Types of material:** full-length plays, translations, solo pieces. **Special interests:** dynamic contemporary plays; unconventional comedies. **Facilities:** Mainstage, 200 seats, proscenium stage. **Best submission time:** year-round. **Response time:** 2 months letter; 6 months script. **Special programs:** Discovery Series: monthly readings of new plays presented for the public and followed by audience discussion.

FAMOUS DOOR THEATRE
(Founded 1987)
Box 57029, Chicago, IL 60657; (773) 404-8283, FAX 404-8292;
    email theatre@famousdoortheatre.org;
    Web site http://www.famousdoortheatre.org
Karen Kessler, *Artistic Director*
Submission procedure: accepts unsolicited scripts. **Types of material:** full-length plays, translations, adaptations. **Facilities:** Theatre Building North Theatre, 150 seats, thrust stage. **Best submission time:** Nov-Mar. **Response time:** 3 months script. **Special programs:** 8th Annual Women at the Door Staged Reading Series (see Development).

FIRST STAGE MILWAUKEE
(Founded 1987)
929 North Water St; Milwaukee, WI 53202; (414) 273-2314,
FAX 273-5595; email goodman@firststage.org;
Web site http://www.firststage.org
Rob Goodman, *Producer/Artistic Director*
Submission procedure: no unsolicited scripts; synopsis, resume and letter of inquiry. **Types of material:** works for young audiences, including translations, adaptations and musicals. **Facilities:** Marcus Center for the Performing Arts's Todd Wehr Theater, 500 seats, thrust stage. **Best submission time:** spring-summer. **Response time:** 1 month letter; 3 months script.

FLEETWOOD STAGE
(Founded 1993)
44 Wildcliff Dr; New Rochelle, NY 10805; (914) 654-8533,
FAX 235-4459
Lewis Arlt, *Producing Director*
Submission procedure: accepts unsolicited scripts; prefers professional recommendation. **Types of material:** full-length plays. **Facilities:** Playhouse at Wildcliff, 100 seats, proscenium stage. **Production considerations:** cast limit of 8; prefers unit set. **Best submission time:** year-round. **Response time:** 6-9 months. **Special programs:** Playwright's Forum: developmental program for playwrights in Westchester and Fairfield Counties; send SASE for application and guidelines.

FLORIDA STAGE
(Founded 1987)
262 South Ocean Blvd; Manalapan, FL 33462; (561) 585-3404,
FAX 588-4708; email info@floridastage.org;
Web site http://www.floridastage.org
Louis Tyrrell, *Producing Director*
Submission procedure: no unsolicited scripts; agent submission. **Types of material:** full-length plays, plays for young audiences. **Special interests:** contemporary issues and ideas. **Facilities:** Florida Stage, 250 seats, thrust stage. **Production considerations:** cast limit of 2-6; 1 set. **Best submission time:** year-round. **Response time:** 3-4 months. **Special programs:** reading series.

FLORIDA STUDIO THEATRE
(Founded 1973)
1241 North Palm Ave; Sarasota, FL 34236; (941) 366–9017
James Ashford, *Casting & Literary Coordinator*
Submission procedure: no unsolicited scripts; synopsis and letter of inquiry.
Types of material: full-length plays, translations, adaptations, musicals,
cabaret/revues, solo pieces. **Facilities:** Florida Studio Theatre, 173 seats, semi-
thrust stage; FST Cabaret Club, 100 seats, cabaret space. **Best submission time:**
Aug-Apr. **Response time:** 1-2 weeks letter; 6 months script. **Special programs:**
Sarasota Festival of New Plays: 4-tier festival includes Young Playwrights Festival:
workshop productions of plays by playwrights grades 2-12; *deadline:* 1 Apr
2001; *dates:* May 2001. Burdick New Play Festival: workshop productions of 3
new plays; playwright receives stipend, travel, housing; scripts selected through
theatre's normal submission procedure; *dates:* May 2001. New Play Summer Fest:
workshop productions of 3 new plays; playwright receives stipend, travel,
housing; scripts selected through theatre's normal submission procedure; *dates:*
Jul-Aug 2001. Fall staged reading series. Florida Shorts Contest (see Prizes).

THE FOOTHILL THEATRE COMPANY
(Founded 1977)
Box 1812; Nevada City, CA 95959; (530) 265–9320
Gary Wright, *Literary Manager*
Submission procedure: accepts unsolicited scripts. **Types of material:** full-
length plays, one-acts, translations, adaptations, plays for young audiences, solo
pieces. **Facilities:** The Nevada Theatre, 246 seats, proscenium stage; also rents
small spaces with 50-100 seats. **Production considerations:** very limited fly and
wing space. **Best submission time:** year-round. **Response time:** 6-12 months.
Special programs: New Voices of the Wild West: annual fall reading series of 4
plays dealing with issues pertaining to rural American West.

FORD'S THEATRE
(Founded 1968)
511 Tenth St NW; Washington, DC 20004; (202) 638–2941,
    FAX 737–3017
Brian J. Laczko, *Managing Director*
Submission procedure: no unsolicited scripts; synopsis, sample pages and letter
of inquiry. **Types of material:** full-length plays, musicals. **Special interests:** small-
scale musicals and works celebrating the African-American experience. **Facilities:**
Ford's Theatre, 699 seats, proscenium/thrust stage. **Production considerations:**
cast limit of 15. **Best submission time:** spring–summer. **Response time:** 3 months
letter; 6-12 months script.

THE FOUNTAIN THEATRE

(Founded 1990)

5060 Fountain Ave; Los Angeles, CA 90029; (323) 663-2235,
    FAX 663-1629

Simon Levy, *Producing Director/Dramaturg*

Submission procedure: no unsolicited scripts; synopsis and letter of inquiry. **Types of material:** full-length plays, translations, adaptations. **Special interests:** lyrical dramas; contemporary comedies; works with dance; adaptations of American literature. **Facilities:** Fountain Theatre Mainstage, 78 seats, thrust stage. **Production considerations:** cast limit of 12; 1 set; no fly space; low ceiling. **Best submission time:** year-round. **Response time:** 3 months letter; 6 months script.

FREE STREET PROGRAMS

(Founded 1969)

1419 West Blackhawk St; Chicago, IL 60622; (773) 772-7248,
    FAX 772-7248; email free@mcs.net

Ron Bieganski, *Artistic Director*
David Schein, *Executive Director*

Submission procedure: no unsolicited scripts; letter from writer with "a concept for a show or a brilliant idea for a new theatre program for inner-city kids/teens." **Types of material:** plays and performance pieces, including shows to be performed in public places or outdoors. **Special interests:** inner-city kids/teenagers; "cultural empowerment of new populations"; developing works with communities; enhancing literacy through the arts; new work by Chicago-area artists. **Facilities:** national/international touring company (teens). **Production considerations:** no expensive production demands. **Response time:** 2 months letter; 2 months script.

FREEDOM REPERTORY THEATRE

(Founded 1966)

1346 North Broad St; Philadelphia, PA 19121; (215) 765-2793,
    FAX 765-4191

Barbara Silzle, *Director of Artistic Initiatives*

Submission procedure: no unsolicited scripts; synopsis, 5-10-page work sample, resume and letter of inquiry. **Types of material:** full-length plays, musicals, cabaret/revues. **Special interests:** contemporary plays with African-American themes. **Facilities:** John E. Allen Theatre, 299 seats, proscenium stage; Freedom Cabaret Theatre, 120 seats, flexible stage. **Best submission time:** year-round. **Response time:** 6-12 weeks. **Special programs:** Freedom Fest: play reading series; resident playwright program; commissioning program; all programs are by invitation only.

FRONTERA @ HYDE PARK THEATRE
(Founded 1992)
2832 East Milk Blvd, Suite 104; Austin, TX 78702; (512) 479-7530,
FAX 479-7531
Vicky Boone, *Artistic Director*
Submission procedure: no unsolicited scripts; synopsis and letter of inquiry.
Types of material: full-length plays, translations, adaptations, musicals, solo
pieces. **Facilities:** Hyde Park Theatre, 90 seats, flexible. **Best submission time:**
year-round. **Response time:** 3 months letter; 6 months script.

FULTON OPERA HOUSE/ACTOR'S COMPANY OF PENNSYLVANIA
(Founded 1963)
Box 1865; Lancaster, PA 17608-1865; (717) 394-7133,
FAX 397-3780; email artdir@fultontheatre.org;
Web site http://www.fultontheatre.org
Michael Mitchell, *Artistic Director*
Submission procedure: no unsolicited scripts; synopsis and letter of inquiry.
Types of material: full-length plays, adaptations. **Special interests:** mainstream
works on contemporary issues; plays that embrace diversity. **Facilities:** Fulton
Opera House, 630 seats, proscenium stage; Studio Theatre, 100 seats, black box.
Production considerations: cast limit of 10. **Best submission time:** fall.
Response time: 3-6 months letter; 6 months script. **Special programs:** Mondays
in May: annual concert reading series of new plays.

GALA HISPANIC THEATRE
(Founded 1976)
Box 43209; Washington, DC 20010; (202) 234-7174,
FAX 332-1247; email galadc@aol.com;
Web site http://www.galadc.org
Hugo J. Medrano, *Producing/Artistic Director*
Submission procedure: no unsolicited scripts; synopsis/description of play and
letter of inquiry. **Types of material:** full-length plays, solo pieces. **Special
interests:** plays by Spanish, Latino or Hispanic-American writers in Spanish or
English only; prefers Spanish-language works with accompanying English
translation; works that reflect sociocultural realities of Hispanics in Latin
America, the Caribbean or Spain, as well as the Hispanic-American experience.
Facilities: GALA Hispanic Theatre, 200 seats, proscenium stage. **Production
considerations:** cast limit of 6-8. **Best submission time:** Apr-May. **Response
time:** 1 month letter; 12 months script. **Special programs:** poetry onstage.

GEFFEN PLAYHOUSE

(Founded 1995)

10886 LeConte Ave; Los Angeles, CA 90024; (310) 208-6500,
    FAX 208-0341

Amy Levinson, *Literary Manager*

Submission procedure: no unsolicited scripts; synopsis, dialogue sample and letter of inquiry. **Types of material:** full-length plays, adaptations, musicals. **Facilities:** Geffen Playhouse, 498 seats, proscenium stage. **Best submission time:** year-round. **Response time:** 6 weeks letter; 6 months script.

GEORGE STREET PLAYHOUSE

(Founded 1974)

9 Livingston Ave; New Brunswick, NJ 08901; (732) 846-2895,
    FAX 247-9151; Web site http://www.georgestplayhouse.org

Literary Associate

Submission procedure: no unsolicited scripts; synopsis, 10-page dialogue sample, character breakdown and letter of inquiry. **Types of material:** full-length plays; one-acts. **Special interests:** social issue one-acts suitable for touring to schools (not seeking any other kind of one-acts); comedies and dramas that present a fresh perspective on our society; "work that tells a compelling, personal, human story while entertaining, challenging and stretching the imagination." **Facilities:** Mainstage, 367 seats, proscenium/thrust stage. **Production considerations:** prefers cast limit of 7. **Best submission time:** year-round. **Response time:** 8-10 months. **Special programs:** Next Stage Festival: workshops of 1-3 new plays. The Diva & Gentle Man Projects: presentation of new material written and performed by 8 solo artists.

GEORGIA REPERTORY THEATRE

(Founded 1990)

Department of Drama, University of Georgia;
    Athens, GA 30602-3154; (706) 542-2836, FAX 542-2080;
    email longman@arches.uga.edu

Stanley V. Longman, *Dramaturg*

Submission procedure: no unsolicited scripts; letter of inquiry. **Types of material:** full-length plays. **Special interests:** plays not produced professionally. **Facilities:** Fine Arts Theatre, 750 seats, proscenium stage; Cellar Theatre, 100 seats, proscenium stage; Seney Stovall Theatre, 250 seats, proscenium stage. **Production considerations:** cast limit of 8; minimal set. **Best submission time:** Jun-Sep only. **Response time:** 3-6 months.

GERMINAL STAGE DENVER

(Founded 1974)
2450 West 44th Ave; Denver, CO 80211; (303) 455-7108;
email gsden@privatei.com;
Web site http://www2.privatei.com/gsden
Ed Baierlein, *Director/Manager*

Submission procedure: no unsolicited scripts; synopsis, 5-page dialogue sample and letter of inquiry with SASP for response. **Types of material:** full-length plays, translations, adaptations. **Special interests:** adaptations that use both dialogue and narration. **Facilities:** Germinal Stage Denver, 100 seats, thrust stage. **Production considerations:** cast limit of 10; minimal production requirements. **Best submission time:** year-round. **Response time:** 2 weeks letter; 6 months script.

GEVA THEATRE

(Founded 1972)
75 Woodbury Blvd; Rochester, NY 14607-1717; (716) 232-1366
Jean Ryon, *New Plays Coordinator*

Submission procedure: no unsolicited scripts; synopsis, dialogue sample, production history, resume and letter of inquiry. **Types of material:** full-length plays, translations, adaptations. **Facilities:** Elaine P. Wilson Theatre, 552 seats, modified thrust stage; Ronald and Donna Fielding Nextstage, 180 seats, modified proscenium. **Best submission time:** year-round. **Response time:** 1 month letter; 6 months script. **Special programs:** American Voices New Play Reading Series; Hibernatus Interruptus, A Winter Festival of New Plays: 2-week workshops of 3 plays; Regional Playwrights and Young Writers Festival; scripts for all special programs selected through theatre's regular submission procedure.

THE GLINES

(Founded 1976)
240 West 44th St; New York, NY 10036; (212) 354-8899

Submission procedure: accepts unsolicited scripts with SASE for response. **Types of material:** full-length plays. **Special interests:** plays dealing with gay experience only; plays not previously produced in New York City. **Facilities:** no permanent facility. **Best submission time:** year-round. **Response time:** 2 months.

GOODMAN THEATRE

(Founded 1925)
As of Nov 2000: 170 North Dearborn St; Chicago, IL 60601;
Prior to Nov 2000: 200 South Columbus Dr; Chicago, IL 60603;
    (312) 443-3811, FAX 263-6004;
    email staff@goodman-theatre.org
Susan V. Booth, *Director of New Play Development*
Submission procedure: no unsolicited scripts; synopsis, professional recommendation and letter of inquiry. **Types of material:** full-length plays, translations, musicals, solo pieces. **Special interests:** social or political themes. **Facilities:** Albert Ivar Goodman Theatre, 830 seats, proscenium stage; Owen Bruner Goodman Theatre, 200–400 seats, flexible stage. **Best submission time:** year-round. **Response time:** 2-3 months letter; 6-8 months script.

GOODSPEED OPERA HOUSE

(Founded 1963)
Box A; East Haddam, CT 06423; (860) 873-8664, FAX 873-2329;
    email info@goodspeed.org; Web site http://www.goodspeed.org
Sue Frost, *Associate Producer*
Submission procedure: no unsolicited scripts; synopsis, sample cassette and letter of inquiry. **Types of material:** original musicals only. **Facilities:** Goodspeed Opera House, 400 seats, proscenium stage; Goodspeed-at-Chester, 200 seats, adaptable proscenium stage. **Best submission time:** Jan–Mar. **Response time:** 3 months letter; 12 months script.

GREAT AMERICAN HISTORY THEATRE

(Founded 1978)
30 East Tenth St; St. Paul, MN 55101; (612) 292-4323,
    FAX 292-4322
Ron Peluso, *Artistic Director*
Submission procedure: no unsolicited scripts; direct solicitation to playwright or agent. **Types of material:** full-length plays, adaptations, musicals, solo pieces. **Special interests:** full-length plays involving Midwest or Minnesota history only; no pageants. **Facilities:** Crawford Livingston Theatre, 597 seats, thrust stage. **Production considerations:** cast limit of 6; moderate production demands; small musicals only.

GRETNA THEATRE
(Founded 1926)
Box 578; Mt. Gretna, PA 17064; (717) 964-3322, FAX 964-2189

Submission procedure: no unsolicited scripts; synopsis, 5-page dialogue sample, character list with descriptions, production history and letter of inquiry; include cassette for musicals. **Types of material:** full-length plays, musicals. **Special interests:** plays suitable for summer audiences; prefers comedies; musicals. **Facilities:** Mt. Gretna Playhouse, 700 seats, proscenium stage. **Production considerations:** open-air facility; 14' ceiling over stage. **Best submission time:** Aug-Apr. **Response time:** 1 month letter; 3 months script.

THE GROUP AT THE STRASBERG ACTING STUDIO
(Founded 2000)
7936 Santa Monica Blvd, West Hollywood, CA 90046;
   (323) 650-7777, FAX 650-7770;
   Web site http://www.strasberg.com
Jay Dysart, *Director of Production*

Submission procedure: no unsolicited scripts; 1-page synopsis, 10-page dialogue sample, cast breakdown, resume and letter of inquiry with SASE for response. **Types of material:** full-length plays, translations, adaptations. **Facilities:** Marilyn Monroe Theatre, 99 seats, endstage; Studio Stras, 49 seats; endstage; Stage Lee, 49 seats, endstage. **Best submission time:** year-round. **Response Time:** 2-3 months letter, 6-10 months script. **Special programs:** workshop production series, reading series.

THE GUTHRIE THEATER
(Founded 1963)
725 Vineland Place; Minneapolis, MN 55403; (612) 347-1185,
   FAX 347-1188; email joh@guthrietheater.org
Literary Department

Submission procedure: no unsolicited scripts; professional recommendation with SASE for response. **Types of material:** full-length plays, translations, adaptations. **Special interests:** well-crafted, highly theatrical works of depth and significance; richly poetic language dealing with universal themes in today's context; adaptations of classic literature; no sitcoms. **Facilities:** Guthrie Theater, 1309 seats, thrust stage; Guthrie Lab, 350 seats, flexible stage. **Best submission time:** year-round. **Response time:** 3-4 months.

HANGAR THEATRE

(Founded 1964)
Box 205; Ithaca, NY 14850; (607) 273-8588, FAX 273-4516;
    Web site http://www.hangartheatre.org
Jamie Grady, *Managing Director*
Submission procedure: no unsolicited scripts; agent submission. **Types of material:** full-length plays, one-acts. **Facilities:** Mainstage, 377 seats, thrust stage. **Best submission time:** Sep-Dec. **Response time:** 3 months.

THE HARBOR THEATRE

(Founded 1998)
160 West 71st St, PHA; New York, NY 10023; (212) 787-1945
Stuart Warmflash, *Artistic Director*
Submission procedure: no unsolicited scripts; synopsis and letter of inquiry. **Types of material:** full-length plays, musicals. **Facilities:** no permanent facility. **Best submission time:** year-round. **Response time:** 2 weeks letter; 3 months script. **Special programs:** The Harbor Theatre Workshop (see Membership and Service Organizations).

HARTFORD STAGE COMPANY

(Founded 1964)
50 Church St; Hartford, CT 06103; (860) 525-5601, FAX 525-4420
Christopher Baker, *Literary Director*
Submission procedure: no unsolicited scripts; direct solicitation to playwright or agent. **Types of material:** full-length plays, translations, adaptations. **Facilities:** John W. Huntington Theatre, 489 seats, thrust stage.

HEDGEROW THEATRE

(Founded 1923)
146 West Rose Valley Rd; Wallingford, PA 19086;
    (610) 565-4211; Web site http://www.hedgerowtheatre.org
Walt Vail, *Literary Manager*
Submission procedure: no unsolicited scripts; synopsis and letter of inquiry. **Types of material:** full-length plays. **Special interests:** new plays by DE, NJ and PA playwrights; mysteries; comedies. **Facilities:** Mainstage, 144 seats, proscenium stage. **Production considerations:** small stage; minimal production demands. **Best submission time:** year-round. **Response time:** 2 months letter; 4 months script.

HIDDEN THEATRE

(Founded 1994)
2301 Franklin Ave E; Minneapolis, MN 55406; (612) 339–4949,
FAX 332–6037; Web site http://www.hiddentheatre.org
David Pisa, *Audience Services Manager*
Submission procedure: no unsolicited scripts; synopsis, 10-page dialogue sample, bio and letter of inquiry. **Types of material:** full-length plays, translations, adaptations. **Special interests:** theatrically inventive new material that asks challenging questions suitable for core ensemble 20-30 years old. **Facilities:** no permanent facility. **Best submission time:** year-round. **Response time:** 6-10 weeks letter; 6-10 months script.

HIP POCKET THEATRE

(Founded 1977)
Box 136758; Fort Worth, TX 76136; (817) 246–9775,
FAX 246–5651; email dsimons@hippocket.org;
Web site http://hippocket.org
Johnny Simons, *Artistic Director*
Submission procedure: accepts unsolicited scripts; include cassette for musicals. **Types of material:** full-length plays, translations, adaptations, plays for young audiences, musicals, solo pieces, multimedia works. **Special interests:** well-crafted stories with poetic, mythic slant that incorporate ritual and ensemble; works utilizing masks, puppetry, music, dance, mime and strong visual elements. **Facilities:** Oak Acres Amphitheatre, 175 seats, outdoor amphitheatre. **Production considerations:** simple sets. **Best submission time:** Oct–Feb. **Response time:** 6 weeks.

THE HIPPODROME STATE THEATRE

(Founded 1973)
25 Southeast Second Place; Gainesville, FL 32601–6596;
(352) 373–5968, FAX 371–9130; Web site http://hipp.gator.net
Tamerin Dygert, *Dramaturg*
Submission procedure: no unsolicited scripts; professional recommendation. **Types of material:** full-length plays, one-acts. **Special interests:** multicultural plays. **Facilities:** Mainstage Theatre, 266 seats, thrust stage; Second Stage, 87 seats, flexible stage. **Production considerations:** cast limit of 6; unit set. **Best submission time:** May-Aug. **Response time:** 1-2 months letter; 3-5 months script. **Special programs:** informal play reading series: possibility of production on the second stage or in site-specific gallery and bar spaces; scripts selected through theatre's normal submission procedure.

HONOLULU THEATRE FOR YOUTH

(Founded 1955)
2846 Ualena St; Honolulu, HI 96819-1910; (808) 839-9885,
 FAX 839-7018; email mark_lutwak@juno.com;
 Web site http://www.htyweb.org
Mark Lutwak, *Artistic Director*
Submission procedure: no unsolicited scripts; synopsis, resume and letter of
inquiry. **Types of material:** plays for young audiences. **Special interests:** plays
with contemporary themes for audiences from pre-school through high school;
small-cast adaptations of classics; new works based on Pacific Rim cultures; plays
with compelling language that are imaginative and socially relevant. **Facilities:**
Richardson Theatre, 800 seats, proscenium stage; Leeward Community College
Theatre, 650 seats, proscenium stage; McCoy Pavilion, 300 seats, flexible stage;
Tenney Theatre, 300 seats, flexible stage; shows also tour to school theatres,
gymnasiums and cafeterias. **Production considerations:** cast limit of 6. **Best
submission time:** year-round. **Response time:** 1 month letter; 4-5 months script.

HORIZON THEATRE COMPANY

(Founded 1983)
Box 5376; Atlanta, GA 31107; (404) 523-1477, FAX 584-8815;
 email horizonco@mindspring.com;
 Web site http://www.mindspring.com/horizonco
Stephanie Harvey, *Literary Manager*
Submission procedure: no unsolicited scripts except for Festival (see below);
synopsis, resume and letter of inquiry. **Types of material:** full-length plays,
translations, adaptations, musicals. **Special interests:** contemporary issues; plays
by women; southern urban themes; comedies. **Facilities:** Horizon Theatre, 170-
200 seats, flexible stage. **Production considerations:** plays cast from ensemble
of up to 12 actors. **Best submission time:** year-round. **Response time:** 6 months
letter; 12 months script. **Special programs:** Teen Ensemble: one-acts about teen
issues to be performed by teens. Senior Citizens Ensemble: one-acts about senior
citizen issues to be performed by senior citizens. New South for the New Century
Festival: annual festival of readings, workshops and full productions of plays by
playwrights speaking from, for and about the South; *deadline:* 1 Mar 2001;
notification: 1 Apr 2001; *dates:* Jun-Jul 2001.

HORSE CAVE THEATRE
(Founded 1977)
Box 215; Horse Cave, KY 42749; (270) 786–1200,
    FAX 786–5298; email hctstaff@scrtc.com;
    Web site http://www.horsecavetheatre.org
Warren Hammack, *Artistic Director*
Submission procedure: no unsolicited scripts; professional recommendation.
Types of material: full-length plays. **Special interests:** KY-based plays by KY playwrights. **Facilities:** Horse Cave Theatre, 346 seats, thrust stage. **Production considerations:** cast limit of 10; 1 set. **Best submission time:** Oct-Apr.
Response time: varies.

HUDSON THEATRE
(Founded 1991)
6539 Santa Monica Blvd; Hollywood, CA 90038; (323) 856–4252,
    FAX 856–4316; email hudsonthr@aol.com
Elizabeth Reilly, *Artistic Director*
Submission procedure: no unsolicited scripts; synopsis and letter of inquiry.
Types of material: full-length plays, one-acts, musicals, solo pieces. **Facilities:** Mainstage, 99 seats, modified thrust stage; Avenue Theatre, 99 seats, runway; Guild Theatre, 43 seats, proscenium stage. **Best submission time:** year-round.
Response time: 3-6 months letter; 1 year script.

THE HUMAN RACE THEATRE COMPANY
(Founded 1986)
126 North Main St, Suite 300; Dayton, OH 45402–1710;
    (937) 461–3823, FAX 461–7223; email hrtheatre@aol.com;
    Web site http://www.humanracetheatre.org
Tony Dallas, *Playwright in Residence*
Submission procedure: no unsolicited scripts; professional recommendation.
Types of material: full-length plays, one-acts, adaptations; plays for young audiences. **Special interests:** OH playwrights; adaptations and original works for junior and senior high school audiences; contemporary issues. **Facilities:** The Loft, 219 seats, thrust stage. **Production considerations:** small cast; no fly space; plays for young audiences tour to schools. **Best submission time:** Dec-Feb.
Response time: 6 months.

HUNTINGTON THEATRE COMPANY

(Founded 1981)
264 Huntington Ave; Boston MA 02115-4606; (617) 266-7900,
FAX 353-8300
Christopher Wigle, *Associate Artistic Director*
Submission procedure: no unsolicited scripts; agent submission only. **Types of material:** full-length plays, translations, adaptations. **Facilities:** Huntington Theatre, 850 seats, proscenium stage. **Best submission time:** year-round. **Response time:** 6 months.

HYPOTHETICAL THEATRE CO., INC.

(Founded 1992)
344 East 14th St; New York, NY 10003; (212) 780-0800, ext 254,
FAX 780-0859; email htc@nyc.rr.com
Literary Manager
Submission procedure: synopsis, 10-page dialogue sample, character breakdown with SASE for response. **Types of material:** full-length plays, one-acts. **Special interests:** contemporary, ground-breaking plays. **Facilities:** Hypothetical Theatre, 99 seats, proscenium stage. **Best submission time:** year-round. **Response time:** 2 months letter; 6 months script. **Special programs:** Hypothetically Speaking: annual festival for 10-30-minute plays; send complete script for festival.

ILLINOIS THEATRE CENTER

(Founded 1976)
Box 397; Park Forest, IL 60466; (708) 481-3510,
FAX 481-3693; email ilthctr@bigplanet.com;
Web site http://www.ilthctr.org
Etel Billig, *Producing Director*
Submission procedure: no unsolicited scripts; synopsis and letter of inquiry with SASE for response. **Types of material:** full-length plays, musicals. **Facilities:** Illinois Theatre Center, 180 seats, proscenium/thrust stage. **Production considerations:** cast limit of 9 for plays, 14 for musicals. **Best submission time:** year-round. **Response time:** 1 month letter; 2 months script.

ILLUSION THEATER

(Founded 1974)
528 Hennepin Ave, Suite 704; Minneapolis, MN 55403;
(612) 339-4944, FAX 337-8042;
email illusiontheater@juno.com
Michael Robins, *Executive Producing Director*
Submission procedure: no unsolicited scripts; professional recommendation.
Types of material: full-length plays, one-acts, translations, adaptations, musicals,
solo pieces. **Special interests:** writers to collaborate on new works with company.
Facilities: Illusion Theater, 250 seats, semi-thrust stage. **Best submission time:**
Jul-Nov. **Response time:** 6-12 months. **Special programs:** Fresh Ink Series: 5-6
plays each presented with minimal set and costumes for 1 weekend; post-
performance discussion with audience, who are seated onstage; scripts selected
through theatre's normal submission procedure.

INDIANA REPERTORY THEATRE

(Founded 1972)
140 West Washington St; Indianapolis, IN 46204-3465;
(317) 635-5277, FAX 236-0767
Literary Manager
Submission procedure: no unsolicited scripts; synopsis and letter of inquiry with
SASE for response. **Types of material:** full-length plays, translations, adaptations,
solo pieces. **Special interests:** adaptations of classic literature; plays that explore
cultural/ethnic issues "with a Midwestern voice." **Facilities:** Mainstage, 600 seats,
modified proscenium stage; Upperstage, 300 seats, modified thrust stage.
Production considerations: cast limit of 6-8. **Best submission time:** year-round
(season chosen by Jan each year). **Response time:** 3-4 months letter; 6 months
script. **Special programs:** Discovery Series: presentation of plays for family
audiences with a focus on youth and culturally/ethnically diverse plays with an
emphasis on history and literature; scripts selected through theatre's normal
submission procedure.

INFERNAL BRIDEGROOM PRODUCTIONS

(Founded 1993)
Box 131644; Houston, TX 77219-1644; (713) 522-8443,
    FAX 630-5208; email infernalbridegroom@hotmail.com
Anthony Barilla, *Associate Director*
Submission procedure: accepts unsolicited scripts. **Types of material:** full-length plays, one-acts, translations, adaptations, plays for young audiences, musicals, solo pieces. **Special interests:** new works by new voices; highly theatrical, "hyper-real works." **Facilities:** no permanent facility; uses 99-seat theatres. **Best submission time:** year-round. **Response time:** 6-12 months script.

INTAR HISPANIC AMERICAN ARTS CENTER

(Founded 1966)
Box 756; New York, NY 10108; (212) 695-6134, ext 11,
    FAX 268-0102
Lorenzo Mans, *Artistic Associate*
Submission procedure: accepts unsolicited scripts. **Types of material:** full-length plays. **Special interests:** new plays by Hispanic-American writers and translations and adaptations of Hispanic works only. **Facilities:** INTAR 53, 74 seats, black box. **Production considerations:** small cast and modest production values. **Best submission time:** year-round (season chosen late summer-early fall). **Response time:** 3 months. **Special programs:** NewWorks Lab: workshop productions; reading series.

INTERACT THEATRE COMPANY

(Founded 1988)
2030 Sansom St; Philadelphia, PA 19103; (215) 568-8077,
    FAX 568-8095; email interact@interacttheatre.org;
    Web site http://www.interacttheatre.org
Seth Rozin, *Producing Artistic Director*
Larry Loebell, *Literary Manager*
Submission procedure: no unsolicited scripts; synopsis, 10-page dialogue sample and letter of inquiry. **Types of material:** full-length plays. **Special interests:** contemporary plays that theatrically explore issues of cultural, political and/or social significance. **Facilities:** The Adrienne, 106 seats, proscenium stage. **Production considerations:** cast limit of 10. **Best submission time:** year-round. **Response time:** 1 month letter; 3 months script. **Special programs:** annual Showcase of New Plays in Jan, including both developmental and fully staged readings; primarily local playwrights.

INTIMAN THEATRE

(Founded 1972)
Box 19760; Seattle, WA 98109; (206) 269-1901, FAX 269-1928;
  email scripts@intiman.org;
  Web site http://www.intiman.org
Mame Hunt, *Artistic Associate*
Submission procedure: no unsolicited scripts; professional recommendation.
Types of material: full-length plays, translations, adaptations. **Special interests:**
plays of complex ideas; unique use of form; language-oriented plays; no domestic
realism; no solo pieces. **Facilities:** Intiman Playhouse, 480 seats, modified thrust
stage. **Best submission time:** Nov-Mar. **Response time:** 4 months.

INVISIBLE THEATRE

(Founded 1976)
1400 North 1st Ave; Tucson, AZ 85719; (520) 882-9721,
  FAX 884-5410
Deborah Dickey, *Literary Manager*
Submission procedure: no unsolicited scripts; professional recommendation.
Types of material: full-length plays, one-acts, musicals, solo pieces. **Special
interests:** mainly but not exclusively works with contemporary settings; works
with strong female roles; social and political issues. **Facilities:** Invisible Theatre,
78 seats, black box. **Production considerations:** cast limit of 10; simple set;
minimal props; small-cast musicals only. **Best submission time:** Oct-Dec.
Response time: 6-12 months.

IRONDALE ENSEMBLE PROJECT

(Founded 1983)
Box 1314, Old Chelsea Station; New York, NY 10011-1314;
  (212) 633-1292, FAX 633-2078; email irondalert@aol.com;
  Web site http://www.irondale.org
Jim Niesen, *Artistic Director*
Submission procedure: no unsolicited scripts; letter of inquiry from playwright
interested in developing work with ensemble through ongoing workshop process.
Types of material: full-length plays, adaptations, plays with music. **Special
interests:** works with political or social relevance. **Facilities:** no permanent
facility. **Production considerations:** cast limit of 8-9. **Best submission time:**
Apr-Sep. **Response time:** 10 weeks.

JEWISH ENSEMBLE THEATRE

(Founded 1989)
6600 West Maple Rd; West Bloomfield, MI 48322-3002;
(248) 788-2900, FAX 788-5160; email jetplay@aol.com;
Web site http://www.comnet.org/jet
Evelyn Orbach, *Artistic Director*
Submission procedure: accepts unsolicited scripts. **Types of material:** full-length plays, one-acts, plays for young audiences. **Special interests:** works on Jewish themes and/or by Jewish writers; work not produced professionally. **Facilities:** Aaron DeRoy Theatre, 193 seats, thrust stage. **Production considerations:** no fly space. **Best submission time:** late spring–early fall. **Response time:** 6 months. **Special programs:** Festival of New Plays in Staged Readings: 4 plays given readings, possibly leading to mainstage production; scripts selected through theatre's normal submission procedure.

JOHN DREW THEATER

(Founded 1931)
158 Main St; East Hampton, NY 11937; (631) 324-0806,
FAX 324-2722; email joshgladstone@guildhall.org;
Web site http://www.guildhall.org
Josh Gladstone, *Director*
Submission procedure: no unsolicited scripts; 1-page synopsis, character/set breakdown and letter of inquiry. **Types of material:** full-length plays, solo pieces. **Special interests:** comedies; plays with contemporary setting. **Facilities:** John Drew Theater, 387 seats, proscenium stage. **Production considerations:** cast limit of 4; unit set; no fly space. **Best submission time:** year-round. **Response time:** 3 months letter; 3 months script.

JOMANDI PRODUCTIONS

(Founded 1978)
1444 Mayson St NE; Atlanta, GA 30324; (404) 876-6346,
FAX 872-5764; email jomandi@bellsouth.net
Literary Manager
Submission procedure: no unsolicited scripts; synopsis, dialogue sample, resume and letter of inquiry. **Types of material:** full-length plays, adaptations, plays for young audiences, musicals, solo pieces. **Special interests:** historical or contemporary portrayals of the African-American experience; adaptations of African-American literature. **Facilities:** 14th Street Playhouse, 370 seats, proscenium/thrust stage. **Production considerations:** produces some large-cast plays but prefers cast of 7; prefers unit set. **Best submission time:** spring–summer. **Response time:** 3 months letter; 4-6 months script.

THE JOSEPH PAPP PUBLIC THEATER/NEW YORK SHAKESPEARE FESTIVAL

(Founded 1954)
The Joseph Papp Public Theater; 425 Lafayette St;
New York, NY 10003; (212) 539-8530, FAX 539-8505
John Dias, *Literary Director*
Wiley Hausam*, Associate Producer, Musicals*
Submission procedure: no unsolicited scripts; synopsis, 10-page sample scene and letter of inquiry; include cassette of 3-5 songs for musicals and operas. **Types of material:** full-length plays, translations, adaptations, musicals, operas, solo pieces. **Facilities:** Newman Theater, 299 seats, proscenium stage; Anspacher Theater, 275 seats, thrust stage; Martinson Hall, 200 seats, proscenium stage; LuEsther Hall, 150 seats, flexible stage; Shiva Theater, 100 seats, flexible stage. **Best submission time:** year-round. **Response time:** 1 month letter; 6 months script.

JUNGLE THEATER

(Founded 1990)
2951 South Lyndale Ave; Minneapolis, MN 55408; (612) 822-4002,
FAX 822-9408; email info@jungletheater.com
Bain Boehlke, *Artistic Director*
Submission procedure: no unsolicited scripts; synopsis, sample pages, resume and letter of inquiry. **Types of material:** full-length plays. **Facilities:** The Jungle Theater, 135 seats, proscenium stage. **Best submission time:** year-round. **Response time:** 1 month letter; 3 months script. **Special programs:** Emerging Playwrights Reading Series: sit-down and staged readings of new plays by early-career playwrights; scripts selected through theater's normal submission procedure and by professional recommendation; *dates:* Aug 2001.

THE KAVINOKY THEATRE

(Founded 1981)
320 Porter Ave; Buffalo, NY 14221; (716) 881-7652,
FAX 881-7790
David Lamb, *Artistic Director*
Submission procedure: no unsolicited scripts; professional recommendation. **Types of material:** full-length plays, adaptations. **Special interests:** comedies. **Facilities:** Kavinoky Theatre, 260 seats, proscenium/thrust stage. **Production considerations:** prefers cast limit of 7; no fly and limited wing space. **Best submission time:** Jun-Aug. **Response time:** 1 month.

KITCHEN DOG THEATER COMPANY
(Founded 1990)
3120 McKinney Ave; Dallas, TX 75204; (214) 953–1055,
FAX 953–1873; email kitchendog@mindspring.com
Dan Day, *Artistic Director*
Submission procedure: accepts unsolicited scripts. **Types of material:** full-length plays, translations, adaptations, solo pieces. **Special interests:** plays by TX and Southwest playwrights. **Facilities:** The McKinney Avenue Contemporary, 100–150 seats, thrust stage; Second Space, 75–100 seats, black box. **Production considerations:** cast limit of 5; moderate production demands; moderate set. **Best submission time:** year-round. **Response time:** 6–8 months. **Special programs:** New Works Festival: annual presentation of new plays, including one full production, staged readings, mini workshops and artist residencies; submit script with SASP for response; *deadline:* 15 Mar 2001; *notification:* 15 Apr 2001; *dates:* Jun–Jul 2001.

KUMU KAHUA THEATRE
(Founded 1971)
46 Merchant St; Honolulu, HI 96813; (808) 536–4222,
FAX 536–4226
Harry Wong III, *Artistic Director*
Submission procedure: accepts unsolicited scripts with SASE for response. **Types of material:** full-lenth plays, one-acts, adaptations. **Special interests:** plays set in Hawaii or dealing with the Hawaiian experience. **Facilities:** Kumu Kahua Theatre, 100 seats, black box. **Best submission time:** year-round. **Response time:** 3–4 months. **Special programs:** Kumu Kahua Theatre/UHM Theatre Department Playwriting Contest: includes the Hawai'i Prize, Pacific/Rim Prize and Resident Prize (see Prizes).

L. A. THEATRE WORKS
(Founded 1974)
681 Venice Blvd; Venice, CA 90291; (310) 827–0808,
FAX 827–4949; email latworks@aol.com
Susan Raab, *Associate Producer*
Submission procedure: no unsolicited scripts; agent submission. **Types of material:** full-length plays, one-acts, adaptations. **Special interests:** highly theatrical, nonrealistic new plays; contemporary adaptations of classic themes. **Facilities:** no permanent facility. **Best submission time:** year-round. **Response time:** 4-6 months.

LA JOLLA PLAYHOUSE

(Founded 1947)
Box 12039; La Jolla, CA 92039; (858) 550-1070, FAX 550-1075
Elizabeth Bennett, *Literary Manager*

Submission procedure: no unsolicited scripts; synopsis, 10-page dialogue sample and letter of inquiry. **Types of material:** full-length plays, translations, musicals. **Special interests:** material pertinent to the lives we are leading at the start of this new century; innovative form and language. **Facilities:** Mandell Weiss Center for the Performing Arts, 500 seats, proscenium stage; Weiss Forum, 400 seats, thrust stage. **Best submission time:** Jun-Nov. **Response time:** 1 month letter; 10 months script.

LA MAMA EXPERIMENTAL THEATER CLUB

(Founded 1961)
74A East 4th St; New York, NY 10003; (212) 254-6468,
 FAX 254-7597; email lamama@lamama.org;
 Web site http://www.lamama.org
Ellen Stewart, *Artistic Director*
Beverly Petty, *Associate Director*

Submission procedure: no unsolicited scripts; accepts unsolicited videotapes of projects with synopsis; prefers professional recommendation. **Types of material:** full-length plays, one-acts, musicals, solo pieces, performance art. **Special interests:** culturally diverse works with music, movement and media. **Facilities:** Annex Theater, 199 seats, flexible stage; The Club Theater, 99 seats, black box; First Floor Theater, 99 seats, black box. **Best submission time:** year-round. **Response time:** 2-6 months. **Special programs:** Experiment 2000: a weekly concert play reading series curated by George Ferencz. Cross Cultural Institute of Theater Art Studies (C.C.I.T.A.S): theatrical workshops and premiere productions involving collaboration among artists of varying geographic and ethnic origins that promote intercultural understanding and artistic exchange. La MaMa Umbria: summer artist's residency program outside of Spoleto in Umbria, Italy; contact theatre for more information.

LAMB'S PLAYERS THEATRE
(Founded 1971)
Box 182229; Coronado, CA 92178; (619) 437-6050, FAX 437-6053
Jeffrey S. Miller, *Director of Outreach*
Submission procedure: no unsolicited scripts; synopsis, maximum 10-page dialogue sample and letter of inquiry; include cassette for musicals. **Types of material:** full-length plays, one-acts, plays for young audiences, musicals, cabaret/revues. **Facilities:** Harder Stage, 350 seats, thrust stage; Hahn, 250 seats, proscenium stage; Lyceum, 200 seats, flexible stage. **Best submission time:** year-round. **Response time:** 4-6 weeks letter; 4-6 months script.

LIFELINE THEATRE
(Founded 1982)
6912 North Glenwood Ave; Chicago, IL 60626; (773) 761-0667,
    FAX 761-4582; email lifeline@suba.com
Dorothy Milne, *Artistic Director*
Submission procedure: no unsolicited scripts; synopsis and letter of inquiry. **Types of material:** adaptations only. **Facilities:** Lifeline Theatre, 100 seats, proscenium stage. **Best submission time:** year-round. **Response time:** 1 month letter; 6 months script.

LINCOLN CENTER THEATER
(Founded 1966)
150 West 65th St; New York, NY 10023; (212) 362-7600;
    Web site http://www.lct.org
Anne Cattaneo, *Dramaturg*
Submission procedure: no unsolicited scripts; agent submission. **Types of material:** full-length plays, one-acts, translations, adaptations, musicals. **Facilities:** Vivian Beaumont, 1000 seats, thrust stage; Mitzi E. Newhouse, 300 seats, thrust stage. **Best submission time:** year-round. **Response time:** 2-4 months.

LIVE BAIT THEATRICAL COMPANY
(Founded 1987)
3914 North Clark; Chicago, IL 60613; (773) 871-1212,
    FAX 871-3191; email info@livebaittheater.org
    Web site http://www.livebaittheater.org
Ryan C. LaFleur, *Managing Director*
Submission procedure: no unsolicited scripts; synopsis and letter of inquiry
from Chicago-area playwrights only; no other submissions accepted. **Types of
material:** full-length plays, translations, adaptations, solo pieces, performance
art. **Special interests:** nonrealistic plays; performance poetry; performance art;
multimedia works; works that emphasize visual aspects of staging. **Facilities:** Live
Bait Theater, 70 seats, black box. **Production considerations:** prefers cast limit
of 9; 1 set; no fly or wing space. **Best submission time:** year-round. **Response
time:** 6 weeks letter; 6 months script.

LONG BEACH PLAYHOUSE
(Founded 1929)
5021 East Anaheim St; Long Beach, CA 90804; (562) 494-1014,
    FAX 961-8616; Web site http://www.longbeachplayhouse.com
Robert Leigh, *Managing Director*
Submission procedure: accepts unsolicited scripts. **Types of material:** full-
length plays, translations, adaptations, plays for young audiences. **Special
interests:** plays not produced professionally; ethnically inclusive and diverse
projects with strong social themes and/or unusual theatricality. **Facilities:**
Mainstage, 200 seats, thrust stage; Studio, 98 seats, proscenium stage. **Production
considerations:** simple sets; no wing space. **Best submission time:** year-round.
Response time: 3-6 months. **Special programs:** New Works Festival: 4 plays
chosen for annual staged reading attended by professional critics who provide
written and oral feedback; playwright receives $100 honorarium and videotape
of reading; plays must be submitted with submission form (available on Web site
or by fax); *deadline:* 1 Nov 2000; *notification:* Feb 2001; *dates:* spring 2001.

LONG WHARF THEATRE
(Founded 1965)
222 Sargent Dr; New Haven, CT 06511; (203) 787–4284,
    FAX 776–2287
Stefan Lanfer, *Literary Associate*
Submission procedure: no unsolicited scripts; synopsis, 10-page dialogue sample, resume and letter of inquiry with SASE for response. **Types of material:** full-length plays, translations, adaptations. **Special interests:** dramatic plays and comedies about human relationships, social concerns, ethical and moral dilemmas. **Facilities:** Newton Schenck Stage, 484 seats, thrust stage; Stage II, 199 seats, proscenium stage. **Best submission time:** year-round. **Response time:** 2 months letter; 6–12 months script.

MABOU MINES
(Founded 1970)
150 First Ave; New York, NY 10009; (212) 473–0559,
    FAX 473–2410
Sharon Fogarty, *Managing Director*
Submission procedure: no unsolicited scripts; professional recommendation. **Types of material:** full-length plays, one-acts, translations, adaptations. **Special interests:** contemporary works on contemporary issues. **Facilities:** The TOny, ROn, NAncy & DAvid–TORO NADA: NO BULL Theater at the 122 Community Center, 60 seats, flexible stage. **Best submission time:** year-round. **Response time:** 6 months.

MAD RIVER THEATER WORKS
(Founded 1978)
Box 248; West Liberty, OH 43357; (937) 465–6751;
    email madriver@bright.net
Jeff Hooper, *Producing Director*
Submission procedure: no unsolicited scripts; direct solicitation to playwright or agent. **Types of material:** full-length plays, one-acts, adaptations. **Special interests:** company-developed works; Midwestern or rural subject matter. **Facilities:** Center Stage, 150 seats, flexible stage. **Production considerations:** cast limit of 6; simple set and costumes. **Best submission time:** year-round. **Response time:** 3–4 months.

MADISON REPERTORY THEATRE
(Founded 1969)
122 State St, Suite 201; Madison, WI 53703–2500; (608) 256–0029,
  FAX 256–7433; email postmaster@madisonrep.org
D. Scott Glasser, *Artistic Director*
Submission procedure: no unsolicited scripts; synopsis and letter of inquiry.
Types of material: full-length plays, translations, adaptations, musicals. **Facilities:**
Isthmus Playhouse, 330 seats, thrust stage. **Production considerations:** cast limit
of 15; no fly space. **Best submission time:** year-round. **Response time:** 4-6
months letter; 4-6 months script. **Special programs:** reading series for plays in
development.

MAGIC THEATRE
(Founded 1967)
Fort Mason Center, Bldg D; San Francisco, CA 94123;
  (415) 441–8001, FAX 771–5505
Laura Hope Owen, *Literary Manager*
Submission procedure: no unsolicited scripts; synopsis, first 10 pages of play,
resume and letter of inquiry. **Types of material:** full-length plays. **Special
interests:** new plays that are innovative and/or nonlinear in form and content;
political themes. **Facilities:** Magic Theatre Southside, 170 seats, proscenium stage;
Magic Theatre Northside, 155 seats, thrust stage. **Production considerations:**
prefers cast limit of 6. **Best submission time:** Sep-May. **Response time:** 6 weeks
letter; 6-8 months script.

MAIN STREET ARTS
(Founded 1993)
94 Main St; Nyack, NY 10960; (914) 358–7701, FAX 358–7701;
  email msapaul@cs.com
Literary Manager
Submission procedure: no unsolicited scripts; synopsis, dialogue sample and
letter of inquiry. **Types of material:** full-length plays, one-acts. **Facilities:**
Mainstage, 65 seats, black box. **Production considerations:** cast limit of 6 for full-
length plays; cast limit of 4 for one-acts. **Best submission time:** year-round.
Response time: 3 weeks letter; 6 weeks script. **Special programs:** Developmental
Reading Series: monthly rehearsed reading of one new play with director and
actors followed by audience question and answer period; local authors preferred.
Midsummernights Shorts One Act Festival: festival of 6-9 one-acts; *deadline:* 1 Mar
2001; no submissions prior to 1 Nov 2000; *notification:* 31 Mar 2001; *dates:* Jul-
Aug 2001. Flying Blind Festival: presentation of short one-acts with no set
requirements; $5 reading fee; *deadline:* 30 Jun 2001; *notification:* 15 July 2001;
dates: Sep-Oct 2001.

MANHATTAN THEATRE CLUB

(Founded 1972)

311 West 43rd St, 8th Floor; New York, NY 10036; (212) 399–3000,
FAX 399–4329; Web site http://www.mtc–nyc.org

Christian Parker, *Literary Manager*

Clifford Lee Johnson III, *Director of Musical Theatre Program*

Submission procedure: no unsolicited scripts; agent submission. **Types of material:** full-length plays, musicals. **Facilities:** Stage I at City Center, 299 seats, proscenium stage; Stage II, 150 seats, thrust stage. **Production considerations:** prefers cast of 6-8; 1 set or unit set. **Best submission time:** year-round. **Response time:** 4 months. **Special programs:** readings and workshop productions of new musicals. "First-hearing" readings: in-house readings of new plays or first drafts. Manhattan Theatre Club Playwriting Fellowships (see Fellowships and Grants).

MARIN SHAKESPEARE COMPANY

(Founded 1989)

Box 4053; San Rafael, CA 94913; (415) 499–1108, FAX 499–1492;
Web site http://www.marinshakespeare.org

Robert Currier, *Artistic Director*

Submission procedure: no unsolicited scripts; synopsis, production history and letter of inquiry. **Types of material:** full-length plays, translations, adaptations. **Special interests:** classical, family-oriented or Shakespeare-related plays suitable for outdoor production. **Facilities:** Forest Meadows Amphitheatre, 600 seats, proscenium/thrust stage. **Best submission time:** year-round. **Response time:** 2 months letter; 2 months script.

MARIN THEATRE COMPANY

(Founded 1967)

397 Miller Ave; Mill Valley, CA 94941; (415) 388–5200,
FAX 388–0768; email info@marintheatre.org
Web site http://www.marintheatre.org

Lee Sankowich, *Artistic Director*

Submission procedure: no unsolicited scripts; agent submission. **Types of material:** full-length plays, translations, adaptations, plays for young audiences. **Facilities:** Marin Theatre, 250 seats, proscenium stage; 2nd theatre, 109 seats, black box. **Best submission time:** Jun–Aug. **Response time:** 6 months.

MARK TAPER FORUM
(Founded 1967)
135 North Grand Ave; Los Angeles, CA 90012; (213) 972-8033
Pier Carlo Talenti, *Literary Manager*
Submission procedure: no unsolicited scripts; synopsis, 5-10 sample pages and letter of inquiry. **Types of material:** full-length plays, one-acts, translations, adaptations, plays for young audiences, musicals, literary cabaret, solo pieces, performance art. **Facilities:** Mark Taper Forum, 742 seats, thrust stage. **Best submission time:** year-round. **Response time:** 4-6 weeks letter; 8-10 weeks script. **Special programs:** Performing for Los Angeles Youth: 55-minute plays that tour Southern CA schools; maximum 6 actors; suitable for grades K-8; scripts selected through theatre's normal submission procedure. Mark Taper Forum Developmental Programs (see Development).

MCC THEATER
(Founded 1986)
120 West 28th St; New York, NY 10001; (212) 727-7722,
    FAX 727-7780
Stephen Willems, *Literary Manager*
Submission procedure: no unsolicited scripts; synopsis, 10-page dialogue sample and letter of inquiry with SASE or SASP for response. **Types of material:** full-length plays, one-acts, translations, adaptations, musicals. **Facilities:** MCC Theater, 99 seats, black box. **Production considerations:** cast limit of 10. **Best submission time:** year-round. **Response time:** 2 weeks letter; 2 months script.

MCCARTER THEATRE CENTER FOR THE PERFORMING ARTS
(Founded 1972)
91 University Place; Princeton, NJ 08540; (609) 683-9100,
    FAX 497-0369; email literary@mccarter.org;
    Web site http://www.mccarter.org
Charles McNulty, *Literary Manager*
Submission procedure: no unsolicited scripts; synopsis, 10-page dialogue sample and letter of inquiry. **Types of material:** full-length plays, musicals. **Facilities:** McCarter Theatre, 1077 seats, proscenium stage. **Best submission time:** Sep-May. **Response time:** 1 month letter; 3 months script.

MERRIMACK REPERTORY THEATRE

(Founded 1979)

50 East Merrimack St; Lowell, MA 01852; (978) 454-6324,
   FAX 934-0166; Web site http://www.mrtlowell.com

David G. Kent, *Producing Artistic Director*

Submission procedure: no unsolicited scripts; synopsis and letter of inquiry. **Types of material:** full-length plays, translations, adaptations, plays for young audiences, musicals. **Special interests:** well-crafted stories with a poetic and human focus; varied ethnic tapestries of American life and love. **Facilities:** Liberty Hall, 372 seats, thrust stage. **Production considerations:** moderate cast size; simple set. **Best submission time:** spring-summer. **Response time:** 1 month letter (if interested); 6 months script.

MERRY-GO-ROUND PLAYHOUSE

(Founded 1958)

Box 506; Auburn, NY 13021; (315) 255-1305, FAX 252-3815;
   email mgrplays@dreamscape.com;
   Web site http://www.merry-go-round.com

Holly Ford, *Literary Manager*

Submission procedure: accepts unsolicited scripts. **Types of material:** full-length plays, translations, adaptations, plays for young audiences, musicals. **Special interests:** participatory plays for young audiences with cast limit of 3-4; plays for grades K-12. **Facilities:** Merry-Go-Round Playhouse (adaptable), 364 seats, proscenium stage or 100 seats, thrust stage. **Production considerations:** cast limit of 6. **Best submission time:** Jan-Feb. **Response time:** 2 months.

METRO THEATER COMPANY

(Founded 1973)

8308 Olive Blvd; St. Louis, MO 63132-2814; (314) 997-6777,
   FAX 997-1811; email bravomtc@aol.com

Carol North, *Artistic Director*

Submission procedure: no unsolicited scripts; professional recommendation. **Types of material:** plays for young audiences. **Special interests:** no works longer than 60 minutes; plays with music that are not dramatically limited by traditional concepts of "children's theatre." **Facilities:** no permanent facility; touring company. **Production considerations:** works cast from ensemble of 5; sets suitable for touring. **Best submission time:** year-round. **Response time:** 2-3 months. **Special programs:** new play readings; commissioning program; interested writers send letter of inquiry with recommendations from theatres who have produced writer's work.

METROSTAGE
(Founded 1984)
1201 North Royal St; Alexandria, VA 22314; (703) 548-9044, FAX 548-9089
Carolyn Griffin, *Producing Artistic Director*
Submission procedure: no unsolicited scripts; synopsis, first 10 pages of dialogue, list of productions/readings and letter of inquiry. **Types of material:** full-length plays. **Facilities:** MetroStage, 150 seats, thrust stage. **Production considerations:** cast limit of 8, prefers 4; prefers 1 set. **Best submission time:** year-round. **Response time:** 1 month letter; 1 month script. **Special programs:** First Stage: staged reading series Oct–May.

MILL MOUNTAIN THEATRE
(Founded 1964)
1 Market Square SE; Roanoke, VA 24011-1437; (540) 342-5749, FAX 342-5745; email mmtmail@millmountain.org; Web site http://www.millmountain.org
Literary Manager
Submission procedure: accepts unsolicited one-acts only; synopsis, 10-page dialogue sample and letter of inquiry for all other submissions; include cassette for musicals. **Types of material:** full-length plays, one-acts, musicals, solo pieces. **Special interests:** plays with racially mixed casts. **Facilities:** Mill Mountain Theatre, 400 seats, flexible proscenium stage; Theatre B, 125 seats, flexible stage. **Production considerations:** cast limit of 15 for plays, 24 for musicals; prefers unit set. **Best submission time:** year-round. **Response time:** 6 weeks letter; 6-8 months script. **Special programs:** Centerpieces: monthly lunchtime staged readings of one-acts by emerging playwrights; unpublished one-acts 25-35 minutes long (no 10-minute plays). The Mill Mountain Theatre New Play Competition: The Norfolk Southern Festival of New Works (see Prizes).

MILWAUKEE CHAMBER THEATRE
(Founded 1975)
158 North Broadway; Milwaukee, WI 53202; (414) 276-8842, FAX 277-4477; email mail@chamber-theatre.com
Montgomery Davis, *Artistic Director*
Submission procedure: no unsolicited scripts; professional recommendation. **Types of material:** full-length plays, one-acts, translations, adaptations. **Special interests:** strong, well-crafted plays; plays about Shaw for annual Shaw Festival. **Facilities:** Broadway Theatre Center: Cabot Theatre, 358 seats, proscenium stage; studio, 96 seats, black box. **Production considerations:** 1 set or unit set. **Best submission time:** summer. **Response time:** 4 months.

MILWAUKEE PUBLIC THEATRE

(Founded 1974)
626 East Kilbourn Ave, #802; Milwaukee, WI 53202-3237;
   (414) 347-1685, FAX 347-1690; email bleigh@execpc.com;
   Web site http://www.execpc.com/mpt
Barbara Leigh, *Co-Artistic/Producing Director*
Submission procedure: no unsolicited scripts; direct solicitation to playwright or agent. **Types of material:** full-length plays, one-acts, translations, adaptations, plays for young audiences, solo pieces, cabaret/revues, clown/vaudeville shows. **Special interests:** works with cast of 1-3 playing multiple roles; political satire; social-political and regional or local themes; plays dealing with disabilities; interart works; new clown/vaudeville shows; works for young and family audiences. **Facilities:** no permanent facility. **Production considerations:** simple production demands; productions tour. **Response time:** 12 months. **Special programs:** outdoor park performances.

MILWAUKEE REPERTORY THEATER

(Founded 1954)
108 East Wells St; Milwaukee, WI 53202; (414) 224-1761,
   FAX 224-9097; email pkosidowski@milwaukeerep.com
Paul Kosidowski, *Literary Manager*
Submission procedure: no unsolicited scripts; agent submission. **Types of material:** full-length plays, translations, adaptations, cabaret/revues. **Facilities:** Quadracci Powerhouse Theatre, 720 seats, thrust stage; Stiemke Theatre, 200 seats, flexible stage; Stackner Cabaret, 100 seats, cabaret stage. **Production considerations:** works for cabaret must not exceed 80 minutes in length. **Best submission time:** year-round. **Response time:** 2-3 months.

MISSOURI REPERTORY THEATRE

(Founded 1964)
4949 Cherry St; Kansas City, MO 64110-2263; (816) 235-2727,
   FAX 235-5367; email theatre@umkc.edu;
   Web site http://www.missourireptheatre.org
Peter Altman, *Producing Artistic Director*
Submission procedure: no unsolicited scripts; agent submission only. **Types of material:** full-length plays, translations, adaptations. **Facilities:** Helen F. Spencer Theatre, 730 seats, modified thrust stage.

MIXED BLOOD THEATRE COMPANY
(Founded 1975)
1501 South Fourth St; Minneapolis, MN 55454; (612) 338-0937
David Kunz, *Script Czar*
Submission procedure: no unsolicited scripts; synopsis and letter of inquiry.
Types of material: full-length plays, musicals, cabaret/revues. **Special interests:** comedies dealing with racial issues, politics or sports. **Facilities:** Main Stage, 200 seats, flexible stage. **Best submission time:** Aug-Jan. **Response time:** 2 months letter; 3-6 months script. **Special programs:** We Don't Need No Stinkin' Dramas (see Prizes).

MOVING ARTS
(Founded 1992)
514 South Spring St; Los Angeles, CA 90013; (213) 622-8906,
    FAX 622-8946; email treynichols@movingarts.org;
    Web site http://www.movingarts.org
Trey Nichols, *Literary Director*
Submission procedure: no unsolicited scripts; synopsis, dialogue sample, resume and letter of inquiry. **Types of material:** full-length plays, translations, adaptations. **Special interests:** work previously unproduced in Los Angeles area. **Facilities:** 60-seat black box at the Los Angeles Theatre Center. **Production considerations:** modest production demands; limited wing and fly space. **Best submission time:** year-round. **Response time:** 1-3 months letter; 6-9 months script. **Special Programs:** Premiere One-Act Festival: annual fall festival of one-acts chosen from one-act competition. (See Premiere One-Act Competition in Prizes.)

MUSIC-THEATRE GROUP
(Founded 1971)
30 West 26th St, Suite 1001; New York, NY 10010;
    (212) 366-5260, ext 22, FAX 366-5265
Lyn Austin, *Producing Director*
Submission procedure: no unsolicited scripts; direct solicitation to playwright or agent. **Types of material:** music-theatre works, operas, cabaret. **Special interests:** experimental musical works; collaborations between music-theatre, dance and the visual arts. **Facilities:** no permanent facility; various sites in New York City, The Berkshires and other national and international venues.

NATIONAL THEATRE OF THE DEAF
(Founded 1967)
Box 659; Chester, CT 06412; (860) 526-4971 (voice), -4974 (TTY),
    FAX 526-0066; email bookntd@aol.com
Jerry Goehring, *Executive Director*
Submission procedure: no unsolicited scripts; synopsis, character breakdown,
sample pages and letter of inquiry with SASE for response. **Types of material:**
full-length plays, adaptations, plays for young audiences. **Special interests:** work
not produced professionally; deaf issues; culturally diverse plays. **Facilities:** no
permanent facility; touring company. **Production considerations:** cast limit of
10; production must tour. **Best submission time:** year-round. **Response time:**
1 month letter; 3-6 months script.

NEBRASKA THEATRE CARAVAN
(Founded 1976)
6915 Cass St; Omaha, NE 68132; (402) 553-4890, FAX 553-6288;
    email caravan@radiks.net
Marya Lucca-Thyberg, *Director of the Caravan*
Submission procedure: no unsolicited scripts; synopsis and letter of inquiry.
Types of material: adaptations, plays for young audiences, musicals. **Special
interests:** work suitable for elementary, intermediate and high school
audiences only. **Facilities:** no permanent facility; touring company. **Production
considerations:** cast limit of 6; 1 set. **Best submission time:** Sep-Dec.
Response time: 1 month letter; 3 months script.

NEVADA SHAKESPEARE FESTIVAL
(Founded 1996)
Box 871; Virginia City, NV 89440; (775) 324-4198;
    email information@nevada-shakespeare.org;
    Web site http://www.nevada-shakespeare.org
Martha Quarkziz, *Communications Director*
Submission procedure: no unsolicited scripts; synopsis, resume and letter of
inquiry. **Types of material:** full-length plays, translations, adaptations, plays for
young audiences, musicals, caberet/revues, solo pieces. **Special interests:** avant-
garde, innovative treatments of imaginative literature. **Facilities:** Piper's Opera
House, 350-500 seats, proscenium stage; NSF Studio, 100 seats, thrust stage. **Best
submission time:** year-round. **Response time:** 1 month letter; 1 month script.

NEW AMERICAN THEATER
(Founded 1972)
118 North Main St; Rockford, IL 61101; (815) 963-9454,
   FAX 963-7215; Web site http://www.newamericantheater.com
William Gregg, *Producing Artistic Director*
Submission procedure: no unsolicited scripts; synopsis and SASE for response.
Types of material: full-length plays. **Facilities:** David W. Knapp Stage, 282 seats,
thrust stage; Amcore Cellar, 90 seats, flexible stage. **Production considerations:**
small-to-medium cast size; modest production demands. **Best submission time:**
fall. **Response time:** 3 months letter; 3 months script. **Special Programs:** New
Voices in the Heartland: annual festival of staged readings.

THE NEW CONSERVATORY THEATRE CENTER
(Founded 1981)
25 Van Ness, Lower Lobby; San Francisco, CA 94102;
   (415) 861-4914, FAX 861-6988; email nctcsf@yahoo.com;
   Web site http://www.nctcsf.org
Ed Decker, *Artistic/Executive Director*
Submission procedure: no unsolicited scripts; synopsis and letter of inquiry.
Types of material: full-length plays, plays for young audiences; musicals. **Special
interests:** gay plays for adult audiences; plays with traditional or progressive
themes. **Facilities:** Decker Theatre, 132 seats, proscenium stage; Walker Theatre,
75 seats, black box; City Theatre, 55 seats, black box. **Best submission time:**
year-round. **Response time:** 3 months letter; 6 months script.

NEW DRAMATISTS
See Membership and Service Organizations.

NEW FEDERAL THEATRE
(Founded 1970)
292 Henry St; New York, NY 10002; (212) 353-1176,
   FAX 353-1088; email newfederal@metrobase.com;
   Web site http://www.metrobase.com/newfederal
Woodie King, Jr., *Producing Director*
Submission procedure: no unsolicited scripts; professional recommendation.
Types of material: full-length plays. **Special interests:** social and political issues;
family and community themes related to minorities and women. **Facilities:** Henry
Street Settlement: Harry Dejour Playhouse, 300 seats, proscenium stage;
Experimental Theatre, 100 seats, black box; Recital Hall, 100 seats, thrust stage.
Production considerations: small cast; no more than 2 sets. **Best submission
time:** year-round. **Response time:** 5 months.

NEW GEORGES
(Founded 1992)
90 Hudson St, #2E; New York, NY 10013; (212) 620-0113,
    FAX 334-9239; email newgeorges@aol.com;
    Web site http://www.newgeorges.org
Susan Bernfield, *Artistic Director*
Submission procedure: accepts unsolicited scripts. **Types of material:** full-length plays. **Special interests:** plays by women only; works with "vigorous use of language and heightened perspectives on reality." **Facilities:** no permanent facility. **Best submission time:** year-round. **Response time:** 3 months letter; 6-9 months script.

THE NEW GROUP
(Founded 1991)
43 West 33rd St, Suite 400; New York, NY 10001;
    email newgroup1@earthlink.net;
    Web site http://newgrouptheater.com
Kevin Scott, *Literary Manager*
Submission procedure: accepts unsolicited scripts with resume (only 1 submission per playwright per year). **Types of material:** full-length plays. **Special interests:** works not previously produced in New York City; "plays which reflect the spirit of our times and tell their stories with immediacy, fearlessness and discipline." **Facilities:** no permanent facility. **Best submission time:** year-round. **Response time:** 6-9 months. **Special programs:** Playwrights Unit: weekly developmental workshop with playwrights and actors; writers admitted based on quality of submitted script.

NEW JERSEY REPERTORY COMPANY
(Founded 1997)
179 Broadway; Long Branch, NJ 07740; (732) 229-3166,
    FAX 229-3167; email info@njrep.org;
    Web site http://www.njrep.org
SuzAnne Barabas, *Artistic Director*
Submission procedure: accepts unsolicited scripts with synopsis and character breakdown. **Types of material:** full-length plays, one-acts, musicals. **Special interests:** work not produced professionally; social, humanistic themes. **Facilities:** Main Stage, 72 seats, black box; Second Stage, 50 seats, flexible stage. **Production considerations:** cast limit of 7; unit or simple set. **Best submission time:** year-round. **Response time:** 6-12 months. **Special programs:** Script-in-Hand: year-round reading series for more than 20 plays; of these, up to 6 selected for Main Stage production.

NEW REPERTORY THEATRE

(Founded 1985)
Box 610418; Newton Highlands, MA 02461; (617) 928-9831;
email adamnewrep@aol.com;
Web site http://www.newrep.org
Rick Lombardo, *Producing Artistic Director*
Submission procedure: no unsolicited scripts; synopsis, dialogue sample and letter of inquiry. **Types of material:** full-length plays, translations, adaptations. **Special interests:** plays of ideas that center around pressing issues of our time; multicultural themes; intimate, interpersonal themes. **Facilities:** New Repertory Theatre, 160 seats, thrust stage. **Production considerations:** cast limit of 7. **Best submission time:** May-Aug. **Response time:** 2 months letter; 6 months script. **Special programs:** reading series.

NEW STAGE THEATRE

(Founded 1966)
1100 Carllisle; Jackson, MS 39202; (601) 948-0143,
FAX 948-3538
John Maxwell, *Artistic Director*
Submission procedure: no unsolicited scripts; synopsis and letter of inquiry. **Types of material:** full-length plays, one-acts, solo pieces. **Facilities:** Meyer Crystal Auditorium, 364 seats, proscenium stage. **Production considerations:** cast limit of 3-8. **Best submission time:** summer-fall. **Response time:** 1 month letter; 3 months script. **Special programs:** Eudora Welty New Play Series; theatre produces one new play every season.

NEW TUNERS THEATRE/THE THEATRE BUILDING

(Founded 1969)
1225 West Belmont; Chicago, IL 60657;
(773) 929-7367, ext 22, FAX 327-1404; email tbtuners@aol.com
John Sparks, *Artistic Director*
Submission procedure: no unsolicited scripts; synopsis, 1 scene, 3-song cassette, bio and letter of inquiry. **Types of material:** musicals. **Facilities:** 3 theatres, 150 seats each, black box. **Best submission time:** year-round. **Response time:** 4 months letter; 6 months script. **Special programs:** Annual STAGES Festival held every summer; New Tuners Workshop: musical developmental workshop. Monthly reading series.

NEW YORK STAGE AND FILM

(Founded 1984)
151 West 30th St, Suite 905; New York, NY 10001; (212) 239-2334,
FAX 239-2996
Johanna Pfaelzer, *Managing Producer*
Submission procedure: no unsolicited scripts; synopsis, resume and letter of inquiry. **Types of material:** full-length plays. **Facilities:** Powerhouse Theatre, 135 seats, proscenium stage; Coal Bin, 110 seats, black box. **Best submission time:** 1 Sep-31 Oct only. **Response time:** 2 months letter; 3 months script.

NEW YORK STATE THEATRE INSTITUTE

(Founded 1974)
155 River St; Troy, NY 12180; (518) 274-3200, FAX 274-3815;
email nysti@capital.net; Web site http://www.nysti.org
Ed Lange *Associate Artistic Director*
Submission procedure: no unsolicited scripts; synopsis, cast/scene breakdown and letter of inquiry. **Types of material:** full-length plays, adaptations, musicals. **Special interests:** works for family audiences only. **Facilities:** Schacht Fine Arts Center, 800 seats, proscenium stage. **Best submission time:** Mar-Sep. **Response time:** 2 months letter; 6 months script. **Special programs:** new work developmental workshops; playwrights receive staged reading or workshop production, negotiable remuneration, travel and housing.

NEW YORK THEATRE WORKSHOP

(Founded 1979)
79 East 4th St; New York, NY 10003; (212) 780-9037
Mandy Mishell Hackett, *Artistic Associate/Literary Department*
Submission procedure: no unsolicited scripts; synopsis, 10-page sample scene, resume and letter of inquiry. **Types of material:** full-length plays, one-acts, translations, music-theatre works, solo pieces, proposals only for performance art. **Special interests:** socially relevant and/or minority issues; innovative form and language. **Facilities:** 79 East 4th Street Theatre, 180 seats, proscenium stage. **Best submission time:** fall-spring. **Response time:** 1 month letter; 5 months script. **Special programs:** Mondays at Three: reading series, developmental workshops and symposia. Summer writing residency. New York Theatre Workshop Playwriting Fellowship for emerging writers of color based in New York (see Fellowships and Grants).

NEXT ACT THEATRE
(Founded 1990)
Box 394; Milwaukee, WI 53201; (414) 278-7780, FAX 278-5930
David Cecsarini, *Artistic Director/Producer*
Submission procedure: no unsolicited scripts; agent submission of synopsis, cast list, production requirements and letter of inquiry. **Types of material:** full-length plays, adaptations, solo pieces. **Facilities:** Stiemke Theatre, 198 seats, flexible stage; Studio Space, 99 seats, thrust stage. **Production considerations:** small cast size; minimal production demands. **Best submission time:** spring. **Response time:** 1 month letter; 6 months script.

NEXT THEATRE COMPANY
(Founded 1981)
927 Noyes St; Evanston, IL 60201; (847) 475-6763,
    FAX 475-6767; email tucker@lightoperaworks.org;
    Web site http://www.nexttheatre.org
Stephanie Tackett, *General Manager*
Submission procedure: no unsolicited scripts; direct solicitation to playwright or agent. **Types of material:** full-length plays, translations, adaptations. **Facilities:** Mainstage, 165 seats, proscenium stage.

NORTH SHORE MUSIC THEATRE
(Founded 1955)
62 Dunham Rd; Beverly, MA 01915; (978) 232-7203,
    FAX 921-0793; Web site http://www.nsmt.org
John LaRock, *Associate Producer*
Submission procedure: no unsolicited scripts; synopsis and letter of inquiry with SASE for response; include cassette for musicals. **Types of material:** musicals. **Special interests:** musicals only. **Facilities:** Main Stage, 1800 seats, arena stage; Workshop, 100 seats, flexible stage. **Production considerations:** prefers cast limit of 12 for Workshop productions. **Best submission time:** year-round. **Response time:** 1 month letter; 3-6 months script. **Special programs:** New Works Development Program: spring and fall workshop productions of new works with authors in residence; theatre pays (rate varies) and houses writers; contact theatre for information.

NORTH STAR THEATRE
(Founded 1991)
347 Gerard St; Mandeville, LA 70448; (504) 624–5266,
FAX 626–1692
Lori Bennett, *Producing Director*
Submission procedure: accepts unsolicited scripts with SASE for response.
Types of material: full-length plays, one-acts, plays for young audiences. **Special interests:** one-act plays suitable for children. **Facilities:** North Star Theatre, 150 seats, thrust stage. **Production considerations:** minimal production demands; simple sets. **Best submission time:** year-round. **Response time:** 3 months.

THE NORTHEASTERN THEATRE (TNT)
(Founded 1992)
Box 765; Scranton, PA 18501–0765; (570) 969–1770;
email tnttheatre@excite.com
Web site http://tnt.pa.webjump.com
Alicia Grega–Pikul, *Producer*
Submission procedure: no unsolicited scripts; send SASE for guidelines. **Types of material:** full-length plays, translations, cabaret/revues, solo pieces, performance art texts, spoken word/poetry performance. **Special interests:** writer-directors, contemporary themes, multicultural artists. **Facilities:** Shopland Theatre, 99-150 seats, flexible stage. **Production considerations:** small cast (prefers 1-6); minimal production demands. **Best submission time:** May–Aug. **Response time:** 1 month letter; 1 month script. **Special programs:** staged reading series. Written and Directed By: annual series culminating in production for 1 writer-director.

NORTHLIGHT THEATRE
(Founded 1975)
9501 North Skokie Blvd; Skokie, IL 60076; (847) 679–9501,
FAX 679–1879; email gwitt@northlight.org
Gavin Witt, *Dramaturg/Literary Manager*
Submission procedure: no unsolicited scripts; synopsis, cast list and letter of inquiry. **Types of material:** full-length plays, translations, adaptations, musicals. **Special interests:** translations and adaptations of "lost" plays; the public world and public issues; plays of ideas; works that are passionate and/or hilarious; stylistic exploration and complexity. **Facilities:** Center East Theatre, 850 seats, proscenium stage; Northlight Theatre, 345 seats, thrust stage. **Production considerations:** cast limit of 2-8; 1 unit or flexible set. **Best submission time:** year-round. **Response time:** 1 month letter; 4 months script.

ODYSSEY THEATRE ENSEMBLE
(Founded 1969)
2055 South Sepulveda Blvd; Los Angeles, CA 90025;
 (310) 477-2055
Sally Essex-Lopresti, *Director of Literary Programs*

Submission procedure: no unsolicited scripts; synopsis, 8-10-page dialogue sample, play's production history (if any), resume and letter of inquiry with SASE for response; include cassette for musicals. **Types of material:** full-length plays, translations, adaptations, musicals. **Special interests:** culturally diverse works; works with innovative form or provocative subject matter; works exploring the enduring questions of human existence and the possibilities of the live theatre experience; works with political or sociological impact. **Facilities:** Odyssey 1, 99 seats, flexible stage; Odyssey 2, 99 seats, thrust stage; Odyssey 3, 99 seats, endstage. **Production considerations:** plays must be 90 minutes or longer. **Best submission time:** year-round. **Response time:** 2-4 weeks letter; 6 months script.

OLDCASTLE THEATRE COMPANY
(Founded 1972)
Box 1555; Bennington, VT 05201-1555; (802) 447-1267,
 FAX 442-3704
Eric Peterson, *Producing Artistic Director*

Submission procedure: accepts unsolicited scripts. **Types of material:** full-length plays, musicals. **Facilities:** Bennington Center for the Arts, 300 seats, modified proscenium stage. **Best submission time:** winter. **Response time:** 4-6 months.

OLNEY THEATRE CENTER FOR THE ARTS
(Founded 1937)
2001 Olney-Sandy Spring Rd; Olney, MD 20832; (301) 924-4485,
 FAX 924-2654
David Jackson, *Literary Manager*

Submission procedure: no unsolicited scripts; professional recommendation. **Types of material:** full-length plays, translations, adaptations, solo pieces. **Facilities:** Mainstage, 500 seats, proscenium stage. **Production considerations:** cast limit of 8. **Best submission time:** year-round. **Response time:** 6 months.

OMAHA THEATER COMPANY FOR YOUNG PEOPLE

(Founded 1949)
2001 Farnam St; Omaha, NE 68102; (402) 345-4852,
    FAX 344-7255
James Larson, *Artistic Director*
Submission procedure: no unsolicited scripts; professional recommendation.
Types of material: one-acts. **Special interests:** plays for family audiences only;
plays based on children's literature and contemporary issues; multicultural
themes. **Facilities:** Omaha Theater Company, 932 seats, proscenium stage; second
stage, 175 seats, black box. **Production considerations:** cast limit of 10; prefers
unit set. **Best submission time:** year-round. **Response time:** 6 months.

ONTOLOGICAL-HYSTERIC THEATER

(Founded 1968)
260 West Broadway; New York, NY 10013; (212) 941-8911,
    FAX 334-5149
Submission procedure: no unsolicited scripts; direct solicitation to playwright
or agent. **Types of material:** full-length plays. **Facilities:** Ontological at St. Mark's
Theater, 80 seats, black box.

THE OPEN EYE THEATER

(Founded 1972)
Box 959; Margaretville, NY 12455; (914) 586-1660, FAX 586-1660;
    email openeye@catskill.net;
    Web site http://www.theopeneye.com
Amie Brockway, *Producing Artistic Director*
Submission procedure: no unsolicited scripts; synopsis and letter of inquiry with
SASE for response. **Types of material:** full-length plays, one-acts, translations,
adaptations, plays for young audiences. **Special interests:** plays for young and
multigenerational audiences; culturally diverse themes; plays with music;
ensemble plays; plays of any length (10 minutes or more); Catskill Mountain-area
writers. **Facilities:** no permanent facility. **Production considerations:** minimal
set. **Best submission time:** Oct–Apr. **Response time:** 1 week letter (if interested);
3-6 months script. **Special programs:** New Play Works: new-play developmental
program of readings and workshop productions.

OREGON SHAKESPEARE FESTIVAL

(Founded 1935)

Box 158; Ashland, OR 97520; (541) 482-2111, FAX 482-0446

Lue Douthit, *Literary Manager*

Submission procedure: no unsolicited scripts; professional recommendation. **Types of material:** full-length plays. **Special interests:** plays of ideas; language-oriented plays; women and minority writers encouraged. **Facilities:** Elizabethan Theatre, 1194 seats, outdoor Elizabethan stage; Angus Bowmer Theatre, 600 seats, thrust stage; Black Swan, 140 seats, black box. **Best submission time:** fall. **Response time:** 3 months. **Special programs:** reading series; commissioning programs.

ORGANIC THEATER COMPANY

(Founded 1969)

1420 Maple Ave; Evanston, IL 60201; (847) 475-0600,
    FAX 475-9200

Ina Marlowe, *Producing Artistic Director*

Submission procedure: no unsolicited scripts; direct solicitation to playwright or agent. **Types of material:** full-length plays, long one-acts. **Facilities:** Mainstage, 200 seats, modified thrust stage.

PAN ASIAN REPERTORY THEATRE

(Founded 1977)

47 Great Jones St; New York, NY 10012; (212) 505-5655,
    FAX 505-6014; email panasian@aol.com;
    Web site http://www.panasianrep.org

Tisa Chang, *Artistic/Producing Director*

Submission procedure: no unsolicited scripts; synopsis and letter of inquiry. **Types of material:** full-length plays, translations, adaptations, musicals. **Special interests:** Asian or Asian-American themes only. **Facilities:** Playhouse 91, 199 seats, proscenium stage; Theatre Four, 288 seats, proscenium stage. **Production considerations:** prefers cast limit of 7. **Best submission time:** summer. **Response time:** 9 months letter; 9 months script. **Special programs:** staged readings and workshops.

PANGEA WORLD THEATER

2509 Dupont Ave S, #209; Minneapolis, MN 55405;
   (612) 377-1728, FAX 377-1728;
   email quest@pangeaworldtheater.org;
   Web site http://www.pangeaworldtheater.org
Meena Natarajan, *Executive & Literary Director*
Submission procedure: accepts unsolicited scripts. **Types of material:** full-length plays, one-acts, translations, adapatations, solo pieces. **Special interests:** adaptations of international literature; multi-ethnic works. **Facilities:** The Litte Theater, 120 seats, flexible stage. **Best submission time:** year-round. **Response time:** 3-6 months.

THE PASADENA PLAYHOUSE

(Founded 1917)
80 South Lake Ave, Suite 500; Pasadena, CA 91101;
   (626) 792-8672, FAX 792-7343;
   email patroninfo@pasadenaplayhouse.com;
   Web site http://www.pasadenaplayhouse.org
David A. Tucker II, *Literary Manager*
Submission procedure: no unsolicited scripts; agent submission. **Types of material:** full-length plays, musicals. **Facilities:** The Pasadena Playhouse, 686 seats, proscenium stage. **Production considerations:** cast limit of 2-7; 1 set or unit set; modest musical requirements. **Best submission time:** year-round. **Response time:** 6-12 months.

PEGASUS PLAYERS

(Founded 1978)
1145 West Wilson; Chicago, IL 60640; (773) 878-9761,
   FAX 271-8057; email pegasusp@megsinet.net
Alex Levy, *Literary Manager*
Submission procedure: no unsolicited scripts; synopsis and letter of inquiry. **Types of material:** full-length plays, translations, adaptations, musicals, solo pieces. **Facilities:** The O'Rourke Center for the Performing Arts, 250 seats, proscenium stage. **Best submission time:** year-round. **Response time:** 1 month letter; 4-6 months script. **Special programs:** Chicago Young Playwrights Festival: annual Jan festival of plays by Chicago-area high school students; write for information.

PEGASUS THEATRE

(Founded 1985)
3916 Main St; Dallas, TX 75226-1228; (214) 821-6005,
FAX 826-1671; Web site http://www.pegasustheatre.com
Steve Erwin, *Literary Manager*
Submission procedure: no unsolicited scripts; synopsis, 10-page dialogue sample, character breakdown and letter of inquiry. **Types of material:** full-length plays. **Special interests:** comedies only, especially contemporary satire; no mysteries. **Facilities:** Mainstage, 141 seats, proscenium stage. **Production considerations:** cast limit of 10; single set; limited fly space. **Best submission time:** Mar-Jun. **Response time:** 1 month letter; 6 months script.

PENDRAGON THEATRE

(Founded 1980)
148 River St; Saranac Lake, NY 12983-2031; (518) 891-1854,
FAX 891-7012; email pdragon@northnet.org;
Web site http://www.northnet.org/pendragon
Bob Pettee, *Managing Director*
Submission procedure: no unsolicited scripts; synopsis, dialogue sample and letter of inquiry with SASP for response. **Types of material:** full-length plays, plays for young audiences. **Special interests:** plays suitable for performance by adolescents ages 11-16. **Facilities:** Pendragon Theatre, 132 seats, black box. **Production considerations:** cast limit of 8; simple set. **Best submission time:** year-round. **Response time:** 3-4 weeks letter; 3 months script.

PENGUIN REPERTORY COMPANY

(Founded 1977)
Box 91; Stony Point, NY 10980; (914) 786-2873, FAX 786-3638
Joe Brancato, *Artistic Director*
Submission procedure: no unsolicited scripts; agent submission only. **Types of material:** full-length plays, adaptations. **Facilities:** Barn Playhouse, 108 seats, proscenium stage. **Production considerations:** cast limit of 5; simple set. **Best submission time:** Dec-Feb. **Response time:** 3 months.

PENOBSCOT THEATRE COMPANY

(Founded 1974)
183 Main St; Bangor, ME 04401; (207) 942-3333, FAX 947-6678;
 email penthtr@agate.net
Mark Torres, *Producing Artistic Director*
Submission procedure: no unsolicited scripts; direct solicitation to playwright or agent;. **Types of material:** full-length plays. **Facilities:** Bangor Opera House, 299 seats, proscenium/thrust stage; Penobscot Theatre, 132 seats, proscenium/thrust stage.

THE PENUMBRA THEATRE COMPANY

(Founded 1976)
The Martin Luther King Bldg; 270 North Kent St;
 St. Paul, MN 55102-1794; (651) 224-4601, FAX 224-7074
Lou Bellamy, *Artistic Director*
Submission procedure: accepts unsolicited scripts with resume. **Types of material:** full-length plays, one-acts, translations, adaptations, plays for young audiences, musicals. **Special interests:** works that address the African-American experience and the African diaspora. **Facilities:** Hallie Q. Brown Theatre, 260 seats, proscenium/thrust stage. **Best submission time:** year-round. **Response time:** 6-9 months. **Special programs:** Cornerstone Dramaturgy and Development Project (see Development).

THE PEOPLE'S LIGHT AND THEATRE COMPANY

(Founded 1974)
39 Conestoga Rd; Malvern, PA 19355-1798; (215) 647-1900
Alda Cortese, *Literary Manager*
Submission procedure: no unsolicited scripts; synopsis, cast list, 10-page dialogue sample and letter of inquiry. **Types of material:** full-length plays, translations, adaptations. **Special interests:** intelligent, original scripts for a family audience. **Facilities:** People's Light and Theatre, 350 seats, flexible stage; Steinbright Stage, 99-150 seats, flexible stage. **Production considerations:** 1 set or unit set. **Best submission time:** year-round. **Response time:** 2 weeks letter; 8-10 months script.

PERFORMANCE RIVERSIDE

(Founded 1983)
4800 Magnolia Ave; Riverside, CA 92506; (909) 222-8399,
    FAX 222-8940
Steven A. Glaudini, *Executive Director*
Submission procedure: no unsolicited scripts; synopsis and letter of inquiry.
Types of material: musicals only. **Facilities:** Landis Auditorium, 850 seats,
proscenium stage. **Production considerations:** cast limit of 25, inclusive of
chorus; limited backstage and wing space. **Best submission time:** year-round.
Response time: 1 month letter; 3 months script.

PERSEVERANCE THEATRE

(Founded 1979)
914 3rd St; Douglas, AK 99824; (907) 364-2421, FAX 364-2603;
    email info@perseverancetheatre.org;
    Web site http://www.juneau.com/pt/
Peter DuBois, *Artistic Director*
Submission procedure: no unsolicited scripts; synopsis, dialogue sample and
letter of inquiry from AK playwrights only. **Types of material:** full-length plays,
one-acts, solo pieces, musicals. **Special interests:** AK playwrights; gay/lesbian
playwrights and themes; women playwrights; Native American playwrights and
themes; political/social issues; musicals. **Facilities:** Mainstage, 150 seats, thrust
stage; Phoenix, 50-75 seats, flexible stage. **Best submission time:** year-round.
Response time: 1 month letter; 3 months script. **Special programs:** Voices from
the Edge Playreading Festival: annual spring presentation of diverse new work
from across AK and the country; Native Playreading and Performance Festival:
annual Nov presentation of Native American work.

PHILADELPHIA THEATRE COMPANY

(Founded 1974)
230 South 15th St, 4th Floor; Philadelphia, PA 19102;
    (215) 568-1920, FAX 568-1944
Michele Volansky, *Dramaturg*
Submission procedure: no unsolicited scripts; agent submission. **Types of
material:** full-length plays, small-scale musicals, solo pieces. **Special interests:**
new American plays; social/humanistic themes; no mysteries or plays for young
audiences. **Facilities:** Plays and Players Theater, 324 seats, proscenium stage. **Best
submission time:** year-round. **Response time:** 6-8 months. **Special programs:**
STAGES: program of staged readings.

PHOENIX THEATRE

(Founded 1920)
100 East McDowell Rd; Phoenix, AZ 85004; (602) 258-1974,
    FAX 253-3626; Web site http://www.phoenixtheatre.net
Michael Barnard, *Artistic Director*
Submission procedure: no unsolicited scripts; synopsis, production history (if any) and letter of inquiry with SASE for response. **Types of material:** plays for young audiences, musicals, cabaret/revues. **Special interests:** plays with strong narratives suitable for a general audience. **Facilities:** Mainstage, 346 seats, proscenium stage; Cookie Company, 150 seats, arena stage. **Best submission time:** year-round. **Response time:** 6 months letter; 6 months script.

THE PHOENIX THEATRE

(Founded 1983)
749 North Park Ave; Indianapolis, IN 46202; (317) 635-7529,
    FAX 635-0010; email phoenixt@oaktree.net;
    Web site http://www.phoenixtheatre.org
Bryan Fonseca, *Producing Director*
Submission procedure: no unsolicited scripts; agent submission. **Types of material:** full-length plays, one-acts. **Facilities:** Mainstage, 150 seats, proscenium stage; Underground, 75 seats, black box. **Best submission time:** Jan–Feb. **Response time:** 1 week letter; 3 months script. **Special programs:** The Festival of Emerging American Theatre (FEAT) Competition (direct solicitation to playwright only).

PILLSBURY HOUSE THEATRE

(Founded 1992)
3501 Chicago Ave S; Minneapolis, MN 55407; (612) 825-0459
Brian Goranson, *Dramaturg*
Submission procedure: no unsolicited scripts; synopsis and letter of inquiry. **Types of material:** full-length plays, one-acts, translations, adaptations. **Facilities:** Pillsbury House Theatre, 100 seats, proscenium stage. **Best submission time:** year-round. **Response time:** 5 months letter; 6 months script.

PING CHONG & COMPANY
(Founded 1975)
47 Great Jones St, 2nd Floor; New York, NY 10012; (212) 529-1557,
FAX 529-1703; email pingchong@earthlink.net
Submission procedure: no unsolicited scripts; direct solicitation to play-wright. **Types of material:** full-length works by company only. **Facilities:** no permanent facility.

PIONEER THEATRE COMPANY
(Founded 1962)
University of Utah; Salt Lake City, UT 84112; (801) 581-6356,
FAX 581-5472
Charles Morey, *Artistic Director*
Submission procedure: no unsolicited scripts; synopsis and letter of inquiry.
Types of material: full-length plays, translations, adaptations, musicals.
Facilities: Simmons Pioneer Memorial Theatre, 912 seats, proscenium stage. **Best submission time:** fall. **Response time:** 1 month letter; 6 months script.

PITTSBURGH PUBLIC THEATER
(Founded 1975)
621 Penn Ave; Pittsburgh, PA 15222; (412) 316-8200,
FAX 316-8216; email rrickard@ppt.org;
Web site http://www.ppt.org
Becky Rickard, *Assistant to the Artistic Director*
Submission procedure: no unsolicited scripts; synopsis, dialogue sample and letter of inquiry with SASE for response. **Types of material:** full-length plays, translations, adaptations, musicals. **Facilities:** O'Reilly Theater, 650 seats, thrust stage. **Best submission time:** Feb-Apr. **Response time:** 2 months letter; 6 months script.

PLAYHOUSE ON THE SQUARE
(Founded 1968)
51 South Cooper St; Memphis, TN 38104; (901) 725-0776,
FAX 272-7530
Jackie Nichols, *Executive Producer*
Submission procedure: accepts unsolicited scripts. **Types of material:** full-length plays, musicals. **Facilities:** Playhouse on the Square, 250 seats, proscenium stage; Circuit Playhouse, 136 seats, proscenium stage. **Best submission time:** year-round. **Response time:** 3-5 months. **Special programs:** Playhouse on the Square New Play Competition (see Prizes).

PLAYMAKERS REPERTORY COMPANY
(Founded 1976)
CB# 3235 Center for Dramatic Art; Country Club Rd;
   Chapel Hill, NC 27599-3235; (919) 962-2484, FAX 962-4069
David Hammond *Artistic Director*
Submission procedure: no unsolicited scripts; agent submission. **Types of material:** full-length plays, translations, adaptations. **Facilities:** Paul Green Theatre, 498 seats, thrust stage. **Best submission time:** Aug-May. **Response time:** 6 months.

THE PLAYWRIGHTS' CENTER
See Membership and Service Organizations.

PLAYWRIGHTS HORIZONS
(Founded 1971)
416 West 42nd St; New York, NY 10036-6896; (212) 564-1235,
   FAX 594-0296; Web site http://www.playwrightshorizons.org
Sonya Sobieski, *Literary Manager*
Submission procedure: accepts unsolicited scripts with resume and cover letter; if necessary, will accept synopsis, dialogue sample and letter of inquiry; for musicals, send script and cassette (no synopses) to musical theatre department. **Types of material:** full-length plays, musicals. **Special interests:** works by American writers only; works with strong sense of language that take theatrical risks; no adaptations, translations, solo pieces or one-acts. **Facilities:** Mainstage, 145 seats, proscenium stage; Studio Theater, 72 seats, black box. **Best submission time:** year-round. **Response time:** 2 months letter; 6 months script.

PLAYWRIGHTS PROJECT
(Founded 1985)
450 B St, Suite 1020; San Diego, CA 92101-8093; (619) 239-8222,
   FAX 239-8225; email youth@playwright.com;
   Web site http://www.playwrightsproject.com
Deborah Salzer, *Executive Director*
Submission procedure: accepts unsolicited scripts. **Types of material:** one-acts. **Special Interests:** CA playwrights under 19 only. **Facilities:** Old Globe Theatre/Cassius Carter Center Stage, 225 seats, arena stage. **Best submission time:** Jan-Apr. **Response time:** 3-4 months.

PLOWSHARES THEATRE COMPANY

(Founded 1989)
2870 East Grand Blvd, Suite 600; Detroit, MI 48202–3146;
   (313) 872–0279, FAX 872–0067;
   email plowshares@earthlink.net;
   Web site http://www.plowshares.org
Gary Anderson, *Producing Artistic Director*
Submission procedure: no unsolicited scripts; direct solicitation to playwright or agent only. **Types of material:** full-length plays, one-acts, translations, adaptations, plays for young audiences, musicals, cabaret/revues, solo performance. **Special interests:** plays by African-American writers only; plays that pertain to the African-American experience. **Facilities:** Anderson Center Theatre, 597 seats, proscenium stage; Charles Wright Theatre, 317 seats, thrust stage. **Best submission time:** Sep–Jan. **Response time:** 3 months. **Special programs:** Kidsplay: Year-round playwriting program for young writers culminating in production of 1 play. Performing Arts Training Program: write for guidelines. New Voices Play Development Program (see Development).

PORTLAND CENTER STAGE

(Founded 1988)
1111 Southwest Broadway; Portland, OR 97205; (503) 248–6309,
   FAX 796–6509; Web site http://www.pcs.org
Chris Coleman, *Artistic Director*   kelsey@pcs.org
Submission procedure: no unsolicited scripts; synopsis and letter of inquiry.
Types of material: full-length plays, translations, adaptations. **Facilities:** Newmark Theatre, Portland Center for the Performing Arts, 860 seats, proscenium stage. **Production considerations:** prefers cast limit of 8–12. **Best submission time:** year-round. **Response time:** 1–2 months letter; 2–3 months script. **Special programs:** playwriting festival and readings (write for submission guidelines).

PORTLAND STAGE COMPANY

(Founded 1970)
Box 1458; Portland, ME 04104; (207) 774–1043, FAX 774–0576;
   email portstage@aol.com;
   Web site http://www.portlandstage.com
Lisa DiFranza, *Literary and Education Director*
Submission procedure: no unsolicited scripts; synopsis, 10-page dialogue sample and letter of inquiry. **Types of material:** full-length plays, translations, adaptations. **Facilities:** Performing Arts Center Theatre, 290 seats, proscenium stage; PSC Rehearsal Hall, 90 seats, flexible stage (readings only). **Best submission time:** May–Jan. **Response time:** 3 months letter; 6 months script.

PRIMARY STAGES

(Founded 1983)
131 West 45th St; New York, NY 10036; (212) 333-7471,
    FAX 333-2025; Web site http://nytheatre.com/primary.htm
Tricia McDermott, *Literary Manager*
Submission procedure: no unsolicited scripts; synopsis, 10-page dialogue sample, description of play style, resume and letter of inquiry with SASE for response; include cassette for musicals. **Types of material:** full-length plays, musicals. **Special interests:** plays not previously produced in New York City only; highly theatrical works by American playwrights for American or New York City premiere; plays by women and minorities; no strict realism or standard film and television fare. **Facilities:** Primary Stages Theatre, 99 seats, proscenium stage; Phil Bosakowski Theatre, 65 seats, proscenium stage. **Production considerations:** cast limit of 2-8; unit set or simple set changes; no fly or wing space. **Best submission time:** Sep-Jun. **Response time:** 2-4 months letter; 6 months-1 year script.

THE PUBLIC THEATRE

(Founded 1991)
2 Great Falls Plaza, Box 7; Auburn, ME 04210; (207) 782-2211,
    FAX 784-3856; Web site http://www.thepublictheatre.org
Janet Mitchko, *Associate Artistic Director*
Submission procedure: no unsolicited scripts; synopsis, dialogue sample and letter of inquiry. **Types of material:** full-length plays. **Facilities:** The Public Theatre, 307 seats, proscenium stage. **Production considerations:** cast limit of 7; minimal production demands. **Best submission time:** late spring-fall. **Response time:** 5 months letter; 10 months script.

THE PURPLE ROSE THEATRE COMPANY

(Founded 1991)
Box 220; Chelsea, MI 48118; (734) 475-5817, FAX 475-0802;
    email purplerose@earthlink.net;
    Web site http://www.purplerosetheatre.org
Anthony Caselli, *Literary Manager*
Submission procedure: no unsolicited scripts; synopsis, dialogue sample and letter of inquiry. **Types of material:** full-length plays. **Special interests:** plays that speak to a middle-American audience. **Facilities:** Garage Theatre, 160 seats, thrust stage. **Production considerations:** cast limit of 10; no fly or wing space. **Best submission time:** year-round. **Response time:** 2 months letter; 6-9 months script.

RED BARN THEATRE
(Founded 1981)
Box 707; Key West, FL 33040; (305) 293-3035, FAX 293-3035;
   email mmcdon3444@aol.com
Mimi McDonald, *Managing Director*
Submission procedure: no unsolicited scripts; synopsis and letter of inquiry with professional recommendation. **Types of material:** full-length plays, musicals, cabaret/revues. **Facilities:** Red Barn Theatre, 88 seats, proscenium stage. **Production considerations:** cast limit of 8; small band for musicals; no fly space; limited wing space. **Best submission time:** Mar-Jul. **Response time:** 6 months letter (if interested); 6 months script.

RED EYE
(Founded 1983)
15 West 14th St; Minneapolis, MN 55403-2301; (612) 870-7531;
   email redeye@mtn.org; Web site http://www.theredeye.org
Steve Busa, *Artistic Director*
Submission procedure: no unsolicited scripts; synopsis, 10-page dialogue sample and letter of inquiry; materials will not be returned. **Types of material:** full-length plays, solo pieces, performance art. **Special interests:** experimental drama and multimedia works only. **Facilities:** Mainstage, 76-120 seats, proscenium stage. **Best submission time:** year-round. **Response time:** 6 months letter (if interested); 6-9 months script. **Special programs:** Isolated Acts: annual multidisciplinary festival held Feb-Apr; by invitation only.

REPERTORIO ESPAÑOL
(Founded 1968)
138 East 27th St; New York, NY 10016
Robert Weber Federico, *Artistic Associate Producer*
Submission procedure: no unsolicited scripts; synopsis and letter of inquiry. **Types of material:** full-length plays, adaptations, plays for young audiences, musicals, operas. **Special interests:** plays dealing with Hispanic themes. **Facilities:** Gramercy Arts Theatre, 130 seats, proscenium stage. **Production considerations:** small cast. **Best submission time:** summer. **Response time:** 1 month letter; 6 months script.

THE REPERTORY THEATRE OF ST. LOUIS

(Founded 1966)
Box 191730; St. Louis, MO 63119; (314) 968-7340;
    email sgregg@repstl.org
Susan Gregg, *Associate Artistic Director*
Submission procedure: no unsolicited scripts; synopsis, character breakdown, technical requirements and letter of inquiry. **Types of material:** full-length plays. **Special interests:** nonnaturalistic plays; contemporary social and political issues. **Facilities:** Main Stage, 750 seats, thrust stage; Studio Theatre, 130 seats, black box. **Production considerations:** small cast; modest production demands. **Best submission time:** year-round. **Response time:** 1 month letter; 2 years script. **Special programs:** developmental workshop for new plays; scripts selected through theatre's normal submission procedure.

RIVERSIDE THEATRE

(Founded 1981)
Box 1651; Iowa City, IA 52244; (319) 338-7672, FAX 887-1362;
    email artistic@riversidetheatre.org;
    Web site http://www.riversidetheatre.org
Ron Clark and Jody Hovland, *Artistic Directors*
Submission procedure: no unsolicited scripts; synopsis and letter of inquiry. **Types of material:** full-length plays, translations, adaptations, cabaret/revues, solo pieces. **Facilities:** Riverside Theatre, 118 seats, flexible stage. **Production considerations:** small cast; simple set. **Best submission time:** year-round. **Response time:** 1 month letter (if interested); 3-5 months script.

ROADSIDE THEATER

(Founded 1975)
91 Madison Ave; Whitesburg, KY 41858; (606) 633-0108,
    FAX 633-1009; email roadside@appalshop.org;
    Web site http://www.appalshop.org/rst
Dudley Cocke, *Director*
Submission procedure: no unsolicited scripts; synopsis, dialogue sample and letter of inquiry. **Types of material:** full-length plays. **Special interests:** plays about the Appalachian region only. **Facilities:** Appalshop Theater, 150 seats, thrust stage. **Production considerations:** small cast; simple sets suitable for touring. **Best submission time:** year-round. **Response time:** 3 weeks letter; 2 months script. **Special programs:** reading and workshop series. Playwright residencies initiated by theatre; playwright may not apply.

ROADWORKS PRODUCTIONS
(Founded 1992)
1144 West Fulton Market, Suite 105; Chicago, IL 60607;
   (312) 492-7150, FAX 492-7155; email shade@roadworks.org;
   Web site http://www.roadworks.org
Shade Murray, *Artistic Director*
Submission procedure: no unsolicited scripts; professional recommendation.
Types of material: full-length plays. **Special interests:** scripts suitable for ensemble aged 20-30; "explosive, high-energy" plays. **Facilities:** no permanent facility. **Best submission time:** Sep-Nov. **Response time:** 2 months.

ROUND HOUSE THEATRE
(Founded 1978)
12210 Bushey Dr, Suite 101; Silver Spring, MD 20902;
   (301) 933-9530, FAX 933-2321;
   Web site http://www.Round-House.org
Production Department
Submission procedure: no unsolicited scripts; synopsis, 10-page dialogue sample, cast breakdown, technical requirements, resume and SASE for response.
Types of material: full-length plays, translations, adaptations, plays for young audiences, musicals, solo pieces. **Special interests:** contemporary issues; new translations of lesser-known classics; experimental works; humorous plays.
Facilities: Round House Theatre, 218 seats, modified thrust stage. **Production considerations:** cast limit of 8; prefers 1 set. **Best submission time:** year-round.
Response time: 2 months letter; minimum 1 year script. **Special programs:** Round the Edges Series: reading series showcasing smaller more experimental pieces; solo work preferred; scripts selected through theatre's regular submission procedure. New Voices Play Reading Series: Monday night reading series of new, unproduced plays and musicals by regional (DC, MD, VA) playwrights; submit full-length plays, one-acts, musicals and ten-minute plays to Nick Olcott, Associate Artistic Director/New Voices Coordinator; *deadline:* spring 2001; *dates:* Jun 2001.

SACRAMENTO THEATRE COMPANY
(Founded 1942)
1419 H St; Sacramento, CA 95814; (916) 446-7501, FAX 446-4066
   Web site http://www.sactheatre.org
Peggy Shannon, *Artistic Director*
Submission procedure: no unsolicited scripts; agent submission. **Types of material:** full-length plays, adaptations, cabaret/revues. **Special interests:** contemporary social and political issues; "craftsmanship, theatricality, vital language." **Facilities:** McClatchy Mainstage, 300 seats, proscenium stage; Stage II, 90 seats, black box. **Production considerations:** cast limit of 3-5. **Best submission time:** Jun-Dec. **Response time:** 6 months.

THE SALT LAKE ACTING COMPANY
(Founded 1970)
168 West 500 N; Salt Lake City, UT 84103; (801) 363–0526,
    FAX 532–8513
David Mong, *Literary Manager*
Submission procedure: no unsolicited scripts; synopsis, 5-10-page dialogue sample, resume and letter of inquiry with SASE for response. **Types of material:** full-length plays, translations, adaptations, musicals. **Special interests:** western American writers "who understand the unique synergistic effect that playwright, actor and audience enjoy when a work is produced for the stage." **Facilities:** Upstairs, 150 seats, thrust stage; Chapel Theatre, 99 seats, thrust stage. **Best submission time:** year-round. **Response time:** 4 months letter; 8 months script. **Special programs:** reading series four times annually.

SAN JOSE REPERTORY THEATRE
(Founded 1980)
101 Paseo de San Antonio; San Jose, CA 95113; (408) 367–7266,
    FAX 367–7237; Web site http://www.sjrep.com
Nakissa Etemad, *Literary Manager/Dramaturg*
Submission procedure: no unsolicited scripts; agent submission. **Types of material:** full-length plays, translations, adaptations, musicals, solo pieces. **Special interests:** small-cast musicals. **Facilities:** San Jose Repertory Theatre, 525 seats, proscenium stage. **Best submission time:** Sep–Nov. **Response time:** 3-6 months.

SEACOAST REPERTORY THEATRE
(Founded 1986)
125 Bow St; Portsmouth, NH 03801; (603) 433–4793,
    FAX 431–7818; email info@seacoastrep.org;
    Web site http://www.seacoastrep.org
Roy M. Rogosin, *Producing Artistic Director*
Submission procedure: no unsolicited scripts; agent submission (1-page synopsis only; include cassette for musicals). **Types of material:** full-length plays, plays for young audiences, musicals. **Special interests:** new American plays; small-scale musicals; plays for young audiences. **Facilities:** Seacoast Repertory Theatre, 230 seats, thrust stage. **Best submission time:** year-round. **Response time:** 3-6 months.

SEASIDE MUSIC THEATER
(Founded 1977)
Box 2835; Daytona Beach, FL 32120; (904) 252-3394,
    FAX 252-8991; Web site http://www.seasidemusictheater.org
Lester Malizia, *General Manager*
Submission procedure: no unsolicited scripts; synopsis, CD or cassette of music and letter of inquiry. **Types of material:** musicals for young and adult audiences, cabaret/revues. **Facilities:** Winter Theater, 576 seats, proscenium stage; Summer Theater, 500 seats, proscenium stage; Theater for Children, 576 seats, proscenium stage. **Production considerations:** cast limit of 20 for Winter Theater, 30 for Summer Theater, 10 for Theater for Children; small musical combo for Theater for Children and Winter Theater, 25-member orchestra for Summer Theater; no wing or orchestra space in Winter Theater; no fly space except in Summer Theater. **Best submission time:** Sep-Nov. **Response time:** 1-3 months letter; 3-6 months script.

SEATTLE CHILDREN'S THEATRE
(Founded 1975)
Box 9640; Seattle, WA 98109-0640; (206) 443-0807;
    Web site http://www.sct.org
Literary Manager
Submission procedure: accepts unsolicited scripts for Drama School Summerstages only; professional recommendation for mainstage. **Types of material:** full-length plays for family audiences, translations, adaptations, musicals, solo pieces. **Special interests:** sophisticated works for young audiences that also appeal to adults. **Facilities:** Charlotte Martin Theatre, 485 seats, proscenium stage; Eve Alvord Theatre, 280 seats, modified proscenium. **Best submission time:** year-round. **Response time:** 8 months. **Special programs:** Drama School Summerstages: one-act plays, 30-60 minutes long for student performance; must have roles for 12-18 actors, ages 8-19; submit script with SASE for response to Don Fleming; Program Director; *deadline:* 1 Dec 2000.

SEATTLE REPERTORY THEATRE
(Founded 1963)
155 Mercer St; Seattle, WA 98109; (206) 443-2210
Christine Sumption, *Artistic Associate*
Submission procedure: no unsolicited scripts; direct solicitation to playwright or agent. **Types of material:** full-length plays, translations, adaptations, solo pieces. **Facilities:** Bagley Wright Theatre, 856 seats, proscenium stage; Leo K. Theatre, 284 seats, proscenium stage. **Special programs:** New Plays in Process: annual workshop production program.

SECOND STAGE THEATRE

(Founded 1979)

Box 1807, Ansonia Station; New York, NY 10023; (212) 787–8302, FAX 877–9886

Christopher Burney, *Associate Artistic Director*

Submission procedure: no unsolicited scripts; synopsis, 5-10-page dialogue sample, resume, production history and letter of inquiry. **Types of material:** full-length plays, adaptations, musicals. **Special interests:** new and previously produced American plays; "heightened" realism; sociopolitical issues; plays by women and minority writers. **Facilities:** Midtown Theatre, 296 seats, proscenium stage; McGinn/Cazale Theatre, 108 seats, endstage. **Best submission time:** year-round. **Response time:** 1 month letter; 5-6 months script. **Special programs:** annual series of 4-6 readings of new and previously produced plays.

SEVEN ANGELS THEATRE

(Founded 1991)

Box 3358; Waterbury, CT 06705; (203) 591–8223, FAX 591–8223

Semina De Laurentis, *Artistic Director*

Submission procedure: no unsolicited scripts; professional recommendation. **Types of material:** full-length plays, musicals. **Facilities:** Seven Angels Theatre, 350 seats, proscenium stage. **Production considerations:** cast limit of 10; prefers unit set; no fly space. **Best submission time:** year-round. **Response time:** 3-6 months letter; 3-6 months script

7 STAGES

(Founded 1979)

1105 Euclid Ave NE; Atlanta, GA 30307; (404) 522–0911

Web site http://www.7stages.org

Del Hamilton, *Artistic Director*

Submission procedure: no unsolicited scripts, direct solicitation to playwright or agent. **Types of material:** full-length plays, translations, adaptations, performance art. **Special interests:** nonrealistic plays and performance texts focusing on social, political or spiritual themes. **Facilities:** 7 Stages, 250 seats, thrust stage; Back Door, 100 seats, flexible stage.

SHAKESPEARE & COMPANY

(Founded 1978)

The Mount; Box 865; Lenox, MA 01240; (413) 637-1199,
  FAX 637-4274; email epstein@shakespeare.org;
  Web site http://www.shakespeare.org

Ariel Bock, *Artistic Associate for Submissions*

Submission procedure: no unsolicited scripts; synopsis, 4-page dialogue sample and letter of inquiry. **Types of material:** full-length and one-act adaptations. **Special interests:** plays based on or adapted from works by Edith Wharton and other women or Henry James. **Facilities:** Mainstage Theatre, 600 seats, outdoor amphitheatre; Duffin Theatre, 500 seats, proscenium stage; Oxford Court, 200 seats, outdoor amphitheatre; Stables Theatre, 108 seats, thrust stage; Salon Theatre, 90 seats, endstage. **Production considerations:** minimal set pieces only; small casts; most theatre spaces part of historic estate (former home of Edith Wharton). **Best submission time:** fall, winter. **Response time:** 6 months letter (if interested); 6 months script.

SHAKESPEARE SANTA CRUZ

(Founded 1981)

Performing Arts Complex; University of California–Santa Cruz;
  1156 High St; Santa Cruz, CA 95064; (831) 459-2121,
  FAX 459-3316; Web site http://shakespearesantacruz.org

Sara Danielson, *Education and Outreach Director*

Submission procedure: no unsolicited scripts; direct solicitation to playwright or agent. **Types of material:** full-length plays, one-acts, plays for young audiences. **Special interests:** Shakespearean spinoffs, i.e., plays that use Shakespeare's characters or plots. **Facilities:** Sinsheimer-Stanley Glen, 500-800 seats, outdoor amphitheatre; Performing Arts Theater, 500 seats, thrust stage.

THE SHAKESPEARE THEATRE

(Founded 1986)

516 8th St; Washington, DC 20003-3808; (202) 547-3230,
  FAX 547-0226; email smazzola@shakespearedc.org;
  Web site http://www.shakespearedc.org

Steven Scott Mazzola, *Assistant to the Artistic Director*

Submission procedure: no unsolicited scripts; professional recommendation. **Types of material:** translations, adaptations. **Special interests:** translations and adaptations of classics only. **Facilities:** The Shakespeare Theatre, 449 seats, proscenium stage. **Best submission time:** summer. **Response time:** 2 months.

SIGNATURE THEATRE

(Founded 1990)
3806 South Four Mile Run Dr; Arlington, VA 22206; (703) 820-9771
Marcia Gardner, *Literary Manager*
Submission procedure: accepts unsolicited scripts from DC playwrights only; agent submission for all other plays. **Types of material:** full-length plays, adaptations, musicals. **Special interests:** work not produced professionally only; social issues; comedies. **Facilities:** Signature Theatre, 126 seats, black box. **Production considerations:** prefers cast limit of 10; no fly space. **Best submission time:** Sep-May. **Response time:** 6 months. **Special programs:** Stages: staged readings of new plays-in-process; scripts selected through theatre's normal submission procedure; On the Edge Series: full production of 1 new play a year.

SIGNATURE THEATRE COMPANY, INC.

(Founded 1991)
534 West 42nd St; New York, NY 10036-6809;
    (212) 967-1913, FAX 967-2957
James Houghton, *Founding Artistic Director*
Submission procedure: no unsolicited scripts; direct solicitation to playwright or agent. **Types of material:** full-length plays, one-acts. **Special interests:** playwrights with substantial body of work to be produced over course of season. **Facilities:** The Peter Norton Space, 160 seats, endstage.

SOCIETY HILL PLAYHOUSE

(Founded 1959)
507 South 8th St; Philadelphia, PA 19147; (215) 923-0210,
    FAX 923-1789; email shpcerols.com;
    Web site http://www.erols.com/shp
Walter Vail, *Literary Manager*
Submission procedure: no unsolicited scripts; direct solicitation to playwright or agent. **Types of material:** full-length plays, musicals. **Special interests:** musicals and comedies with casts of 5-7. **Facilities:** Society Hill Playhouse, 223 seats, proscenium stage; Second Space, 90 seats, flexible stage. **Production considerations:** prefers small cast.

SOHO REPERTORY THEATRE
(Founded 1975)
46 Walker St; New York, NY 10013; (212) 941-8632, FAX 941-7148
Alexandra Conley, *Executive Director*
Submission procedure: accepts unsolicited scripts for Summer Camp only (see below); direct solicitation to playwright or agent for all other plays. **Types of material:** full-length plays, one-acts, solo pieces. **Facilities:** Soho Rep, 74 seats, black box. **Special programs**: Summer Camp: annual Jul festival of unproduced full-length plays, one-acts, solo pieces; *deadline*: 1 Feb 2001; *notification:* May 2001.

SOURCE THEATRE COMPANY
(Founded 1978)
1835 14th St NW; Washington, DC 20009; (202) 462-1073
Keith Parker, *Literary Manager*
Submission procedure: accepts unsolicited scripts for Literary Prize only (see below); direct solicitation to playwright or agent for all other plays. **Types of material:** full-length plays, one-acts, musicals, solo pieces. **Facilities:** Source Theatre Company, 100-140 seats, flexible stage. **Special programs:** 21st Annual Washington Theatre Festival: a summer festival of new-play workshop productions and staged readings; *deadline:* 15 Jan 2001; *dates:* 11 Jul-11 Aug 2001. Source Theatre Company 2001 Literary Prize (see Prizes).

SOUTH COAST REPERTORY
(Founded 1964)
Box 2197; Costa Mesa, CA 92628-2197; (714) 708-5500
Jerry Patch, *Dramaturg*
John Glore, *Literary Manager*
Submission procedure: no unsolicited scripts; synopsis, dialogue sample and letter of inquiry. **Types of material:** full-length plays, translations, adaptations, musicals. **Facilities:** Mainstage, 507 seats, modified thrust stage; Second Stage, 161 seats, thrust stage. **Best submission time:** year-round. **Response time:** 1-3 weeks letter; 2-4 months script. **Special programs:** COLAB (Collaboration Laboratory) New Play Program: developmental program culminating in readings, staged readings, workshop productions and full productions; playwright receives grant, commission and/or royalties depending on nature of project. Pacific Playwrights Festival: annual 3-week developmental program for playwrights from across the nation culminating in staged readings, workshop productions and full productions performed for the public and theatre colleagues; plays are chosen through theatre's normal submission procedure and by invitation; not-for-profit theatres are also welcome to submit work; *dates:* Jun 2001.

SPOKANE INTERPLAYERS ENSEMBLE

(Founded 1981)
Box 1961; Spokane, WA 99210; (509) 455-7529, FAX 624-9348;
    email interplayers@interplayers.com;
    Web site http://www.interplayers.com
Robert A. Welch, *Managing Director*
Submission procedure: no unsolicited scripts; synopsis, dialogue sample, cast list, set requirements, production history, reviews (if any) and letter of inquiry. **Types of material:** full-length plays. **Facilities:** Spokane Interplayers Ensemble, 256 seats, thrust stage. **Production considerations:** prefers cast limit of 8; 1 set. **Best submission time:** year-round. **Response time:** 3 months letter (if interested); 3-6 months script.

ST. LOUIS BLACK REPERTORY COMPANY

(Founded 1976)
634 North Grand Blvd, Suite 10-F; St. Louis, MO 63103;
    (314) 534-3807, FAX 534-8456;
    email theblackrep@hotmail.com
Ronald J. Himes, *Producing Director*
Submission procedure: no unsolicited scripts; synopsis, 3-5-page dialogue sample, resume and letter of inquiry. **Types of material:** full-length plays, plays for young audiences, musicals. **Special interests:** works by African-American and Third World playwrights. **Facilities:** Grandel Theatre, 470 seats, thrust stage. **Best submission time:** Jun-Aug. **Response time:** 2 months letter; 2 months script. **Special programs:** touring company presenting works for young audiences.

STAGE ONE: THE LOUISVILLE CHILDREN'S THEATRE

(Founded 1946)
501 West Main; Louisville, KY 40202-2957; (502) 589-5946,
    FAX 588-5910; email stageone@kca.org;
    Web site http://www.stageone.org
Moses Goldberg, Producing Director
Submission procedure: accepts unsolicited scripts. **Types of material:** plays for young audiences. **Special interests:** plays about young people in the real world; good, honest treatments of familiar titles. **Facilities:** Moritz von Bomard Theater, 610 seats, thrust stage; Louisville Gardens, 300 seats, arena stage. **Production considerations:** prefers cast limit of 12; some productions tour. **Best submission time:** Oct-Dec. **Response time:** 3 months. **Special programs:** Tomorrow's Playwrights: annual one-act competition open to high school students throughout KY region; 3 finalists receive staged readings and prepare rewrite to determine placement; cash awards for winners and sponsoring schools; submit play through school; *deadline*: 1 Mar 2001

STAGES REPERTORY THEATRE
(Founded 1978)
3201 Allen Prkwy, #101; Houston, TX 77019; (713) 527-0220,
  FAX 527-8669
Rob Bundy, *Artistic Director*
Submission procedure: accepts unsolicited scripts. **Types of material:** full-length plays, plays for young audiences. **Special interests:** nonrealistic, edgy works. **Facilities:** Stages Repertory Theatre, 235 seats, arena stage; Stages Repertory Theatre, 180 seats, thrust stage. **Production considerations:** cast limit of 6; maximum 1 hour running time for children's shows. **Best submission time:** year-round. **Response time:** 9 months. **Special programs:** Southwest Festival for New Plays (see Development).

STAGEWORKS
(Founded 1993)
133 Warren St; Hudson, NY 12534-3118; (518) 828-7843;
  FAX 828-4026; email stagewrk@mhonline.net;
  Web site http://www.mhonline.net/~stagewrk
Laura Margolis, *Producing Artistic Director*
Submission procedure: no unsolicted scripts; synopsis and letter of inquiry. **Types of material:** full-length plays, translations, adaptations, musicals, solo pieces. **Facilities:** North Pointe, 90 seats, proscenium/thrust stage. **Production considerations:** cast limit of 10; 1 set or unit set; no fly space. **Best submission time:** year-round. **Response time:** 4-6 months letter; 6-8 months script. **Special programs:** Ten by Ten: annual festival of new short plays; participation by invitation only.

STAMFORD THEATRE WORKS
(Founded 1988)
95 Atlantic St; Stamford, CT 06901; (203) 359-4414, FAX 356-1846
Jane Desy, *Literary Manager*
Submission procedure: no unsolicited scripts; synopsis, dialogue sample and letter of inquiry; include cassette for musicals. **Types of material:** full-length plays, translations, adaptations, musicals. **Special interests:** plays that are contemporary, innovative and thought-provoking; socially and culturally relevant; challenging and entertaining. **Facilities:** Center Stage, 150 seats, modified thrust stage. **Production considerations:** prefers small cast; unit set. **Best submission time:** year-round. **Response time:** 2 months letter; 6 months script. **Special programs:** Windows on the Work: developmental workshop for 3 new plays; each play receives rehearsals, staged readings and audience discussions; scripts selected through theatre's normal submission procedure; plays not produced professionally only; *dates:* Feb-Mar.

STATE THEATER COMPANY

(Founded 1982)
719 Congress Ave; Austin, TX 78701; (512) 472–5143,
  FAX 472–7199; email admin@statetheatercompany.com;
  Web site http://www.statetheatercompany.com
John Walch, *Literary Office*
Submission procedure: accepts unsolicited scripts from TX playwrights only; others send synopsis, 15-page dialogue sample and letter of inquiry. **Types of material:** full-length plays, adaptations, solo pieces. **Special interests:** work not produced professionally; TX plays; comedies. **Facilities:** State Theater, 350 seats, proscenium stage; Horton Foote Theatre, 90 seats, proscenium stage. **Best submission time:** 1 Jan–1 May only. **Response time:** 6–9 months letter; 6–9 months script (most scripts returned in the fall). **Special programs:** Harvest Festival of New American Plays (see Prizes).

STEPPENWOLF THEATRE COMPANY

(Founded 1976)
1650 North Halsted; Chicago, IL 60614; (312) 335–1888, FAX 335–0808
Literary Manager
Submission procedure: no unsolicited scripts; synopsis, 10-page dialogue sample and letter of inquiry. **Types of material:** full-length plays. **Special interests:** ensemble pieces with dynamic acting roles. **Facilities:** Mainstage, 510 seats, proscenium stage; Studio, 50–300 seats, flexible stage. Garage, 60 seats, flexible stage. **Best submission time:** year-round. **Response time:** 1–3 months letter, 6–9 months script.

STRATFORD FESTIVAL THEATER

(Founded 1996)
1850 Elm St; Stratford, CT 06615; (203) 378–1200,
  FAX 378–9777
J. Wishnia, *Dramaturg*
Submission procedure: no unsolicited scripts; synopsis and letter of inquiry with SASE for response. **Types of material:** full-length plays, plays for young audiences, musicals, cabaret/revues. **Facilities:** Festival Stage, 1500 seats, proscenium stage. **Best submission time:** year-round. **Response time:** 2 months letter; 6 months script. **Special programs:** The Play's the Thing: readings of 4–6 new plays each season by celebrity actors; scripts chosen through theatre's normal selection process.

STRAWDOG THEATRE COMPANY

(Founded 1988)
3829 North Broadway; Chicago, IL 60613; (773) 528-9889,
 FAX 528-7238; email strawdogtc@aol.com
Sarah Stray, *Literary Manager*
Submission procedure: no unsolicited scripts; direct solicitation to playwright or agent. **Types of material:** full-length plays, one-acts, translations, adaptations. **Special interests:** scripts suitable for ensemble aged 25-35; "off-the-wall," dark comedies. **Facilities:** Mainstage, 74 seats, black box. **Production considerations:** no fly or wing space.

STUDIO ARENA THEATRE

(Founded 1965)
710 Main St; Buffalo, NY 14202-1990; (716) 856-8025,
 FAX 856-3415; Web site http://www.studioarena.org
Gavin Cameron, *Artistic Director*
Submission procedure: no unsolicited scripts; agent submission. **Types of material:** full-length plays, translations, adaptations. **Special interests:** plays of local interest; plays of a theatrical nature; American history and culture; ethnic cultures, including plays about minorities. **Facilities:** Studio Arena Theatre, 637 seats, thrust stage. **Production considerations:** cast limit of 6; no fly system and limited wing space. **Best submission time:** year-round. **Response time:** 6 months.

THE STUDIO THEATRE

(Founded 1979)
1333 P St NW; Washington, DC 20005; (202) 232-7267,
 FAX 588-5262; email studio@studiotheatre.org;
 Web site http://studiotheatre.org
Serge Seiden, *Literary Manager*
Submission procedure: no unsolicited scripts; direct solicitation to playwright or agent. **Types of material:** full-length plays, translations, adaptations, musicals, solo pieces. **Special interests:** contemporary American and British plays. **Facilities:** Mead Theatre, 200 seats, thrust stage; Milton Theatre, 200 seats, thrust stage; Secondstage, 50 seats, flexible stage. **Response time:** 6 months.

SYRACUSE STAGE
(Founded 1973)
820 East Genesee St; Syracuse, NY 13210-1508; (315) 443-4008,
FAX 443-9846; email geisler@syr.edu;
Web site http://www.syracusestage.org
Garrett Eisler, *Literary Manager*
Submission procedure: accepts unsolicited scripts. **Types of material:** full-length plays. **Facilities:** John D. Archbold Theatre, 499 seats, proscenium stage. **Production considerations:** prefers small cast. **Best submission time:** year-round. **Response time:** 6 months.

TADA!
(Founded 1984)
120 West 28th St, 2nd Floor; New York, NY 10001; (212) 627-1732,
FAX 243-6736; email tada@tadatheater.com;
Web site http://www.tadatheater.com
Janine Nina Trevens, *Artistic Director*
Submission procedure: accepts unsolicited scripts. **Types of material:** one-acts, plays for young audiences, musicals. **Special interests:** work to be performed by children and teenagers. **Facilities:** Mainstage, 98 seats, black box. **Production considerations:** modest production demands. **Best submission time:** year-round. **Response time:** 6 months.

TAMPA BAY PERFORMING ARTS CENTER
(Founded 1987)
1010 North W. C. MacInnes Place; Tampa, FL 33602;
(813) 222-1000; FAX 222-1057; Web site http://www.tbpac.org
Karla Hartley, *Artistic Associate*
Submission procedure: accepts unsolicited scripts. **Types of material:** full-length plays. **Special interests:** plays by women writers. **Facilities:** Carol Morsani Hall, 2500 seats, proscenium stage; Playhouse, 1000 seats, proscenium stage; Jaeb, 300 seats, proscenium stage; Off Center, 150 seats, black box. **Production considerations:** small cast; 1 set. **Best submission time:** summer. **Response time:** 1 month.

TAPROOT THEATRE
(Founded 1976)
Box 30946; Seattle, WA 98103-0946; (206) 781-9705;
  email taproot@taproottheatre.org;
  Web site http://www.taproot.org/taproot
M. Christopher Boyer, *Director*
Submission procedure: no unsolicited scripts; direct solicitation to playwright or agent. **Types of material:** full-length plays, plays for young audiences, musicals. **Special interests:** social issue plays for children suitable for touring; plays of hope. **Facilities:** Taproot Theatre, 224 seats, thrust stage. **Production considerations:** cast limit of 12-15 for mainstage shows; cast limit of 5 for touring shows; no fly space. **Special programs:** readings of 8-10 new plays each year; participation by invitation.

TENNESSEE REPERTORY THEATRE
(Founded 1985)
427 Chestnut St; Nashville, TN 37203-4826; (615) 244-4878,
  FAX 244-1232; Web site http://www.tnrep.org
Todd Olson, *Associate Artistic Director*
Submission procedure: accepts unsolicited scripts with SASE for response; include synopsis and CD or cassette for musicals. **Types of material:** full-length plays, musicals, revues. **Facilities:** War Memorial Auditorium, 1400 seats, proscenium stage; Polk Theatre, 1100 seats, proscenium stage; Johnson Theatre, 88 seats, black box. **Production considerations:** small cast; small orchestra; minimal technical requirements. **Best submission time:** Jun-Sep. **Response time:** 4-6 weeks letter; 9-12 months script.

THALIA SPANISH THEATRE
(Founded 1977)
Box 4368; Sunnyside, NY 11104; (718) 729-3880, FAX 729-3388;
  email thaliaspan@aol.com;
  Web site http://www.queensnewyork.com/cultural/thalia
Angela Gil Orrios, *Artistic/Executive Director*
Submission procedure: accepts unsolicited scripts. **Types of material:** full-length plays, translations, adaptations. **Special interests:** plays in Spanish. **Facilities:** Thalia Spanish Theatre, 74 seats, proscenium stage. **Best submission time:** year-round. **Response time:** 3 months.

THEATER AT LIME KILN

(Founded 1984)
Lime Kiln Arts; 14 South Randolph St; Lexington, VA 24450;
 (540) 463-7088, FAX 463-1082; email limekiln@cfw.com
Brian Desmond, *Artistic Director*
Submission procedure: no unsolicited scripts; direct solicitation to playwright or agent. **Types of material:** full-length plays, adaptations, musicals. **Special interests:** work not produced professionally only; issues, language and music indigenous to VA and region; nontraditional staging. **Facilities:** The Kiln, 299 seats, outdoor amphitheatre. **Production considerations:** prefers cast limit of 9.

THE THEATER AT MONMOUTH

(Founded 1970)
Box 385; Monmouth, ME 04259-0385; (207) 933-2952,
 FAX 933-2952; email tamoffice@theateratmonmouth.org;
 Web site http://www.theateratmonmouth.org
David Greenham, *Managing Director*
Submission procedure: no unsolicited scripts; synopsis and letter of inquiry. **Types of material:** adaptations, plays for young audiences. **Special interests:** large-cast adaptations of classic literature for young audiences. **Facilities:** Cumston Hall, 275 seats, thrust stage. **Production considerations:** simple set. **Best submission time:** Sep. **Response time:** 4-6 weeks letter; 4-6 months script.

THEATER BY THE BLIND

(Founded 1979)
306 West 18th St; New York, NY 10011; (212) 243-4337,
 FAX 243-4337; email ashiotis@panix.com;
 Web site http://www. tbtb.org
Ike Schambelan, *Artistic Director*
Submission procedure: accepts unsolicited scripts. **Types of material:** full-length plays, one-acts, musicals. **Special interests:** work by and about the blind. **Facilities:** no permanent facility; company performs in various 99-seat venues. **Best submission time:** year-round. **Response time:** 2 months.

THEATRE DE LA JEUNE LUNE

(Founded 1979)
105 First St N; Minneapolis, MN 55401; (612) 332-3968,
 FAX 332-0048
Barbara Berlovitz, *Co-Artistic Director*
Submission procedure: no unsolicited scripts; synopsis and letter of inquiry.
Types of material: full-length plays, translations, adaptations, musicals,
cabaret/revues. **Special interests:** large-cast plays dealing with universal themes.
Facilities: Theatre de la Jeune Lune, 500 seats, flexible stage. **Best submission
time:** year-round. **Response time:** 8-10 weeks letter; 4 months script.

THEATER EMORY

(Founded 1985)
Rich Building, Room 230; Emory University; Atlanta, GA 30322;
 (404) 727-3465, FAX 727-6253; email vmurphy@emory.edu;
 Web site http://www.emory.edu/arts/
Vincent Murphy, *Artistic Producing Director*
Submission procedure: accepts unsolicited scripts through members of
Southeast Playwrights Project, Atlanta, GA, only; professional recommendation
from artistic director for all others. **Types of material:** full-length plays, one-acts,
translations, adaptations. **Special interests:** adaptations and translations of
literary and classic works. **Facilities:** MGM-I, 200 seats, thrust stage; MGM-II, 70
seats, flexible stage; Annex Studio, 60 seats, flexible stage. **Production
considerations:** cast limit of 20; no fly or wing space. **Best submission time:**
year-round. **Response time:** 2 months letter; 4 months script. **Special programs:**
Brave New Works: biennial staged reading marathon of new plays in conjunction
with the Southeast Playwrights Project; scripts chosen through regular
submission procedure; *deadline:* fall 2001; *dates:* spring 2002. The Playwriting
Center of Theater Emory: biennial 5-13 week residency of major playwright to
develop new work and teach playwriting workshop; *remuneration:* $25,000;
residency during 2001-02 academic year.

THEATRE FOR A NEW AUDIENCE

(Founded 1979)
154 Christopher St, Suite 3D; New York, NY 10014-2839;
 (212) 229-2819
Submission procedure: no unsolicited scripts; direct solicitation to playwright
or agent. **Types of material:** translations or adaptations of classic texts only.
Facilities: American Place Theatre, 299 seats, thrust stage.

THEATER FOR THE NEW CITY

(Founded 1970)
155–57 First Ave; New York, NY 10003–2906; (212) 254–1109
Crystal Field, *Executive Artistic Director*
Submission procedure: accepts unsolicited scripts with SASE for response.
Types of material: full-length plays. **Special interests:** plays with no previous mainstage production; experimental American works; plays with poetry, music and dance; social issues. **Facilities:** Joyce and Seward Johnson Theater, 200 seats, flexible stage; 2nd theatre, 75 seats, flexible stage; 3rd theatre, 100 seats, flexible stage. **Best submission time:** summer. **Response time:** 9-12 months.

THEATRE IV

(Founded 1975)
114 West Broad St; Richmond, VA 23220; (804) 783–1688,
    FAX 775–2325; email bmiller@theatreiv.org
    Web site http://www.theatreiv.org
Bruce Miller, *Artistic Director*
Submission procedure: no unsolicited scripts; synopsis and letter of inquiry.
Types of material: plays for young audiences only, including full-length plays, translations and adaptations. **Special interests:** scripts adaptable for touring with cast of 3-5. **Facilities:** Empire Theatre, 604 seats, proscenium stage; Little Theatre, 84 seats, flexible space. **Best submission time:** year-round. **Response time:** 2 months letter; 2 years script.

THEATRE IV ARTREACH

(Founded 1976)
3567 Edwards Rd, #5; Cincinnati, OH 45208; (513) 871–2300,
    FAX 533–1295; email artreach@zoomtown.com
    Web site http://www.theatreiv.org
Kelly Germain, *Associate Artistic Director*
Submission procedure: no unsolicited scripts; direct solicitation to playwright or agent. **Types of material:** plays for young audiences only. **Facilities:** no permanent facility; touring company.

THEATRE IN THE SQUARE

(Founded 1982)
11 Whitlock Ave; Marietta, GA 30064; (770) 422-8369, FAX 424-2637
Literary Manager
Submission procedure: no unsolicited scripts; synopsis and letter of inquiry.
Types of material: full-length plays, one-acts, translations, musicals. **Special interests:** world and southeastern premieres. **Facilities:** Mainstage, 225 seats, proscenium stage; Alley Stage, up to 120 seats, flexible stage. **Production considerations:** cast limit of 9; unit set; no fly space. **Best submission time:** Dec-Feb. **Response time:** 1 month letter (if interested); 6 months script.

THEATER MU

(Founded 1992)
711 West Lake St, Suit 212; Minneapolis, MN 55408;
    (612) 824-4804, FAX 824-3396; email info@theatermu.org;
    Web site http://www.theatermu.org
Rick Shiomi, *Artistic Director*
Submission procedure: no unsolicited scripts; synopsis, sample pages and letter of inquiry. **Types of material:** full-length plays, one-acts, adaptations, plays for young audiences. **Special interests:** plays combining traditional Asian performance with western theatre styles; short plays suitable for touring to schools. **Facilities:** no permanent facility; company performs in various proscenium venues with approximately 150 seats. **Production considerations:** cast limit of 10; simple sets. **Best submission time:** year-round. **Response time:** 2 months letter; 3 months script. **Special programs:** annual weekend staged reading series; touring and outreach programs.

THEATER OF THE FIRST AMENDMENT

(Founded 1990)
MS 3E6; George Mason University; Fairfax, VA 22030-4444;
    (703) 993-2195, FAX 993-2191; email rdavi4@gmu.edu
Rick Davis, *Artistic Director*
Submission procedure: no unsolicited scripts; synopsis, sample pages, resume and letter of inquiry. **Types of material:** full-length plays, one-acts, translations, adaptations, plays for young audiences. **Special interests:** sophisticated plays for younger audiences; "cultural history made dramatic as opposed to history dramatized; large battles joined; hard questions asked; word and image stretched." **Facilities:** TheaterSpace, 150-200 seats, flexible space. **Production considerations:** roles for younger actors welcome as TFA works with training program. **Best submission time:** Aug-Jan. **Response time:** 2 weeks letter; 6 months script. **Special programs:** readings, workshops and other development activities tailored to work that is under serious consideration for production.

THEATRE ON THE SQUARE

(Founded 1982)

450 Post St; San Francisco, CA 94102; (415) 433–6461,
    FAX 433–2910; email tots@wenet.net

Jonathan Reinis, *Owner*

Submission procedure: no unsolicited scripts; synopsis and letter of inquiry.
Types of material: full-length plays, musicals. **Facilities:** Theatre on the Square,
750 seats, proscenium/thrust stage. **Production considerations:** no fly space. **Best
submission time:** year-round. **Response time:** 6 months letter; 1 year script.

THEATRE PREVIEWS AT DUKE

(Founded 1986)

Box 90680; 209 Bivins Building; Durham, NC 27708–0680;
    (919) 660–3347, FAX 684–8906; email zannie@duke.edu

Zannie Giraud Voss, *Managing Director*

Submission procedure: no unsolicited scripts; synopsis and letter of inquiry.
Types of material: full-length plays, translations, adaptations, musicals.
Facilities: Reynolds Theatre, 600 seats, proscenium stage; Sheafer Theatre, 110
seats, black box. **Best submission time:** spring. **Response time:** 3 months
letter; 2-6 months script.

THEATRE THREE

(Founded 1969)

Box 512; Port Jefferson, NY 11777–0512; (631) 928–9202,
    FAX 928–9120

Jeffrey Sanzel, *Artistic Director*

Submission procedure: no unsolicited scripts; send SASE for guidelines. **Types
of material:** one-acts. **Special interests:** previously unproduced works only.
Facilities: Second Stage, 80-100 seats, black box. **Production considerations:**
prefers cast limit of 2-6; 1 set; minimal production demands. **Best submission
time:** year-round. **Response time:** 1 month letter; 6 months script (if requested).
Special programs: Annual Festival of One-Act Plays: fully staged productions;
send SASE to theatre for guidelines; *deadline:* 30 Sep 2000; *notification:* 30 Dec
2000; *dates:* Feb-Mar 2001.

THEATRE THREE, INC.
(Founded 1961)
2800 Routh St; Dallas, TX 75201; (214) 871-2933,
 FAX 871-3139; email theatre3@airmail.net;
 Web site http://www.vline.net/theatre3/
Jac Alder, *Executive Producer/Director*
Submission procedure: no unsolicited scripts; agent submission. **Types of material:** full-length plays, musicals. **Facilities:** Theatre Three, 242 seats, arena stage; Theatre Too, 60 seats, black box. **Best submission time:** year-round; prefers Sep-Dec. **Response time:** 3 months.

THEATRE X
(Founded 1969)
158 North Broadway; Milwaukee, WI 53202; (414) 278-0555
David Ravel, *Producing Director*
Submission procedure: no unsolicited scripts; synopsis with SASE for response. **Types of material:** full-length plays. **Special interests:** contemporary plays; "pseudo-naturalism and self-conscious theatricality involving the ongoing fruits of interdisciplinary collaboration." **Facilities:** Black Box, 99 seats, flexible stage. **Production considerations**: theatre uses core acting company of 3 women and 2 men, late forties, early fifties. **Best submission time:** year-round. **Response time:** 6 months.

THEATRE VIRGINIA
(Founded 1955)
2800 Grove Ave; Richmond, VA 23221-2466; (804) 353-6100
George Black, *Producing Artistic Director*
Submission procedure: no unsolicited scripts; agent submission. **Types of material:** full-length plays, musicals. **Facilities:** Main Stage, 500 seats, proscenium stage. **Best submission time:** year-round. **Response time:** 3-8 months. **Special programs:** New Voices for the Theatre: playwriting competition open to VA students grades 5-12; winners grades 9-12 attend 3-week summer residency program and receive dramaturgical assistance and professional staged reading; contact Education and Outreach Department for more information; *deadline*: 1 Feb 2001.

THEATREWORKS
(Founded 1969)
1100 Hamilton Ct; Menlo Park, CA 94025; (650) 463-7126,
FAX 463-1963; email jeannie@theatreworks.org;
Web site http://www.theatreworks.org
Jeannie Barroga, *Literary Manager*
Submission procedure: accepts unsolicited full-length plays and musicals; for translations and adaptations, send letter of inquiry with SASP for response. **Types of material:** full-length plays, translations, adaptations, musicals. **Special interests:** works offering opportunities for multiethnic casting. **Facilities:** Mountain View Center, 625 seats, proscenium stage; Stage II, 117 seats, thrust stage. **Best submission time:** Jul-Nov. **Response time:** 1 month letter; 4 months script. **Special programs:** New Works Forum: developmental reading series for plays, musicals and music-theatre pieces.

THEATREWORKS/USA
(Founded 1961)
151 West 26th St, 7th Floor; New York, NY 10001; (212) 647-1100,
FAX 924-5377; email info@theatreworksusa.org
Barbara Pasternack, *Artistic Director*
Submission procedure: accepts unsolicited scripts; prefers synopsis, sample scene(s) and songs (include cassette and lyric sheet) and letter of inquiry. **Types of material:** plays and musicals for young audiences. **Special interests:** literary adaptations; historical/biographical themes; fairy tales; contemporary issues. **Facilities:** Promenade Theatre, 398 seats, proscenium stage; also tours. **Production considerations:** cast limit of 5-6 (can play multiple roles); sets suitable for touring. **Best submission time:** summer. **Response time:** 1 month letter; 6 months script. **Special programs:** Theatreworks/USA Commissioning Program (see Development).

THEATRICAL OUTFIT
(Founded 1976)
Box 1555; Atlanta, GA 30301; (404) 577-5257, FAX 577-5259;
email kate.warner@theatricaloutfit.org;
Web site http://www.theatricaloutfit.org
Kate Warner, *Managing Director/Artistic Associate*
Submission procedure: no unsolicited scripts; 1-page synopsis and letter of inquiry with SASP for response. **Types of material:** full-length plays, adaptations, solo pieces. **Facilities:** Theatrical Outfit, 800 seats, proscenium stage. **Best submission time:** Apr-Jun. **Response time:** 2 months letter; 2 months script.

TOTEM POLE PLAYHOUSE
(Founded 1950)
Box 603; Fayetteville, PA 17222; (717) 352-2164, FAX 352-8870
Carl Schurr, *Producing Artistic Director*
Submission procedure: no unsolicited scripts; synopsis, sample pages and letter of inquiry. **Types of material:** full-length plays, one-acts, musicals. **Special interests:** light comedies and musicals that appeal to a general audience. **Facilities:** Mainstage, 453 seats, proscenium stage. **Best submission time:** year-round. **Response time:** 1-2 months letter; 6 months script.

TOUCHSTONE THEATRE
(Founded 1981)
321 East 4th St; Bethlehem, PA 18015; (610) 867-1689,
    FAX 867-0561; email touchstone@nni.com;
    Web site http://www.touchstone.org
Mark McKenna, *Artistic Director*
Submission procedure: no unsolicited scripts; letter of inquiry. **Types of material:** proposals for works to be created in collaboration with company's ensemble only. **Facilities:** Touchstone Theatre, 74 seats, black box. **Production considerations:** 18' x 21' playing area. **Best submission time:** year-round. **Response time:** 1 month.

TRINITY REPERTORY COMPANY
(Founded 1964)
201 Washington St; Providence, RI 02903; (401) 521-1100,
    FAX 521-0447; Web site http://www.trinityrep.com
Craig Watson, *Literary Manager*
Submission procedure: no unsolicited scripts; synopsis, dialogue sample and letter of inquiry. **Types of material:** full-length plays, translations, adaptations, musicals, solo pieces. **Facilities:** Upstairs Theatre, 500 seats, thrust stage; Downstairs Theatre, 297 seats, thrust stage. **Best submission time:** year-round. **Response time:** 2 months letter; 3 months script.

TRUSTUS THEATRE
(Founded 1985)
Box 11721; Columbia, SC 29211-1721; (803) 254-9732,
FAX 771-9153; email trustus88@aol.com;
Web site http://www.trustus.org
Jon Tuttle, *Literary Manager*
Submission procedure: accepts unsolicited scripts. **Types of material:** one-acts.
Special interests: experimental, hard-hitting, off-the-wall comedies or
"dramadies" for Late-Night series; no musicals or plays for young audiences.
Facilities: Mainstage, 100 seats, flexible proscenium stage. **Production
considerations:** small cast; moderate production demands. **Best submission
time:** Aug-Dec. **Response time:** 2-4 months. **Special programs:** Trustus
Playwrights' Festival (see Prizes).

TURNIP THEATRE COMPANY
(Founded 1991)
145 West 46th St; New York, NY 10036; (212) 768-4016;
Literary Committee
Submission procedure: no unsolicited scripts; direct solicitation to playwright.
Types of material: full-length plays. **Special interests:** New York-area
playwrights. **Facilities:** no permanent facility. **Best submission time:** theatre not
currently accepting scripts. **Special programs:** 15 Minute Play Festival; send SASE
for guidelines; *deadline:* 1 Nov 2000 for guideline submission, 1 Dec 2000 for
submission; *notification:* Feb 2001; *dates:* Apr 2001.

TWO RIVER THEATRE COMPANY
(Founded 1994)
Box 8035; Red Bank, NJ 07702; (732) 345-1400, FAX 345-1414;
email info@tworivertheatre.org
Jonathan Fox, *Artistic Director*
Submission procedure: no unsolicited scripts; synopsis, first 10 pages of script
and letter of inquiry with SASE for response. **Types of material:** full-length plays,
adaptations. **Facilities:** Algonquin Arts Theatre, 500 seats, proscenium stage.
Production considerations: cast limit of 10. **Best submission time:** year-round.
Response time: 1 month letter; 8-10 months script.

UBU REPERTORY THEATER

(Founded 1982)
95 Wall St, 21st Floor; New York, NY 10005; (212) 509-1455,
FAX 509-1635; email uburep@spacelab.net
Françoise Kourilsky, *Founder/Artistic Director*
Submission procedure: no unsolicited scripts; synopsis and letter of inquiry.
Types of material: full-length plays, one-acts, translations. **Special interests:** French-language plays or their translations only; contemporary plays from French-speaking countries and regions. **Facilities:** no permanent facility.
Production considerations: cast limit of 7; 1 set or simple sets. **Best submission time:** year-round. **Response time:** 2 months letter; 6 months script.

UNICORN THEATRE

(Founded 1974)
3828 Main St; Kansas City, MO 64111; (816) 531-7529, ext 18,
FAX 531-0421; Web site http://www.unicorntheatre.org
Herman Wilson, *Literary Assistant*
Submission procedure: accepts unsolicited scripts. **Types of material:** full-length plays. **Special interests:** contemporary social issues. **Facilities:** Unicorn Theatre, 180 seats, thrust stage. **Best submission time:** Sep-Apr. **Response time:** 4-6 months. **Special programs:** Unicorn Theatre National Playwrights' Award (see Prizes).

UTAH SHAKESPEAREAN FESTIVAL

(Founded 1961)
351 West Center St; Cedar City, UT 84720-2498; (435) 586-7880,
FAX 865-8003; email phillips@suu.edu;
Web site http://www.bard.org
Douglas N. Cook, *Producing Artistic Director*
George Judy, *Director of New Plays Series*
Submission procedure: no unsolicited scripts; synopsis, professional recommendation and letter of inquiry. **Types of material:** full-length plays.
Special interests: plays with no previous mainstage production only; plays by writers from western United States or plays with western themes; plays with classical themes; plays about minorities or the underserved. **Facilities:** Downtown Cinema Theatre, 150 seats, proscenium stage. **Production considerations:** cast limit of 10-12; no sets, minimal props and costumes; 5-rehearsal limit; 2 staged readings; no full productions. **Best submission time:** May-Dec. **Response time:** 1 Mar of the year following submission.

VICTORY GARDENS THEATER

(Founded 1974)
2257 North Lincoln Ave; Chicago, IL 60614; (773) 549–5788,
    FAX 549–2779
Sandy Shinner, *Associate Artistic Director*
Submission procedure: accepts unsolicited scripts from Chicago-area writers only; others send synopsis, 10-page dialogue sample and letter of inquiry with SASE for response. **Types of material:** full-length plays, adaptations, musicals. **Special interests:** Chicago and Midwest playwrights; plays by women and writers of color. **Facilities:** Mainstage One, 195 seats, modified thrust stage; Mainstage Two, 200 seats, thrust stage; 2 studio theaters, 70 seats each, black box. **Production considerations:** prefers cast limit of 10; simple set; small-cast musicals only. **Best submission time:** Mar–Jun. **Response time:** 2 months letter; 9 months script. **Special programs:** Victory Gardens Playwrights Ensemble: core group of twelve resident writers. Readers Theater: staged readings of works-in-progress by area writers twice a month. Artist Development Workshop: playwriting class offered throughout the year that brings people with and without disabilities together in a creative environment.

THE VICTORY THEATRE

(Founded 1979)
3326 West Victory Blvd; Burbank, CA 91505; (818) 841–4404,
    FAX 841–6328; email thevictory@mindspring.com
    Web site http://www.thevictorytheatres.com
Tom Ormeny, *Artistic Director*
Submission procedure: no unsolicited scripts; synopsis, first 15 pages of script, resume and letter of inquiry. **Types of material:** full-length plays, adaptations. **Special interests:** plays involving social and political issues; "well-made, but cutting-edge" plays. **Facilities:** The Victory Theatre, 91 seats, arena stage; The Little Victory, 48 seats, arena stage. **Production considerations:** prefers cast limit of 12; maximum 2 simple sets; no fly space. **Best submission time:** year-round. **Response time:** 2 months letter; 3 months script.

THE VINEYARD PLAYHOUSE

Founded (1982)
Box 2452, 24 Church St; Vineyard Haven, MA 02568;
   (508) 693-6450
M. J. Bruder Munafo, Producer & Artistic Director
Submission procedure: no unsolicited scripts; direct solicitation to playwright or agent. **Types of material:** full-length plays, translations, adaptations, plays for young audiences, solo pieces. **Special interests:** contemporary American works; culturally diverse plays; plays that address social issues. **Facilities:** The Vineyard Playhouse, 120 seats, black box. **Production considerations:** prefers cast limit of 10; simple sets.

VINEYARD THEATRE

(Founded 1981)
108 East 15th St; New York, NY 10003-9689; (212) 353-3366,
   FAX 353-3803
Douglas Aibel, *Artistic Director*
Submission procedure: no unsolicited scripts; synopsis or project description, 10-page dialogue sample and letter of inquiry; include cassette for musicals. **Types of material:** full-length plays, musicals. **Special interests:** plays that incorporate music in a unique way; musicals with strong narrative; "nervy, eccentric theatrical forms." **Facilities:** Vineyard Dimson Theatre, 120 seats, flexible stage; Vineyard 26th Street Theatre, 71 seats, thrust stage. **Best submission time:** year-round. **Response time:** 6-12 months letter; 6 months script. **Special programs:** New Works at the Vineyard: developmental lab productions for new plays and musicals.

VIRGINIA STAGE COMPANY

(Founded 1979)
Box 3770; Norfolk, VA 23514; (757) 627-6988, FAX 628-5958;
   Web site http://www.vastage.com
Patricia Darden, *Assistant to the Directors*
Submission procedure: no unsolicited scripts; synopsis and letter of inquiry. **Types of material:** full-length plays, musicals. **Special interests:** plays by VA writers; world premieres; works about "twenty-somethings" and youth culture; poetic drama and comedy; hard-hitting, issue-oriented plays. **Facilities:** Mainstage, 700 seats, proscenium stage; laboratory theatre, 99 seats, flexible stage. **Best submission time:** year-round. **Response time:** 1 month letter; 6 months script.

THE WALNUT STREET THEATRE COMPANY

(Founded 1809)

825 Walnut St; Philadelphia, PA 19107-5107; (215) 574-3550,
FAX 574-3598

Beverly Elliott, *Literary Manager*

Submission procedure: no unsolicited scripts; synopsis, cast list, 10-20-page dialogue sample and letter of inquiry with SASE for response from Dramatist Guild members only; include professional-quality cassette for musicals. **Types of material:** full-length plays, musicals. **Special interests:** original, socially relevant musicals with uplifting themes; commercially viable works for Main Stage; meaningful comedies and dramas with some broad social relevance for Studio 3. **Facilities:** Main Stage, 1050 seats, proscenium stage; Studio 3, 80 seats, flexible stage. **Production considerations:** cast limit of 4 for Studio 3. **Response time:** 3 months letter; 6 months script.

WATERTOWER THEATRE, INC.

(Founded 1976)

15650 Addison Rd; Addison, TX 75001; (972) 450-6220,
FAX 450-6244; Web site http://www.watertowertheatre.com

Terry Martin, *Artistic Director*

Submission procedure: no unsolicited scripts; synopsis, dialogue sample, resume and letter of inquiry with SASE for response. **Types of material:** full-length plays, musicals, solo pieces. **Special interests:** comedies; plays that make creative use of flexible space. **Facilities:** Addison Conference & Theatre Centre, 100-300 seats, flexible stage. **Response time:** 3 months letter; 6 months script. **Special programs:** Stone Cottage New Works Festival: readings of previously unproduced full-length plays; submit synopsis, character breakdown and SASE for response; *deadline:* 15 Feb 2001; *notification:* 30 May 2001; *dates:* Jul 2002.

WEISSBERGER THEATER GROUP

(Founded 1992)

909 Third Ave, 27th Floor; New York, NY 10022-9998;
(212) 339-5529, FAX 486-8996

Jay Harris, *Producer*

Submission procedure: no unsolicited scripts; synopsis and letter of inquiry. **Types of material:** full-length plays. **Special interests:** topical issue-oriented plays. **Facilities:** no permanent facility. **Production considerations:** cast limit of 7. **Best submission time:** year-round. **Response time:** 1 month letter; 2 months script.

WEST COAST ENSEMBLE
(Founded 1982)
Box 38728; Los Angeles, CA 90038; (323) 876-9337,
    FAX 876-8916
Les Hanson, *Artistic Director*
Submission procedure: accepts unsolicited scripts. **Types of material:** full-length plays, one-acts, translations, adaptations, musicals. **Special interests:** plays not previously produced in Southern CA only; musicals; short plays. **Facilities:** Mainstage, 85 seats, proscenium stage. **Production considerations:** simple set; no fly space. **Best submission time:** Jun-Dec. **Response time:** 6 months. **Special programs:** staged readings of new plays. West Coast Ensemble Contests (see Prizes).

WESTBETH THEATRE CENTER
(Founded 1977)
151 Bank St; New York, NY 10014; (212) 691-2272, FAX 924-7185
    Web site http://www.westbeththeatre.com
Arnold Engelman, *Producing Director*
Submission procedure: no unsolicited scripts; synopsis, project proposal and letter of inquiry with SASE for response. **Types of material:** full-length plays, musicals, solo pieces. **Special interests:** "fresh, unique" and contemporary works. **Facilities:** Music Hall, 100-250 seats, proscenium; Big Room, 99 seats, black box; Studio Theatre, 85 seats, black box; Café, 50-70 seats, cabaret. **Production considerations:** modest technical demands. **Best submission time:** year-round. **Response time:** 2 months letter; 4 months script. **Special programs:** Westbeth Theatrical Development Program (see Development).

THE WESTERN STAGE
(Founded 1974)
156 Homestead Ave; Salinas, CA 93901; (831) 755-6990, FAX 755-6954
Michael Roddy, *Literary Manager*
Submission procedure: no unsolicited scripts; synopsis and letter of inquiry; include cassette for musicals; for adaptations of work not in public domain, enclose copy of letter granting rights. **Types of material:** full-length plays, adaptations, plays for young audiences, musicals, cabaret/revues. **Special interests:** adaptations of works of literary significance; large-cast plays. **Facilities:** Mainstage, 500 seats, proscenium stage; Cabaret, 250 seats, proscenium stage; Studio, 100 seats, thrust stage. **Best submission time:** year-round. **Response time:** 4-6 weeks letter; 3 months script.

WILL GEER THEATRICUM BOTANICUM

(Founded 1973)

Box 1222; Topanga, CA 90290; (310) 455-2322, FAX 455-3724;
   email theatricum@aol.com

Ellen Geer, *Artistic Director*

Submission procedure: no unsolicited scripts; synopsis, dialogue sample and letter of inquiry; include cassette for musicals. **Types of material:** full-length plays, musicals. **Special interests:** work suitable for large outdoor playing space. **Facilities:** Will Geer Theatricum Botanicum, 300 seats, outdoor amphitheatre. **Production considerations:** cast limit of 4-10; simple sets. **Best submission time:** Sep. **Response time:** 1 month letter; 6 months script.

WILLIAMSTOWN THEATRE FESTIVAL

(Founded 1955)

Sep-May: 100 East 17th St, 3rd Floor; New York, NY 10003;
   (212) 228-2286, FAX 228-9091;
   Web site http://www.wtfestival.org

Jun-Aug: Box 517; Williamstown, MA 01267-0517; (413) 458-3200,
   FAX 458-3147

Michael Ritchie, *Producer*

Submission procedure: no unsolicited scripts; agent submission only. **Types of material:** full-length plays, adaptations, musicals, solo pieces. **Facilities:** Main Stage, 521 seats, proscenium stage; 2nd stage, 96 seats, thrust stage. **Best submission time:** 1 Oct-15 Feb. **Response time:** 6-12 months. **Special programs:** New Play Staged Readings Series.

WILLOWS THEATRE COMPANY

(Founded 1977)

1975 Diamond Blvd, Suite B-230; Concord, CA 94520;
   (925) 798-1300, FAX 676-5726; email rich@willowstheatre.org;
   Web site http://www.willowstheatre.org

 Richard H. Elliott, *Artistic Director*

Submission procedure: no unsolicited scripts; synopsis, character breakdown and letter of inquiry. **Types of material:** full-length plays, adaptations, musicals. **Special interests:** musicals and plays based on figures and events drawn from American history, especially CA history; contemporary comedies. **Facilities:** Willows Theatre, 210 seats, proscenium stage. **Production considerations:** cast limit of 35. **Best submission time:** 1 Jan-1 Apr. **Response time:** 3 months letter; 6-12 months script. **Special programs:** staged readings and workshop development productions.

THE WILMA THEATER

(Founded 1972)

265 South Broad St; Philadelphia, PA 19107; (215) 893-9456,
FAX 893-0895; email info@wilmatheater.org;
Web site http://www.wilmatheater.org

Literary Manager/Dramaturg

Submission procedure: no unsolicited scripts; professional recommendation.
Types of material: full-length plays, translations, adaptations, musicals. **Special interests:** new translations and adaptations from the international repertoire with emphasis on innovative, bold staging; world premieres; ensemble works; works with poetic dimension; plays with music; multimedia works; social issues. **Facilities:** Wilma Theater, 300 seats, flexible/proscenium stage. **Production considerations:** prefers cast limit of 12; stage 44' x 46'. **Best submission time:** year-round. **Response time:** 9-12 months.

WINGS THEATRE COMPANY, INC.

(Founded 1986)

154 Christopher St; New York, NY 10014; (212) 627-2960,
FAX 462-0024; email ejeffer@brainlink.com;
Web site http://www.brainlink.com/~cjeffer/

Tricia Gilbert, *Literary Manager*

Submission procedure: accepts unsolicited scripts. **Types of material:** full-length plays, musicals. **Special interests:** new musicals or gay-themed plays only. **Facilities:** Wings Theatre, 74 seats, proscenium stage. **Best submission time:** year-round. **Response time:** plays received by 1 May receive response in Sep of that year; plays received after 1 May receive response Sep of following year.

WOMEN'S PROJECT & PRODUCTIONS

(Founded 1978)

55 West End Ave; New York, NY 10023; (212) 765-1706,
FAX 765-2024; email wpp@earthlink.net;
Web site http://www.womensproject.org

Lisa McNulty, *Literary Manager*

Submission procedure: no unsolicited scripts; synopsis, 10-page dialogue sample and letter of inquiry with SASE for response. **Types of material:** full-length plays. **Special interests:** plays by women only. **Facilities:** Theatre Four, 199 seats, proscenium stage. **Best submission time:** year-round. **Response time:** 2 months letter; 8 months script. **Special programs:** Playwrights Lab and Directors Forum: developmental program including play readings and work-in-progress presentations; participation by invitation only. Commissioning program.

WOOLLY MAMMOTH THEATRE COMPANY
(Founded 1981)
1401 Church St NW; Washington, DC 20005; (202) 234-6130,
   ext 513; email Woollymamm@aol.com
Mary Resing, *Literary Manager*
Submission procedure: no unsolicited scripts; professional recommendation.
Types of material: full-length plays, translations, adaptations, solo pieces.
Special interests: theatrical and provocative plays which combine elevated
language with edgy situations and complex characters. **Facilities:** MainStage, 132
seats, thrust stage. **Production considerations:** prefers cast limit of 6; minimal
staging requirements. **Best submission time:** Jun. **Response time:** 12 months.
Special programs: Foreplay: reading series of 5-6 plays each year under
consideration for MainStage production.

THE WOOSTER GROUP
(Founded 1969)
Box 654, Canal Street Station; New York, NY 10013;
   (212) 966-9796, FAX 226-6576; email woostergrp@aol.com;
   Web site http://www.thewoostergroup.org
Kim Whitener, *Managing Director*
Submission procedure: no unsolicited scripts (company customarily collaborates
on its own original work). **Types of material:** full-length plays. **Special interests:**
experimental works. **Facilities:** The Performing Garage, 99 seats, black box.

WORCESTER FOOTHILLS THEATRE COMPANY
(Founded 1974)
100 Front St, Suite 137; Worcester, MA 01608; (508) 754-3314,
   FAX 767-0676
Michael Walker, *Executive Producer/Artistic Director*
Submission procedure: no unsolicited scripts; synopsis and letter of inquiry.
Types of material: full-length plays, translations, adaptations. **Special interests:**
plays suited to multigenerational audiences. **Facilities:** Worcester Foothills
Theatre, 349 seats, proscenium stage. **Production considerations:** prefers cast
limit of 10, simple set. **Best submission time:** Sep. **Response time:** 3 months
letter; 4 months script.

WRITERS' THEATRE CHICAGO
(Founded 1992)
c/o Books on Vernon; 664 Vernon Ave; Glencoe, IL 60022;
 (847) 835-7366, FAX 835-5332; email writerstheatre@aol.com
Marilyn Campbell, *Artistic Associate*
Submission procedure: accepts unsolicited scripts with professional recommendation if possible. **Types of material:** full-length plays, translations, adaptations. **Special interests:** highly literary plays by or about great writers and writing. **Facilities:** Nicholas Pennell Theatre, 50 seats, thrust stage. **Production considerations:** small cast; small space; minimal production demands. **Best submission time:** year-round. **Response time:** 3 months.

YALE REPERTORY THEATRE
(Founded 1965)
Box 208244, Yale Station; New Haven, CT 06520-8244;
 (203) 432-1560, FAX 432-1550;
 email catherine.sheehy@yale.edu
Catherine Sheehy, *Resident Dramaturg*
Submission procedure: no unsolicited scripts; synopsis and letter of inquiry. **Types of material:** full-length plays, translations, adaptations, solo pieces. **Special interests:** new work; new translations of classics; contemporary foreign plays. **Facilities:** University Theatre, 654 seats, proscenium stage; Yale Repertory Theatre, 487 seats, modified thrust stage. **Best submission time:** year-round. **Response time:** 2 months letter; 3 months script.

THE YORK THEATRE COMPANY
(Founded 1968)
The Theatre at St Peter's Church; Citicorp Center;
 619 Lexington Ave; New York, NY 10022-4610;
 (212) 935-5824, FAX 832-0037
Literary Department
Submission procedure: no unsolicited scripts; synopsis and letter of inquiry with SASE for response. **Types of material:** musicals, revues. **Special interests:** small-cast musicals. **Facilities:** The Theatre at Saint Peter's Church, 177 seats, flexible stage. **Best submission time:** year-round. **Response time:** 1-2 months letter; 6-8 months script.

YOUNG PLAYWRIGHTS INC.

See Young Playwrights Festival in Prizes and Young Playwrights Inc. in Organizations.

ZACHARY SCOTT THEATRE CENTER (ZACH)

(Founded 1933)
1510 Toomey Rd; Austin, TX 78704–1078; (512) 476–0594,
   FAX 476–0314; email zach@io.com;
   Web site http://www.zachscott.com
Dave Steakley, *Producing Artistic Director*
Submission procedure: no unsolicited scripts; direct solicitation to playwright or agent. **Types of material:** full-length plays, plays for young audiences. **Facilities:** Mainstage 1, 200 seats, thrust stage; Mainstage 2, 130 seats, arena stage. **Production considerations:** plays for young audiences that tour easily. **Best submission time:** Jan. **Response time:** 6 months.

PRIZES

What competitions are included here?

All the playwriting contests we know of that offer prizes of at least $200 or, in the case of awards to playwrights 19 or under, the equivalent in production or publication. Most awards for which the playwright cannot apply—the Joseph Kesselring Award, the Pulitzer Prize—are not listed. Exceptions are made when, as with the Susan Smith Blackburn Prize, the nominating process allows playwrights to encourage nomination of their work by theatre professionals.

How can I give myself the best chance of winning?

Send your script in well before the deadline, when the readers are fresh and enthusiastic rather than buried by an avalanche of submissions. Assume the deadline is the date your script must be received (not the postmark date). Make sure you don't mistake a notification date for the submission deadline. If a listing specifies "write for guidelines," be sure to follow this instruction. It usually means that we don't have space in our brief listing to give you all the information you need; also contests may change their rules or their deadlines after this book has been published. Always send an SASE with your submission, if you expect your materials to be returned.

Should I enter contests that charge entry fees?

It's true that a number of listings require a fee. Many contest sponsors are unable to secure sufficient funding to cover their costs, which are considerable. We have not included those listings with unusually high fees. Some playwrights will not pay fees as a matter of principle, others consider it part of doing business. It's up to you.

How can I find out about new prizes and updates throughout the year?

Write for guidelines to ensure that you have the most recent rules. Also refer to the Membership and Service Organizations, Useful Publications and Online Resources sections in this book for those groups that list current contest news.

A couple of *Sourcebook* reminders:

"Full-length play" means a full-length, original work without a score or libretto. One-acts, musicals, adaptations, translations, plays for young audiences and solo pieces are listed separately.

Sourcebook entries are alphabetized by first word (excluding "the") even if the title starts with a proper name. So, for instance, you'll find the "Harold Morton Landon Translation Award" under H. In the index, you will also find this prize cross-listed under L. And, we alphabetize listings word-by-word, e.g., "A. D. Players" would be listed before "Academy Theatre." We've included listings of biennial prizes with deadlines after the dates of this *Sourcebook* (September 2000–August 2001), so please read the deadlines carefully—don't mistake a March 2002 deadline for 2001.

AMERICAN RENEGADE PLAYWRITING CONTEST

American Renegade Theatre; 11136 Magnolia Blvd;
North Hollywood, CA 91601; (818) 763-4430

David A. Cox, *Artistic Director*

Types of material: full-length plays. **Frequency:** annual. **Remuneration:** $500 1st prize; full production; 5% of box office gross; 2 runners-up receive staged readings. **Guidelines:** unpublished work not produced professionally. **Submission procedure:** script and $20 fee (checks payable to ARTC). **Deadline:** 1 Oct 2000. **Notification:** 15 Nov 2000. (See Production.)

AMERICAN TRANSLATORS ASSOCIATION AWARDS

225 Reinekers Ln, Suite 590; Alexandria, VA 22314;
FAX (703) 683-6122; email ata@atanet.org
Courtney Searls-Ridge, *Chair, ATA Honors and Awards*

GERMAN LITERARY TRANSLATION PRIZE

Types of material: translations of full-length plays and one-acts. **Frequency:** biennial. **Remuneration:** $1000; up to $500 expenses to attend ATA annual conference. **Guidelines:** translation from German published in U.S. by American publisher during 2 years before deadline as single volume or in collection. **Submission procedure:** no submission by translator; publisher nominates translation and submits 2 copies of book plus 10 consecutive pages of German original, extra jacket and any advertising copy; vita of translator. **Deadline:** 15 May 2001. **Notification:** fall 2001.

LEWIS GALANTIERE LITERARY TRANSLATION PRIZE

Types of material: translations of full-length plays and one-acts. **Frequency:** biennial. **Remuneration:** $1000; up to $500 expenses to attend ATA annual conference. **Guidelines:** translation from any language except German published in U.S. by American publisher during 2 years before deadline as single volume or in collection. **Submission procedure:** no submission by translator; publisher nominates translation and submits 2 copies of book plus 10 consecutive pages of original, extra jacket and any advertising copy; vita of translator. **Deadline:** 30 Mar 2002. **Notification:** fall 2002.

ANNA ZORNIO MEMORIAL CHILDREN'S THEATRE PLAYWRITING AWARD

Department of Theatre and Dance; University of New Hampshire;
  Paul Creative Arts Center; 30 College Rd;
  Durham, NH 03824-3538; (603) 862-3044, FAX 862-0298
Julie Brinker, *Director of Theatre Education*

Types of material: plays and musicals for young audiences. **Frequency:** every 4 years. **Remuneration:** $1000; production by UNH Theatre in Education Program in May 2002. **Guidelines:** U.S. or Canadian resident; unpublished work not produced professionally and not more than 1 hour long; prefers single or unit set; 2-submission limit. **Submission procedure:** script with brief synopsis, character breakdown and statement of design/technical considerations; SASP for acknowledgment of receipt; include cassette for musical; write for guidelines. **Deadline:** 1 Sep 2001. **Notification:** May 2002; exact date TBA.

THE ANNUAL BLANK THEATRE COMPANY YOUNG PLAYWRIGHTS FESTIVAL

1301 Lucile Ave; Los Angeles, CA 90026-1519; (323) 662-7734;
  email info@theblank.com;
  Web site http://www.theblank.com
Christopher Steele, *Producer*

Types of material: full-length plays, one-acts, plays for young audiences, musicals, operas, solo pieces. **Frequency:** annual. **Remuneration:** workshop production for approximately 9 playwrights; some scripts receive full production. **Guidelines:** playwright 19 years of age or younger as of deadline date; original play of any length on any subject; send SASE in late Jan 2001 for guidelines. **Submission procedure:** script with cover sheet containing name, date of birth, home address, phone number and name of school (if any). **Deadline:** 1 Apr 2001. **Notification:** May 2001.

ASF Translation Prize

The American-Scandinavian Foundation; 15 East 65th St;
New York, NY 10021; (212) 879-9779, FAX 249-3444;
email agyongy@amscan.org
Publishing Office

Types of material: translations. **Frequency:** annual. **Remuneration:** $2000; publication of excerpt in *Scandinavian Review*, $500 for runner-up. **Guidelines:** unpublished translation from a Scandinavian language into English of work written by a Scandinavian author after 1800; manuscript must be at least 50 pages long if prose drama, 25 pages if verse drama, and must be conceived as part of a book. **Submission procedure:** 4 copies of translation, 1 of original; permission letter from copyright holder; write for guidelines. **Deadline:** 1 Jun 2001. **Notification:** fall 2001.

Attic Theatre Ensemble's One-Act Marathon

Attic Theatre Centre; 65621/2 Santa Monica Blvd;
Hollywood, CA 90038; (323) 469-3786, FAX 463-9571;
Web site http://www.attictheatre.org
James Carey, *Producing Artistic Director*

Types of material: one-acts. **Frequency:** annual. **Remuneration:** $250 1st prize; $100 2nd prize; $50 3rd prize; 12 finalists get productions. **Guidelines:** previously unproduced one-act no longer than 45 minutes long; no adaptations. **Submission procedure:** send SASE for application and guidelines or visit Web site. **Deadline:** 30 Sep 2000. **Notification:** Jan 2001. **Dates:** Jun 2001. (See listing in Production.)

Aurand Harris Memorial Playwriting Award

The New England Theatre Conference; Northeastern University;
306 Huntington Ave; Boston, MA 02115; (617) 424-9275,
FAX 424-1057; email netc@world.com;
Web site http://www.netheatreconference.org

Types of material: plays for young audiences. **Frequency:** annual. **Remuneration:** $1000 1st prize, $500 2nd prize. **Guidelines:** resident of CT, MA, ME, NH, RI, VT or member of The New England Theatre Conference (NETC); unpublished work not produced professionally; 1 submission limit. **Submission procedure:** bound script, synopsis, character breakdown and statement that play has not been published or professionally produced and is not under consideration for publication or production prior to 1 Sep 2000; $20 fee (fee is waived for NETC members); send SASP for acknowledgment of receipt; script will not be returned; send SASE for guidelines. **Deadline:** 1 May 2001. **Notification:** Sep 2001 (winners only).

AURICLE AWARD

Plays on Tape; Box 5789; Bend, OR 97708–5789; (541) 923–6246,
　　FAX 923–9679; email theatre@playsontape.com;
　　Web site http://www.playsontape.com
Silvia Gonzalez S., *Literary Manager*
Types of material: full-length plays, long one-acts. **Frequency:** annual.
Remuneration: $500 and 10 audio copies if play is produced as audio recording;
$100 prize to winner if cost of producing audio recording is prohibitively
expensive, i.e., too large a cast, too complicated sound effects, etc. **Guidelines:**
any play that has not been audio-produced; running time approximately 74
minutes; prefers 2–5 character play; special interest in plays by women and
minorities. **Submission procedure:** script, synopis and $3 fee per script with
SASE; write for guidelines. **Deadline:** 31 Dec 2000. **Notification:** 1 Feb 2001.

BAKER'S PLAYS HIGH SCHOOL PLAYWRITING CONTEST

Baker's Plays; Box 699222; Quincy, MA 02269–9222;
　　(617) 745–0805, FAX 745–9891; email raypape@hotmail.com;
　　Web site http://www.bakersplays.com
Ray Pape, *Associate Editor*
Types of material: full-length plays, one-acts, plays for young audiences,
musicals. **Frequency:** annual. **Remuneration:** $500 1st prize, publication; $250
2nd prize; $100 3rd prize. **Guidelines:** high school student, sponsored by high
school drama or English teacher; prefers play that has been produced or given
public reading. **Submission procedure:** script with signature of sponsoring
teacher; write for guidelines. **Deadline:** 31 Jan 2001. **Notification:** May 2001.

BEVERLY HILLS THEATRE GUILD PLAYWRITING AWARDS

2815 North Beachwood Dr; Los Angeles, CA 90068–1923;
　　(323) 465–2703
Dick Dotterer, Competition Coordinator

JULIE HARRIS PLAYWRITING AWARD

Types of material: full-length plays (no adaptations or musicals). **Frequency:**
annual. **Remuneration:** $5000 1st prize; $2500 2nd prize; $1500 3rd prize;
possible staged reading for all winners. **Guidelines:** U.S. citizen or legal resident;
plays must be written in English; 1 submission, not previously submitted,
published, produced, optioned or winner of any other major competition.
Submission guidelines: signed entry form and bound script; script will not be
returned; send SASE for guidelines and entry form. **Deadline:** 1 Nov 2000.
Notification: Jun 2001.

THE MARILYN HALL AWARD

Types of material: 2 categories: plays suitable for grades 6-8, approximately 60 minutes or less; plays suitable for grades 3-5, approximately 30 minutes or less; adaptations, translations, plays for young audiences, plays with songs (no musicals). **Frequency:** annual. **Remuneration:** category 1: $750, possible staged reading; category 2: $250, possible staged reading. **Guidelines:** U.S. citizen or legal resident; plays must be written in English; not previously submitted, published, under professional option, or winner of any other major competition; plays may have had one non-professional or educational theatre production; authors may submit 1 script in each category. **Submission procedure:** signed entry form and bound script; scripts will not be returned; send SASE for guidelines and entry form. **Deadline:** 28 Feb 2001; no submission postmarked before 15 Jan 2001. **Notification:** Jun 2001.

BIENNIAL PROMISING PLAYWRIGHT AWARD

Colonial Players, Inc; Box 2167; Annapolis, MD 21404
Frances Marchand, *Contest Coordinator*
Types of material: full-length plays, adaptations. **Frequency:** biennial. **Remuneration:** $750; production (playwright must be available to attend rehearsals). **Guidelines:** resident of CT, DC, DE, GA, MA, MD, NC, NH, NJ, NY, PA, RI, SC, VA or WV; play not produced professionally, suitable for arena stage; between 90-120 minutes; 2-set limit; cast limit of 10; only adaptation of material in public domain. **Submission procedure:** script and SASP for acknowledgment of receipt; send SASE for guidelines. **Deadline:** 31 Dec 2000; no submission before 1 Sep 2000. **Notification:** Jun 2001.

CALIFORNIA YOUNG PLAYWRIGHTS CONTEST

Playwrights Project; 450 B St, Suite 1020;
    San Diego, CA 92101-8002; (619) 239-8222, FAX 239-8225;
    email youth@playwright.com;
    Web site http://www.playwrightsproject.com
Deborah Salzer, *Director*
Types of material: full-length plays, one-acts, musicals, solo pieces. **Frequency:** annual. **Remuneration:** $100, professional production or staged reading, travel and housing to attend rehearsals to each of several winners (4 in 1999); all entrants receive written evaluation of work. **Guidelines:** CA writer or collaborating writers under 19 years of age as of deadline date; work at least 10 pages long; previous submissions ineligible. **Submission procedure:** 2 copies of script, brief bio and cover letter; script will not be returned; write for guidelines. **Deadline:** 1 Apr 2001. **Notification:** summer 2001.

CLAUDER COMPETITION FOR EXCELLENCE IN PLAYWRITING

Box 383259; Cambridge, MA 02238-3259; (781) 322-3187;
    email bcarpenter@harvard.edu
Betsy Carpenter, *Director*
Types of material: full-length plays. **Frequency:** biennial. **Remuneration:** $3000
1st prize; production by Portland Stage Company (see Production); $500 prize
and staged reading for several runners-up. **Guidelines:** resident of or student
attending school or college in CT, MA, ME, NH, RI or VT; play not produced
professionally and minimum 45 minutes long. **Submission procedure:** script
and production history, if any; write for guidelines. **Deadline:** 1 Sep 2000.
Notification: TBA.

COLUMBUS SCREENPLAY DISCOVERY AWARDS

Christopher Columbus Society; 433 North Camden Dr, Suite 600;
    Beverly Hills, CA 90210; (310) 288-1881, FAX 288-0257;
    email writing@screenwriters.com;
    Web site http://screenwriters.com
Carlos de Abreu and Janice Pennington, *Co-Founders*
Types of material: screenplays. **Frequency:** annual. **Remuneration:** Discovery
of the Year Award: up to $10,000 for 1-3 scripts a year optioned by Society;
Discovery of the Month Award: up to 3 scripts a month selected for development.
Guidelines: unproduced feature screenplay not under option. **Submission
procedure:** application, screenplay, release form and $45 fee; screenplay will not
be returned; write for guidelines. **Deadline:** 1 Dec 2000 for Discovery of the Year;
developmental deadline ongoing.

THE CUNNINGHAM PRIZE FOR PLAYWRITING

The Theatre School; DePaul University; 2135 North Kenmore;
    Chicago, IL 60614-4111; (773) 325-7938, FAX 325-7920;
    email lgoetsch@wppost.depaul.edu;
    Web site http://theatreschool.depaul.edu/prize.htm
Lara Goetsch, *Director of Marketing and Public Relations*
Types of material: full-length plays, plays for young audiences, musicals, solo
pieces. **Frequency:** annual. **Remuneration:** $5000. **Guidelines:** Chicago-area
playwright; play which "affirms the centrality of religion, broadly defined, and the
human quest for meaning, truth and community." **Submission procedure:** script
and brief statement which connects work to purpose of prize; write for
guidelines. **Deadline:** 1 Dec 2000. **Notification:** 1 Mar 2001.

DAYTON PLAYHOUSE FUTUREFEST

1301 East Siebenthaler Ave; Dayton, OH 45414; (937) 333-7469,
FAX 277-9539

Fran Pesch, *Interim Theatre Manager*

Types of material: full-length plays. **Frequency:** annual. **Remuneration:** $1000
1st prize, 5 $100 runners-up; 3 plays receive full productions, 3 plays receive
reading at Jul 2001 FutureFest weekend; travel and housing to attend weekend.
Guidelines: unproduced, unpublished play. **Submission procedure:** bound script
and resume; send SASE or fax number for guidelines. **Deadline:** postmarked by
30 Oct 2000. **Notification:** Apr 2001.

DOROTHY SILVER PLAYWRITING COMPETITION

Jewish Community Center of Cleveland; 3505 Mayfield Rd; Cleveland
Heights, OH 44118; (216) 382-4000, ext 275, FAX 382-5401

Lisa Kollins, *Managing Director*

Types of material: full-length plays. **Frequency:** annual. **Remuneration:** $1000
(including $500 to cover residency expenses); staged reading; possible
production. **Guidelines:** unproduced play that provides "fresh and significant"
perspective on the range of the Jewish experience. **Submission procedure:**
script only. **Deadline:** 15 Dec 2000. **Notification:** Aug 2001.

DRAMARAMA

The Playwrights' Center of San Francisco; Box 460466;
San Francisco, CA 94146-0466; (415) 626-4603,
FAX 863-0901; email playctrsf@aol.com;
Web site http://www.playwrights.org

Sheppard Kominars, *Chairman*

LONG PLAY CONTEST

Types of material: full-length plays, solo pieces. **Frequency:** annual.
Remuneration: $500; up to 4 scripts given 4-5 rehearsals and staged readings
at fall festival. **Guidelines:** unproduced play minimum 60 minutes long.
Submission procedure: send SASE for guidelines and application with $25 fee.
Deadline: 15 Mar 2001. **Notification:** 15 Aug 2001. **Dates:** Oct 2001.

SHORT PLAY CONTEST

Types of material: one-acts, solo pieces. **Frequency:** annual. **Remuneration:** $500;
up to 4 scripts given 4-5 rehearsals and staged readings at fall festival. **Guidelines:**
unproduced play maximum 60 minutes long. **Submission procedure:** send SASE
for guidelines and application with $25 fee. **Deadline:** 15 Mar 2001. **Notification:**
15 Aug 2001. **Dates:** Oct 2001.

DRURY UNIVERSITY ONE-ACT PLAY COMPETITION

Drury University; 900 North Benton Ave; Springfield, MO 65802;
(417) 873-7430, FAX 873-7432; email sasher@lib.drury.edu;
Web site http://www.drury.edu/Academics/PLAYATT.html
Sandy Asher, *Writer-in-Residence*
Types of material: one-acts. **Frequency:** biennial. **Remuneration:** $300 1st prize, 2 runners-up receive $150; possible production; winners recommended to The Open Eye Theater (see Production). **Guidelines:** unproduced, unpublished play 20-45 minutes long; prefers small cast, 1 set; 1-submission limit. **Submission procedure:** script only; send SASE for guidelines. **Deadline:** 1 Dec 2000. **Notification:** 1 Apr 2001.

DUBUQUE FINE ARTS PLAYERS NATIONAL ONE-ACT PLAYWRITING CONTEST

330 Clarke Dr; Dubuque, IA 52001; (319) 588-0646
Jennie G. Stabenow, *Coordinator*
Types of material: one-acts, one-act adaptations. **Frequency:** annual. **Remuneration:** $600 1st prize, $300 2nd prize, $200 3rd prize; possible production for all 3 plays. **Guidelines:** unproduced, unpublished play maximum 35 pages and 40 minutes long; prefers cast limit of 5; 1 set; no submission limit; only adaptations of material in public domain. **Submission procedure:** entry form, 2 copies of script, 1-paragraph synopsis and $10 fee per submission; optional SASE for critique and optional SASP for acknowledgment of receipt; send SASE for guidelines. **Deadline:** 31 Jan 2001; no submission before 1 Nov 2000. **Notification:** 30 Jun 2001.

EAST WEST PLAYERS NEW VOICES PLAYWRITING COMPETITION

East West Players; 244 South San Pedro St; Suite 301;
Los Angeles, CA 90012; (213) 625-7000, FAX 625-7111;
email info@eastwestplayers.org;
Web site http://www.eastwestplayers.org
Ken Narasaki, *Literary Manager*
Types of material: full-length plays, plays for young audiences, musicals. **Frequency:** annual. **Remuneration:** $1000 1st prize, reading, possible workshop or production; $500 2nd prize, reading, possible workshop or production. **Guidelines:** English-language play not produced professionally; prefers Asian-Pacific writers and works with Asian-Pacific themes and cast. **Submission procedure:** 2 copies of script, character breakdown, cover letter and SASP for acknowledgment of receipt. **Deadline:** TBA; see Web site for deadlines. **Notification:** TBA. (See Production and David Henry Hwang Writers Institute in Development.)

EMERGING PLAYWRIGHT AWARD
Urban Stages; 17 East 47th St; New York, NY 10017;
(212) 421-1380, FAX 421-1387; email urbanstage@aol.com;
Web site http://www.mint.net/urbanstages
T. L. Reilly, *Producing Director*
Types of material: full-length plays; plays for young audiences; solo pieces. **Frequency:** annual. **Remuneration:** $500, production, travel to attend rehearsals; housing. **Guidelines:** play unproduced in New York; submissions from minority playwrights and plays with ethnically diverse casts encouraged. **Submission procedure:** script, production history (if any) and bio. **Deadline:** ongoing; best submission time Jul-Aug. (See Urban Stages in Production.)

FESTIVAL OF FIRSTS PLAYWRITING COMPETITION
Sunset Center; Box 1950; Carmel, CA 93921; (831) 624-3996
Director
Types of material: full-length plays. **Frequency:** annual. **Remuneration:** up to $1000; possible production. **Guidelines:** unproduced play. **Submission procedure:** entry form, script, character breakdown, synopsis and $15 entry fee; send SASE for guidelines. **Deadline:** 31 Aug 2001; no submission before 15 Jun 2001. **Notification:** Sep 2001.

FESTIVAL OF NEW AMERICAN THEATRE
Essential Theatre; 995 Greenwood Ave, #6; Atlanta, GA 30306;
(404) 876-8471
Peter Hardy, *Producing Artistic Director*
Types of material: full-length plays. **Frequency:** annual. **Remuneration:** $300; full production. **Guidelines:** resident of GA; unproduced play. **Submission procedure:** script with SASE for response. **Deadline:** 15 May 2001. **Notification:** 1 Sep 2001. **Dates:** Jan-Feb 2002.

FLORIDA SHORTS CONTEST
(Formerly American Sketches Contest)
Florida Studio Theatre; 1241 North Palm Ave; Sarasota, FL 34236
Types of material: short plays and cabaret sketches. **Frequency:** annual. **Remuneration:** $500; production for winning script and up to 12 others as part of evening of short works. **Guidelines:** residents of FL; sketch of 5 pages or less on specified theme TBA. **Submission procedure:** script only; write for guidelines. **Deadline:** 30 Mar 2001.

THE FRANCESCA PRIMUS PRIZE

Denver Center Theatre Company; 1050 13th St; Denver, CO 80204

Bruce K. Sevy, *Associate Artistic Director/New Play Development*

Types of material: full-length plays. **Frequency:** annual. **Remuneration:** $2000–3000; workshop; reading as part of Denver Center Theatre Company US WEST Theatre Fest (see Development); travel and housing to attend rehearsals; possible full production. **Guidelines:** plays by women only. **Submission procedure:** script, cover letter and SASE for response; send SASE for guidelines. **Deadline:** 1 Jul 2001. **Notification:** Mar–Apr 2002.

GEORGE R. KERNODLE PLAYWRITING CONTEST

Department of Drama; 619 Kimpel Hall; University of Arkansas;
    Fayetteville, AR 72701; (501) 575-2953, FAX 575-7602

Director

Types of material: one-acts. **Frequency:** annual. **Remuneration:** $300 1st prize, $200 2nd prize, $100 3rd prize; possible staged reading or production. **Guidelines:** U.S. or Canadian playwright; unproduced, unpublished play; maximum 1 hour long; cast limit of 8; 3-submission limit. **Submission procedure:** script with statement that play has not received full production, $3 fee per submission and optional SASE or SASP for acknowledgment of receipt; write for guidelines. **Deadline:** 1 Jun 2001; no submission before 1 Jan 2001. **Notification:** 1 Nov 2001.

GILMAN AND GONZALEZ-FALLA THEATRE FOUNDATION MUSICAL THEATRE AWARD

109 East 64th St; New York, NY 10021; (212) 734-8011,
    FAX 734-9606; email soncel@aol.com

Ela Majchrzak, *Coordinator*

Types of material: musicals. **Frequency:** annual. **Remuneration:** $25,000. **Guidelines:** writer(s) must have had a musical produced by commercial or not-for-profit theatre. **Submission procedure:** write for guidelines. **Deadline:** 31 Dec 2000.

GOSHEN COLLEGE PEACE PLAYWRITING CONTEST

Goshen College; 1700 South Main St; Goshen, IN 46526;
(219) 535-7393, FAX 535-7660; email douglc@goshen.edu
Douglas Caskey, *Director of Theatre*

Types of material: one-acts. **Frequency:** biennial. **Remuneration:** $500; production; room and board to attend rehearsals and/or production. **Guidelines:** 1 unproduced submission, 30-50 minutes long, exploring a contemporary peace or justice theme "broadly defined." **Submission procedure:** script, 1-paragraph synopsis and resume. **Deadline:** 31 Dec 2001. **Notification:** 1 May 2002.

GREAT PLAINS PLAY CONTEST

University Theatre; 317 Murphy Hall; University of Kansas;
Lawrence, KS 66045; (785) 864-3381, FAX 864-5251
Delbert Unruh, *Director*

Types of material: full-length plays, musicals, operas, plays/musicals for young audiences. **Frequency:** annual. **Remuneration:** $2000 1st prize, production, $500 to cover travel and housing; $500 2nd prize. **Guidelines:** play not produced professionally dealing with any historical or contemporary aspect of the Great Plains; 2nd prize gives theatre option to produce work. **Submission procedure:** script only. **Deadline:** 1 Sep 2000. **Notification:** 15 Jan 2001.

GREAT PLATTE RIVER PLAYWRIGHTS' FESTIVAL

University of Nebraska-Kearney Theatre; Kearney, NE 68849-5260;
(308) 865-8406, FAX 865-8806; email garrisonj@unk.edu
Jack Garrison, *Artistic Director*

Types of material: full-length plays, one-acts, plays for young audiences, musicals. **Frequency:** annual. **Remuneration:** $500 1st prize, $300 2nd prize, $200 3rd prize; production, travel and housing to attend rehearsals. **Guidelines:** unproduced, unpublished original work; submission of works-in-progress for possible development encouraged. **Submission procedure:** script, resume and cover letter; include cassette for musical. **Deadline:** 1 Apr 2001. **Notification:** 31 Jul 2001.

THE GREGORY KOLOVAKOS AWARD

PEN American Center; 568 Broadway; New York, NY 10012;
(212) 334-1660, FAX 334-2181; email jm@pen.org
John Morrone, *Awards Coordinator*
Types of material: translations. **Frequency:** triennial. **Remuneration:** $2000.
Guidelines: U.S. writer, critic or translator whose work has made a sustained
contribution over time to the cause of Latin American literature, as well as
their Iberian counterparts, in English; primarily recognizes work from Spanish
but contributions from other Hispanic languages also considered; candidate
must be nominated by editor or colleague. **Submission procedure:** letter from
nominator documenting candidate's qualifications with particular attention to
depth and vision of his or her work, candidate's vita; supporting materials may
be requested from finalists; write for guidelines. **Deadline:** 1 Dec 2000.
Notification: finalists mid-Jan 2001; winner mid-May 2001.

HAROLD MORTON LANDON TRANSLATION AWARD

The Academy of American Poets; 584 Broadway, Suite 1208;
New York, NY 10012; (212) 274-0343, FAX 274-9427;
email academy@poets.org; Web site http://www.poets.org
Michael Tyrell, *Awards Administrator*
Types of material: translations. **Frequency:** annual. **Remuneration:** $1000.
Guidelines: U.S. citizen; published translation of verse, including verse
drama, from any language into English verse; book must have been published
in 2000. **Submission procedure:** 3 copies of book (no manuscripts).
Deadline: 31 Dec 2000.

HARVEST FESTIVAL OF NEW AMERICAN PLAYS
State Theater Company; 719 Congress Ave; Austin, TX 78757;
(512) 472-5143, ext 18, FAX 472-7199;
email admin@statetheatercompany.com;
Web site http://www.statetheatercompany.com
John Walch, *Literary Manager*
Types of material: full-length plays, adaptations, solo pieces. **Frequency:** annual. **Remuneration:** $1000 1st prize Best New American Play Award, staged reading, travel and housing to attend rehearsals and festival, considered for full production in following season; $500 2nd prize Larry L. King Outstanding Texas Playwright Award, staged reading, travel and housing to attend rehearsals and festival, considered for full production in following season; up to 4 additional plays receive staged reading in festival. **Guidelines:** U.S. citizen; play that has not had professional production; adaptations in public domain only. **Submission procedure:** script from TX playwright or agent only; script with professional recommendation; other playwrights send synopsis, 15-page dialogue sample, resume; send SASE for guidelines. **Deadline:** 1 Apr 2001. **Notification:** fall 2001.

HENRICO THEATRE COMPANY ONE-ACT PLAYWRITING COMPETITION
The County of Henrico; Division of Recreation and Parks;
Box 27032; Richmond, VA 23273; (804) 501-5138,
FAX 501-5284; email per22@co.henrico.va.us
Amy A. Perdue, *Cultural Arts Coordinator*
Types of material: one-acts, musicals, solo pieces. **Frequency:** annual. **Remuneration:** $300 1st prize, production; $200 2nd prize, possible production and video. **Guidelines:** unproduced, unpublished work; no controversial themes or "excessive language"; prefers small cast, simple set. **Submission procedure:** 2 copies of script; write for guidelines. **Deadline:** 1 Jul 2001. **Notification:** 31 Dec 2001.

HRC'S ANNUAL PLAYWRITING CONTEST
Hudson River Classics, Inc; Box 940; Hudson, NY 12534;
(518) 828-0175
Jan M. Grice, *President*
Types of material: full-length plays. **Frequency:** annual. **Remuneration:** $500; staged reading. **Guidelines:** Northeast playwright; 60-90-minute unpublished play. **Submission procedure:** script, bio and $5 fee. **Deadline:** 1 Jun 2001; no submission before 1 Mar 2001. **Notification:** Sep 2001.

IHT/SRT INTERNATIONAL PLAYWRIGHTING COMPETITION
Singapore Repertory Theatre; Telok Ayer Performing Arts Centre;
182 Cecil St; Singapore 069547; 65-221-5585,
FAX 65-221-1936; email singrep@cyberway.com.sg;
Web site http://www.singrep.com
Sasha Fong, *Marketing Executive*
Types of material: full-length plays. **Frequency:** annual. **Remuneration:** $15,000
(U.S. dollars), full production, transportation, lodging and per diem to attend
rehearsals and performances. **Guidelines:** playwright of any nationality or
ethnicity; English-language play, not produced professionally dealing with some
aspect of modern Asian indentity. **Submission procedure:** script only; 1
submission; script will not be returned. **Deadline:** 31 Mar 2001. **Notification:**
May 2001.

JACKIE WHITE MEMORIAL NATIONAL CHILDREN'S PLAYWRITING CONTEST
309 Parkade Blvd; Columbia, MO 65202; (573) 874-5628
Betsy Phillips, *Director*
Types of material: plays and musicals to be performed by young actors.
Frequency: annual. **Remuneration:** $250; optional production by Columbia
Entertainment Company Children's Theatre School; room, board and partial
travel to attend performance; all entrants receive written evaluation. **Guidelines:**
unpublished original work, 60-90 minutes in length, with 20-30 speaking
characters of all ages, at least 10 developed in some detail, to be played by
students ages 10-15. **Submission procedure:** completed entry form, script,
character breakdown, act/scene synopsis, resume and $10 fee; include cassette
for musical; send SASE for guidelines. **Deadline:** 1 Jun 2001. **Notification:** 30
Aug 2001.

JAMES D. PHELAN AWARD IN LITERATURE
Intersection for the Arts/The San Francisco Foundation;
446 Valencia St; San Francisco, CA 94103; (415) 626-2787,
FAX 626-1636; email info@theintersection.org
Awards Coordinator
Types of material: full-length plays, one-acts, plays for young audiences.
Frequency: annual. **Remuneration:** $2000. **Guidelines:** CA-born author 20-35
years of age as of 31 Jan 2001; unpublished play-in-progress. **Submission
procedure:** application and script. **Deadline:** 31 Jan 2001; no submission before
15 Nov 2000. **Notification:** 15 Jun 2001.

JANE CHAMBERS PLAYWRITING AWARD

c/o Department of Theatre Arts; Wright State University;
Dayton, OH 45435-0001;
Web site http://wright.edu/academics/theatre/chambers_announce.html

Mary Donahoe, *Administrator*

Types of material: full-length plays, one-acts, solo pieces, performance-art pieces. **Frequency:** annual. **Remuneration:** $1000; free registration and rehearsed reading at the Women and Theatre Conference in late July; student submissions eligible for $250 Student Award. **Guidelines:** work by a woman that reflects a feminist perspective and contains a majority of roles for women; special interest in works by and about women from a diversity of positions in respect to race, class, sexual preference, physical ability, age and geographical region; experimentation with dramatic form encouraged; 1-submission limit; award administered by the Association for Theatre in Higher Education (see Membership and Service Organizations). **Submission procedure:** application, 3 copies of script, synopsis and resume; if possible, professional recommendation; optional SASP for acknowledgment of receipt; send SASE for guidelines and application. **Deadline:** 15 Feb 2001. **Notification:** 30 Jun 2001.

JEWEL BOX THEATRE PLAYWRIGHTING AWARD

3700 North Walker; Oklahoma City, OK 73118-7099;
(405) 521-1786, FAX 525-6562

Charles Tweed, *Production Director*

Types of material: full-length plays. **Frequency:** annual. **Remuneration:** $500; possible production. **Guidelines:** unproduced ensemble play with emphasis on character rather than spectacle. **Submission procedure:** entry form, 2 copies of script, playwright's agreement and $10 fee; send SASE in Oct for guidelines and forms. **Deadline:** 15 Jan 2001. **Notification:** Apr 2001.

JOHN GASSNER MEMORIAL PLAYWRITING AWARD

The New England Theatre Conference; Northeastern University;
306 Huntington Ave; Boston, MA 02115; (617) 424-9275,
FAX 424-1057; email netc@world.com;
Web site http://www.netheatreconference.org

Types of material: full-length plays. **Frequency:** annual. **Remuneration:** $1000 1st prize, $500 2nd prize; staged reading; possible publication. **Guidelines:** New England resident or NETC member (see Membership and Service Organizations); unpublished play that has not had professional full production and is not under consideration for publication or professional production; 1-submission limit. **Submission procedure:** script with cover page, character breakdown, brief synopsis and statement that play has not been published or professionally produced and is not under consideration; SASP for acknowledgment of receipt; $10 fee, except for NETC members; script will not be returned; send SASE for guidelines. **Deadline:** 15 Apr 2001. **Notification:** 1 Sep 2001 (winners only).

KENNEDY CENTER AMERICAN COLLEGE THEATER FESTIVAL: MICHAEL KANIN PLAYWRITING AWARDS PROGRAM

The John F. Kennedy Center for the Performing Arts;
Washington, DC 20566-0001; (202) 416-8857, FAX 416-8802
John Lion, *Producing Director*

ANCHORAGE PRESS THEATER FOR YOUTH PLAYWRITING AWARD

Types of material: full-length plays, adaptations, musicals. **Frequency:** annual. **Remuneration:** $1000; $1250 fellowship to attend either the New Visions/New Voices Festival (see Development) or the National Youth Theatre Symposium (see Waldo M. and Grace C. Bonderman IUPUI/IRT Playwriting Event for Young Audiences in this section); possible publication by Anchorage Press with royalties. **Guidelines:** writer enrolled as full-time student at college or university during year of production or during either of the 2 years preceding the production; play on theme appealing to young people from kindergarten–12th grade produced by an ACTF-participating college or university; write for KC/ACTF brochure. **Submission procedure:** college or university which has entered production of work in ACTF registers work for awards program. **Deadline:** 1 Dec 2000. **Dates:** 23 Apr–30 Apr 2001.

THE FOURTH FREEDOM FORUM PLAYWRITING AWARD

Types of material: full-length plays. **Frequency:** annual. **Remuneration:** $5000 1st prize for playwright, publication by Palmetto Play Service, all-expense-paid 9-day residency at Sundance Theatre Laboratory (see Development), which includes consultation with Sundance directors and dramaturgs and reading by Lab actors, $1500 to producing college or university; $2500 2nd prize to playwright, $1000 to producing college or university. **Guidelines:** writer enrolled as full-time student at college or university during year of production or during either of the 2 years preceding the production; play on themes of world peace and international disarmament produced by an ACTF-participating college or university; write for KC/ACTF brochure. **Submission procedure:** college or university which has entered production of work in ACTF registers work for awards program. **Deadline:** 1 Dec 2000. **Dates:** 23 Apr–30 Apr 2001.

THE JEAN KENNEDY SMITH PLAYWRITING AWARD

Types of material: full-length plays, adaptations, musicals. **Frequency:** annual. **Remuneration:** $2500 plus Dramatists Guild (see Membership and Service Organizations) membership and fellowship to attend a prestigious playwriting program. **Guidelines:** writer enrolled as full-time student at college or university during year of production; play that explores the human experience of living with disabilities produced by an ACTF-participating college or university; write for KC/ACTF brochure. **Submission procedure:** college or university which has entered production of work in ACTF registers work for awards program. **Deadline:** 1 Dec 2000. **Dates:** 23 Apr–30 Apr 2001.

THE KC/ACTF MUSICAL THEATER AWARD

Types of material: musicals. **Frequency:** annual. **Remuneration:** $1000 for lyrics; $1000 for music; $1000 for book to producing college or university. **Guidelines:** at least 50% of writing team must be enrolled as full-time student(s) at college or university during year of production or during either of the 2 years preceding the production; original and copyrighted work produced by an ACTF-participating college or university; write for KC/ACTF brochure. **Submission procedure:** college or university which has entered production of work in ACTF registers work for awards program. **Deadline:** 1 Dec 2000. **Dates:** 23 Apr–30 Apr 2001.

THE LORRAINE HANSBERRY PLAYWRITING AWARD

Types of material: full-length plays. **Frequency:** annual. **Remuneration:** $2500 1st prize for playwright, internship at the National Playwrights Conference at the O'Neill Theater Center (see Development), publication of play by The Dramatic Publishing Company (see Publication), $750 to producing college or university; $1000 2nd prize to playwright, $500 to producing college or university. **Guidelines:** writer enrolled as full-time student at college or university during year of production or during either of the 2 years preceding the production; play dealing with the black experience produced by an ACTF-participating college or university; write for KC/ACTF brochure. **Submission procedure:** college or university which has entered production of work in ACTF registers work for awards program. **Deadline:** 1 Dec 2000. **Dates:** 23 Apr–30 Apr 2001.

THE NATIONAL AIDS FUND CFDA-VOGUE INITIATIVE AWARD FOR PLAYWRITING

Types of material: full-length plays, adaptations, musicals. **Frequency:** annual. **Remuneration:** $2500 plus fellowship to attend Bay Area Playwrights Festival (see Development). **Guidelines:** writer enrolled as full-time student at college or university during year of production or during either of the 2 years preceding the production; play concerning personal or social implications of HIV/AIDS produced by an ACTF-participating college or university; write for KC/ACTF brochure. **Submission procedure:** college or university which has entered production of work in ACTF registers work for awards program. **Deadline:** 1 Dec 2000. **Dates:** 23 Apr–30 Apr 2001.

THE NATIONAL STUDENT PLAYWRITING AWARD

Types of material: full-length plays, adaptations, musicals. **Frequency:** annual. **Remuneration:** $2500 for playwright, production at Kennedy Center during festival, publication by Samuel French (see Publication) with royalties, fellowship to attend Sundance Theatre Laboratory (see Development), Dramatists Guild membership (see Membership and Service Organizations); $1000 to producing college or university. **Guidelines:** writer enrolled as full-time student at college or university during year of production or during either of the 2 years preceding the production; work must be produced by an ACTF-participating college or university; write for KC/ACTF brochure. **Submission procedure:** college or university which has entered production of work in ACTF registers work for awards program. **Deadline:** 1 Dec 2000. **Dates:** 23 Apr–30 Apr 2001.

THE SHORT PLAY AWARDS PROGRAM

Types of material: one-acts, one-act adaptations. **Frequency:** annual. **Remuneration:** $1000 for 3 or less playwrights, publication by Samuel French (see Publication); Dramatists Guild of America membership (see Membership and Service Organizations). **Guidelines:** writer enrolled as full-time student at college or university during year of production or during either of the 2 years preceding the production; one-act must be produced by an ACTF-participating college or university; simple production demands (minimal setup and strike time); write for KC/ACTF brochure. **Submission procedure:** college or university which has entered production of work in ACTF registers work for awards program. **Deadline:** 1 Dec 2000. **Dates:** 23 Apr–30 Apr 2001.

KUMU KAHUA THEATRE/UHM DEPARTMENT OF THEATRE & DANCE PLAYWRITING CONTEST

Kumu Kahua Theatre; 46 Merchant St; Honolulu, HI 96813;
(808) 536–4222, FAX 536–4226
Harry Wong III, *Artistic Director, Kumu Kahua Theatre*

HAWAI'I PRIZE

Types of material: full-length plays. **Frequency:** annual. **Remuneration:** $500. **Guidelines:** play set in HI or dealing with some aspect of HI experience; unproduced play; previous entries ineligible. **Submission procedure:** write for entry brochure. **Deadline:** 1 Jan 2001. **Notification:** 1 May 2001.

PACIFIC RIM PRIZE

Types of material: full-length plays. **Frequency:** annual. **Remuneration:** $400. **Guidelines:** play set in or dealing with Pacific Islands, Pacific Rim or Pacific Asian-American experience; unproduced play; previous entries ineligible. **Submission procedure:** write for entry brochure. **Deadline:** 1 Jan 2001. **Notification:** 1 May 2001.

RESIDENT PRIZE

Types of material: full-length plays, one-acts. **Frequency:** annual. **Remuneration:** $200. **Guidelines:** resident of HI at time of submission; previous entries ineligible. **Submission procedure:** write for entry brochure. **Deadline:** 1 Jan 2001. **Notification:** May 2001.

L. ARNOLD WEISSBERGER AWARD

Box 428; Williamstown, MA 01267-0428; (413) 458-3200,
FAX 458-3147
Jenny Gersten, *Associate Producer*
Types of material: full-length plays only. **Frequency:** annual. Remuneration: $5000; publication by Samuel French (see Publication). **Guidelines:** 1 unpublished script not professionally produced. **Submission Procedure:** direct solicitation to playwright or theatre; administered by Williamstown Theatre Festival (see Production and Development). **Deadline:** postmarked by 15 Jun 2001; no submission before 1 Jan 2001. **Notification:** Nov 2001.

LAMIA INK! INTERNATIONAL ONE-PAGE PLAY COMPETITION

Box 202; Prince St Station; New York, NY 10012
(Ms.) Cortland Jessup, *Artistic Director*
Types of material: 1-page plays. **Frequency:** annual. **Remuneration:** $200; reading in New York City and publication in magazine (see Lamia Ink! in Publication) for winner and 11 other best plays; at least $50 2nd prize, $25 3rd prize. **Guidelines:** 3-submission limit. **Submission procedure:** script, SASE for response and $2 fee per submission or $5 for 3 submissions; send SASE for guidelines. **Deadline:** 15 Mar 2001. **Notification:** 15 May 2001.

THE LITTLE THEATRE OF ALEXANDRIA NATIONAL ONE-ACT PLAYWRITING COMPETITION

Little Theatre of Alexandria; 600 Wolfe St; Alexandria, VA 22314;
(703) 683-5778, FAX 683-1378; email ltlthtre@erols.com
Chairman, One-Act Playwriting Competition
Types of material: one-acts. **Frequency:** annual. **Remuneration:** $350 1st prize, $250 2nd prize, $150 3rd prize; possible production. **Guidelines:** unpublished, unproduced work; prefers plays with running times of 20-60 minutes, few scenes and 1 set; 2-submission limit. **Submission procedure:** script, synopsis, character breakdown and $5 fee; send SASE for guidelines. **Deadline:** 30 Apr 2001; no submission before 1 Dec 2000. **Notification:** Sep 2001.

LOIS AND RICHARD ROSENTHAL NEW PLAY PRIZE

Cincinnati Playhouse in the Park; Box 6537;
   Cincinnati, OH 45206-0537; (513) 345-2242

Associate Artistic Director

Types of material: full-length plays, musicals. **Frequency:** annual. **Remuneration:** $10,000, production, travel and housing to attend rehearsals. **Guidelines:** unpublished work not professionally produced; no translations or adaptations. **Submission procedure:** 5-page dialogue sample, 2-page maximum abstract including synopsis, character breakdown and bio; include cassette for musicals; 1-submission limit. **Deadline:** 31 Dec 2000. **Notification:** 6-8 months.

LOS ANGELES DESIGNERS' THEATRE COMMISSIONS

Box 1883; Studio City, CA 91614-0883; (323) 650-9600 (voice),
   654-2700 (TDD), FAX 654-3260; email ladesigners@juno.com

Richard Niederberg, *Artistic Director*

Types of material: full-length plays, bills of related one-acts, translations, adaptations, plays for young audiences, musicals, solo pieces, operas. **Frequency:** ongoing. **Remuneration:** negotiable commissioning fee; possible travel to attend rehearsals if developmental work is needed. **Guidelines:** commissioning program for work with commercial potential which has not received professional full production, is not under option and is free of commitment to specific director, actors or other personnel; large casts and multiple sets welcome; prefers controversial material. **Submission procedure:** proposal or synopsis and resume; include cassette for musical; materials will not be returned. **Deadline:** ongoing. **Notification:** at least 4 months.

LOVE CREEK ANNUAL SHORT PLAY FESTIVAL

Love Creek Productions; c/o 162 Nesbit St; Weehawken, NJ 07087-6817

Cynthia Granville-Callahan, *Festival Literary Manager/Chair, Reading Committee*

Types of material: one-acts. **Frequency:** annual. **Remuneration:** minimum of 60 finalists receive mini-showcase production in New York City during festival; cash prize for best play of festival. **Guidelines:** unpublished play not produced in NYC area within past year; maximum length of 40 minutes; cast of 2 or more, simple sets and costumes; 2-submission limit; strongly prefers women in major roles and predominantly female cast; mini-festivals centered around specific themes; upcoming themes include "Fear of God," gay and lesbian themes, political plays. **Submission procedure:** script with letter giving theatre permission to produce play if chosen and specifying whether Equity showcase is acceptable; send SASE for themes and deadlines. **Deadline:** ongoing. **Dates:** year-round.

THE MARC A. KLEIN PLAYWRITING AWARD

Department of Theater Arts; Case Western Reserve University;
    10900 Euclid Ave; Cleveland, OH 44106-7077; (216) 368-4868,
    FAX 368-5184; email ksg@po.cwru.edu
John Orlock, *Chair, Reading Committee*
Types of material: full-length plays, bills of related one-acts. **Frequency:** annual.
Remuneration: $1000 ($500 is used to cover residency expenses); production.
Guidelines: student currently enrolled at U.S. college or university; work
endorsed by faculty member of university theatre department that has not
received professional full production or trade-book publication. **Submission
procedure:** completed entry form and script. **Deadline:** 15 May 2001.
Notification: 1 Aug 2001.

MAXIM MAZUMDAR NEW PLAY COMPETITION

Alleyway Theatre; 1 Curtain Up Alley; Buffalo, NY 14202-1911;
    (716) 852-2600, FAX 852-2266; email email@alleyway.com
Literary Manager
Types of material: full-length plays, one-acts, musicals. **Frequency:** annual.
Remuneration: $400, production with royalty, and travel and housing to attend
rehearsals for full-length play or musical; $100 and production for one-act play or
musical. **Guidelines:** unproduced full-length work minimum 90 minutes long with
cast limit of 10 and unit set or simple set, or unproduced one-act work less than
40 minutes long with cast limit of 6 and simple set; prefers work with
unconventional setting that explores the boundaries of theatricality; 1-submission
limit in each category. **Submission procedure:** script, character breakdown and
resume; include cassette of complete score for musicals; $5 fee per playwright.
Deadline: 1 Jul 2001. **Notification:** 1 Oct 2001 for finalists; 1 Feb 2002 for winners.

MCLAREN MEMORIAL COMEDY PLAYWRITING COMPETITION

Midland Community Theatre; 2000 West Wadley Ave;
    Midland, TX 79705; (915) 682-2544, FAX 682-6136;
    Web site http://www.mct-cole.org
Coordinator
Types of material: full-length plays, one-acts, translations, adaptations, plays for
young audiences, musicals, solo pieces. **Frequency:** annual. **Remuneration:** $400
1st prize, staged reading; 3 finalists receive staged reading. **Guidelines:** comedies
only; prefers work that has not received professional full production. **Submission
procedure:** script and $5 fee. **Deadline:** 31 Jan 2001; no submission before 1 Dec
2000. **Notification:** May 2001.

MIDWEST THEATRE NETWORK ORIGINAL PLAY COMPETITION/ ROCHESTER PLAYWRIGHT FESTIVAL

5031 Tongen Ave NW; Rochester, MN 55901; (507) 281-8887;
    email sweens@uswest.net
Joan Sween, *Executive Director/Dramaturg*

Types of material: full-length plays, collections of one-acts, plays for young audiences, musicals, full-length solo pieces, satirical revues. **Frequency:** biennial. **Remuneration:** 4-8 awards of $300-1000 each (contingent on funding); full production by cooperating theatres; travel, room and board to attend festival. **Guidelines:** unpublished work not produced professionally. **Submission procedure:** 1 entry form per script; include cassette for musical; send SASE for guidelines and entry form. **Deadline:** exact date TBA.

MILDRED AND ALBERT PANOWSKI PLAYWRITING AWARD

Forest A. Roberts Theatre; Northern Michigan University;
    Marquette, MI 49855; (906) 227-2553, FAX 227-2567
James A. Panowski, *Director*

Types of material: full-length plays, adaptations, solo pieces. **Frequency:** annual. **Remuneration:** $2000; production; travel, room and board for 1-week residency. **Guidelines:** 1 unpublished, unproduced submission; rewrites of previous entries ineligible. **Submission procedure:** entry form and script; write for guidelines. **Deadline:** 21 Nov 2000. **Notification:** Apr 2001.

THE MILL MOUNTAIN THEATRE NEW PLAY COMPETITION: THE NORFOLK SOUTHERN FESTIVAL OF NEW WORKS

1 Market Square SE, 2nd Floor; Roanoke, VA 24011-1437;
    (540) 342-5730, FAX 342-5745;
    email mmtmail@millmountain.org;
    Web site http://www.millmountain.org
New Play Competition Coordinator

Types of material: full-length plays, one-acts, musicals, solo pieces. **Frequency:** annual. **Remuneration:** $1000; staged reading and possible full production; travel stipend and housing for limited residency. **Guidelines:** U.S. resident; 1 unproduced, unpublished submission; cast limit of 10; no 10-minute plays. **Submission procedure:** agent submission or script with professional recommendation by director, literary manager or dramaturg; include cassette for musical; send SASE for guidelines. **Deadline:** 1 Jan 2001; no submission before 1 Oct 2000. **Notification:** Aug 2001.

MORTON R. SARETT NATIONAL PLAYWRITING COMPETITION

Department of Theatre; University of Nevada, Las Vegas;
  4505 Maryland Pkwy, Box 455036; Las Vegas, NV 89154–5036;
  (702) 895–3666
Corrine A. Bonate, *Coordinator*
Types of material: full-length plays, musicals. **Frequency:** biennial.
Remuneration: $3000; production; travel and housing to attend rehearsals and
opening performance. **Guidelines:** unpublished, unproduced play or musical; no
adaptations. **Submission procedure:** application, 2 bound copies of script and
50-word synopsis; send SASE for guidelines. **Deadline:** 15 Dec 2001; no
submission before 1 Sep 2001. **Notification:** Jun 2002.

MOVING ARTS PREMIERE ONE-ACT COMPETITION

514 South Spring St; Los Angeles, CA 90013; (213) 622–8906,
  FAX 622–8946; email rrasmussen@movingarts.org;
  Web site http://www.movingarts.org
Rebecca Rasmussen, *Mangaing Director*
Types of material: one-acts. **Frequency:** annual. **Remuneration:** $200,
production in annual fall one-act festival. **Guidelines:** play not previously
produced in L.A. area; single set; modest technical requirements. **Submission
procedure:** script without author's name or address, cover letter and $8 fee per
script payable to Moving Arts (see Production). **Deadline:** 28 Feb 2001.
Notification: Jul 2001.

NANTUCKET SHORT PLAY FESTIVAL AND COMPETITION

Nantucket Theatrical Productions; Box 2177; Nantucket, MA 02584;
  (508) 228–5002
Jim Patrick, *Artistic Director*
Types of material: one-acts. **Frequency:** annual. **Remuneration:** $200; 1 or more
staged readings for winning play and selected additional plays as part of summer
festival. **Guidelines:** unpublished play which has not received Equity production;
maximum length of 40 pages; simple production demands. **Submission
procedure:** script and $8 fee; send SASE for guidelines. **Deadline:** ongoing.
Notification: ongoing. **Dates:** Jul 2001.

NATF SCRIPT COMPETITION

The National Audio Theatre Festivals; 115 Dikeman St;
   Hempstead, NY 11550; (516) 483-8321, FAX 538-7583;
   Web site http://www.natf.org

Sue Zizza, *Executive Director*

Types of material: radio plays. **Frequency:** annual. **Remuneration:** $800 split between 2-4 winners; workshop production; published in NATF Scriptbook. **Guidelines:** radio plays only, 25 minutes or less; "dialogue that demonstrates how sound can color content"; strong female roles and multicultural viewpoints; 1-submission limit. **Submission procedure:** 3 copies of script in radio format, cover letter stating authorship and $20 fee; visit Web site for guidelines. **Deadline:** 15 Nov 2000. **Notification:** Apr 2001. (See The Audio Theatre Workshop in Development.)

NATIONAL CHILDREN'S THEATRE FESTIVAL

Actors' Playhouse at the Miracle Theatre; 280 Miracle Mile;
   Coral Gables, FL 33134; (305) 444-9293, ext 615,
   FAX 444-4181; Web site http://www.actorsplayhouse.org

Earl Maulding, *Director of Theatre for Young Audiences*

Types of material: musicals for young audiences. **Frequency:** annual. **Remuneration:** $500 prize, production, travel and housing to attend festival. **Guidelines:** unpublished musical for young people ages 5-12, 45-60 minutes long, with cast limit of 8 (may play multiple roles) and minimal sets suitable for touring; translations and adaptations eligible only if writer owns copyright to material; special interest in works dealing with social issues including multiculturalism in today's society. **Submission procedure:** completed entry form, script and $10 fee; include score and cassette for musical; write for guidelines. **Deadline:** 1 Aug 2001. **Notification:** Nov 2001. **Dates:** Jan 2002.

NATIONAL HISPANIC PLAYWRITING AWARD

Arizona Theatre Company; Box 1631; Tucson, AZ 85702;
   (520) 884-8210, FAX 628-9129

Elaine Romero, *Contest Director*

Types of material: full-length plays, adaptations. **Frequency:** annual. **Remuneration:** $1000; possible staged reading; travel, room and board to attend rehearsals and performance. **Guidelines:** playwright of Hispanic heritage residing in U.S., U.S. territories or Mexico; 1 unproduced, unpublished submission written in English, Spanish or both languages. **Submission procedure:** script (with English translation if original in Spanish), 1-page cover letter including production history (if any) and bio. **Deadline:** 31 Oct 2000. **Notification:** spring 2001.

NATIONAL NEW PLAY AWARD

Department of Theatre Arts; Humboldt State University;
 Arcata, CA 95521; (707) 826-4606, FAX 826-5494;
 email mtk3@axe.humboldt.edu;
 Web site http://www.humboldt.edu/~mtk3
Margaret Thomas Kelso, *Assistant Professor of Theatre Arts*
Types of material: full-length plays. **Frequency:** triennial. **Remuneration:** 2 awards of $1000; full production; 2-week residency. **Guidelines:** unproduced, unpublished play. **Submission procedure:** script only; 2-submission limit. **Deadline:** 30 Jan 2002; no submission before 1 Dec 2001. **Notification:** spring 2002.

NATIONAL PLAY AWARD

Box 286; Hollywood, CA 90078; (323) 465-9517,
 FAX 417-4722; email nrtf@nrtf.com;
 Web site http://www.nrtf.org
C. Raul Espinoza, *Chair, National Repertory Theatre Foundation*
Types of material: full-length plays. **Frequency:** annual. **Remuneration:** $5000 1st prize; $500 each for 4 runners-up; all finalists receive staged reading in fall festival. **Guidelines:** unpublished play, not produced with paid Equity cast, which has not won major award; previous entries ineligible. **Submission procedure:** script and $25 fee (check payable to NRTF); visit Web site for guidelines. **Deadline:** postmarked by 31 Mar 2001; no submission before 1 Jan 2001. **Notification:** 1 Aug 2001 for finalists; 31 Dec 2001 for winner.

NATIONAL TEN-MINUTE PLAY CONTEST

Actors Theatre of Louisville; 316 West Main St;
 Louisville, KY 40202-4218; (502) 584-1265, FAX 584-1265
Michael Bigelow Dixon, *Literary Manager*
Amy Wegener, *Assistant Literary Manager*
Types of material: 10-minute plays. **Frequency:** annual. **Remuneration:** $1000 Heideman Award; possible production with royalty. **Guidelines:** U.S. citizen or resident; play 10 pages long or less which has not had Equity production; 1 submission limit; previous entries ineligible. **Submission procedure:** script only; script will not be returned; write for guidelines. **Deadline:** postmarked before 1 Dec 2000. **Notification:** fall 2001.

NEW AMERICAN COMEDY (NAC) FESTIVAL

Ukiah Players Theatre; 1041 Low Gap Rd; Ukiah, CA 95482;
(707) 462-1210, FAX 462-1790
Michael Ducharme, *Executive Director*
Types of material: full-length plays. **Frequency:** biennial. **Remuneration:** $50 per performance for play selected for full production (6 to 8 performances); $25 each per performance for 2 plays chosen as staged readings; up to $400 travel and $25 per diem to attend 1-week workshop. **Guidelines:** playwright must be available to participate in 1-week developmental workshop; unproduced, unpublished comedy; prefers small cast, simple set. **Submission procedure:** application, script with 1-page plot summary, scenic requirements, character breakdown, estimated running time, resume; write for guidelines. **Deadline:** 30 Nov 2001. **Notification:** Feb 2002. **Dates:** May–Jun 2002.

NEW PROFESSIONAL THEATRE WRITERS FESTIVAL

Box 799; New York, NY 10108; (212) 398-2666,
FAX 398-2924; email newprof@aol.com
Literary Manager
Types of material: full-length plays. **Frequency:** annual. **Remuneration:** $2000; 2-week residency with dramaturg; staged reading; busniess seminar; possible production. **Guidelines:** African-American writer. **Submission procedure:** script, resume and SASP for acknowledgment of receipt. **Deadline:** 1 Jun 2001. **Notification:** Sep 2001.

NEW YORK CITY HIGH SCHOOL PLAYWRITING CONTEST

Young Playwrights Inc; 321 West 44th St, Suite 906;
New York, NY 10036; (212) 307-1140, FAX 307-1454;
email writeaplay@aol.com; Web site http://youngplaywrights.org
Sheri M. Goldhirsch, *Artistic Director*
Types of material: full-length plays, one-acts. **Frequency:** annual. **Remuneration:** varies. **Guidelines:** New York City high school student; writers under 18 years of age automatically entered in Young Playwrights Festival National Playwriting Contest (see listing this section). **Submission procedure:** script with playwright's name, date of birth, home address, phone number, school and grade on title page; write for guidelines. **Deadline:** 15 Apr 2001. **Notification:** 1 Jun 2001.

Oglebay Institute Towngate Theatre Contests

Oglebay Institute; Stifel Fine Arts Center; 1330 National Rd;
 Wheeling, WV 26003; (304) 242-7700, FAX 242-7767
Performing Arts Department

Playwriting Contest

Types of material: full-length plays. **Frequency:** annual. **Remuneration:** $300; production; partial travel to attend performances. **Guidelines:** unpublished, unproduced play; simple set. **Submission procedure:** script and resume. **Deadline:** 30 Dec 2000. **Notification:** 1 May 2001.

Playwriting Contest for College Students

Types of material: full-length plays. **Frequency:** annual. **Remuneration:** $100; production. **Guidelines:** unpublished, unproduced play, simple set. **Submission procedure:** script only. **Deadline:** 15 Mar 2001. **Notification:** 1 Jun 2001.

Paul Green Playwrights Prize

c/o North Carolina Writer's Network; 3501 Highway 54 W; Studio C;
 Chapel Hill, NC 27516; email mail@ncwriters.org;
 Web site http://www.ncwriters.org

Types of material: full-length plays, one-acts, solo pieces. **Frequency:** annual. **Remuneration:** $500. **Guidelines:** unpublished, unproduced play. **Submission procedure:** 2 copies of script, synopsis and $12 fee for nonmembers or $10 fee for members; do not list name on manuscript, include separate cover sheet with title, name and contact information; include SASE for winners list; send SASE for guidelines. **Deadline:** 30 Sep 2000. **Notification:** Feb 2001. (See North Carolina Writer's Network in Membership and Service Organizations.)

PEN Center USA West Literary Awards

672 South Lafayette Park Pl, Suite 41; Los Angeles, CA 90057;
 (213) 365-8500, FAX 365-9616; email pen@pen-usa-west.org;
 Web site http://www.pen-usa-west.org
Eric Chow, *Membership & Awards Coordinator*

Types of material: full-length plays, screenplays, teleplays. **Frequency:** annual. **Remuneration:** $1000 award in each of several categories, including drama, screenwriting and television writing. **Guidelines:** writer residing west of Mississippi River; only full-length (original or adapted) screenplays and teleplays; script first produced during 2000 calendar year. **Submission procedure:** 4 copies of script, playbill or press materials verifying eligibility and cover letter giving title of work, author's name and state of residence, name of producer and production dates. **Deadline:** 31 Jan 2001.

PEN-BOOK-OF-THE-MONTH CLUB TRANSLATION PRIZE
PEN American Center; 568 Broadway; New York, NY 10012;
(212) 334-1660, FAX 334-2181; email jm@pen.org
John Morrone, *Literary Awards Manager*
Types of material: translations. **Frequency:** annual. **Remuneration:** $3000.
Guidelines: book-length translation from any language into English published in U.S. during current calendar year. **Submission procedure:** 3 copies of book. **Deadline:** 15 Dec 2000. **Notification:** spring 2001.

PEN/LAURA PELS FOUNDATION AWARD FOR DRAMA
PEN American Center; 568 Broadway; New York, NY 10012-3225;
(212) 334-1660, FAX 334-2181; email jm@pen.org
John Morrone, *Literary Awards Manager*
Types of material: full-length plays. **Frequency:** annual. **Remuneration:** $5000.
Guidelines: mid-career American playwright who has had at least 2 full-length plays professionally produced in theatres 299 seats or larger. **Submission procedure:** playwright must be nominated by a professional colleague through a letter of support accompanied by a list of candidate's produced work. **Deadline:** 3 Jan 2001. **Notification:** spring 2001.

PERISHABLE THEATRE WOMEN'S PLAYWRITING FESTIVAL
Box 23132; Providence, RI 02903; (401) 331-2695, FAX 331-7811;
email perishable@as220.org;
Web site http://www.perishable.org
Vanessa Gilbert, *Festival Director*
Types of material: one-acts. **Frequency:** annual. **Remuneration:** 3 awards of $500; production; publication in anthology. **Guidelines:** unproduced one-act, no more than 40 minutes in length, by woman playwright; 2-submission limit. **Submission procedure:** script, resume and $5 fee. **Deadline:** 15 Dec 2000. **Notification:** 31 Mar 2001.

PETERSON EMERGING PLAYWRIGHT COMPETITION
Theatre Arts Department, Catawba College; 2300 West Innes St;
    Salisbury, NC 28144; (704) 637–4771, FAX 637–4207
    email jepperso@catawba.edu
James R. Epperson, *Chair, Theatre Arts Department*
Types of material: full-length plays, musicals. **Frequency:** annual. **Remuneration:** $2000; full production; transportation, room and board to attend rehearsals and performances. **Guidelines:** unpublished, unproduced full-length work by an emerging playwright; two one-acts with common theme accepted. **Submission procedure:** script and bio; send SASP for acknowledgment of receipt. **Deadline:** 15 Feb 2001. **Notification:** 1 May 2001.

PLAYHOUSE ON THE SQUARE NEW PLAY COMPETITION
Playhouse on the Square; 51 South Cooper St; Memphis, TN 38104;
    (901) 725–0776, 726–4498
Jackie Nichols, *Executive Director*
Types of material: full-length plays, musicals. **Frequency:** annual. **Remuneration:** $500; production. **Guidelines:** unproduced work; small cast; full arrangement for piano for musical; prefers southern playwrights. **Submission procedure:** script only. **Deadline:** 1 Apr 2001.

PLAYS FOR THE 21ST CENTURY
The Playwrights Theater; Box 803305; Dallas, TX 75380;
    (972) 980–7390, FAX 980–7480;
    email jackmarsh@earthlink.net;
    Web site http://www.playwrighttheatertexas.org
Jack Marshall, *Artistic Director*
Types of material: full-length plays. **Frequency:** annual. **Remuneration:** $1500 1st prize; 4 finalists receive full production in week-long festival. **Guidelines:** play not produced professionally. **Submission procedure:** application, script, synopsis, character breakdown, set requirements and $15 fee. **Deadline:** 31 Jan 2001. **Notification:** 30 Jun 2001. **Dates:** fall 2001.

PLAYWRIGHTS FIRST AWARD
c/o The National Arts Club; 15 Gramercy Park S;
    New York, NY 10003; (212) 249–6299
Types of material: full-length plays. **Frequency:** annual. **Remuneration:** $1000 for best play; reading for selected plays; introductions to theatre professionals. **Guidelines:** 1 unproduced play written within last 2 years (no translations, adaptations or musicals). **Submission procedure:** script and resume; script will not be returned. **Deadline:** 15 Oct 2000. **Notification:** May 2001.

QRL POETRY SERIES AWARDS

Quarterly Review of Literature; Princeton University; 26 Haslet Ave;
   Princeton, NJ 08540
Renée Weiss, *Co-Editor*
Types of material: full-length plays, one-acts, translations. **Frequency:** annual.
Remuneration: $1000; publication in QRL Poetry Series; 100 complimentary
paperback copies. **Guidelines:** up to 6 awards a year for poetry and poetic drama
only; play 50-100 pages in length. **Submission procedure:** submissions accepted
in Nov and May only; must be accompanied by $20 subscription for books
published in series; send SASE for guidelines.

REVA SHINER FULL-LENGTH PLAY CONTEST

Bloomington Playwrights Project; 308 South Washington St;
   Bloomington, IN 47401; (812) 334-1188;
   email bppwrite@bluemarble.net;
   Web site http://www.newplays.org
Artistic Director
Types of material: full-length plays, musicals. **Frequency:** annual. **Remuneration:**
$500; staged reading; production. **Guidelines:** unpublished, unproduced work 75-
150 minutes long, suitable for production in small 65-seat theatre; welcomes
innovative works; small-scale musicals; simple set. **Submission procedure:** script,
cover letter and $5 fee; include cassette for musical; write or visit Web site for
guidelines. **Deadline:** 15 Jan 2001. **Notification:** Apr 2001.

ROBERT J. PICKERING AWARD FOR PLAYWRITING EXCELLENCE

Coldwater Community Theater; 89 Division St; Coldwater, MI 49036;
   (517) 278-2389, FAX 279-8095
J. Richard Colbeck, *Award Chairman*
Types of material: full-length plays, one-acts, adaptations, plays for young
audiences, musicals. **Frequency:** annual. **Remuneration:** $200; full production;
room and board. **Guidelines:** unproduced play. **Submission procedure:**
application and script. **Deadline:** 31 Dec 2000. **Notification:** 15 Jan 2001.

SHORT GRAIN CONTEST

Grain Magazine; Box 1154; Regina, SK S4P 3B4; Canada;
  (306) 244-2828, FAX 244-0255;
  email grain.mag@sk.sympatico.ca;
  Web site http://www.skwriter.com

Jennifer Still, *Business Manager*

Types of material: monologues. **Frequency:** annual. **Remuneration:** $500 1st prize, $250 2nd prize, $125 3rd prize (Canadian dollars); winners and honorable mentions receive payment for publication in magazine. **Guidelines:** unpublished, unproduced monologue not submitted elsewhere; 500-word maximum. **Submission procedure:** U.S. and international entries: entry form and $22 fee plus $4 U.S. postage for subscription mailing cost; Canadian entries: entry form and $22 fee for first 2 entries ($5 fee for each additional entry); fee includes 1-year subscription; write or email for guidelines. **Deadline:** 31 Jan 2001. **Notification:** 30 Apr 2001.

SHUBERT FENDRICH MEMORIAL PLAYWRITING CONTEST

Pioneer Drama Service; Box 4267; Englewood, CO 80155-4267;
  (303) 779-4035, FAX 779-4315;
  email editors@pioneerdrama.com;
  Web site http://www.pioneerdrama.com

Beth Somers, *Editor*

Types of material: full-length plays, one-acts, translations, adaptations, plays for young audiences, musicals. **Frequency:** annual. **Remuneration:** publication with $1000 advance on royalties (10% book royalty, 50% performance royalty); all entries considered for publication. **Guidelines:** produced, unpublished work not more than 90 minutes long; subject matter and language appropriate for schools and community theatres; prefers works with a preponderance of female roles; minimal set requirements. **Submission procedure:** script with proof of production (e.g., program, reviews); include score or cassette for musical; send SASE for guidelines. **Deadline:** 1 Mar 2001 (scripts received after deadline will be considered for 2002 contest). **Notification:** 1 Jun 2001.

SIENA COLLEGE INTERNATIONAL PLAYWRIGHTS COMPETITION

Department of Creative Arts; Siena College; 515 Loudon Rd;
Loudonville, NY 12211-1462; (518) 783-2381, FAX 783-4293;
email maciag@siena.edu;
Web site http://www.siena.edu/theatre
Gary Maciag, *Director of Theatre*
Types of material: full-length plays. **Frequency:** biennial. **Remuneration:** $2000;
production; maximum $1000 to cover residency expenses. **Guidelines:** playwright
available for 6-week residency in Jan/Feb 2003; play that has had no previous
workshop or full production; prefers play suitable for college audience and
featuring characters suitable for college-age performers; prefers small cast and
unit set or minimal set change. **Submission procedure:** application and script;
send SASE for application and guidelines after 1 Nov 2001. **Deadline:** 30 Jun
2002; no submission before 1 Feb 2002. **Notification:** 30 Sep 2002.

6TH ANNUAL EMPIRE SCREENPLAY CONTEST

Box 811098; Los Angeles, CA 90081-1098;
email empirecontact@yahoo.com;
Web site http://www.geocities.com/empirecontact/
Michael J. Farrand, *Contest Administrator*
Types of material: screenplays; screenplay proposals. **Frequency:** annual.
Remuneration: 2 $2,000 prizes; Final Draft screenplay software; winners
announced at the Sundance Film Festival. **Guidelines:** narrative screenplays; no
submission limit. **Submission procedure:** application, signed certification form,
screenplay or first 20 pages and 2-page synopsis for proposal and letter of
inquiry with $45 fee per submission ($50 for late submission); send SASE for
guidelines and application. **Deadline:** 15 Jul 2001; 15 Aug 2001 late submission.
Notification: Jan 2002, exact date TBA.

SOURCE THEATRE COMPANY 2001 LITERARY PRIZE

1835 14th St NW; Washington, DC 20009; (202) 462-1073
Keith Parker, *Literary Manager*
Types of material: full-length plays, one-acts, musicals, solo pieces. **Frequency:**
annual. **Remuneration:** $250; staged reading, possible production in 21st Annual
Washington Theatre Festival (12 Jul-12 Aug 2001). **Guidelines:** work not
produced professionally. **Submission procedure:** script, synopsis, resume and
$10 fee; 1-submission limit; send SASE for response; materials will not be
returned. **Deadline:** postmarked before 15 Jan 2001. **Notification:** 15 May 2001.

SOUTH FLORIDA WRITERS CONTEST

South Florida Chapter National Writers Association; Box 570415;
  Miami, FL 33257–0415; (305) 275–8666

Steve Liebowitz, *President*

Types of material: full-length plays, one-acts. **Frequency:** annual. **Remuneration:** $300 1st prize, staged reading; $150 2nd prize, staged reading. **Guidelines:** unpublished, unproduced work. **Submission procedure:** script, cover letter and $12 fee; script will not be returned. **Deadline:** 15 Nov 2000. **Notification:** Feb 2001.

SOUTHEASTERN THEATRE CONFERENCE NEW PLAY PROJECT

Box 9868; Greensboro, NC 27429–0868; (336) 272–3645

Stephen Hancock, *Coordinator*

Types of material: full-length plays, collection of related one-acts. **Frequency:** annual. **Remuneration:** $1000; staged reading at SETC Annual Convention; travel, room and board to attend convention. **Guidelines:** resident of state in SETC region (AL, FL, GA, KY, MS, NC, SC, TN, VA, WV); unproduced work; collection of one-acts bound in 1 cover; limit of 1 full-length submission or collection of one-acts. **Submission procedure:** application and script. **Deadline:** 1 Jun 2001. **Notification:** Nov 2001.

SOUTHERN PLAYWRIGHTS COMPETITION

228 Stone Center; Jacksonville State University;
  Jacksonville, AL 36265; (256) 782–5411, FAX 782–5441;
  email swhitton@jsucc.jsu.edu;
  Web site http://www.jsu.edu/depart/english/southpla.htm

Steven J. Whitton, *Coordinator*

Types of material: full-length plays, solo pieces. **Frequency:** annual. **Remuneration:** $1000; production; housing to attend rehearsals. **Guidelines:** native or resident of AL, AR, FL, GA, KY, LA, MS, NC, SC, TN, TX, VA or WV; 1 unpublished, original submission that deals with the southern experience and has not received Equity production. **Submission procedure:** entry form, script and synopsis; write for guidelines after Sep 2000. **Deadline:** 15 Feb 2001. **Notification:** 1 May 2001.

THE STANLEY DRAMA AWARD

Wagner College Theatre; 1 Campus Rd; Staten Island, NY 10301;
(718) 390-3325, FAX 390-3323

Types of material: full-length plays, one-acts, plays for young audiences, musicals. **Frequency:** annual. **Remuneration:** $2000; production; travel to attend rehearsals and room and board during performances. **Guidelines:** unpublished, unproduced play or collection of one-acts; 1-submission limit. **Submission procedure:** application, script and $20 fee; cassette for musicals. **Deadline:** 1 Oct 2000. **Notification:** Mar 2001.

SUMMERFIELD G. ROBERTS AWARD

The Sons of the Republic of Texas; 1717 8th St; Bay City, TX 77414;
(409) 245-6644, FAX 245-6644; email srttexas@srttexas.org;
Web site http://www.srttexas.org
Melinda Williams

Types of material: full-length plays. **Frequency:** annual. **Remuneration:** $2500 given to work from 1 of several genres, including playwriting. **Guidelines:** play about living in the Republic of Texas, completed during calendar year preceding deadline. **Submission procedure:** 5 copies of script; scripts will not be returned. **Deadline:** 15 Jan 2001. **Notification:** early Apr 2001.

THE SUSAN SMITH BLACKBURN PRIZE

3239 Avalon Pl; Houston, TX 77019; (713) 308-2842,
FAX 654-8184
Emilie S. Kilgore, *Board of Directors*

Types of material: full-length plays. **Frequency:** annual. **Remuneration:** $10,000 1st prize plus signed Willem de Kooning print, made especially for Blackburn Prize; $500 to each of 8-11 other finalists. **Guidelines:** woman playwright of any nationality writing in English; unproduced play or play produced within one year of deadline; previous winners are not eligible. **Submission procedure:** no submission by playwright; professional artistic directors of specified theatres are invited to nominate play and submit 2 copies of script; playwright may bring script to attention of eligible nominator; send 55¢-postage SASE for guidelines and list of theatres eligible to nominate. **Deadline:** 20 Sep 2000. **Notification:** Jan 2001 for finalists; Feb 2001 for winner.

SWTA NATIONAL NEW PLAY CONTEST

Southwest Theatre Association, Inc;
   c/o University of Texas at Arlington; Theatre Arts Program;
   700 West 2nd St; Box 19103; Arlington, TX 76019-0103;
   (817) 272-3141, -5708; email gaupp@uta.edu
Andrew Gaupp and Dennis Maher, *New Plays Committee Co-Chairs*
Types of material: full-length plays, one-acts. **Frequency:** annual.
Remuneration: $200 1st prize; reading at SWTA conference in Nov 2001;
possible excerpt publication in SWTA journal, *Theatre Southwest*; 1-year
membership in SWTA. **Guidelines:** U.S. resident; unproduced, unpublished
play; 1-submission limit. **Submission procedure:** bound script, 1-page
synopsis, 1-page bio and $10 fee (check payable to SWTA). **Deadline:** 15 Mar
2001. **Notification:** Sep 2001. **Dates:** Nov 2001.

THEATRE CONSPIRACY ANNUAL NEW PLAY CONTEST

Theatre Conspiracy, Inc; 10091 McGregor Blvd; Ft. Myers, FL 33919;
   (941) 936-3239
Bill Taylor, *Artistic Director*
Types of material: full-length plays. **Frequency:** annual. **Remuneration:** $500;
production. **Guidelines:** play not previously produced; cast limit of 8; simple
production demands. **Submission procedure:** script, 1-page synopsis, character
breakdown, technical requirements, bio and $10 fee. **Deadline:** 31 Nov 2000.
Notification: Mar 2001. **Dates:** late May-early Jun 2001.

THEATREFEST REGIONAL PLAYWRITING CONTEST

Montclair State University; Upper Montclair, NJ 07043;
   (973) 655-7496, FAX 655-5335;
   Web site http://www.montclair.edu
John Wooten, *Artistic Director*
Types of material: full-length plays. **Frequency:** annual. **Remuneration:** $1500
John Golden Prize; full production; housing; $500 to 2 runners-up. **Guidelines:**
playwright, resident of CT, NJ or NY; unproduced, unpublished work exploring
contemporary issues; cast limit of 8. **Submission procedure:** 1-5 page synopsis,
5-page dialogue sample and SASE for response; write for guidelines. **Deadline:** 1
Jan 2001. **Notification:** 15 Feb 2001.

THEODORE WARD PRIZE FOR AFRICAN-AMERICAN PLAYWRIGHTS

Columbia College Chicago Theater/Music Center; 72 East 11th St;
 Chicago, IL 60605; (312) 344-6136, FAX 344-8077;
 email chigochuck@aol.com
Chuck Smith, *Facilitator*
Types of material: full-length plays, translations, adaptations, solo pieces.
Frequency: annual. **Remuneration:** $2000 1st prize, production, travel and housing to attend rehearsals; $500 2nd prize, staged reading; 3rd prize, staged reading at Goodman Theatre (see Production). **Guidelines:** African-American U.S. resident; 1 full-length submission not produced professionally; translations and adaptations of material in public domain only. **Submission procedure:** script, short synopsis, production history and brief resume; write for guidelines. **Deadline:** 1 Jul 2001; no submission before 1 Apr 2001. **Notification:** Nov 2001.

TOWSON UNIVERSITY PRIZE FOR LITERATURE

Towson University; Towson, MD 21252; (410) 830-2128
Dean, College of Liberal Arts
Types of material: book or book-length manuscript; all literary genres eligible, including plays. **Frequency:** annual. **Remuneration:** $2000. **Guidelines:** author no more than 40 years of age, MD resident for 3 years and at time prize awarded; work published within 3 years prior to submission or scheduled for publication within the year. **Submission procedure:** publisher or playwright submits application and 5 copies of work; write for guidelines. **Deadline:** 15 Jun 2001. **Notification:** 1 Dec 2001.

TRUSTUS PLAYWRIGHTS' FESTIVAL

Trustus Theatre; Box 11721; Columbia, SC 29211-1721;
 (803) 254-9732, FAX 771-9153; email Trustus88@aol.com;
 Web site http://www.trustus.org
Jon Tuttle, *Literary Manager*
Types of material: full-length plays. **Frequency:** annual. **Remuneration:** $500 1st prize, full production with travel and housing to attend opening; $250 2nd prize, staged reading. **Guidelines:** work not produced professionally; cast limit of 8; no musicals or plays for young audiences. **Submission procedure:** application, 2 copies of synopsis and resume; send SASE for application and guidelines. **Deadline:** 1 Mar 2001; no submission before 1 Jan 2001. **Notification:** 1 Jun 2001.

Unicorn Theatre National Playwrights' Award
3828 Main St; Kansas City, MO 64111; (816) 531-7529, ext 18,
FAX 531-0421
Herman Wilson, *Literary Assistant*
Types of material: full-length plays. **Frequency:** no set dates. **Remuneration:** $1000; production; possible travel and residency. **Guidelines:** unpublished play not produced professionally; special interest in social issues; contemporary (post-1950) themes and settings only; no musicals; cast limit of 10; 2-submission limit. **Submission procedure:** synopsis, at least 10 pages of dialogue, character breakdown, resume, cover letter and SASE for response; no scripts. **Deadline:** ongoing. **Notification:** 4 weeks; 4-8 months if script is requested.

University of Louisville Grawemeyer Award for Music Composition
Grawemeyer Music Award Committee; School of Music;
University of Louisville; Louisville, KY 40292; (502) 852-6907,
FAX 852-0520; email mlgreeo1@gwise.louisville.edu;
Web site http://www.louisville.edu/ur/onpi/grawemeyer
Paul Brink, *Chair*
Types of material: works in major musical genres, including music-theatre works and operas. **Frequency:** annual. **Remuneration:** $200,000 (paid in 5 annual installments of $40,000). **Guidelines:** work premiered between 1996-2000; entry must be sponsored by professional music organization or individual. **Submission procedure:** application, score, cassette, supporting materials and $40 fee submitted jointly by composer and sponsor; write for guidelines. **Deadline:** 29 Jan 2001. **Notification:** TBA. **Dates:** spring 2002 for presentation of award.

Vermont Playwrights Award
The Valley Players; Box 441; Waitsfield, VT 05673-0441;
(802) 496-3751
Jennifer Howard, *Coordinator*
Types of material: full-length plays. **Frequency:** annual. **Remuneration:** $1000; probable production. **Guidelines:** resident of ME, NH or VT; unproduced, unpublished play, suitable for community group, that has not won playwriting competition; moderate production demands. **Submission procedure:** entry form and 2 copies of script; send SASE for guidelines. **Deadline:** 1 Feb 2001.

VSA ARTS PLAYWRIGHT DISCOVERY AWARD

1300 Connecticut Ave NW, Suite 700; Washington, DC 20036;
    (800) 933–8721 (voice), (202) 737–0645 (TTY),
    FAX (202) 737–0725; email playwright@vsarts.org;
    Web site http://www.vsarts.org

Types of material: one-acts. **Frequency:** annual. **Remuneration:** awards in 2 categories: $2500 for playwright 22 years of age or older, $500 for playwright 21 years of age or younger; professional production at Kennedy Center; travel, room and board to attend performance. **Guidelines:** U.S. citizen; play less than 40 pages in length dealing with some aspect of disability by writer with a disability; family audience; previous submission ineligible; 1-submission limit. **Submission procedure:** application and 2 copies of script; send SASE for ackowledgment of receipt; scripts will not be returned; write or visit Web site for application and guidelines. **Deadline:** Apr 2001, exact date TBA.

WALDO M. AND GRACE C. BONDERMAN IUPUI/IRT PLAYWRITING EVENT FOR YOUNG AUDIENCES

IUPUI University Theatre; 425 University Blvd, Suite 309;
    Indianapolis, IN 46202; (317) 274–2095, FAX 278–1025;
    email dwebb@iupui.edu;
    Web site http://iupui.edu/~comstudy/playsym/symhome.html
Mark McCreary, *Literary Manager*

Types of material: plays for young audiences. **Frequency:** biennial. **Remuneration:** 4 prizes of $1000; 1 week of developmental work culminating in showcase reading at National Youth Theatre Playwriting Symposium; travel from within continental U.S. and housing during residency. **Guidelines:** writer must be available for week-long developmental residency; unpublished play at least 45 minutes long with strong storyline, compelling characters and careful attention to language; not previously produced by Equity company. **Submission procedure:** send SASE for entry form and guidelines or visit Web site. **Deadline:** 8 Sep 2000. **Notification:** Dec 2000. **Dates:** Apr-May 2001 for residency; 4-6 May for Showcase/Symposium.

WE DON'T NEED NO STINKIN' DRAMAS

Mixed Blood Theatre Company; 1501 South 4th St;
  Minneapolis, MN 55454; (612) 338–0937
David Kunz, *Script Czar*
Types of material: full-length comedies, musical comedies. **Frequency:** annual. **Remuneration:** $2000 if theatre chooses to produce play; $1000 if not. **Guidelines:** unproduced, unpublished work by U.S. citizen who has had at least 1 work produced or workshopped professionally or by educational institution; comedies; plays minimum 65 pages long about race issues, sports or with a political edge; 2-submission limit (dual entries must be sent under separate cover). If interested in MBTC but not sure if work is suitable, send brief cover letter and 1-page-maximum synopsis to MBTC. **Submission procedure:** script; resume (optional); write for guidelines. **Deadline:** 1 Feb 2001. **Notification:** fall 2001.

WEST COAST ENSEMBLE CONTESTS

Box 38728; Los Angeles, CA 90038; (323) 876–9337,
  FAX 876–8916
Les Hanson, *Artistic Director*

WEST COAST ENSEMBLE FULL-LENGTH PLAY COMPETITION

Types of material: full-length plays. **Frequency:** annual. **Remuneration:** $500; production; royalty on any performances beyond 8-week run. **Guidelines:** 1 submission not produced in southern CA; cast limit of 12. **Submission procedure:** script with SASE or SASP for acknowledgment of receipt. **Deadline:** 31 Dec 2000. **Notification:** Jul 2001.

WEST COAST ENSEMBLE MUSICAL STAIRS

Types of material: musical theatre works. **Frequency:** annual. **Remuneration:** $500; production; royalty on any performances beyond 8-week run. **Guidelines:** 1 unpublished musical submission not produced in southern CA; all genres and styles eligible, including pop, rock, country and western, etc.; cast limit of 12. **Submission procedure:** script, cassette of music (include score and lead sheets if available). **Deadline:** 30 Jun 2001. **Notification:** Jan 2002.

WHITE BIRD PLAYWRITING CONTEST

White Bird Productions, Inc;138 South Oxford St;
   Brooklyn, NY 11217; (718) 369-3308, FAX 369-3308
Kathryn Dickinson, *Artistic Director*
John Istel, *Literary Manager*
Types of material: full-length plays. **Frequency:** annual. **Remuneration:** $200; staged reading; possible travel to attend rehearsals. **Guidelines:** play with theme, plot and/or central idea that deals in a general or specific way with the environment; 2-submission limit. **Submission procedure:** script and resume. **Deadline:** 15 Feb 2001. **Notification:** Oct 2001.

WICHITA STATE UNIVERSITY PLAYWRITING CONTEST

University Theatre; Wichita State University; 1845 Fairmount;
   Wichita, KS 67260-0153; (316) 978-3368, FAX 978-3951
Leroy Clark, *Contest Director*
Types of material: full-length plays, bills of related one-acts. **Frequency:** annual. **Remuneration:** production; expenses for playwright to attend production. **Guidelines:** unpublished, unproduced work at least 90 minutes long by student currently enrolled at U.S. college or university; no musicals or plays for young audiences. **Submission procedure:** bound script with unbound cover sheet containing author's name, address and phone number (no author's name on script); send SASP for acknowlegment of receipt; write for guidelines. **Deadline:** 15 Feb 2001. **Notification:** 15 Apr 2001.

WRITER'S DIGEST WRITING COMPETITION

1507 Dana Ave; Cincinnati, OH 45207-1005; (513) 531-2690,
   ext 328, FAX 531-1843; email competitions@fwpubs.com
Competition Coordinator
Types of material: full-length plays, screenplays, teleplays. **Frequency:** annual. **Remuneration:** $1500 Grand Prize, expenses paid to New York City to meet with editors and agents or to 2001 Maui Writer's Conference; $750 1st prize, $350 2nd prize, $250 3rd prize, each with $100 worth of Writer's Digest books; $100 4th prize with current *Writer's Market* and 1-year subscription to *Writer's Digest* magazine; $25 5th prize with current *Writer's Market* and 1-year subscription to *Writer's Digest* magazine. **Guidelines:** unproduced, unpublished work, not accepted by publisher or producer at time of submission; previous entries ineligible. **Submission procedure:** entry form, 1-page synopsis, first 15 pages of script, indication of projected market for work and $10 fee; send SASE for guidelines. **Deadline:** 31 May 2001. **Notification:** fall 2001.

Year-End-Series (Y.E.S.) New Play Festival

Department of Theatre; Northern Kentucky University;
   Highland Heights, KY 41099; (606) 572-6362, FAX 572-6057;
   email forman@nku.edu

Sandra Forman, *Project Director*

Types of material: full-length plays, adaptations, musicals. **Frequency:** biennial. **Remuneration:** 4 awards of $500; production; travel and expenses to attend late rehearsals and performance. **Guidelines:** unproduced work in which majority of roles can be handled by students; small orchestra for musicals; 1-submission limit. **Submission procedure:** application and script. **Deadline:** 31 Oct 2000. **Notification:** Jan 2001. **Dates:** 19-29 Apr 2001.

Young Connecticut Playwrights Festival

Maxwell Anderson Playwrights Series; Box 671;
   West Redding, CT 06896; (203) 938-2770

Bruce Post, *Dramaturg*

Types of material: full-length plays, one-acts, musicals, translations, adaptations, plays for young audiences, solo pieces. **Frequency:** annual. **Remuneration:** staged reading in May festival; certificate. **Guidelines:** CT resident ages 12-19 only; script maximum 60 pages in length. **Submission procedure:** bound script with playwright's name, date of birth, home address, phone number and name of school on title page; send SASE for guidelines. **Deadline:** 27 Mar 2001. **Notification:** May 2001. **Dates:** May 2001.

Young Playwrights Festival National Playwriting Contest

Young Playwrights Inc; 321 West 44th St, Suite 906;
   New York, NY 10036; (212) 307-1140;
   email writeaplay@aol.com; Web site http://youngplaywrights.org

Sheri M. Goldhirsch, *Artistic Director*

Types of material: full-length plays, one-acts. **Frequency:** annual. **Remuneration:** staged reading or production with royalty; travel and residency; 1-year Dramatists Guild membership (see Membership and Service Organizations). **Guidelines:** playwright 18 years of age or younger as of 1 Dec 2000; submissions from playwrights of all backgrounds encouraged. **Submission procedure:** script with playwright's name, date of birth, home address and phone number on title page; write for guidelines. **Deadline:** 1 Dec 2000.

PUBLICATION

What is listed in this section?

Those who are primarily or exclusively play publishers, and literary magazines and small presses, all who accept work of unpublished writers. For online publication and production opportunities, see the Online Resources chapter.

How can I determine the best places to submit my play?

Think of these publishers as highly individual people looking for very particular kinds of material, which means you should find out as much as possible about their operations before submitting scripts. One of the best sources is the Council of Literary Magazines and Presses (154 Christopher St, Suite 3C; New York, NY 10014-2839; 212-741-9110), and their *Directory of Literary Magazines 2000* ($12.95 paper, plus $3.00 for 1st-class postage and handling), a descriptive listing of hundreds of magazines, including many which publish plays. Other leads may be found in the *The International Directory of Little Magazines and Small Presses: 1999–2000* (Dustbooks; Box 100; Paradise, CA 95967; 530-877-6110; $34.95 paper, $55.00 cloth, plus $6.00 shipping and handling). You should also write to individual publishers listed here and ask for style sheets, catalogs, sample copies, etc. Don't forget that when publishers say they accept unsolicited scripts, they *always* require you to enclose an SASE for return of the manuscript.

AMELIA MAGAZINE

329 "E" St; Bakersfield, CA 93304; (661) 323-4064, FAX 323-5326;
email amelia@lightspeed.net
Frederick A. Raborg, Jr., *Editor*
Types of material: one-acts, including translations and solo pieces.
Remuneration: $150 prize; 10 complimentary copies. **Guidelines:** winner of
annual Frank McClure One-Act Play Award published in magazine; unpublished
play maximum 45 minutes long. **Submission procedure:** accepts unsolicited
scripts with list of any productions and $15 fee; sample copy $10.95.
Deadline: 15 May 2001. **Notification:** 15 Sep 2001.

ANCHORAGE PRESS

Box 8067; New Orleans, LA 70182; (504) 283-8868, FAX 866-0502
Orlin Corey, *Editor*
Types of material: works for young audiences, including full-length plays, one-
acts, translations, adaptations and musicals. **Remuneration:** negotiated royalty.
Guidelines: specialty house publishing quality works for young audiences only;
only works produced a minimum of 3 times considered. **Submission procedure:**
accepts unsolicited scripts with proof of production. **Response time:** 2-3 months.

ARTE PÚBLICO PRESS

University of Houston; Houston, TX 77204-2174; (713) 743-2841,
FAX 743-2847
Nicolás Kanellos, *Publisher*
Types of material: full-length plays, one-acts, adaptations, plays for young
audiences, musicals. **Remuneration:** negotiated royalty; complimentary copies.
Guidelines: unpublished works in English or Spanish by Hispanic writers only.
Submission procedure: accepts unsolicited scripts. **Response time:** 6 months.

ASIAN PACIFIC AMERICAN JOURNAL

16 West 32nd St, Suite 10A; New York, NY 10001;
(212) 494-0061, FAX 228-7718; email desk@aaww.org;
Web site http://www.aaww.org
Hanya Yanagihara, *Editor*
Types of material: one-acts. **Remuneration:** 2 complimentary copies.
Guidelines: semiannual literary journal publishing work by and/or of interest
to Asian-Americans; plays maximum 4000 words. **Submission procedure:**
accepts unsolicited scripts; send 4 copies of script. **Response time:** 3 months.

AUDREY SKIRBALL-KENIS PLAY COLLECTION

630 West 5th St; Los Angeles, CA 90071; (213) 228-7327,
   FAX 228-7339; Web site http://www.askplay.org
Tom Harris, *Project Director*
Types of material: full-length plays, one-acts, translations, adaptations, plays for young audiences, musicals, solo pieces, performance-art texts. **Remuneration:** descriptive listing of work in *Southern California Unpublished Plays Collection,* catalog of plays housed in Central Library in downtown Los Angeles. **Guidelines:** unpublished plays professionally produced in Southern California only. **Submission procedure:** accepts unsolicited scripts.

BAKER'S PLAYS

Box 699222; Quincy, MA 02269-9222; (617) 745-0805,
   FAX 745-9891; email raypape@hotmail.com;
   Web site http://www.bakersplays.com
Ray Pape, *Associate Editor*
Types of material: full-length plays, one-acts, plays for young audiences, musicals, chancel dramas. **Remuneration:** negotiated book and production royalty. **Guidelines:** prefers produced plays; prefers plays suitable for high school, community and regional theatres; "Plays from Young Authors" division features plays by high school playwrights. **Submission procedure:** accepts unsolicited scripts with resume; include press clippings if play has been produced. **Response time:** 2-6 months. **Special programs:** Baker's Plays High School Playwriting Contest (see Prizes).

BROADWAY PLAY PUBLISHING, INC.

56 East 81st St; New York, NY 10028-0202; (212) 772-8334,
   FAX 772-8358; email BroadwayPl@aol.com;
   Web site http://www.broadwayplaypubl.com
Types of material: full-length plays. **Remuneration:** 10% book royalty, 80% amateur royalty, 90% stock royalty; 10 complimentary copies. **Guidelines:** major interest is in original, innovative work by American playwrights; no historical or autobiographical plays. **Submission procedure:** no unsolicited scripts; letter of inquiry. **Response time:** 2 months letter; 4 months script.

CALLALOO

322 Bryan Hall; Department of English; University of Virginia;
 Box 400121; Charlottesville, VA 22904–4121; (804) 924–6637,
 FAX 924–6472; email callaloo@virginia.edu;
 Web site http://www.people.virginia.edu/~callaloo
Charles H. Rowell, *Editor*
Types of material: one-acts (including translations), excerpts of longer plays.
Remuneration: complimentary copies and offprints. **Guidelines:** quarterly
journal of African-American and African arts and letters published by Johns
Hopkins University Press. **Submission procedure:** accepts unsolicited scripts;
send 3 copies of script with SASE for response. **Response time:** 6 months.

COLLAGES & BRICOLAGES

Box 360; Shippenville, PA 16254; email cb@penn.com
Marie-José Fortis, *Editor*
Types of material: one-acts. **Remuneration:** 2 complimentary copies (50%
discount on additional copies). **Guidelines:** annual journal of international
writing publishing poetry, fiction, drama and criticism, including 1–5 plays a
year; minimalist plays; avant-garde and feminist work; innovative plays less
than 30 pages long; plays must relate to issue theme (2001 theme is Love).
Submission procedure: accepts unsolicited scripts; no simultaneous
submissions; submit 1 Aug–1 Dec only. **Response time:** 2 weeks–3 months.

CONFRONTATION

English Department; C.W. Post College of Long Island University;
 Greenvale, NY 11548; (516) 299–2720, FAX 299–2735;
 email mtucker@liu.edu
Martin Tucker, *Editor*
Types of material: one-acts. **Remuneration:** $15–75; 1 complimentary copy.
Guidelines: general magazine for "literate" audience; unpublished plays.
Submission procedure: accepts unsolicited scripts. **Response time:** 8–10 weeks.

CONTEMPORARY DRAMA SERVICE

Meriwether Publishing, Ltd; 885 Elkton Dr;
Colorado Springs, CO 80907; (719) 594-4422, FAX 594-9916
Theodore Zapel, *Executive Editor*

Types of material: one-acts, adaptations, plays for young audiences, musicals, readers' theatre, monologues. **Remuneration:** book royalties or payment for amateur and professional performance rights. **Guidelines:** publishes works suitable for teenage, high school and college market, as well as collections of scenes and practical books on theatre arts; prefers comedies; prefers produced works. **Submission procedure:** accepts unsolicited scripts; send $2 for sample catalog and guidelines. **Response time:** 2 months.

DESCANT

Box 314, Station P; Toronto, Ontario; Canada M5S 2S8;
(416) 593-2557; Web site http://www.descant.on.ca
Nathan Whitlock, *Managing Editor*
Karen Mulhallen, *Editor*

Types of material: full-length plays, one-acts, performance-art texts. **Remuneration:** $100 honorarium; 1-year subscription; 1 complimentary copy (40% discount on additional copies). **Guidelines:** quarterly literary magazine publishing an average of 2 plays a year; unpublished plays; visit Web site for more information. **Submission procedure:** accepts unsolicited scripts; send SASE for response (Canadian postage or IRC only). **Response time:** 6 months.

THE DRAMATIC PUBLISHING COMPANY

311 Washington St; Box 129; Woodstock, IL 60098;
(815) 338-7170, FAX 338-8981;
email plays@dramaticpublishing.com;
Web site http://www.dramaticpublishing.com
Linda Habjan, *Editor*

Types of material: full-length plays, one-acts, translations, adaptations, plays for young audiences, musicals. **Remuneration:** standard royalty; 10 complimentary copies (33% discount on additional copies). **Guidelines:** works for professional, stock and amateur markets; prefers produced plays. **Submission procedure:** accepts unsolicited scripts. **Response time:** 4-8 months.

DRAMATICS MAGAZINE

2343 Auburn Ave; Cincinnati, OH 45219; (513) 421–3900,
  FAX 421–7077; email dcorathers@etassoc.org
Don Corathers, *Editor*
Types of material: full-length plays, one-acts and solo pieces for young performers. **Remuneration:** payment for 1-time serial rights; complimentary copies. **Guidelines:** educational theatre magazine; plays suitable for high school production; prefers produced plays. **Submission procedure:** accepts unsolicited scripts. **Response time:** 2–3 months.

DRAMATISTS PLAY SERVICE, INC.

440 Park Avenue South; New York, NY 10016; (212) 683–8960,
  FAX 213–1539; email postmaster@dramatists.com;
  Web site http://www.dramatists.com
Stephen Sultan, *President*
Types of material: full-length plays, musicals. **Remuneration:** possible advance against royalties; 10% book royalty, 80% amateur royalty, 90% stock royalty; 10 complimentary copies (40% discount on additional copies). **Guidelines:** works for stock and amateur market; prefers works produced in New York City. **Submission procedure:** no unsolicited scripts; 1-page synopsis and letter of inquiry. **Response time:** 4–6 months letter; 4–6 months script.

ELDRIDGE PUBLISHING COMPANY

Box 1595; Venice, FL 34284–1595; (800) HI–STAGE;
  email info@histage.com; Web site http://www.histage.com
Nancy S. Vorhis, *Editor*
Types of material: full-length plays, one-acts, musicals. **Remuneration:** outright purchase of religious material only; all other works, 10% book royalty, 50% amateur and educational royalty; complimentary copies (50% discount on additional copies). **Guidelines:** publishes 50–75 plays and musicals a year for school, church and community theatre; comedies, mysteries or serious drama. **Submission procedure:** accepts unsolicited scripts; if possible, include cassette for musicals. **Response time:** 2 months.

ENCORE PERFORMANCE PUBLISHING
Box 692; Orem, UT 84057; (801) 225-0605
Michael C. Perry, *President*
Types of material: full-length plays, one-acts, translations, adaptations, plays for young audiences, musicals, solo pieces. **Remuneration:** 10% book royalty, 50% performance royalty; 10 complimentary copies (discount on additional copies). **Guidelines:** publishes 10-30 plays and musicals a year; works must have had a minimum of 2 amateur or professional productions; special interest in works with strong family or Judeo-Christian message and in Christmas, Halloween and other holiday plays. **Submission procedure:** no unsolicited scripts; synopsis, production information and letter of inquiry; best submission time May-Aug. **Response time:** 2-4 weeks letter; 2-3 months script.

FREELANCE PRESS
Box 548; Dover, MA 02030; (508) 785-8250, FAX 785-8291
Narcissa Campion, *Managing Editor*
Types of material: musicals. **Remuneration:** 10% book royalty, 70% performance royalty; 1 complimentary copy. **Guidelines:** unpublished issue-oriented musicals and musical adaptations of classics; approximately 1 hour long; suitable for performing by young people only. **Submission procedure:** accepts unsolicited scripts. **Response time:** 3 months.

HEUER PUBLISHING COMPANY
Box 248; Cedar Rapids, IA 52406; (319) 364-6311, FAX 364-1771;
    email editor@hitplays.com; Web site http://www.hitplays.com
C. Emmett McMullen, *Editor and Publisher*
Types of material: works for young audiences, including full-length plays, one-acts and musicals. **Remuneration:** outright purchase or performance royalty; complimentary copies. **Guidelines:** dramatic works suitable for middle school or high school students; plays appropriate for family audiences. **Submission procedure:** accepts unsolicited scripts. **Response time:** 1-2 months.

I. E. CLARK PUBLICATIONS
Box 246; Schulenburg, TX 78956-0246; (979) 743-3232,
    FAX 743-4765; email ieclark@cvtv.net;
    Web site http://www.ieclark.com
Donna Cozzaglio, *Editorial Department*
Types of material: full-length plays, one-acts, translations, adaptations, plays
for young audiences, musicals. **Remuneration:** book and performance
royalties. **Guidelines:** publishes for worldwide professional, amateur and
educational markets; prefers produced works. **Submission procedure:** accepts
unsolicited scripts; cassette or videotape must accompany musical; include
proof of production with reviews and photos for produced works; send $3 for
catalog; send SASE for submission guidelines. **Response time:** 2-6 months.

INTERNATIONAL READERS' THEATRE (IRT)
PUBLISH-ON-DEMAND SCRIPT SERVICE
Blizzard Publishing; 73 Furby St; Winnipeg; Canada MB R3C 2A2
    (204) 775-2923, (800) 694-9256, FAX (204) 775-2947;
    email irt@blizzard.mb.ca;
    Web site http://www.blizzard.mb.ca/catalog
David Fuller, *Production Coordinator*
Types of material: full-length plays, one-acts, plays for young audiences,
monologues. **Remuneration:** 10% book royalty. **Guidelines:** publishes more than
60 plays a year in chapbook format; submissions also considered for Blizzard
Publishing trade paperback publishing program; previously produced work only.
Submission procedure: accepts unsolicited scripts with submission forms and
SASE for response; write for submission guidelines and forms. **Response time:**
4-6 months.

KALLIOPE, A JOURNAL OF WOMEN'S LITERATURE & ART
Florida Community College; 3939 Roosevelt Blvd;
    Jacksonville, FL 32205; Web site http://www.fccj.org/kalliope
Mary Sue Koeppel, *Editor*
Types of material: one-acts, including solo pieces. **Remuneration:** 2
complimentary copies or free 1-year subscription. **Guidelines:** triannual journal
of women's literature and art publishing short fiction, poetry, artwork,
photography, interviews, reviews and an average of 1 play a year; unpublished
plays, less than 20 pages long, by women only; "no trite themes or erotica."
Submission procedure: accepts unsolicited scripts. **Response time:** 3-6 months.

THE KENYON REVIEW

Kenyon College; Gambier, OH 43022; (740) 427–5208,
FAX 427–5417; email kenyonreview@kenyon.edu;
Web site http://www.kenyonreview.org
David H. Lynn, *Editor*
Types of material: one-acts, solo pieces, excerpts from full-length plays.
Remuneration: cash payment; 2 complimentary copies. **Guidelines:** literary
journal publishing an average of 2 plays a year; unproduced, unpublished works
maximum 30 pages long. **Submission procedure:** no unsolicited scripts; sample
pages and letter of inquiry. **Response time:** 3-4 months.

LAMIA INK!

Box 202; Prince St Station; New York, NY 10012
(Ms.) Cortland Jessup, *Artistic Director*
Types of material: very short monologues and performance pieces; 1-page
plays for contest (see below). **Remuneration:** 4 complimentary copies.
Guidelines: biannual "art rag" magazine; experimental theatre pieces
maximum 5 pages long, prefers 2-3 pages; special interest in Japanese, Pacific
Rim and Native American writers, and poets' theatre, performance poems,
theatre manifestos and essays. **Submission procedure:** accepts unsolicited
scripts with SASE for response. **Response time:** 2-3 weeks minimum. Special
programs: Lamia Ink! International One-Page Play Competition (see Prizes).

LILLENAS DRAMA RESOURCES

Lillenas Publishing Company; Box 419527; Kansas City, MO 64141;
(816) 931–1900, (800) 877–0700, FAX (816) 412–8390;
email drama@lillenas.com;
Web site http://www.lillenas.com/drama
Kimberly R. Messer, *Manager/Editor*
Types of material: full-length plays, one-acts, collections of sketches, playlets,
children's recitations. **Remuneration:** outright purchase or royalty. **Guidelines:**
unpublished "creatively conceived and practically producible scripts and
outlines that provide church and school with an opportunity to glorify God and
his creation in drama." **Submission procedure:** accepts unsolicited scripts;
send SASE for guidelines and current need letter. **Response time:** 3 months.

NEW PLAYS

Box 5074; Charlottesville, VA 22905; (804) 979-2777,
    FAX 984-2230; email patwhitton@aol.com;
    Web site http://www.newplaysforchildren.com
Patricia Whitton Forrest, *Publisher*

Types of material: plays for young audiences. **Remuneration:** 10% book royalty, 50% performance royalty. **Guidelines:** innovative material not duplicated by other sources of plays for young audiences; produced plays, directed by someone other than author. **Submission procedure:** accepts unsolicited scripts. **Response time:** 1-2 months minimum.

PERFORMING ARTS JOURNAL

Box 260; Village Station; New York, NY 10014-0260;
    (212) 243-3885, FAX 243-3885; email pajpub@aol.com
Bonnie Marranca and Gautam Dasgupta, *Co-Publishers and Editors*

Types of material: short full-length plays, one-acts, translations, solo pieces. **Remuneration:** fee. **Guidelines:** publishes plays and critical essays on international performance, drama, video, music, film and photography; special interest in translations; plays less than 40 pages long. **Submission procedure:** no unsolicited scripts; synopsis and letter of inquiry. **Response time:** 1-2 months letter; 1-2 months script.

PIONEER DRAMA SERVICE

Box 4267; Englewood, CO 80155-4267; (303) 779-4035,
    FAX 779-4315; email editors@pioneerdrama.com;
    Web site http://www.pioneerdrama.com

Types of material: full-length plays, one-acts, plays for young audiences, musicals. **Remuneration:** royalty. **Guidelines:** produced work suitable for educational theatre, including melodramas and Christmas plays. **Submission procedure:** accepts unsolicited scripts; prefers synopsis and letter of inquiry. **Response time:** 2 weeks letter; 3-4 months script. **Special programs:** Shubert Fendrich Memorial Playwriting Contest (see Prizes).

PLAYERS PRESS
Box 1132; Studio City, CA 91614-0132; (818) 789-4980
Robert W. Gordon, *Senior Editor*
Types of material: full-length plays, one-acts, translations, adaptations, plays for young audiences, musicals, solo pieces, monologues, scenes, teleplays, screenplays. **Remuneration:** cash option and/or outright purchase or royalty; complimentary copies (20% discount on additional copies). **Guidelines:** theatre press publishing technical and reference books and scripts; produced works for professional, amateur and educational markets. **Submission procedure:** accepts unsolicited scripts with proof of production, resume and 2 business-size SASEs; prefers synopsis, proof of production, resume and letter of inquiry with SASE for response. **Response time:** 1-6 weeks letter; 1-6 months script.

PLAYS ON TAPE
Box 5789; Bend, OR 97708-5789; (541) 923-6246, FAX 923-9679;
    email theatre@playsontape.com;
    Web site http://www.playsontape.com
Silvia Gonzalez S., *Literary Manager*
Types of material: full-length plays, one-acts. **Remuneration:** negotiable fee and royalty; 10 complimentary copies of audiotape or CD. **Guidelines:** audiobook company marketing primarily to theatre gift bookstores and libraries; "works that do not diminish in quality due to restrictions of audiotape" only; special interest in works by women and minorities; maximum 74 minutes. **Submission procedure:** accepts unsolicited scripts; prefers synopsis, letter of inquiry and up to 10 pages of dialogue with SASE or email address for response; accepts scripts and synopses via email or floppy disk; send SASE for guidelines. **Response time:** 3 months letter; 5-6 months script.

PLAYS, THE DRAMA MAGAZINE FOR YOUNG PEOPLE
Box 600160; Newton, MA 02460; (262) 796-8776;
    email lizpreston@mediaone.net;
    Web site http://www.writermag.com
Elizabeth Preston, *Managing Editor*
Types of material: one-act plays for young audiences, including adaptations of material in the public domain. **Remuneration:** $75-175 depending on length of play. **Guidelines:** publishes 70 plays a year; prefers work 20-30 minutes long for junior and senior high school, 15-20 minutes for middle grades, 8-15 minutes for lower grades; no religious plays; magazine acquires all rights. **Submission procedure:** accepts unsolicited original scripts; letter of inquiry for adaptations; prefers format used in magazine (send SASE for style sheet). **Response time:** 1 week letter; 2-3 weeks script.

POEMS & PLAYS

English Department; Middle Tennessee State University;
  Murfreesboro, TN 37132; (615) 898-2712, FAX 898-5098;
  Web site http://www.mtsu.edu/~english/poemplay.html
Gaylord Brewer, *Editor*
Types of material: one-acts and short plays. **Remuneration:** 1 complimentary copy. **Guidelines:** annual magazine of poetry and short plays published Apr, includes an average of 2-3 plays in each issue; unpublished works; prefers produced works not more than 10-15 pages long. **Submission procedure:** accepts unsolicited scripts 1 Oct-15 Jan only; sample issue $6. **Response time:** 1-2 months. **Special programs:** Tennessee Chapbook Prize: annual award for either a one-act play or collection of short plays or poetry, maximum manuscript length 24-30 pages; winning script published as interior chapbook in magazine; playwright receives 50 complimentary copies; submit script and $10 for reading fee and copy of next issue; *deadline:* 15 Jan 2001; no submissions before 1 Oct 2000.

PRISM INTERNATIONAL

Creative Writing Program; University of British Columbia;
  Buch E462-1866 Main Mall; Vancouver, BC; Canada V6T 1Z1;
  (604) 822-2514, FAX 822-3616;
  email prism@interchange.ubc.ca;
  Web site http://www.arts.ubc.ca/prism
Chris LaBonte and Andrea MacPherson, *Co-Editors*
Types of material: one-acts (including translations and solo pieces), excerpts from full-length plays. **Remuneration:** $20-30 per printed page; 1-year subscription. **Guidelines:** quarterly literary magazine; unpublished plays, maximum 40 pages long; send SASE for guidelines. **Submission procedure:** accepts unsolicited scripts, include copy of original with translations. **Response time:** 3-6 months. **Special programs:** UBC's Creative Writing Residency Prize in Stageplay: a 1-month residency at UBC and $25,000 (Canadian) prize (about $16,900 U.S.); call or visit Web site for guidelines.

RAG MAG

Box 12; Goodhue, MN 55027; (651) 923-4590
Beverly Voldseth, *Editor and Publisher*
Types of material: full-length plays, one-acts, solo pieces. **Remuneration:** 1 complimentary copy. **Guidelines:** biannual small-press literary magazine publishing artwork, prose and poetry, with interest in innovative character plays; prefers short one-acts but will consider longer plays with a view to publishing extracts or scenes. **Submission procedure:** accepts unsolicited short one-acts; Sep-May only; send maximum 10-page sample, bio and letter of inquiry for longer plays; include name, address and title on each page of script; 1-submission limit; send SASE for guidelines. **Response time:** 1-2 months.

RESOURCE PUBLICATIONS, INC.

160 East Virginia St, #290; San Jose, CA 95112-5876;
(408) 286-8505, FAX 287-8748; email Ken@rpinet.com;
Web site http://www.rpinet.com
Ken Guentert, *Editor*
Types of material: plays 7-15 minutes long. **Remuneration:** royalty. **Guidelines:** collection of skits suitable for middle school or high school students. **Submission procedure:** accepts unsolicited scripts. **Response time:** 2 months.

ROCKFORD REVIEW

Box 858; Rockford, IL 61105; email dragonldy@prodigy.net;
Web site http://members.tripod.com/~rwguild
David Ross, *Editor*
Types of material: one-acts, including solo pieces. **Remuneration:** 1 complimentary cop; one-acts selected for publication eligible for quarterly "Editor's Choice" prize of $25 (winner invited to reading and reception as guest of honor in Jun). **Guidelines:** quarterly journal publishing poetry, fiction, satire, artwork and an average of 4-5 plays a year; one-acts not more than 10 pages long, preferably of a satirical nature; interested in work that provides new insight into the human dilemma ("to cope or not to cope"). **Submission procedure:** accepts unsolicited scripts; sample copy $5. **Response time:** 1-2 months.

SAMUEL FRENCH, INC.

45 West 25th St; New York, NY 10010-2751; (212) 206-8990,
FAX 206-1429; email samuelfrench@earthlink.net;
Web site http://samuelfrench.com

Lawrence Harbison, *Senior Editor*

Types of material: full-length plays, one-acts, plays for young audiences, musicals, solo pieces. **Remuneration:** 10% book royalty; 10 complimentary copies (40% discount on additional copies). **Guidelines:** "Many of our publications have never been produced in New York; these are generally comprised of light comedies, mysteries, mystery-comedies, a handful of one-acts and plays for young audiences, and plays with a preponderance of female roles; however, do not hesitate to send in your future Pulitzer Prize Winner." **Submission procedure:** accepts unsolicited scripts. **Response time:** 2-4 months minimum.

SINISTER WISDOM

Box 3252; Berkeley, CA 94703; email sinister@serious.com
Editor

Types of material: one-acts, excerpts from full-length plays. **Remuneration:** 2 complimentary copies. **Guidelines:** lesbian quarterly of art and literature; works by lesbians reflecting the diversity of lesbians; no heterosexual themes; excerpts maximum 3000 words; send SASE for current themes. **Submission procedure:** accepts unsolicited scripts. **Response time:** 2-9 months.

SMITH AND KRAUS

Box 127; Lyme, NH 03768; (603) 643-6431, FAX 643-1831;
email sandk@sover.net

Marisa Smith, *President*

Types of material: full-length plays, one-acts, translations, adaptations, plays for young audiences, solo pieces, monologues. **Remuneration:** usually fee or royalty; at least 10 complimentary copies. **Guidelines:** theatre press publishing works of interest to theatrical community, especially to actors, including collections of monologues and an average of 50 full-length plays a year. **Submission procedure:** no unsolicited scripts; synopsis and letter of inquiry. **Response time:** 2-3 weeks letter; 2-4 months script.

Sun & Moon Press
6026 Wilshire Blvd; Los Angeles, CA 90036; (323) 857-1115;
email djmess@sunmoon.com;
Web site http://www.sunmoon.com
American Theater and Literature Program (ATL)
Types of material: full-length plays, one-acts, translations. **Remuneration:** royalty; 10 complimentary copies. **Guidelines:** press publishing average of 10 single-play volumes a year; unpublished plays. **Submission procedure:** accepts unsolicited scripts. **Response time:** 2-6 months.

Theater Magazine
Box 208244; New Haven, CT 06520-8244; (203) 432-1568,
FAX 432-8336; email theater.magazine@yale.edu;
Web site http://www.yale.edu/drama/publications/theater
Erika Munk, *Editor*
Types of material: full-length plays, translations, adaptations, solo pieces. **Remuneration:** maximum fee of $150; complimentary copies. **Guidelines:** triquarterly theatre journal publishing an average of 2 plays in each issue, plus articles and essays; special interest in experimental, innovative work; "no standard psychological realism or TV-script clones." **Submission procedure:** accepts unsolicited scripts with resume and letter of inquiry. **Response time:** 3-6 months.

TheatreForum
Theatre & Dance Department 0344;
University of California-San Diego; 9500 Gilman Dr;
La Jolla, CA 92093-0344; (619) 534-6598, FAX 534-1080;
email TheatreForum@ucsd.edu;
Web site http://www-theatre.ucsd.edu/TF/
Jim Carmody, Adele Edling Shank and Theodore Shank, *Editors*
Types of material: full-length plays, translations, adaptations. **Remuneration:** $200; 10 complimentary copies; discount for additional copies. **Guidelines:** biannual international journal focusing on innovative work, publishing 2 scripts in each issue, plus articles, interviews and photographs; professionally produced, unpublished plays. **Submission procedure:** no unsolicited scripts; professional recommendation. **Response time:** 3 months.

Ubu Repertory Theater Publications
See Membership and Service Organizations.

DEVELOPMENT

What's in this section?

Conferences, festivals, workshops and programs whose primary purpose is to develop plays and playwrights. Also listed are some playwright groups and membership organizations whose main activity is play development. Developmental organizations such as New Dramatists whose many programs cannot be adequately described in the brief format used in this section are listed in Membership and Service Organizations. Some programs listed in Prizes also include a developmental element. Note: Some programs provide writers with stipends or living situations, etc. Others require a small fee. Read the "financial arrangement" section carefully.

How can I get into these programs?

Keep applying to those for which you are convinced your work is suited. If you're turned down one year, you may be accepted the next on the strength of your latest piece. If you're required to submit a script with your application, don't forget your SASE!

ABINGDON THEATRE COMPANY

432 West 42nd St, 4th Floor; New York, NY 10036; (212) 736-6604,
    FAX 736-6608; email atcnyc@aol.com;
    Web site http://www.abingdon-nyc.org
Pamela Paul, *Co-Artistic Director*
Open to: playwrights. **Description:** biweekly in-house readings; 10 plays receive
12 hours of rehearsal and staged readings; of those, 4 plays selected for
workshop production; of those, 2 plays selected for mainstage production.
Financial arrangement: stipend for workshops and mainstage production.
Guidelines: play unproduced in New York. **Application procedure:** script only.
Deadline: ongoing. **Notification:** 6 months. **Dates:** year-round.

ACT/HEDGEBROOK WOMEN PLAYWRIGHTS FESTIVAL

A Contemporary Theatre; The Eagles Building, 700 Union St;
    Seattle, WA 98101-2330; (206) 292-7660, FAX 292-7670;
    Web site http://www.acttheatre.org
Gordon Edelstein, *Artistic Director*
Open to: playwrights. **Description:** 4 playwrights chosen for reading of play with
audience feedback; playwright then goes to Hedgebrook (see Colonies and
Residencies) for a week to work on any revisions that come out of reading.
Financial arrangement: $1000 stipend, travel and lodging. **Guidelines:** woman
playwright; unproduced play. **Application procedure:** professional nomination
only; theatre panel selects finalists. **Deadline:** fall 2000. **Notification:** Mar 2001.
Dates: May 2001.

ANNUAL BACKDOOR THEATRE NEW PLAY PROJECT

Wichita Falls Backdoor Players, Inc; Box 896; Wichita Falls, TX 76307;
    (940) 322-5000, FAX 322-8167;
    email backdoor@wf.net
Linda Bates, *Managing Director*
Open to: playwrights. **Description:** 1 play each Sep receives five weeks of
rehearsal and workshop production with a minimum of 6 performances.
Financial arrangement: $500 honorarium; travel and housing. **Guidelines:**
special interest in playwrights from Texas and surrounding region; full-length
plays which have not received professional production. **Application procedure:**
script, brief synopsis, resume and SASP for acknowledgment of receipt. **Deadline:**
15 Mar 2001. **Notification:** Jul 2001. **Dates:** Sep 2001.

ASCAP MUSICAL THEATRE WORKSHOP

1 Lincoln Plaza; New York, NY 10023; (212) 621-6234

Michael A. Kerker, *Director of Musical Theatre*

Open to: composers, lyricists. **Description:** 10-session workshop under the direction of Stephen Schwartz; works presented to panels of musical theatre professionals. **Financial arrangement:** free. **Guidelines:** write for guidelines and dates. **Application procedure:** resume and cassette of 4 theatrical songs (no pop songs). **Deadline:** 15 Mar 2001. **Notification:** exact date TBA. **Dates:** exact dates TBA.

ASHLAND NEW PLAYS FESTIVAL

ArtWork Enterprises, Inc.; Box 453; Ashland, OR 97520;
(541) 482-4357

Open to: playwrights. **Description:** up to 6 new works given 16-20 hours of rehearsal with actors, director and dramaturg, culminating in 2 public readings. **Financial arrangement:** $500 stipend and housing. **Guidelines:** U.S. resident; previously unproduced full-length play; cast limit of 6; 1-submission limit. **Application procedure:** script and double-spaced, 1-page maximum synopsis. **Deadline:** 1 Apr 2001. **Notification:** 1 Jul 2001. **Dates:** Oct 2001.

ASIAN AMERICAN THEATER COMPANY
EMERGING ARTISTS PROJECT

1840 Sutter St, Suite 207; San Francisco, CA 94115; (415) 440-5545,
FAX 440-5597; email aatc@wenet.net;
Web site http://www.wenet.net/~aatc

Pamela A. Wu, *Producing Director*

Open to: playwrights. **Description:** developmental workshop for 2-4 plays, leading to staged reading or production; plays not selected for workshop considered for inclusion in series of 8-10 readings presented each season. **Financial arrangement:** free; honorarium contingent on funding. **Guidelines:** playwright of Asian-Pacific descent writing in English; prefers plays depicting Asian-Pacific-American perspective. **Application procedure:** script, synopsis and character breakdown. **Deadline:** ongoing. **Notification:** 1-6 months. **Dates:** exact dates TBA.

A.S.K. THEATER PROJECTS
11845 West Olympic Blvd, Suite 1250 West; Los Angeles, CA 90064; (310) 478-3200, FAX 478-5300; email askplay@primenet.com; Web site http://www.askplay.org
Mead K. Hunter, *Director of Literary Programs*
Open to: playwrights. **Description:** approximately 15 playwrights either receive public rehearsed reading of play or participate in private writer's retreat; 2-3 plays receive workshop production. **Financial arrangement:** playwright receives $150 for rehearsed reading, $500 for retreat participation, $1000 for workshop production. **Guidelines:** unproduced full-length play-in-progress. **Application procedure:** script submissions accepted only from agents or by professional recommendation; playwrights may submit sample pages and resume. **Deadline:** ongoing. **Notification:** 4-6 months.

THE AUDIO THEATRE WORKSHOP
The National Audio Theatre Festivals; 115 Dikeman St; Hempstead, NY 11550; (516) 483-8321, FAX 538-7583; Web site http://www.natf.org
Sue Zizza, *Executive Director*
Open to: playwrights. **Description:** 1-week intensive spring workshop held at William Woods University in Fulton, MO; classes in writing, directing, acting, sound design and technical skills for radio production; week culminates in live performance with simultaneous broadcast and Web cast. **Financial arrangement:** $350 plus travel; some scholarships available. **Guidelines:** women and minorities encouraged to apply. **Application procedure:** registration form; contact NATF before 15 Mar 2001 for application materials. **Deadline:** contact NATF or visit Web site for exact deadlines. **Notification:** 15 Apr 2001 for scholarships. **Dates:** Jun 2001, exact dates TBA. (See NATF Script Competition in Prizes.)

BALTIMORE PLAYWRIGHTS FESTIVAL
251 South Ann St; Baltimore, MD 21231; (410) 276-2153
Rodney Bonds, *President*
Open to: playwrights, composers, librettists, lyricists. **Description:** selected plays receive 3-5 developmental readings Sep-Mar; from these, participating theatres choose scripts for full production in summer festival. **Financial arrangement:** $100 honorarium for produced scripts. **Guidelines:** past or current resident of MD; unproduced play; send SASE for guidelines. **Application procedure:** 3 copies of script and letter of inquiry with $5 fee. **Deadline:** 30 Sep 2000. **Notification:** 15 Apr 2001. **Dates:** summer 2001.

BAY AREA PLAYWRIGHTS FESTIVAL

The Playwrights Foundation; Box 460357; San Francisco, CA 94106;
   (415) 263-3986; email bayplays@best.com
Jayne Wenger, *Artistic Director*
Lanny Lighthill, *Producing Director*
Open to: playwrights. **Description:** 6-9 scripts given dramaturgical attention and 2 rehearsed readings separated by 5-6 days for rewrites during 2-week festival; mandatory prefestival weekend retreat for initial brainstorming with directors and dramaturgs. **Financial arrangement:** small stipend, travel. **Guidelines:** unproduced full-length play only. **Application procedure:** script and resume. **Deadline:** 15 Feb 2001. **Notification:** Jun 2001. **Dates:** prefestival weekend Aug 2001; festival Sep or Oct 2001.

BMI-LEHMAN ENGEL MUSICAL THEATRE WORKSHOP

Broadcast Music, Inc.; 320 West 57th St; New York, NY 10019;
   (212) 830-2508, FAX 262-2824; email jbanks@bmi.com
Jean Banks, *Senior Director, Musical Theatre*
Open to: composers, librettists, lyricists. **Description:** 2-year program of weekly workshop meetings; ongoing advanced group for invited alums of Workshop; showcase presentations to invited members of entertainment industry. **Financial arrangement:** free. **Application procedure:** application and work samples. **Deadline:** 1 May 2001 for librettists; 1 Aug 2001 for composers and lyricists. **Notification:** Sep 2001.

BROADWAY TOMORROW

191 Claremont Ave, Suite 53; New York, NY 10027;
   (212) 531-2447, FAX 531-2447
Elyse Curtis, *Artistic Director*
Open to: composers, librettists, lyricists. **Description:** new musicals presented in concert with writers' involvement. **Financial arrangement:** participant pays $50 annual membership fee. **Guidelines:** resident of NY metropolitan area. **Application procedure:** synopsis, resume, cassette of 3 songs with description of scenes in which they occur, reviews if available and SASE for response. **Deadline:** 31 Aug 2001. **Notification:** 3-6 months. **Dates:** year-round.

C. BERNARD JACKSON READERS THEATRE
c/o Inner City Cultural Center; 514 South Spring St;
   Los Angeles, CA 90014; (213) 627-7670, FAX 622-5881

Open to: playwrights, translators. **Description:** cold reading series held first Monday of every month; each reading followed by critique. **Financial arrangement:** free. **Guidelines:** play maximum 90 minutes; special interest in international, multicultural work; write for guidelines. **Application procedure:** synopsis and letter of inquiry. **Deadline:** ongoing. **Dates:** year-round.

CAC PLAYWRIGHT'S UNIT
Contemporary Arts Center; 900 Camp St; New Orleans, LA 70130;
   (504) 528-3805, FAX 528-3828; Web site http://www.cacno.org
Performance Support Coordinator

Open to: playwrights. **Description:** 9-month workshop for 8-15 writers; participants' works developed and given staged readings. **Financial arrangement:** write or call for information. **Guidelines:** writer living in New Orleans area. **Application procedure:** call for information. **Deadline:** ongoing. **Dates:** ongoing.

CARNEGIE MELLON DRAMA'S SUMMER NEW PLAYS PROJECT
Carnegie Mellon Drama; College of Fine Arts; Pittsburgh, PA 15213;
   (412) 268-3284, FAX 621-0281
Peter Frisch and Milan Stitt, *Artistic Directors*

Open to: playwrights, translators, solo performers. **Description:** 3 playwrights each brought in for 2 weeks to work on play with director and Equity company of actors, culminating in 2 public script-in-hand performances. **Financial arrangement:** $1000 stipend, travel and housing. **Guidelines:** full-length play or bill of related one-acts already being developed at established professional regional theatre. **Application procedure:** no submission by playwright; CMU approaches theatre for possible co-production. **Dates:** Jul–Aug 2001.

CHARLOTTE FESTIVAL/NEW PLAYS IN AMERICA
Charlotte Repertory Theatre; 129 West Trade St;
   Charlotte, NC 28244; (704) 333-8587
Claudia Carter Covington, *Literary Manager*
Carol Bellamy, *Literary Associate*

Open to: playrights, translators. **Description:** 4 plays each given 12-16 hours of rehearsal with Equity company, culminating in 2 public staged readings during week-long festival; some scripts subsequently receive full production as part of theatre's regular season. **Financial arrangement:** honorarium, travel and housing. **Guidelines:** only full-length plays and translations that have not received professional production. **Application procedure:** script only. **Deadline:** ongoing. **Dates:** 4-18 Feb 2001.

The Chesterfield Film Company/Writer's Film Project

1158 26th St, Box 544; Santa Monica, CA 90401; (213) 683-3977,
FAX (310) 260-6116; Web site http://www.chesterfield-co.com

Open to: playwrights, screenwriters. **Description:** up to 5 writers annually chosen for year-long screenwriting workshop; writer creates 2 feature-length screenplays; company intends to produce best of year's work. **Financial arrangement:** $20,000 stipend. **Guidelines:** current and former writing-program students encouraged to apply; write or call for information. **Application procedure:** 2 copies of completed application, writing samples and $39.50 fee. **Deadline:** fall 2000; exact date TBA. **Dates:** Jun 2001–Jun 2002.

Cornerstone Dramaturgy and Development Project

Penumbra Theatre Company; 270 North Kent St; St. Paul, MN
55102-1794; (651) 224-4601, FAX 224-7074

Lou Bellamy, *Artistic Director*

Open to: playwrights. **Description:** 1 playwright a year offered mainstage production with possible 3-4 week residency; 1 playwright offered 4-week workshop-residency culminating in staged reading. **Financial arrangement:** varies according to needs of project. **Guidelines:** full-length play dealing with the African-American and/or Pan-African experience which has not received professional full production; one-acts considered. **Application procedure:** script and resume; write for guidelines. **Deadline:** ongoing.

David Henry Hwang Writers Institute

East West Players; 244 South San Pedro St, Suite 301;
Los Angeles, CA 90012; (213) 625-7000, FAX 625-7111;
email info@eastwestplayers.org;
Web site http://www.eastwestplayers.org

Ken Narasaki, *Literary Manager*

Open to: playwrights, screenwriters. **Description:** 2 20-week workshops each year culminating in a public staged reading. **Financial arrangement:** $350 fee; 1 scholarship available. **Application procedure:** completed application form and work sample with $25 nonrefundable deposit. **Deadline:** visit Web site.

Denver Center Theatre Company US WEST Theatre Fest

1050 13th St; Denver, CO 80204

Bruce K. Sevy, *Associate Artistic Director/New Play Development*

Open to: playwrights. **Description:** new plays receive workshops and rehearsed readings during spring festival; most plays given 15-30 hours of rehearsal, culminating in 1 public presentation. **Financial arrangement:** stipend, travel, housing. **Application procedure:** send SASE for guidelines. **Deadline:** 31 Dec 2001. **Dates:** late May–early Jun.

DRAMA LEAGUE NEW DIRECTORS–NEW WORKS SERIES

The Drama League of New York; 165 West 46th St, Suite 601;
New York, NY 10036; (212) 302-2100, FAX 302-2254;
email dlny@echonyc.com; Web site http://www.dramaleague.org

Open to: playwright-director teams. **Description:** 3 projects each summer receive up to 4 weeks of rehearsal space in New York City; development ranges from exploratory rehearsals to workshop production according to needs of collaborative team. **Financial arrangement:** $1000 for each team. **Application procedure:** proposal describing project submitted jointly by director and playwright; bios; write, call or visit Web site for guidelines. **Deadline:** 15 Feb 2001. **Notification:** 1 May 2001.

DRAMA WEST PRODUCTIONS

Box 5022-127; Lake Forest, CA 92630
Catherine Stanley, *Artistic Director*

Open to: playwrights. **Description:** 5-6 plays each month given staged reading, followed by audience feedback. **Financial arrangement:** free. **Guidelines:** one-acts appropriate for a general audience which have not received professional production. **Application procedure:** script only. **Deadline:** ongoing. **Notification:** 2 weeks, if script is accepted.

8TH ANNUAL WOMEN AT THE DOOR STAGED READING SERIES

Famous Door Theatre Company; Box 57029; Chicago, IL 60657;
(773) 404-8283, FAX 404-8292;
Email theatre@famousdoortheatre.org;
Web site http://www.famousdoortheatre.org
Carson Becker, *Producer*

Open to: playwrights. **Description:** 3-5 plays receive 3-4 rehearsals culminating in professional staged readings; plays considered for subsequent workshop and/or mainstage production. **Guidelines:** woman playwright; previously unproduced full-length play; 1-submission limit; no musicals or adaptations. **Financial arrangement:** honorarium contingent on funding; possible housing; visit Web site for information on status of cash prizes. **Application procedure:** 1-page synopsis, first scene or first 10 pages of play and resume. **Deadline:** 1 Nov 2000. **Notification:** finalists 1 Jan 2001; winners 1 Apr 2001. **Dates:** May-Jun 2001.

FIRST STAGE

Box 38280; Los Angeles, CA 90038; (323) 850-6271, FAX 850-6295
Dennis Safren, *Literary Manager*

Open to: playwrights, solo performers, screenwriters. **Description:** organization providing year-round developmental services using professional actors, directors and dramaturgs; weekly staged readings of plays and screenplays followed by discussions; bimonthly playwriting and screenwriting workshops; periodic dramaturgy workshops; annual short-play marathon; annual One-Act Play Contest with $100 first prize, $50 second and third prizes and videotaped staged reading for all winners, *deadline:* 1 Jul 2001 (send SASE for guidelines), *notification:* 1 Nov 2001. **Financial arrangement:** subscription of $160 a year or $45 a quarter for resident of Los Angeles, Orange or Ventura counties; $60 annual subscription for nonresident; nonmember may submit script for reading. **Application procedure:** script only. **Deadline:** ongoing. **Notification:** 2-6 months. **Dates:** year-round.

FLORIDA PLAYWRIGHTS' PROCESS

PACT Institute for the Performing Arts at Ruth Eckerd Hall;
 111 McMullen-Booth Rd; Clearwater, FL 33759;
 (727) 791-7060, ext 354, FAX 791-7449;
 email ensignsp@gte.net; Web site http://www.rutheckerdhall.net
Elizabeth Brincklow, *Program Director*

Open to: playwrights. **Description:** 3 plays (2 by playwright 19 or younger) receive 4-5 months of workshop, rehearsal and staged reading, culminating in workshop production with moderated audience discussion. **Financial arrangement:** $400 and maximum travel stipend of $250. **Guidelines:** FL playwright; unproduced and unpublished full-length play; cast limit of 6; maximum running time 2 hours; simple props and set. **Application procedure:** write or call for guidelines. **Deadline:** 16 Nov 2000. **Notification:** 31 Jan 2001. **Dates:** Feb-May 2001.

THE 42ND STREET WORKSHOP

432 West 42nd St, 5th Floor; New York, NY 10036;
 (212) 695-4173, FAX 695-3384
Sheila Walsh, *Literary Manager*

Open to: playwrights, screenwriters. **Description:** writers meet weekly to develop scripts through in-house readings and critiques; approximately 30 works a year receive staged readings; 3-4 works receive showcase productions. **Financial arrangement:** $25 monthly fee. **Application procedure:** script and letter of reference from company member. **Deadline:** ongoing. **Notification:** 1 Dec 2000. **Dates:** year-round.

THE FRANK SILVERA WRITERS' WORKSHOP

Box 1791; Manhattanville Station; New York, NY 10027; (212) 281-8832, FAX 281-8839 (call first); email playrite@artswire.org; Web site http://www.artswire.org/~playrite

Garland Lee Thompson, *Founding Executive Director*

Open to: playwrights. **Description:** upper Manhattan- and Harlem-based program which includes Monday series of readings of new plays by new and established writers, followed by critiques; Saturday seminars conducted by master playwrights; staged readings; and 2-3 showcases and readers' theatre productions a year. **Financial arrangement:** $35 annual fee plus $10 per Saturday class; Monday-night readings free. **Guidelines:** interested in new plays by writers of all colors and backgrounds. **Application procedure:** attend Sep open house; submitting script and attending a Monday-night session encouraged; call for information.

FREDERICK DOUGLASS CREATIVE ARTS CENTER WRITING WORKSHOPS

270 West 96th St; New York, NY 10025; (212) 864-3375, FAX 864-3474 (call first); email fdcac@aol.com; Web site http://www.fdcac.org

Fred Hudson, *Artistic Director*

Open to: playwrights, screenwriters, television writers. **Description:** 4 cycles a year of 8-week beginning and advanced playwriting workshops; advanced workshops include readings and possible productions; also film and television writing workshops; weekly meetings. **Financial arrangement:** $200 fee per workshop; author of play given staged reading receives $50, author of produced play receives $500. **Application procedure:** contact FDCAC for information. **Deadline:** Sep 2000 for 1st cycle; Jan 2001 for 2nd cycle; May 2001 for 3rd cycle; Jul 2001 for 4th cycle; call for exact dates. **Dates:** Oct-Dec 2000; Jan-Mar 2001; Apr-Jun 2001; Jul-Sep 2001.

FREE PLAY READING SERIES AND PLAYWRIGHT DEVELOPMENT WORKSHOP

American Renaissance Theatre of Dramatic Arts; 10 West 15th St, Suite 325; New York, NY 10011

Rich Stone, *Artistic Director*

Open to: playwrights. **Description:** 1-2 plays-in-progress given 2 rehearsals and a public reading, followed by audience critique; playwright also attends workshop addressing each of the plays and the "business" of playwriting. **Financial arrangement:** free. **Guidelines:** resident of New York city area; unproduced play. **Application procedure:** synopsis, 10-page dialogue sample and SASE for response. **Deadline:** 31 Dec 2000. **Notification:** 30 Mar 2001. **Dates:** Jun 2001; exact dates TBA.

THE GENESIUS GUILD PROGRAMS FOR THE DEVELOPMENT OF NEW PLAYS & MUSICALS

Box 2213; New York, NY 10108–2213; (212) 946–5625;
  email literary@genesiusguild.org;
  Web site http://www.genesiusguild.org
Thomas Morrissey, *Artistic Director*

Open to: playwrights, translators, composers, librettists, lyricists, solo performers. **Description:** program offering range of developmental services including in-house readings; staged readings; workshop and showcase productions; development process varies according to needs of script. **Financial arrangement:** free. **Guidelines:** emerging or established playwright. **Application procedure:** 1- or 2-page synopsis, scene breakdown, cast requirements, production needs, cassette for musical and bio or resume. **Deadline:** ongoing. **Dates:** Sep–May.

HAROLD PRINCE MUSICAL THEATRE PROGRAM

The Directors Company; 311 West 43rd St, Suite 307;
  New York, NY 10036; (212) 246–5877, FAX 246–5882
HPMTP Selection Committee

Open to: playwrights, composers, librettists, lyricists. **Description:** program supports creation, development and production of new musicals; writers and composers work collaboratively with director under guidance of program's artistic directors and Harold Prince; process includes monthly meetings, readings and presentation for invited audience in New York City. **Financial arrangement:** commissioning and optioning fees available. **Guidelines:** musicals in any stage of development; call for guidelines. **Application procedure:** full scripts accepted from agent or with professional recommendation; all others submit synopsis, 15-page dialogue sample and 6-song cassette or CD. **Deadline:** ongoing. **Notification:** 3-6 months.

HEDGEROW HORIZONS

146 West Rose Valley Rd; Wallingford, PA 19086; (610) 565–4211
Walt Vail, *Literary Manager*

Open to: playwrights. **Description:** 5 full-length plays and 2 one-acts each given 1 rehearsal and 1 public reading. **Financial arrangement:** free. **Guidelines:** playwright must be resident of DE, PA or NJ; play not professionally produced. **Application procedure:** send SASE for guidelines. **Deadline:** 28 Feb 2001. **Notification:** 30 Apr 2001. **Dates:** 30 May 2001.

HISPANIC PLAYWRIGHTS PROJECT

South Coast Repertory; Box 2197; Costa Mesa, CA 92628-2197;
(714) 708-5500, ext 5405
Juliette Carrillo, *Project Director*

Open to: playwrights. **Description:** up to 3 scripts given 1-3-week workshop with director, dramaturg and professional cast, culminating in public reading or workshop production and discussion; playwright meets with director and dramaturg prior to workshop. **Financial arrangement:** per diem, travel, housing. **Guidelines:** Hispanic-American playwright; unproduced play preferred but produced play which would benefit from further development will be considered; play must not be written entirely in Spanish; no musicals. **Application procedure:** script, synopsis and bio. **Deadline:** Jan 2001; exact date TBA. **Notification:** Mar 2001. **Dates:** Jun 2001.

KEY WEST THEATRE FESTIVAL

Box 992; Key West, FL 33041; (305) 292-3725, FAX 293-0845;
email theatrekw@attglobal.net
Joan McGillis, *Artistic Director*

Open to: playwrights, translators, solo performers. **Description:** up to 8 plays given staged readings and 5 plays given full productions during 10-day festival, which also includes workshops and seminars. **Financial arrangement:** travel and housing. **Guidelines:** unproduced full-length play, one-act, musical, work for young audiences. **Application procedure:** script, resume and 2 letters of recommendation. **Deadline:** 31 Dec 2000. **Notification:** Apr 2001. **Dates:** 28 Jun-8 Jul 2001.

L. A. BLACK PLAYWRIGHTS

5926 5th Ave; Los Angeles, CA 90043; (323) 292-9438
James Graham Bronson, *President*

Open to: playwrights, librettists, lyricists. **Description:** group meets every second Sunday for guest speakers, private and public readings, and showcases. **Financial arrangement:** free. **Guidelines:** resident of Los Angeles area; members mainly but not exclusively African-American; prefers produced playwright. **Application procedure:** submit full-length play. **Deadline:** ongoing. **Dates:** year-round.

THE LEHMAN ENGEL MUSICAL THEATRE WORKSHOP

335 North Brand Blvd; Glendale, CA 91203; (818) 502-3309,
FAX 502-3365; email jsparksco@aol.com
John Sparks, *Artistic Director*

Open to: composers, librettists, lyricists. **Description:** Sep-Jun workshop; in-house staged readings; skeletal productions (Equity contract). **Financial arrangement:** 1st-year workshop members pay dues of $500, which include nonrefundable application fee (see below); in subsequent years, members pay dues of $300. **Application procedure:** application; 1-page resume; cassette of 3 songs or equivalent for composer; 3 lyrics for lyricist; short scene for librettist; nonrefundable $50 fee. **Deadline:** 15 Aug 2001. **Notification:** Sep 2001. **Dates:** Sep 2001-Jun 2002.

LORNA LITTLEWAY'S JUNETEENTH JAMBOREE OF NEW PLAYS

Box 3463; Louisville, KY 40201-3463; (502) 636-4200;
email juneteenthfest@aol.com
Lorna Littleway, *Founder/Producing Director*
Kristi Papailler-Berkley, *Associate Producer/Artistic Director*

Open to: playwrights. **Description:** 12 plays given professional staged reading during 3-week festival in Jun. **Financial arrangement:** free. **Guidelines:** plays which address the African-American experience and explore any of 5 themes: 19th-century African-American experience; pre- and Harlem Renaissance era; Caribbean/Native American influence on African-Americans; African-American youth and contemporary issues; and new images of women; young writers encouraged to apply. **Application procedure:** 2 copies of script and $10 fee (1 script and fee to Louisville address and 1 script to: 605 Water St, #21B; New York, NY 10002). **Deadline:** 15 Apr 2001; no submission before 15 Dec 2000. **Notification:** 30 Apr 2001. **Dates:** Jun 2001.

MANHATTAN PLAYWRIGHTS UNIT

338 West 19th St, #6B; New York, NY 10011-3982; (212) 989-0948
Saul Zachary, *Artistic Director*

Open to: playwrights, screenwriters. **Description:** developmental workshop meeting weekly for in-house readings and discussions of members' works-in-progress; end-of-season series of staged readings of new plays. **Financial arrangement:** free. **Guidelines:** produced or published writer. **Application procedure:** letter of inquiry, resume and SASE for response. **Deadline:** ongoing.

MARK TAPER FORUM DEVELOPMENTAL PROGRAMS

135 North Grand Ave; Los Angeles, CA 90012; (213) 972–8033
Pier Carlo Talenti, *Literary Manager*
(Also see entry in Production)

ASIAN THEATRE WORKSHOP (ATW)

Open to: playwrights, solo performers. **Description:** ongoing developmental program including Asian Pacific American Friends of Center Theatre Group (APAF) Reading Series; discussions with outside theatre artists; workshop productions. **Financial arrangement:** honorarium. **Guidelines:** Asian-Pacific playwright. **Application procedure:** script and resume. **Deadline:** ongoing.

BLACKSMYTHS

Open to: playwrights, solo performers. **Description:** ongoing developmental program including writers' group, staged readings and workshops. **Financial arrangement:** honorarium. **Guidelines:** African-American playwright; resident of Los Angeles area. **Application procedure:** script and resume. **Deadline:** ongoing.

LATINO THEATRE INITIATIVE (LTI)

Open to: playwrights, solo performers. **Description:** ongoing developmental program including staged readings and workshops. **Financial arrangement:** remuneration varies. **Guidelines:** Latino playwright. **Application procedure:** script and resume. **Deadline:** ongoing.

NEW WORK FESTIVAL

Open to: playwrights, solo performers. **Description:** 16-18 plays given workshops (2 weeks of rehearsal, 2 public presentations) or rehearsed readings. **Financial arrangement:** remuneration varies. **Guidelines:** unproduced, unpublished play. **Application procedure:** brief synopsis, 5-10 sample pages and resume. **Deadline:** 30 Apr 2001.

OTHER VOICES PROJECT

Open to: playwrights, solo performers. **Description:** ongoing developmental program including community and professional development; staged readings; workshops; Summer Chautauqua: biennial week-long seminar. **Financial arrangement:** remuneration varies. **Guidelines:** disabled playwright writing about disability; program designed to increase presence of disabled community in mainstream theatre. **Application procedure:** script and resume; call for guidelines for Summer Chautauqua. **Deadline:** call for information.

MUSICAL THEATRE WORKS

440 Lafayette St; New York, NY 10003; (212) 677–0040,
    FAX 598–0105; email mtw2000@akula.com
Lonny Price, *Artistic Director*
Open to: composers, librettists, lyricists. **Description:** new composers,
librettists and lyricists work with established musical theatre professionals to
develop projects through labs, readings, workshop productions and a 6-week
professional workshop culminating in public presentation; free rehearsal space
and casting, technical, administrative, legal and dramaturgical support.
Financial arrangement: free. **Guidelines:** completed unproduced work.
Application procedure: send letter of inquiry and SASE for guidelines.
Deadline: ongoing.

NATIONAL MUSIC THEATER CONFERENCE

O'Neill Theater Center; 234 West 44th St, Suite 901;
    New York, NY 10036–3909; (212) 382–2790, FAX 921–5538
Paulette Haupt, *Artistic Director*
Michael E. Nassar, *Associate Director*
Open to: composers, librettists, lyricists. **Description:** development period of 2–
4 weeks at O'Neill Theater Center, Waterford, CT for new music-theatre works
of all genres, traditional and nontraditional; some works developed privately,
others presented as staged readings. **Financial arrangement:** stipend, round-trip
travel from NYC, room and board. **Guidelines:** U.S. citizen; unproduced work;
adaptations acceptable if rights have been obtained. **Application procedure:**
send SASE for guidelines and application form after 15 Sep 2000. **Deadline:** 1
Mar 2001; no submission before 1 Nov 2000. **Dates:** Aug 2001.

NATIONAL PLAYWRIGHTS CONFERENCE

O'Neill Theater Center; 234 West 44th St, Suite 901;
    New York, NY 10036–3909; (212) 382–2790, FAX 921–5538
James Houghton, *Artistic Director*
Mary F. McCabe, *Managing Director*
Open to: playwrights. **Description:** 4-week conference at O'Neill Theater
Center, Waterford, CT; 9-12 plays developed and presented as staged readings;
preconference weekend for initial reading and planning. **Financial
arrangement:** stipend, travel, room and board. **Guidelines:** U.S. citizen or
resident. **Application procedure:** send SASE for guidelines after 15 Aug 2000.
Deadline: 1 Nov 2000. **Notification:** Apr 2001. **Dates:** preconference weekend
TBA; conference Jul 2001.

THE NEW HARMONY PROJECT LABORATORY

613 North East St; Indianapolis, IN 46202; (317) 464-1103,
    FAX 635-4201

Anna D. Shapiro, *Artistic Director*

Open to: playwrights, composers, librettists, screenwriters, television writers. **Description:** 4-6 scripts given up to 2 weeks of intensive development with professional community of directors, actors, producers, dramaturgs and musical directors. **Financial arrangement:** $400 stipend; travel, room and board. **Guidelines:** narrative works that "emphasize the dignity of the human spirit and the worth of the human experience." **Application procedure:** 10-page writing sample, project proposal and statement of artistic purpose. **Deadline:** fall 2000, exact date TBA. **Notification:** 15 Mar 2001. **Dates:** May-Jun 2001.

NEW PERSPECTIVES NEW PLAY DEVELOPMENT PROGRAM

New Perspectives Theatre Company; 750 Eighth Ave, #601;
    New York, NY 10036; (212) 730-2030, FAX 730-2030;
    email NPLiteraryMgr@aol.com

Deirdre Hollman, *Literary Manager*

Open to: playwrights. **Description:** 5-10 plays chosen each year for range of developmental services from rehearsed staged readings with audience feedback to full workshop productions; development process varies according to needs of script; special interest in works by women and minority writers and/or works with a multicultural focus; annual staged reading series in May. **Financial arrangement:** free. **Guidelines:** full-length play. **Application procedure:** 15-page dialogue sample, synopsis and character breakdown. **Deadline:** ongoing. **Notification:** 2-6 months from submission date. **Dates:** year-round.

NEW VISIONS/NEW VOICES

The Kennedy Center-Youth and Family Programs; 2700 F Street NW;
    Washington, DC 20566; (202) 416-8880, FAX 416-8297;
    email yfp@kennedy-center.org

Kim Peter Kovac, *Senior Program Director*

Open to: playwrights. **Description:** biennial program; up to 8 plays given rehearsals and staged readings. **Guidelines:** previously unproduced plays for young and family audiences; playwright must be sponsored by theatre; call for information and application. **Financial arrangement:** small stipend. **Application procedure:** sponsoring theatre submits completed application and supporting materials. **Deadline:** 1 Oct 2001. **Notification:** 15 Jan 2002. **Dates:** May 2002.

NEW VOICES PLAY DEVELOPMENT PROGRAM

Plowshares Theatre Company; 2870 East Grand Blvd, Suite 600;
   Detroit, MI 48202-3146; (313) 872-0279, FAX 872-0067;
   email plowshares@earthlink.net;
   Web site http://www.plowshares.org

Gary Anderson, *Producing Artistic Director*

Open to: playwrights, solo performers. **Description:** up to 6 plays-in-progress given 2 weeks of rehearsal with professional company of actors, directors and dramaturgs, culminating in 2 staged readings followed by audience discussion; program provides marketing assistance following development; possible future full production. **Financial arrangement:** $1000 to play chosen best of festival; some travel stipends available. **Guidelines:** African-American playwright; unproduced play addressing the African-American experience. **Application procedure:** 3 copies of script, synopsis, resume and bio. **Deadline:** ongoing. **Dates:** summer 2001. (See Plowshares Theatre Company in Production.)

NEW YORK FOUNDATION FOR THE ARTS
FISCAL SPONSORSHIP PROGRAM

155 Avenue of the Americas, 14th Floor;
   New York, NY 10013-1507; (212) 366-6900, ext 223,
   FAX (646) 486-3285; email sponsor@nyfa.org

Mary Six Rupert, *Program Officer, Services and Technology*

Open to: playwrights, translators, composers, librettists, lyricists, solo performers, screenwriters, television and radio writers. **Description:** program provides fiscal sponsorship, financial services and technical assistance to individuals or organizations without not-for-profit status so that they can seek funds from foundations, corporations and individuals that require not-for-profit status in order to contribute funds. The program has two categories: Artists' Projects (individual artists or collaborating artists); and Emerging Organizations (emerging arts organizations in the process of obtaining not-for-profit status). Program does not offer grants or provide funding. **Financial arrangement:** as a service fee, NYFA retains a percentage of grants and contributions it receives on behalf of a project; $50-100 one time processing fee. **Guidelines:** selection based on artistic excellence, uniqueness and fundability of project, and on artist's previous work and proven ability to complete proposed work. **Application procedure:** write for application form and guidelines. **Deadline:** Nov 2000; Mar 2001; Jul 2001; contact NYFA for exact dates. **Notification:** 6 weeks.

NEWGATE THEATRE NEW PLAY DEVELOPMENT

134 Mathewson St; Providence, RI 02903;
    Web site http://www.newgatetheatre.org
New Works Coordinator

Open to: playwrights, solo performers. **Description:** organization providing year-round developmental services; 3-4 scripts each season receive staged reading, in some cases leading to workshop production. Test Tube Theatre Festival for playwrights interested in deeper rehearsal involvement: 3 full-length plays receive 4-5 weeks of rehearsal culminatng in workshop production. **Financial arrangement:** small stipend and possible housing. **Guidelines:** playwright available for rehearsal process; full-length plays in need of development. **Application procedure:** script, resume and SASE for response. **Deadline:** 15 Oct 2000 for Test Tube Festival; 1 Feb 2001 for regular program. **Dates:** Test Tube Festival: Jan–Feb; regular program: year-round.

THE NEXT STAGE FESTIVAL OF NEW PLAYS

(Formerly The Next Stage)
The Cleveland Play House; 8500 Euclid Ave;
    Cleveland, OH 44106-0189; (216) 795-7010, ext 207,
    FAX 795-7005
Scott Kanoff, *Literary Manager/Resident Director*

Open to: playwrights. **Description:** annual mid-winter festival of 4-8 rehearsed readings over a 1-month period; plays receive 4-6 rehearsal days with director, dramaturg and professional cast and 2 public readings with audience discussion; at least one play will be fully produced in following theatre season. **Financial arrangement:** stipend, travel and housing. **Guidelines:** previously unproduced full-length play or musical; must give theatre 90-day option on future production. **Application procedure:** letter of inquiry, brief synopsis, 10-page dialogue sample, resume, reviews and SASP for acknowledgement of receipt; include cassestte for musicals. **Deadline:** 15 Jun 2001; no submission before 1 May 2001. **Notification:** 2-4 months.

Off-Off Broadway Original Short Play Festival

45 West 25th St; New York, NY 10010–2751; (212) 206–8990,
FAX 206–1429

Karen Keri, *Festival Coordinator*

Open to: playwrights. **Description:** festival production hosted by Love Creek Productions on Theatre Row in New York City; possible publication by Samuel French (see Publication). **Financial arrangement:** free. **Guidelines:** one-acts or segments of full-length plays less than 40 minutes long only; play must have been developed and produced by theatre, professional school or college that has playwriting program; send SASE for application after Jan 2001. **Application procedure:** no submission by playwright; completed application submitted by organization producing work. **Deadline:** May 2001; exact date TBA. **Notification:** within 2 weeks. **Dates:** Jul 2001.

Old Pueblo Playwrights

Box 64914; Tucson, AZ 85728; (520) 743–0940, FAX 743–7245;
email 4stern@azstarnet.com

Chris Stern, *Member*

Open to: playwrights, translators, screenwriters, television and radio writers. **Description:** members meet weekly to develop scripts; staged readings at annual New Play Festival in Jan. **Financial arrangement:** $36 annual dues. **Application procedure:** submit writing sample at weekly meeting. **Deadline:** ongoing. **Dates:** ongoing.

One Acts in Performance

Polaris North, c/o Diane Martella; 1265 Broadway, Room 803;
New York, NY 10001; (212) 684–1985

Diane Martella, *Treasurer/Co-sponsor*

Open to: playwrights. **Description:** approximately every 2 months, 3–5 plays given brief rehearsal period, culminating in workshop production followed by informal audience discussion. **Guidelines:** unproduced one-act play not more than 30 minutes long; 4-character maximum; single set. **Financial arrangement:** free. **Application procedure:** script only. **Deadline:** ongoing. **Notification:** 2–6 weeks. **Dates:** year-round.

ORANGE COUNTY PLAYWRIGHTS' ALLIANCE DEVELOPMENTAL WORKSHOP

Box 6927; Fullerton, CA 92834; (714) 738-3841, 850-1176,
   FAX 738-7833; Web site http://www.ocpaplaywrights.org
Eric Eberwein, *Co-Director*

Open to: playwrights. **Description:** ongoing developmental workshop meeting bimonthly; up to 12 scripts each year receive staged reading or production; annual Page to Stage Contest for one-acts by California writers with $100 1st prize, $50 2nd prize and $25 3rd prize and workshop production for all winners, *deadline:* 1 Jul 2001 (send script with character breakdown and $5 fee), *notification:* Feb 2002. **Financial arrangement:** $80 annual membership fee. **Guidelines:** residents of Orange County and greater Los Angeles area only. **Application procedure:** work sample and resume. **Deadline:** ongoing. **Notification:** 2 months.

PLAYFORMERS

20 Waterside Plaza, Apt 11G; New York, NY 10010; (212) 213-9835
John Fritz, *Executive Director*

Open to: playwrights. **Description:** playwrights' support group meets once a month for readings of works-in-progress and critiques. **Financial arrangement:** $15 initiation fee on acceptance; $75 annual dues. **Guidelines:** playwright invited to attend meetings as guest before applying for membership. **Application procedure:** script and resume. **Deadline:** ongoing. **Dates:** Sep-Jun.

PLAYLABS

The Playwrights' Center; 2301 Franklin Ave;
   Minneapolis, MN 55406-1099; (612) 332-7481;
   email pwcenter@mtn.org; Web site http://www.pwcenter.org
Megan Monaghan, *PlayLabs Artistic Director*

Open to: playwrights, solo performers. **Description:** 4-6 new works given 2 weeks of development with playwright's choice of professional director, dramaturg and Twin Cities actors, culminating in staged reading followed by audience discussion. **Financial arrangement:** honorarium, travel, housing and per diem. **Guidelines:** U.S. citizen or permanent resident; writer must be available to attend entire conference and preconference weekend; unproduced, unpublished play, solo performance piece or mixed-media piece; full-length works preferred. **Application procedure:** application and work sample; send SASE for application after 1 Oct 2000. **Deadline:** 1 Dec 2000. **Notification:** 1 May 2001. **Dates:** preconference weekend May/Jun; 2001, exact dates TBA; conference 8-22 Jul 2001.

PLAYS-IN-PROGRESS FESTIVALS OF NEW WORKS

615 4th St; Eureka, CA 95501; (707) 443-3724

Susan Bigelow-Marsh, *Executive Director*

Open to: playwrights. **Description:** 5 scripts each given full production and 8-10 scripts each given 3-4 weeks of development with actors and directors, culminating in staged reading followed by discussion, in spring or fall festival of new work; ongoing development and August Women's Festival coproduced with Women on Stage, *deadline:* 15 May 2001. **Financial arrangement:** negotiable; housing. **Guidelines:** primarily CA writers; 1 out-of-state writer selected for each festival; unproduced, unpublished play. **Application procedure:** script and resume. **Deadline:** 1 Mar 2001; 1 Jul 2001. **Dates:** Sep 2001; May 2002.

PLAYWRIGHTS' CENTER OF SAN FRANCISCO STAGED READINGS

Box 460466; San Francisco, CA 94146-0466; (415) 626-4603,
    FAX 863-0901; email playctrsf@aol.com;
    Web site http://www.playwrights.org

Sheppard B. Kominars, *Chairman of the Board*

Open to: playwrights. **Description:** developmental program meeting weekly for 1 staged reading, monthly for reading and discussion of works-in-progress. **Financial arrangement:** $55 annual membership fee; some scholarships available for students. **Application procedure:** completed application. **Deadline:** ongoing.

PLAYWRIGHTS FORUM

Box 5322; Rockville, MD 20848; (301) 816-0569; email pforum@erols.com;
    Web site http://www.erols.com/pforum/welcome.htm

Ernest Joselovitz, *President*

Open to: playwrights. **Description:** ongoing developmental program including 3-tier range of membership options: Forum 1, workshop program offering three 3-month sessions a year for apprentice playwrights; Forum 2, professional playwriting groups meeting biweekly; and Associate membership offering participation in many of Forum's auxiliary programs but not in workshops; depending on type of membership, members variously eligible for in-house and public readings, Musical Theatre Wing, mentorships, special classes, including Rewrites and Screenwriting, production observerships, free theatre tickets, Internet activities, semiannual conference, organization's newsletter and handbook, published series of members' scripts, and a commissioning program for original plays for young audiences. **Financial arrangement:** for Forum 1, $90 per 15-week session; for Forum 2, $90 every 4 months; Associate membership $25 fee a year; financial aid available. **Guidelines:** resident of mid-Atlantic area only; for Forum 2, prefers produced playwright or former Forum 1 participant, willing to make long-term commitment; send SASE or visit Web site site for further information. **Application procedure:** for Forum 1, send SASE or call for information; for Forum 2, script and bio; for Associate membership, send annual fee. **Deadline:** for Forum 1, 10 Sep 2000, 10 Jan 2001, 10 May 2001; for Forum 2, ongoing. **Notification:** 4 weeks.

PLAYWRIGHTS GALLERY

Abraham Goodman House: Theatre Wing; 2124 Broadway;
    Box 2700; New York, NY 10023; (212) 595-4597,
    FAX 595-6129; email savadge@juno.com
Deborah Savadge, *Coordinator*

Open to: playwrights, solo performers. **Description:** developmental workshop meeting bimonthly Sep-Jun; plays receive staged readings at 3-day festivals in fall and spring. **Financial arrangement:** playwrights share cost of space rental. **Application procedure:** 15-20 page work sample. **Deadline:** 3 Sep 2000. **Notification:** 1 Oct 2000.

PLAYWRIGHTS' KITCHEN ENSEMBLE

c/o Coronet Theatre; 368 North La Cienega; Los Angeles, CA 90048;
    FAX (310) 652-6401
Dan Lauria, *Artistic Director*

Open to: playwrights. **Description:** 1 play per week given staged reading by celebrity actors and directors for audience including theatre, film and TV professionals. **Financial arrangement:** free. **Guidelines:** full-length play unproduced in Los Angeles. **Application procedure:** script only. **Deadline:** 31 Dec 2000; no submission before 1 Sep 2000.

PLAYWRIGHTS LAB

(Formerly Playwrights Circle)
Pulse Ensemble Theatre; 432 West 42nd St; New York, NY 10036;
    (212) 695-1596, FAX 736-1255
Brian Richardson, *Company Manager*

Open to: playwrights, solo performers, screenwriters. **Description:** 4-month workshop meeting weekly culminating in public staged reading or workshop production in either Open Pulse Arts Lab (OPAL) for one-acts or the Studio Series for full-length plays. **Guidelines:** experienced playwrights residing in NY area only. **Financial arrangement:** $100 monthly fee. **Application procedure:** completed application and professional recommendation. **Deadline:** ongoing. **Notification:** ongoing. **Dates:** year-round.

PLAYWRIGHTS' PLATFORM
164 Brayton Rd; Boston, MA 02135; (617) 630-9704;
    Web site http://www.tiac.net/users/ghorton/playplat.html
Beverly Creasey, *President*
Open to: playwrights. **Description:** ongoing developmental program including
weekly workshop held at Massachusetts College of Art, staged readings,
summer festival of full productions, dramaturgical and referral services.
Financial arrangement: playwright receives percentage of box office for
festival productions; participants encouraged to become members of
organization ($35 annual dues). **Guidelines:** MA resident available for regular
meetings only; unpublished, unproduced play; write for membership
information. **Application procedure:** letter of inquiry only. **Deadline:** ongoing.

PLAYWRIGHTS PROJECT
Henry Street Settlement/Abrons Arts Center; 466 Grand St;
    New York, NY 10002-4804; (212) 598-0400, FAX 388-1418
Jonathon Ward, *Director of Drama Program*
Open to: playwrights. **Description:** 5-6 plays developed during two 5-week
programs, culminating in workshop production. **Financial arrangement:** $500
production budget. **Guidelines:** New York City playwrights only. **Application
procedure:** first act or first 10 pages of script, synopsis, character breakdown,
resume or brief bio; finalists will be interviewed. **Deadline:** ongoing.
Notification: 5 weeks. **Dates:** year-round.

PLAYWRIGHTS THEATRE OF NEW JERSEY
NEW PLAY DEVELOPMENT PROGRAM
33 Green Village Rd; Madison, NJ 07940; (973) 514-1787, ext 18
Peter Hays, *Literary Manager*
Open to: playwrights. **Description:** new plays developed through sit-down
readings, staged readings and productions; liaison with other producing
theatres provided. **Financial arrangement:** playwright receives royalty.
Guidelines: American playwright; previously unproduced play; send SASE for
guidelines. **Application procedure:** 10-page dialogue sample, developmental
history, if any, resume and SASP for acknowledgment of receipt. **Deadline:** 30
Apr 2001; no submission before 1 Sep 2000. **Notification:** 8 months. **Dates:**
year-round.

PLAYWRIGHTS WEEK

The Lark Theatre Company; 939 Eighth Ave, Suite 301;
New York, NY 10019; (212) 246-2676, FAX 246-2609;
email info@larktheatre.org; Web site http://www.larktheatre.org
Literary Department
Open to: playwrights. **Description:** 8 plays-in-progress given 10 hours of rehearsal, culminating in staged reading followed by review with Lark dramaturgical staff; scripts may receive subsequent "BareBones" workshop production. **Financial arrangement:** possible travel and housing. **Guidelines:** 1-submission limit per year. **Application procedure:** script and $15 fee. **Deadline:** 31 Dec 2000. **Notification:** 15 Mar 2001. **Dates:** 3-10 Jun 2001.

PUERTO RICAN TRAVELING THEATRE PLAYWRIGHTS' UNIT

141 West 94th St; New York, NY 10025; (212) 354-1293,
FAX 307-6769
Allen Davis III, *Director*
Open to: playwrights, solo performers. **Description:** 7-9-month workshops comprised of 2 units, 1 for professional playwrights, 1 for beginners; weekly meetings; spring staged reading series; City "In Sight" showcase production series. **Financial arrangement:** $100 fee per workshop cycle. **Guidelines:** resident of New York City area; Latino or other minority playwright or playwright interested in multicultural theatre. **Application procedure:** for professional unit, submit full-length play; beginners contact director. **Deadline:** 30 Sep 2000. **Notification:** within 2 weeks. **Dates:** Oct 2000-Jul 2001.

REMEMBRANCE THROUGH THE PERFORMING ARTS NEW PLAY DEVELOPMENT

Box 162446; Austin, TX 78716; (512) 329-9118,
FAX 329-9118
Marla Macdonald, *Director of New Play Development*
Open to: playwrights. **Description:** 8 playwrights chosen annually for summer developmental workshops, culminating in work-in-progress productions in fall; plays subsequently given referral to nationally recognized theatres for world premieres. **Financial arrangement:** free. **Guidelines:** resident of central TX; full-length play that has not received Equity production. **Application procedure:** script, synopsis, resume and SASE. **Deadline:** ongoing.

THE RICHARD RODGERS AWARDS

American Academy of Arts and Letters; 633 West 155th St;
New York, NY 10032-7599; (212) 368-5900, FAX 491-4615
Richard Rodgers Awards
Open to: playwrights, composers, librettists, lyricists. **Description:** 1 or more works a year given full production, studio/lab production or staged reading by not-for-profit theatre in New York City; writer(s) participate in rehearsal process. **Financial arrangement:** free. **Guidelines:** U.S. citizen or permanent resident; new work by writer/composer not already established in musical theatre; innovative, experimental material encouraged; 1-submission limit; previous submissions ineligible. **Application procedure:** send SASE for application and information. **Deadline:** 1 Nov 2000. **Notification:** Mar 2001.

THE SCHOOLHOUSE

Owens Rd; Croton Falls, NY 10519; (914) 234-7232
Douglas Michael, *Literary Manager*
Open to: playwrights. **Description:** about 6 plays a year receive development with director and actors, culminating in public reading and possible full production; ongoing weekly writer's group. **Financial arrangement:** small fee to help offset costs. **Guidelines:** resident of Westchester or Putnam counties, NY or Fairfield County, CT, who can participate in program; prefers full-length plays. **Application procedure:** script or excerpt (at least 10 pages) and letter of inquiry. **Deadline:** ongoing. **Notification:** 1 month.

THE SCRIPTEASERS

3404 Hawk St; San Diego, CA 92103-3862; (619) 295-4040,
FAX 299-2084
Jonathan Dunn-Rankin, *Corresponding Secretary*
Open to: playwrights, screenwriters, television writers. **Description:** writers, directors and actors meet every other Friday evening in private home for cold readings of new scripts, followed by period of constructive criticism; 1 or 2 rehearsed staged readings a year presented at local theatres as showcases. **Financial arrangement:** donations of $1 accepted at each reading. **Guidelines:** guest writer must attend at least 2 readings before submitting script; unproduced script by new or established writer who is resident of San Diego County; write or call for guidelines. **Application procedure:** write or call for guidelines. **Deadline:** ongoing.

SHENANDOAH INTERNATIONAL PLAYWRIGHTS

ShenanArts; 717 Quick's Mill Rd; Staunton, VA 24401; (540) 248-1868,
    FAX 248-7728; email theatre@shenanarts.org;
    Web site http://www.shenanarts.org
Robert Graham Small, *Artistic Director*
Kathleen Tosco, *Managing Director*
Open to: playwrights, screenwriters. **Description:** 4-week retreat for 4-6
American writers and 4 international writers at Pennyroyal farm in
Shenandoah Valley; program geared to facilitate major rewrite or new draft of
existing script; personal writing balanced by workshops and staged readings
with professional company of dramaturgs, directors and actors. **Financial
arrangement:** travel, room and board. **Guidelines:** competitive admission
based on submitted work. **Application procedure:** 2 copies of completed draft
of script to be worked on at retreat; personal statement of applicant's
background as a writer; SASP for acknowledgment of receipt; write or call for
guidelines. **Deadline:** 1 Feb 2001. **Notification:** after 10 Jun 2001. **Dates:** Jul-
Aug 2001.

SOUTHERN APPALACHIAN PLAYWRIGHTS' CONFERENCE

Southern Appalachian Repertory Theatre; Box 1720;
    Mars Hill, NC 28754; (828) 689-1384, FAX 689-1272;
    email sart@mhc.edu
Milli Way, *Managing Director*
Open to: playwrights. **Description:** up to 5 writers selected to participate in
annual 3-day conference at which 1 work by each writer is given informal
reading and critiqued by panel of theatre professionals; 1 work may be
selected for production as part of summer 2001 season. **Financial
arrangement:** room and board; writer of work selected for production receives
$500 honorarium. **Guidelines:** unproduced, unpublished play. **Application
procedure:** script with synopsis, character breakdown and resume. **Deadline:**
31 Oct 2000. **Dates:** Apr 2001.

SOUTHWEST FESTIVAL FOR NEW PLAYS

Stages Repertory Theatre; 3201 Allen Pkwy, #101;
    Houston, TX 77019; (713) 527-0240, FAX 527-8669
K. David Cochran, *Festival Coordinator*
    (Also see entry in Production)

CHILDREN'S THEATRE PLAYWRIGHTS' DIVISION

Open to: playwrights. **Description:** 4 plays chosen for development with actors and director over period of 1 week, culminating in presentation of scenes; 1 play receives staged reading. **Financial arrangement:** stipend, contingent on funding. **Guidelines:** play for 4-10-year-old audience to be performed by adult actors; maximum 50 minutes long; cast limit of 8; play not produced professionally. **Application procedure:** script only; author's name should not appear on script; include title page with author info. **Deadline:** 14 Feb 2001; no submission before 1 Oct 2000. **Notification:** May 2001. **Dates:** Jun 2001.

LATINO PLAYWRIGHTS' DIVISION

Open to: playwrights. **Description:** 4 plays chosen for development with professional actors and director over period of 1 week, culminating in presentation of scenes; 1 play receives staged reading. **Financial arrangement:** stipend, contingent on funding. **Guidelines:** Latino playwright; play written in Spanish must be sent with English translation; play not produced professionally. **Application procedure:** script only; author's name should not appear on script; include title page with author info. **Deadline:** 14 Feb 2001; no submission before 1 Oct 2000. **Notification:** May 2001. **Dates:** Jun 2001.

TEXAS PLAYWRIGHTS' DIVISION

Open to: playwrights. **Description:** 4 plays chosen for development with dramaturg, director and actors over period of 1 week, some plays receive staged readings. **Financial arrangement:** stipend, contingent on funding. **Guidelines:** TX native or resident or non-TX playwright writing on TX theme; play not produced professionally; prefers small cast. **Application procedure:** script only; author's name should not appear on script; include title page with author info. **Deadline:** 14 Feb 2001; no submission before 1 Oct 2000. **Notification:** May 2001. **Dates:** Jun 2001.

WOMEN'S PLAYWRIGHTS' DIVISION

(Formerly Women's Repertory Project)
Open to: playwrights. **Description:** 4 plays chosen for development with professional actors and director over period of 1 week, some plays receive presentation of scenes; 1 play receives full reading. **Financial arrangement:** stipend, contingent on funding. **Guidelines:** woman playwright; play not produced professionally. **Application procedure:** script only; author's name should not appear on script; include title page with author info. **Deadline:** 14 Feb 2001; no submission before 1 Oct 2000. **Notification:** May 2001. **Dates:** Jun 2001.

STREISAND FESTIVAL OF NEW JEWISH PLAYS

c/o San Diego Center for Jewish Culture; The Lawrence Family JCC;
4126 Executive Dr; La Jolla, CA 92037;
(619) 457-3161, ext 149, FAX 457-2422; email lfjccla@aol.com

Lynette Allen, *Executive Director*

Open to: playwrights, composers, librettists, lyricists. **Description:** 4 plays receive 2½ days of rehearsal, culminating in staged reading followed by audience discussion; possible future full production. **Financial arrangement:** travel and housing. **Guidelines:** play or musical with Jewish content. **Application procedure:** 3 copies of script and resume. **Deadline:** 15 Jan 2001. **Notification:** Apr 2001. **Dates:** Jun 2001.

SUMMERNITE

School of Theatre, Stevens Bldg; Northern Illinois University;
DeKalb, IL 60115-2854; (815) 753-8258, FAX 753-8415

Christopher Markle, *Artistic Director*

Open to: playwrights. **Description:** up to 10 plays receive staged readings during 15-week program; 2 plays chosen for subsequent full production. **Financial arrangement:** royalties for plays chosen for production. **Guidelines:** special interest in large-cast full-length plays or translations not previously produced in Chicago area. **Application procedure:** synopsis and letter of inquiry. **Deadline:** 1 Sep 2000. **Notification:** 1 Dec 2000. **Dates:** May–Aug 2001.

THE SUNDANCE INSTITUTE FEATURE FILM PROGRAM

8557 West Olympic Blvd; Beverly Hills, CA 90211; (310) 360-1981,
FAX 360-1969; Web site http://www.sundance.org

Open to: playwrights, screenwriters, filmmaking teams (e.g., writer/director). **Description:** program includes 5-day Screenwriters Labs each Jan and Jun offering participants one-on-one problem-solving sessions with professional screenwriters; 3-week Filmmakers Lab in Jun in which projects are explored through work with directors, writers, actors, cinematographers, producers, editors and other resource personnel; network/advisory service offers practical and creative assistance to selected projects. **Financial arrangement:** travel, room and board for at least 1 writer/filmmaker per project; possible room and board for additional members of team. **Guidelines:** completed "compelling, original, narrative feature film scripts (they can be based on a true story or be adaptations of plays, novels, short stories, etc.) which represent the unique vision of the writer and/or director"; special interest in supporting new talent and artists in transition (e.g., theatre artist who wants to work in film, writer who wants to direct); send SASE for guidelines. **Application procedure:** completed application, cover letter, first 5 pages of screenplay, synopsis, bios of project participants and $30 fee; applicants who pass 1st round of selection will be asked to send full screenplay. **Deadline:** 5 May 2001. **Notification:** Jul 2001.

THE SUNDANCE THEATRE LABORATORY

8857 West Olympic Blvd; Beverly Hills, CA 90211; (310) 360-1981,
 FAX 360-1969; email philip_himberg@sundance.org;
 Web site http://www.sundance.org
Philip Himberg, *Artistic Director, Sundance Theatre*
Robert Blacker, *Artistic Director, Sundance Theatre Lab*
Open to: playwrights, solo performers. **Description:** 8-10 scripts workshopped
for 18 days. **Financial arrangement:** travel, room and board. **Guidelines:** full-
length play, new adaptation and/or translation of classic material, musical, play
for young audiences, solo piece; playwright-director teams encouraged.
Application procedure: send SASE for guidelines and application. **Deadline:** 15
Dec 2000. **Notification:** Apr 2001. **Dates:** Jul 2001.

THE TEN-MINUTE MUSICALS PROJECT

Box 461194; West Hollywood, CA 90046; (323) 651-4899
Michael Koppy, *Producer*
Open to: composers, librettists, lyricists, solo performers. **Description:** up to 10
brief pieces selected during annual cycle for possible inclusion in full-length
anthology-musicals to be produced at Equity theatres in U.S. and Canada;
occasionally some pieces workshopped using professional actors and director.
Financial arrangement: $250 royalty advance with equal share of licensing
royalties when produced. **Guidelines:** complete work with a definite beginning,
middle and end, 7-14 minutes long, in any musical style or genre; adaptations of
strongly structured material in the public domain, or for which rights have been
obtained, are encouraged; cast of 2-10, prefers 6-10; write for guidelines.
Application procedure: script, lead sheets and cassette of sung material.
Deadline: 31 Aug 2001. **Notification:** 30 Nov 2001.

THEATREWORKS/USA COMMISSIONING PROGRAM

Theatreworks/USA; 151 West 26th St, 7th Floor; New York, NY 10001;
 (212) 647-1100, FAX 924-5377; email info@theatreworksusa.org
Barbara Pasternack, *Artistic Director*
Open to: composers, librettists, lyricists. **Description:** step commissioning
process, possibly leading to 2-week developmental workshop and production.
Financial arrangement: free. **Guidelines:** works dealing with issues relevant to
target audiences; special interest in historical/biographical subject matter and
musical adaptations of fairy tales and traditional or contemporary classics; 1 hour
long; cast of 5-6 actors, set suitable for touring. **Application procedure:** prefers
treatment with sample scenes, lyric sheets and cassette of music; will accept
script only. **Deadline:** ongoing. **Notification:** 6 months.

THE TUESDAY GROUP
321 West 24th St, #16E; New York, NY 10011; (212) 645-3143
Larry Kunofsky, *Coordinator*
Open to: playwrights. **Description:** group meets every 2 weeks to read and discuss members' works; some plays workshopped with resident directors and ensemble; members' work showcased in annual Tuesdayfest short play festival. **Financial arrangement:** $60 fee per trimester. **Guidelines:** New York City playwright. **Application procedure:** writing sample and letter of inquiry with SASE for response. **Deadline:** ongoing. **Notification:** 2 months.

UNIVERSITY OF ALABAMA NEW PLAYWRIGHTS' PROGRAM
Department of Theatre and Dance; University of Alabama;
  Box 870239; Tuscaloosa, AL 35487-0239; (205) 348-9032,
  FAX 348-9048; email pcastagn@woodsquad.as.ua.edu;
  Web site http://www.as.ua.edu/theatre/npp.htm
Paul C. Castagno, *Director and Dramaturg*
Open to: playwrights, composers, librettists, lyricists, solo performers. **Description:** opportunity for writer to develop unproduced script or to pursue further development of produced work, culminating in full production; writer may visit campus several times during rehearsal process and is required to offer limited playwriting workshops during visit(s). **Financial arrangement:** substantial stipend, travel and expenses. **Guidelines:** writer with some previous experience and script that has had some development; special interest in works with Southern themes. **Application procedure:** script or synopsis and letter of inquiry. **Deadline:** submit Aug-Mar only. **Notification:** 6 months. **Dates:** fall-spring. **Special programs:** department will also consider one-acts for festival by its directing students and writers' proposals for workshops with its playwriting and acting students; submit by 1 Oct for Janusfest, a festival of new full-length plays.

THE WATERFRONT ENSEMBLE, INC.
Box 1486; Hoboken, NJ 07030; (201) 963-2235;
  email info@waterfrontensemble.org;
  Web site http://www.waterfrontensemble.org
Jason Grote, *Literary Manager*
Open to: playwrights, translators, solo performers. **Description:** playwright-driven company of actors, directors and playwrights that meets weekly to work on new plays in preparation for productions in New York and New Jersey; 25 one-acts and 3 full-length plays produced each year. **Financial arrangement:** $75 membership fee per year; $25 for 2 months (suggested donation). **Guidelines:** NY/NJ-area playwright. **Application procedure:** up to 30-page writing sample and resume. **Deadline:** ongoing. **Notification:** 4-12 months. **Dates:** year-round. **Special programs:** New Jersey All Ages Playwright Festival, *deadline:* 1 May 2001; *dates:* Jul 2001; call or write for more information.

WESTBETH THEATRICAL DEVELOPMENT PROGRAM

Westbeth Theatre Center; 151 Bank St; New York, NY 10014;
(212) 691-2272, FAX 924-7185;
Web site http://www.westbeththeatre.com
Steven Bloom, *Artistic Associate*
Open to: playwrights, composers. **Description:** program to explore ideas and concepts that eventually mature into dramatic texts; individual development meetings with staff; possible future production. **Financial arrangement:** free. **Guidelines:** send SASE for detailed guidelines. **Application procedure:** no unsolicited scripts; proposal, synopsis and resume. **Deadline:** ongoing. **Notification:** 4-8 months. (See Westbeth Theatre Center in Production.)

WILLIAMSTOWN THEATRE FESTIVAL

100 East 17th St, 3rd Floor; New York, NY 10003; (212) 228-2286,
FAX 228-9091; Web site http://www.wtfestival.org
Michael Ritchie, *Producer*
Open to: playwrights, composers, librettists, lyricists. **Description:** 4 plays each season given public reading. **Financial arrangement:** stipend, travel and housing. **Guidelines:** American playwright; play not professionally produced. **Application procedure:** agent submission only. **Deadline:** 15 Feb 2001; no submission before 1 Oct 2000.

WOMEN OF COLOR PRODUCTIONS

163 East 104th St, Suite 4E; New York, NY 10029; (212) 501-3842
Jacqueline Wade, *Executive Producer*
Open to: playwrights, composers, librettists, lyricists, screenwriters, solo performers. **Description:** monthly reading series; possible inclusion in Through Her Eyes: Women of Color Arts Festival (see below). **Financial arrangement:** $10 fee per reading. **Guidelines:** prefers woman playwright of color or any writer whose work features female characters of color; special interest in one-acts. **Application procedure:** application, 2 copies of script, 1-page synopsis, professional recommendation, character breakdown, resume with SASE for reading series; write for application and guidelines. **Deadline:** ongoing. **Dates:** Sep 2000-Jun 2001 for reading series. **Special programs:** Through Her Eyes: Women of Color Arts Festival: annual 3-week festival held at various venues throughout New York City; 2 producing levels: Tier 1, 10 guest artists receive $300-600 honorarium, rehearsal space, technical staff and marketing support; Tier 2, 40 playwrights contribute to production cost, receive percentage of ticket sales, marketing support and 10-15 hours rehearsal time; send application, professional recommendation, resume and $35 fee for Festival; write for application and guidelines; *deadline:* 1 Dec 2000; *notification:* Jan 2001; *dates:* Mar 2001.

WOMEN PLAYWRIGHTS PROJECT
Centenary Stage Company; 400 Jefferson St;
Hackettstown, NJ 07840; (908) 979–0900, FAX 813–1984
Catherine Rust, *Project Director*
Open to: playwrights. **Description:** 1 play given 1 week of rehearsal with professional actors and director, followed by staged reading and possible mainstage production. **Financial arrangement:** $150-200 honorarium; travel, room and board. **Guidelines:** woman playwright; full-length play preferred. **Application procedure:** script only. **Deadline:** 1 Nov 2000. **Notification:** 1 Jan 2001. **Dates:** Mar 2001.

WOMEN'S WORK PROJECT
New Perspectives Theatre Company; 750 Eighth Ave, Suite 601;
New York, NY 10036; (212) 730–2030, FAX 730–2030
Celia Braxton, *Women's Work Director*
Open to: playwrights. **Description:** 2 playwrights chosen for 6-9 month residency to develop full-length play. **Financial arrangement:** free. **Guidelines:** woman playwright; special interest in works by writers of color; previously unproduced full-length play; call for application and guidelines. **Application procedure:** completed application and script. **Deadline:** 15 May 2001. **Notification:** 1 Aug 2001. **Dates:** year-round.

WORKING STAGES
Colorado Shakespeare Festival; Campus Box 277;
Boulder, CO 80309–0277; (303) 492–1527;
email kevin.brown@colorado.edu
Kevin Brown, *Dramaturg*
Open to: playwrights. **Description:** 3 plays chosen for 1-2 week workshops culminating in staged reading. **Financial arrangement:** travel and housing provided. **Guidelines:** resident of AZ, southern CA, CO, NM, northern TX or UT; professionally unproduced play. **Application procedure:** 2 copies of script, synopsis, character breakdown, resume and letter of inquiry with SASE for response. **Deadline:** 6 Jan 2001. **Notification:** 1 Apr 2001. **Dates:** Jul-Aug 2001.

THE YOUNG PLAYWRIGHTS URBAN RETREAT

Young Playwrights Inc.; 321 West 44th St, Suite 906;
New York, NY 10036; (212) 307-1140, FAX 307-1454;
email writeaplay@aol.com; Web site http://youngplaywrights.org

Coordinator

Open to: playwrights. **Description:** 2-week New York City retreat for young playwrights; guest lectures by prominent American playwrights; one-on-one sessions with teaching artists; 3 intensive daily writing workshops; viewing of Broadway and Off-Broadway plays; development of new short play for public performance with professional actors and director. **Financial arrangement:** $1190 tuition includes meals, transportation in NYC, supervised housing and theatre tickets; limited financial aid available. **Guidelines:** playwright aged 14-21. **Application procedure:** completed application, writing sample, recommendation from teacher or mentor and $100 fee (applied to tuition; refundable if applicant does not attend); call for application. **Deadline:** 1 Apr 2001. **Dates:** 15-23 Jul 2001.

PART TWO
CAREER OPPORTUNITIES

Agents

Fellowships and Grants

Emergency Funds

State Arts Agencies

Colonies and Residencies

Membership and Service Organizations

AGENTS

I'm wondering whether or not I should have an agent. Where can I get information to help me decide?

Send a check or money order for $7 and a 55¢ SASE to the Association of Authors' Representatives, Box 237201, Ansonia Station, New York, NY 10023, to receive their brochure which describes the role of the literary agent, the canon of ethics, and which contains their membership list. The list may be found at AAR's Web site: http://www.AAR-online.org. Also, see Useful Publications for books you may consult on the subject, ask your fellow playwrights, look at copies of scripts for the names of agents and make an intelligent guess as to whether they would be interested in representing your work.

How do I select the names of appropriate agents to contact?

All of the agents listed here represent playwrights. The Dramatists Guild also has a list of agents available to its members, and provides advice on relationships with agents (see Membership and Service Organizations). You may come across names that appear on none of these lists, but be wary, especially if someone tries to charge you a fee to read your script.

How do I approach an agent?

Do not telephone, do not drop in, do not send manuscripts. Write a brief letter describing your work and asking if the agent would like to see a script. Enclose your professional resume; it should show that you have had work produced or published, and make clear that you look at writing as an ongoing career, not an occasional hobby. If you're a beginning writer who's just finished your first play, you'd probably do better to work on getting a production rather than an agent.

ABRAMS ARTISTS AGENCY
275 7th Ave, 26th Floor; New York, NY 10001; (646) 486-4600
Charmaine Ferenczi, Jack Tantleff, *Agents*

THE AGENCY
1800 Ave of the Stars, Suite 400; Los Angeles, CA 90067; (310) 551-3000
Nick Mechanic, Steve Whitney, Jerome Zeitman, *Agents*

ALAN BRODIE REPRESENTATION LTD.
211 Piccadilly; London W1V 9LD; England; 44-171-917-2871
Alan Brodie, Sarah McNair, *Agents*

ANN ELMO AGENCY
60 East 42nd St; New York, NY 10165; (212) 661-2880
Mari Cronin, Letti Lee, *Agents*

THE BARBARA HOGENSON AGENCY, INC.
165 West End Ave, Suite 19C; New York, NY 10023; (212) 874-8084
Barbara Hogenson, *Agent*

BERMAN, BOALS, & FLYNN
208 West 30th St, Suite 401; New York, NY 10001; (212) 868-1068
Judy Boals, Jim Flynn, *Agents*

THE BETHEL AGENCY
311 West 43rd St, Suite 602; New York, NY 10036; (212) 664-0455
Lewis Chambers, *Agent*

BRET ADAMS LTD.
448 West 44th St; New York, NY 10036; (212) 765-5630
Bret Adams, Bruce Ostler, *Agents*

DON BUCHWALD & ASSOCIATES
10 East 44th St; New York, NY 10017; (212) 867-1200
Adeena Kasseboom, *Agent*

THE DRAMATIC PUBLISHING COMPANY
311 Washington St; Box 129; Woodstock, IL 60098; (815) 338-7170
Linda Habjan, Dana Wolworth (musicals), *Agents*

Duva-Flack Associates, Inc.
200 West 57th St, Suite 1008; New York, NY 10019; (212) 957-9600
Robert Duva, *Agent*

Elisabeth Marton Agency
1 Union Square, Room 612; New York, NY 10003-3303; (212) 255-1908
Tonda Marton, *Agent*

Farber Literary Agency
14 East 75th St, 2E; New York, NY 10021; (212) 861-7075
Ann Farber, Seth Farber, *Agents*

Fifi Oscard Associates
24 West 40th St, 17th Floor; New York, NY 10018; (212) 764-1100
Carolyn French, Carmen LaVia, Kevin McShane, Fifi Oscard,
Peter Sawyer, *Agents*

Flora Roberts
157 West 57th St; New York, NY 10019; (212) 355-4165
Sarah Douglas, *Agent*

Gage Group
9255 Sunset Blvd, Suite 515; Los Angeles, CA 90069; (310) 859-8777
Martin Gage, *Agent*

The Gersh Agency
130 West 42nd St, Suite 2400; New York, NY 10036; (212) 997-1818
John Buzzetti, Peter Hagan, Scott Yoselow, *Agents*

Graham Agency
311 West 43rd St; New York, NY 10036; (212) 489-7730
Earl Graham, *Agent*

Harden-Curtis Associates
850 Seventh Ave, Suite 405; New York, NY 10019; (212) 977-8502
Mary Harden, *Agent*

HAROLD MATSON COMPANY, INC.
276 Fifth Ave; New York, NY 10001; (212) 679-4490
Ben Camardi, Jonathan Matson, *Agents*

HELEN MERRILL, LTD.
295 Lafayette St, Suite 915; New York, NY 10012; (212) 226-5015
Beth Blickers, Patrick Herold, Morgan Jenness, *Agents*

INTERNATIONAL CREATIVE MANAGEMENT
40 West 57th St; New York, NY 10019; (212) 556-5600
Mitch Douglas, Sarah Jane Leigh, *Agents*

THE JOYCE KETAY AGENCY
1501 Broadway, Suite 1908; New York, NY 10036; (212) 354-6825
Joyce P. Ketay, Carl Mulert, Wendy Streeter, *Agents*

THE KOPALOFF COMPANY
6399 Wilshire, Suite 414; Los Angeles, CA 90048; (323) 782-1854
Don Kopaloff, Arnold Soloway, *Agents*

LANTZ AGENCY
200 West 57th St, Suite 503; New York, NY 10019; (212) 586-0200
Robert Lantz, *Agent*

PARAMUSE ARTISTS ASSOCIATES, INC.
25 Central Park W; New York, NY 10023; (212) 758-5055
Mike Sbabo, *Agent*

PEREGRINE WHITTLESEY AGENCY
345 East 80th St, #31F; New York, NY 10021; (212) 737-0153
Peregrine Whittlesey, *Agent*

PINDER LANE & GARON-BROOKE ASSOCIATES
159 West 53rd St; New York, NY 10019; (212) 489-0880
Nancy Coffey, Dick Duane, Robert Thixton, *Agents*

ROBERT A. FREEDMAN DRAMATIC AGENCY
1501 Broadway, Suite 2310; New York, NY 10036; (212) 840-5760
Robert A. Freedman, Selma Luttinger, *Agents*

ROSENSTONE/WENDER
3 East 48th St, 4th Floor; New York, NY 10017; (212) 832-8330
Ronald Gwiazda, Howard Rosenstone, Phyllis Wender, *Agents*

SAMUEL FRENCH
45 West 25th St; New York, NY 10010-2751; (212) 206-8990
Lawrence Harbison, *Senior Editor*

SHUKAT COMPANY, LTD.
340 West 55th St, Suite 1A; New York, NY 10019; (212) 582-7614
Maribel Rivas, Scott Shukat, Patricia McLaughlin, *Agents*

STEPHEN PEVNER, INC.
248 West 73rd St, 2nd Floor; New York, NY 10023; (212) 496-0474
Stephen Pevner, *Producer*

THE SUSAN GURMAN AGENCY
865 West End Ave, #15A; New York, NY 10025; (212) 749-4618
Gail Eisenberg, Susan Gurman, *Agents*

SUSAN SCHULMAN A LITERARY AGENCY
454 West 44th St; New York, NY 10036; (212) 713-1633

WILLIAM MORRIS AGENCY
1325 Ave of the Americas; New York, NY 10019; (212) 586-5100
Peter Franklin, David Kalodner, George Lane, Owen Laster, Biff Liff, Gilbert Parker, Roland Scahill, Susan Weaving, *Agents*

WRITERS & ARTISTS AGENCY
19 West 44th St, Suite 1000; New York, NY 10036; (212) 391-1112
Jeff Berger, William Craver, *Agents*

FELLOWSHIPS AND GRANTS

Can I apply directly to all the programs listed in this section?

No. A number of the grant programs we list must be applied to by a producing or presenting organization. However, you should be aware that these programs exist so that you can bring them to the attention of organizations with which you have a working relationship. All or most of the funds disbursed benefit the individual artist by covering commissioning fees, residencies and other expenses related to the creation of new works.

How can I enhance my chances of winning an award?

Apply for as many awards for which you qualify; once you have written the first grant proposal, you can often, with little additional work, adapt it to fit other guidelines. Start early. This is so important that we give full listings to the increasing number of awards offered in alternate years, even when the deadline falls outside the period this *Sourcebook* covers. Use the Submission Calendar in the back of this book to help you plan your campaign. In the case of all awards for which you can apply directly, write for guidelines and application forms months ahead. Study the guidelines carefully and follow them meticulously. Don't hesitate to ask for advice and assistance from the organization to which you are applying. Submit a well-thought-out, clearly written, neatly typed application—and make sure it arrives in the organization's office by the deadline. (Never assume, without checking, that the deadline is the postmark date.)

THE ALFRED HODDER FELLOWSHIP

The Council of the Humanities; Joseph Henry House;
   Princeton University; Princeton, NJ 08544-5264;
   (609) 258-4717, FAX 258-2783;
   Web site http://www.princeton.edu/~humcounc

Open to: playwrights, translators. **Frequency:** annual. **Remuneration:** $45,600
(approx) fellowship. **Guidelines:** emerging artist; writer spends academic year
at Princeton pursuing independent project; prefers writer outside of academia.
Application procedure: maximum 10-page work sample, 2-3 page project
proposal and resume; send SASE for guidelines. **Deadline:** 1 Nov 2000.

THE AMERICAN-SCANDINAVIAN FOUNDATION

56-58 Park Ave; New York, NY 10016; (212) 879-9779,
   FAX 249-3444; email grants@amscan.org;
   Web site http://www.amscan.org

Fellowship Program

Open to: playwrights, translators, composers, librettists, lyricists. **Frequency:**
annual. **Remuneration:** $3000-18,000. **Guidelines:** U.S. citizen or permanent
resident with undergraduate degree; grants and fellowships for research and
study in Scandinavian countries. **Application procedure:** application, sup-
plementary materials and $10 fee. **Deadline:** 1 Nov 2000. **Notification:** Mar 2001.

ARIZONA COMMISSION ON THE ARTS
PERFORMING ARTS FELLOWSHIP

417 West Roosevelt St; Phoenix, AZ 85003; (602) 255-5882,
   FAX 256-0282; email general@arizonaarts.org;
   Web site http://az.arts.asu.edu/artscomm

Claire West, *Performing Arts Director*

Open to: playwrights, composers. **Frequency:** award rotates triennially among
disciplines. **Remuneration:** $5000 fellowship. **Guidelines:** AZ resident 18 years
of age or older who is not enrolled for more than 3 credit hours at college or
university; send SASE for guidelines and application. **Application procedure:**
application and work sample. **Deadline:** Sep 2000 for composers; Sep 2001 for
playwrights, exact dates TBA. **Notification:** Mar 2001 for composers; Mar 2002
for playwrights.

ARTIST TRUST

1402 Third Ave, Suite 404; Seattle, WA 98101-2118;
   (206) 467-8734, FAX 467-9633; email info@artisttrust.org;
   Web site http://www.artisttrust.org
Heather Dwyer, Program Director

FELLOWSHIPS

Open to: playwrights, composers, librettists, lyricists, screenwriters, radio and television writers. **Frequency:** award rotates among disciplines. **Remuneration:** $5500 award. **Guidelines:** WA resident only; practicing professional artist of exceptional talent and demonstrated ability; award based on creative excellence and continuing dedication to an artistic discipline; send SASE for guidelines (available mid-Apr). **Application procedure:** application and work sample. **Deadline:** mid-Jun, exact date TBA (16 Jun in 2000) for composers, librettists, lyricists, screenwriters, radio & television writers; mid-Jun 2002; exact date TBA, for playwrights.

GAP (GRANTS FOR ARTIST PROJECTS)

Open to: playwrights, composers, librettists, lyricists, screenwriters, radio and television writers. **Frequency:** annual. **Remuneration:** grant up to $1200. **Guidelines:** WA resident only; grant provides support for artist-generated projects which can include (but is not limited to) the development, presentation or completion of new work; award based on quality of work as represented by supporting material and on creativity and feasibility of proposed project; write for guidelines (available Dec 2000). **Application procedure:** application and work sample. **Deadline:** 23 Feb 2001.

ARTISTS-IN-BERLIN PROGRAMME

To obtain application only:
German Academic Exchange Service (DAAD); 950 Third Ave,
19th Floor; New York, NY 10022; (212) 758-3223,
FAX 755-5780; email daadny@daad.org;
All applications and inquiries to:
Deutscher Akademischer Austauschdienst (DAAD);
Markgrafenstr 37/Taubenstr 30; D-10117 Berlin, Germany;
49-030-202-2080, FAX 49-030-204-1267;
email bkp.berlin@daad.de; Web site http://www.daad.org

Open to: playwrights, composers. **Frequency:** annual. **Remuneration:** monthly grant to cover living costs and rent during 1-year residency in Berlin (6 months in exceptional cases); workspace provided or paid for; travel for writer and any members of immediate family who will be staying in Berlin for period of residency; health and accident insurance; in some cases specific projects such as readings or publications can be subsidized. **Guidelines:** to enable 15-20 internationally known and qualified young artists to pursue own work while participating in city's cultural life and making contact with local artists; must reside in Berlin for period of grant; German nationals and foreign writers who are resident in Germany ineligible; write for guidelines. **Application procedure:** application; samples of published work (no manuscripts), preferably in German, otherwise in English or French, for playwrights; scores, records, tapes or published work for composers. **Deadline:** 31 Dec 2000. **Notification:** May 2001. **Dates:** residency begins between 1 Jan and 30 Jun 2002.

ARTS INTERNATIONAL/THE FUND FOR U.S. ARTISTS AT INTERNATIONAL FESTIVALS AND EXHIBITIONS

251 Park Ave S, 5th Floor; New York, NY 10010; (212) 674-9744,
FAX 674-9092; email thefund@artsinternational.org;
Web site http://www.artsinternational.org/programs/index.htm

Open to: performing artists and organizations. **Frequency:** triannual. **Remuneration:** grants of up to $25,000 (most grants $1000-10,000) to cover expenses related to festival participation including travel, lodging, artist's fees and per diem. **Guidelines:** U.S. citizen or permanent resident who has been invited to international festival. **Application procedure:** application; work sample; proposal; bio; copy of invitation from festival; full budget showing all costs of participation in festival and festival's contribution to these costs. **Deadline:** 5 Sep 2000; 16 Jan 2001; 2 May 2001. **Notification:** 2 months. (See National Endowment for the Arts International Partnerships in this section.)

ASIAN CULTURAL COUNCIL

437 Madison Ave, 37th Floor; New York, NY 10022;
(212) 812-4300, FAX 812-4299; email acc@accny.org;
Web site http://www.asianculturalcouncil.org

ACC RESIDENCY PROGRAM IN ASIA

Open to: playwrights, composers, librettists, lyricists. **Frequency:** annual. **Remuneration:** amount varies. **Guidelines:** to support American artists, scholars, and specialists undertaking collaborative research, teaching or creative residencies at cultural and educational institutions in East and Southeast Asia. **Application procedure:** write for application, include project description. **Deadline:** 1 Feb 2001.

JAPAN-UNITED STATES ARTS PROGRAM

Open to: playwrights, composers, librettists, lyricists. **Frequency:** annual. **Remuneration:** amount varies. **Guidelines:** to support residencies in Japan for American artists for a variety of purposes, including creative activities (other than performances), research projects, professional observation tours and specialized training. **Application procedure:** write for application, include project description. **Deadline:** 1 Feb 2001.

ATLANTA BUREAU OF CULTURAL AFFAIRS

675 Ponce de Leon Ave; Atlanta, GA 30308; (404) 817-6815,
FAX 817-6827; email bcacas@mindspring.com;
Website http://www.bcaatlanta.org
Camille Russell Love, *Director*

ARTISTS PROJECT

Open to: playwrights, composers, librettists, lyricists. **Frequency:** annual. **Remuneration:** grant up to $4000. **Guidelines:** practicing professional artist; Atlanta resident for at least 1 year prior to deadline. **Application procedure:** write for guidelines and application. **Deadline:** 15 Dec 2000. **Notification:** Mar 2001.

MAYOR'S FELLOWSHIPS IN THE ARTS

Open to: playwrights, composers, librettists, lyricists. **Frequency:** award rotates among disciplines. **Remuneration:** $5000 award. **Guidelines:** practicing professional artist; Atlanta resident for at least 3 consecutive years prior to deadline; playwright may apply under literary or theatre arts; composer, librettist, lyricist apply under music. **Application procedure:** write for guidelines and application. **Deadline:** Dec 2000, exact date TBA, for composers, librettists, lyricists; Dec 2001, exact date TBA, for playwrights. **Notification:** Mar 2001.

AURAND HARRIS CHILDREN'S THEATRE GRANTS AND FELLOWSHIPS

The Children's Theatre Foundation of America; Box 8067;
New Orleans, LA 70182; (504) 283-8868, FAX 866-0502
Orlin Corey, *President*

FELLOWSHIPS

Open to: playwrights. **Frequency:** annual. **Remuneration:** $2500 maximum award. **Guidelines:** U.S. resident; funds to be used for specific projects or professional development of theatre artists who work in the area of children's theatre. **Application procedure:** write for guidelines. **Deadline:** 1 May 2001. **Notification:** 1 Sep 2001.

GRANTS

Open to: not-for-profit theatres. **Frequency:** annual. **Remuneration:** grant up to $3000. **Guidelines:** grant to assist in production costs of premiere of new play for children including expenses to enable playwright to participate in rehearsals and attend performances. **Application procedure:** write for guidelines. **Deadline:** 1 May 2001. **Notification:** 1 Sep 2001.

BUSH ARTIST FELLOWS PROGRAM

The Bush Foundation; E-900 First National Bank Bldg;
332 Minnesota St; St. Paul, MN 55101; (651) 227-5222
Julie Dalgleish, *Program Director*

Open to: playwrights, composers, screenwriters. **Frequency:** award rotates biennially among disciplines. **Remuneration:** $40,000 in equal monthly installments for 12-18 months. **Guidelines:** MN, ND, SD or western WI resident at least 25 years old who is not a student; playwright must have had at least 1 play given full production or workshop production for which admission was charged; screenwriter must have had 1 public staged reading or workshop production for which admission was charged, or screenplay sale or option. **Application procedure:** write for guidelines and application. **Deadline:** next deadline for playwrights, composers and screenwriters Oct 2000, exact date TBA. **Notification:** Apr 2001.

CINTAS FELLOWSHIPS
c/o Institute of International Education;
    U.S. Student Programs Division; 809 United Nations Plaza;
    New York, NY 10017-3580; (212) 984-5565,
    FAX 984-5325; email cintas@iie.org;
    Web site http://www.iie.org/fulbright/cintas
Scott Pentzer, *Program Officer*
Open to: playwrights. **Frequency:** annual; award rotates among artistic disciplines. **Remuneration:** $10,000 paid in quarterly stipends. **Guidelines:** artist of Cuban decent or citizenship living outside of Cuba. **Application procedure:** call or visit Web site after Dec 2000 for guidelines. **Deadline:** exact date TBA.

DOBIE-PAISANO FELLOWSHIP
University of Texas at Austin; J. Frank Dobie House;
    702 East Dean Keeton St; Austin, TX 78705; (512) 471-8542,
    FAX 471-9997; email aslate@mail.utexas.edu
Audrey Slate, *Director*
Open to: playwrights. **Frequency:** annual. **Remuneration:** living allowance to cover 6-month residency at 265-acre ranch; free housing; families welcome. **Guidelines:** native Texan, or playwright who has lived in TX for at least 2 years or has published work about TX; ordinarily 2 writers selected each year. **Application procedure:** write for application after 1 Oct 2000. **Deadline:** 26 Jan 2001. **Notification:** May 2001.

THE DON AND GEE NICHOLL FELLOWSHIPS IN SCREENWRITING
Academy of Motion Picture Arts and Sciences; 8949 Wilshire Blvd;
    Beverly Hills, CA 90211-1972; (310) 247-3059;
    Web site http://www.oscars.org/nicholl
Greg Beal, *Program Coordinator*
Open to: playwrights, screenwriters. **Frequency:** annual. **Remuneration:** up to 5 fellowships of $25,000. **Guidelines:** playwright, screenwriter or fiction writer who has not worked as a professional screenwriter for theatrical films or television or sold screen or television rights to any original story, treatment, stage play, screenplay or teleplay; 1st-round selection based on submission of original screenplay or screen adaptation of writer's own original work, 100-130 pages, written in standard screenplay format; send SASE for guidelines after 1 Jan 2001; application may be obtained from Web site. **Application procedure:** application, screenplay and $30 application fee. **Deadline:** 1 May 2001. **Notification:** 1st-round selection Aug 2001; winners late Oct 2001.

ELECTRONIC ARTS GRANT PROGRAM

Experimental Television Center; 109 Lower Fairfield Rd;
  Newark Valley, NY 13811; (607) 687-4341, FAX 687-4341;
  email etc@experimentaltvcenter.org;
  Web site http://www.experimentaltvcenter.org
Sherry Miller Hocking, *Program Director*

FINISHING FUNDS

Open to: media artists, including writers and composers, involved in creation of film, audio, video or computer-generated time-based works. **Frequency:** annual. **Remuneration:** up to $1000. **Guidelines:** resident of NY State; funds to be used to assist completion of work which is time-based in conception and execution; work must be presented as installation performance, on video, as Web site production or must utilize new technologies; work must be completed before 30 Sep 2001; write for guidelines. **Application procedure:** 3 copies of application, project description, work samples and resume. **Deadline:** 15 Mar 2001. **Notification:** 6-8 weeks.

PRESENTATION FUNDS

Open to: not-for-profit organizations presenting audio, film, video or computer-generated time-based works. **Frequency:** ongoing. **Remuneration:** grant of up to $750 to assist presentation of work and artist's involvement in activities related to presentation. **Guidelines:** NY State organization; event must be open to public; write for guidelines. **Application procedure:** individual may not apply; application and supporting materials submitted by organization well in advance of event. **Deadline:** ongoing. **Notification:** 15th of month following month of submission.

FULBRIGHT SENIOR SCHOLAR AWARDS FOR FACULTY AND PROFESSIONALS

Council for International Exchange of Scholars (CIES);
  3007 Tilden St NW, Suite 5L; Washington, DC 20008-3009;
  (202) 686-7877, FAX 362-3442; email apprequest@cies.iie.org;
  Web site http://www.cies.org

Open to: scholars and professionals in all areas of theatre and the arts, including playwrights, translators, composers, librettists and lyricists. **Frequency:** annual. **Remuneration:** grant for university lecturing or research in one of more than 130 countries for 2-9 months; amount varies with country of award; travel; maintenance allowance for living costs of grantee and possibly family. **Guidelines:** U.S. citizen; Ph.D., MFA or comparable professional qualifications; university or college teaching experience for lecturing awards; application may be obtained from Web site. **Application procedure:** application. **Deadline:** 1 Aug 2001. **Notification:** up to 11 months, depending on country.

GEORGE BENNETT FELLOWSHIP

Phillips Exeter Academy; Exeter, NH 03833–1104;
   Web site http://www.exeter.edu
Charles Pratt, *Coordinator, Selection Committee*

Open to: playwrights. **Frequency:** annual. **Remuneration:** academic-year stipend of $6000; room and board for fellow and family. **Guidelines:** individual who is seriously contemplating or pursuing a career as a writer (in any genre) and who needs time and freedom from material considerations to complete a project in progress; committee favors playwrights who have not yet been produced commercially or at a major not-for-profit theatre; fellow expected to make self and talents available in informal and unofficial way to students interested in writing; send SASE for guidelines and application or visit Web site (no phone inquiries). **Application procedure:** application, work sample, statement concerning work-in-progress, names of 2 references and $5 fee. **Deadline:** 1 Dec 2000. **Notification:** 15 Mar 2001. **Dates:** Sep 2001–Jun 2002.

HARVARD UNIVERSITY BUNTING FELLOWSHIP PROGRAM

(Formerly Bunting Fellowship Program)
The Radcliffe Institute for Advanced Study; Application Office;
   34 Concord Ave; Cambridge, MA 02138; (617) 495–8212,
   FAX 495–8136; Web site http://www.radcliffe.edu/bunting

Open to: playwrights, composers, librettists. **Frequency:** annual. **Remuneration:** up to $40,000 1-year fellowship. **Guidelines:** to provide opportunity and support for professionals of demonstrated accomplishment and exceptional promise to complete substantial project in their field; full-time appointment; fellow required to reside in Boston area and expected to present work-in-progress in public colloquia during year; office or studio space, auditing privileges and access to libraries and other resources at Harvard provided; call, write or visit Web site for guidelines and application. **Application procedure:** application. **Deadline:** 2 Nov 2000. **Notification:** Apr 2001. **Dates:** 15 Sep 2001–15 Aug 2002.

THE JAPAN FOUNDATION
152 West 57th St, 39th Floor; New York, NY 10019;
(212) 489-0299, FAX 489-0409;
Web site http://www.jfny.org/jfny/index.html
Artists Fellowship Program
Open to: specialists in the fields of fine arts, performing arts, music, journalism and creative writing, including playwrights, composers, librettists, lyricists and screenwriters. **Frequency:** annual. **Remuneration:** monthly stipend of ¥370,000 (about $3425) or ¥430,000 (about $4000), depending on grantee's professional career; travel; other allowances. **Guidelines:** U.S. citizen or permanent resident; fellowship of 2-6 months, not to be held concurrently with another major grant, to support project substantially related to Japan. **Application procedure:** write for guidelines and application, stating theme of project, present position and citizenship. **Deadline:** 1 Dec 2000. **Notification:** early-mid Apr 2001. **Dates:** residency begins between 1 Apr 2001 and 31 Mar 2002.

JOHN SIMON GUGGENHEIM MEMORIAL FOUNDATION
90 Park Ave; New York, NY 10016; (212) 687-4470,
FAX 697-3248; email fellowships@gf.org;
Web site http://www.gf.org
Open to: playwrights, composers. **Frequency:** annual. **Remuneration:** 1-year fellowship (in 2000, 182 fellowships with average grant of $34,863). **Guidelines:** citizen or permanent resident of U.S. or Canada; recipient must demonstrate exceptional creative ability; grant to support research in any field of knowledge or creation in any of the arts under the freest possible conditions. **Application procedure:** write for guidelines. **Deadline:** 1 Oct 2000. **Notification:** Apr 2001.

THE KENNEDY CENTER FUND FOR NEW AMERICAN PLAYS

The John F. Kennedy Center for the Performing Arts; 2700 F St NW;
    Washington, DC 20566; (202) 416-8024, FAX 416-8205;
    email rsfoster@kennedy-center.org;
    Web site http://kennedy-center.org/fnap

Max Woodward, *Director*

Rebecca Foster, *Manager*

Open to: not-for-profit professional theatres. **Frequency:** annual. **Remuneration:** $10,000 grant to playwright whose work theatre is producing, plus grant (amount dependent on quality of proposal and need) to theatre (6 in 1999); occasional $2500 Roger L. Stevens Award to playwright whose work shows "extraordinary promise" (4 in 1999). **Guidelines:** grant to theatre covers living and travel expenses for playwright during minimum 4 weeks of rehearsal and during any necessary additional rehearsals and rewrites in course of run; grant also covers expenses exceeding theatre's budget allocation for hiring of director, designer and guest actors; limit of 1 proposal per theatre; translations and musicals ineligible; write or visit Web site for guidelines after 15 Jan 2001. **Application procedure:** playwright may not apply; proposal and supporting materials submitted by theatre. **Deadline:** May 2001, exact date TBA.

THE KLEBAN AWARD

c/o New Dramatists; 424 West 44th St; New York, NY 10036;
    (212) 757-6960

Christie Brown, *Director of Playwright and Literary Services*

Open to: librettists and/or lyricists (TBA). **Frequency:** annual. **Remuneration:** TBA ($100,000 each to lyricist and librettist, paid in installments of $50,000 a year, in 1999-2000). **Guidelines:** applicant whose work has received a full or workshop production, or who has been a member or associate of a professional musical workshop or theatre group (e.g., ASCAP or BMI workshops; see Development); writer whose work has been performed on the Broadway stage for a cumulative period of 2 years ineligible; write for guidelines. **Application procedure:** application and work sample. **Deadline:** Sep 2000; exact date TBA.

MANHATTAN THEATRE CLUB PLAYWRITING FELLOWSHIPS

311 West 43rd St, 8th Floor; New York, NY 10036; (212) 399–3000,
 FAX 399–4329; Web site http://www.mtc-nyc.org
Literary Assistant
Open to: playwrights. **Frequency:** annual. **Remuneration:** $10,000 fellowship.
Guidelines: New York-based playwright who has completed formal education
and can demonstrate financial need; writers from all backgrounds encouraged to
apply; fellowship includes commission for new play, production assistantship, 1-
year residency at MTC; send SASE for guidelines or visit Web site. **Application
procedure:** sample script, resume, statement of purpose and letter of
recommendation from theatre professional or professor. **Deadline:** 31 Dec 2000.

MARIN ARTS COUNCIL INDIVIDUAL ARTIST GRANT

251 North San Pedro Rd; San Rafael, CA 94903; (415) 499–8350,
 FAX 499–8537; email alison@marinarts.org;
 Web site http://www.marinarts.org
Alison DeJung, *Grants Coordinator*
Open to: playwrights, composers. **Frequency:** biennial. **Remuneration:** $2000–
10,000 grant. **Guidelines:** Marin County artist only; award given based on
completion of original work. **Application procedure:** application and work
sample. **Deadline:** Jan 2001; exact date TBA. **Notification:** Jun 2001.

MARY FLAGLER CARY CHARITABLE TRUST
COMMISSIONING PROGRAM

122 East 42nd St, Room 3505; New York, NY 10168;
 (212) 953–7705, FAX 953–7720; email gmorgan@carytrust.org
Gayle Morgan, *Music Program Director*
Open to: performance institutions including theatre and opera companies.
Frequency: biennial. **Remuneration:** grant to help not-for-profit professional
organization commission new musical work from established or emerging
composer; amount varies (total of $400,000 available for 1999 grants).
Guidelines: New York City organization only; funds to be used to compensate
composer and librettist for creative work and to cover copying costs; write for
guidelines. **Application procedure:** individual may not apply; letter of application
and representative audiotape of composer's music submitted by organization.
Deadline: 30 Jun 2001.

MATURE WOMAN SCHOLARSHIP AWARD

The National League of American Pen Women; 1300 17th St NW;
Washington, DC 20036-1973; (202) 785-1997
Mary Jane Hillery, *National Scholarship Chairman*
All inquiries to: 66 Willow Rd; Sudbury, MA 01776-2663

Open to: playwrights, composers, librettists, lyricists. **Frequency:** biennial. **Remuneration:** $1000 grant. **Guidelines:** American woman age 35 and over; 3 awards (1 in art, 1 in music, 1 in letters) to further creative goals of women at age when encouragement can lead to realization of long-term purposes; present and past NLAPW members ineligible; send SASE for guidelines. **Application procedure:** work sample; statement of purpose for which money will be used; proof that applicant is over age 35; statement that applicant is not a member of NLAPW; and $8 fee. **Deadline:** 1 Oct 2001. **Notification:** 1 Mar 2002.

THE MCKNIGHT INTERDISCIPLINARY FELLOWSHIP GRANT

Intermedia Arts; 2822 Lyndale Ave S; Minneapolis, MN 55408;
(612) 871-4444, FAX 871-6927;
email allstaff@intermediaarts.org;
Web site http://www.intermediaarts.org
Sandy Agustín, *Director of Community and Education Programs*

MINNESOTA FELLOWSHIP

Open to: interdisciplinary artists. **Frequency:** annual. **Remuneration:** $25,000 fellowship; $2000 in travel expenses. **Guidelines:** resident of MN for 1 year before application; mid-career interdisciplinary artists; fellowship and technical support to pursue educational/presentational activity during 18-month fellowship period; send SASE for guidelines after Oct 2000. **Application procedure:** application, 1-page maximum artist statement, 10-page maximum work sample, resume and optional SASP for acknowledgment of receipt. **Deadline:** 14 Jan 2001. **Notification:** spring 2001.

NATIONAL MCKNIGHT INTERDISCIPLINARY FELLOW IN RESIDENCE

Open to: interdisciplinary artists. **Frequency:** biennial. **Remuneration:** $10,000 artist's fee; up to $4000 in travel expenses. **Guidelines:** artists with accomplished body of work; must have teaching and/or mentoring experience; must be in Minneapolis for at least 4 weeks (not necessarily consecutive) during 2002; send SASE for guidelines. **Application procedure:** letter of intent no more than 2 pages in length describing artist's body of interdisciplinary work, teaching and/or mentoring experience and previous residency experience. **Deadline:** 1 Jan 2001 intent to apply; Mar 2001 application; exact date TBA. **Notification:** May 2001.

MEET THE COMPOSER GRANT PROGRAMS

2112 Broadway, Suite 505; New York, NY 10023; (212) 787–3601;
FAX 787–3745; email mtrevino@meetthecomposer.org;
Web site http://www.meetthecomposer.org

MEET THE COMPOSER/AMERICAN SYMPHONY ORCHESTRA LEAGUE MUSIC ALIVE

Mark Treviño, *Senior Program Manager*

Open to: composers. **Frequency:** annual. **Remuneration:** grant for composer's fee ($2500 per residency week); composer's expenses (up to one roundtrip fare for every 2-week residency, and up to $175 per day for food and lodging); orchestra expenses (up to $1000 per residency week). **Guidelines:** supports composer residencies ranging from 2 to 8 weeks in duration scheduled in conjunction with performance(s) of the composer's work; the work(s) may be a world premiere or existing work(s) by a living American composer; the performance of a world premiere or commissioned work is not a requirement of the program; residency weeks may be scheduled contiguously or divided into multiple visits and must take place between 1 Sep 2001 and 31 Aug 2002; the minimum duration for each residency visit is 7 days, inclusive of travel; write for complete guidelines or refer to MTC Web site. **Application procedure:** individuals may not apply; orchestras apply on behalf of composer. **Deadline:** 15 Aug 2001.

MEET THE COMPOSER FUND

William Towns, *Program Manager*

Open to: theatre, music-theatre and opera companies; arts presenters; musical organizations; TV production companies, radio stations; performing ensembles of all kinds (jazz, chamber, new music, etc.). **Frequency:** 4 times annually. **Remuneration:** up to $250 per individual composer. **Guidelines:** awards are based solely on the overall quality of the application, including merit of composer participation, level of audience/community involvement, and general strength of compositions; administered by Meet The Composer in New York and by four regional offices that comprise the National Affiliate Network; write for complete guidelines or refer to MTC Web site. **Application procedure:** varies from region to region; individuals may not apply; performing organizations apply on behalf of composer. **Deadlines:** 1 Oct 2000; 2 Jan 2001; 1 Apr 2001; 1 Jun 2001.

MEET THE COMPOSER/NATIONAL ENDOWMENT FOR THE ARTS COMMISSIONING MUSIC/USA

Mark Treviño, *Senior Program Manager*

Open to: theatre, music-theatre and opera companies; arts presenters; public TV and radio stations; performing ensembles of all kinds (jazz, chamber, new music, etc.). **Frequency:** annual. **Remuneration:** commissioning grant up to $30,000 to cover composer, librettist, TV writer and/or radio writer fees and copying costs for opera or music-theatre work (amount based on scope and length of work). **Guidelines:** organizations that have been producing or presenting for at least 3 years; plans must involve full production of new work and a minimum of 4 performances for a single organization or a minimum of 6 for a consortium; write for complete guidelines or refer to MTC Web site. **Application procedure:** individuals may not apply; 1 host organization submits application and supporting materials; application may be from a single organization for grants up to $10,000 or from consortium of organizations for grants up to $30,000. **Deadline:** 15 Jan 2001.

NEW RESIDENCIES

Mark Treviño, *Senior Program Manager*

Open to: theatre, music-theatre and opera companies; arts presenters; musical organizations; performing ensembles of all kinds (jazz, chamber, new music, etc.). **Frequency:** annual. **Remuneration:** grant for composer's salary ($40,000 per annum for 2 years; $20,000 toward 3rd year salary, must be matched 1-to-1 by host organizations); up to $25,000 toward production expenses (each expenditure must be matched 1-to-1 by host organizations); up to $15,000 toward institutional partnership building activities; possible $1500 for composer's relocation costs. **Guidelines:** up to 4 organizations, including at least 2 producing or presenting organizations and at least 1 community-based organization, form Residency Partnerships to sponsor 3-year composer residency; composer writes works for all host organizations and works a minimum of 60 hours per month "making music a positive force in community life" through organizing cultural events, teaching, recruiting other composers to community work, etc.; host organizations produce residency works, provide office space and logistical support, and offer health insurance for composer; write for complete guidelines or refer to MTC Web site. **Application procedure:** individuals may not apply; performing organizations apply on behalf of composer. **Deadline:** 15 Sep 2000.

NATIONAL ENDOWMENT FOR THE ARTS
INTERNATIONAL PARTNERSHIPS

1100 Pennsylvania Ave NW, Room 704; Washington, DC 20506;
(202) 682-5429, FAX 682-5024;
Web site http://www.arts.gov
Pennie Ojeda, *International Coordinator*

ARTSLINK PROJECTS

All applications and inquiries to: CEC International Partners;
12 West 31st St; New York, NY 10001-4415; (212) 643-1985,
FAX 643-1996; email artslink@cecip.org

Open to: creative, interpretive and traditional artists, including playwrights, translators, composers, librettists, lyricists and solo performers; award rotates biennially among disciplines. **Frequency:** annual. **Remuneration:** grant up to $6000 (most grants $1500-3500). **Guidelines:** U.S. citizen or permanent resident; to enable individual artist or groups of up to 5 artists to work with their counterparts in Central or Eastern Europe, the former Soviet Union or the Baltics; mutually beneficial collaborative project that will enrich artist's work and/or create new work that draws inspiration from knowledge and experience gained in country visited; write for guidelines. **Application procedure:** application and supporting materials. **Deadline:** next deadline for playwrights: 16 Jan 2002. **Notification:** Apr 2002.

THE FUND FOR U.S. ARTISTS AT INTERNATIONAL
FESTIVALS AND EXHIBITIONS

All applications and inquiries to: Arts International;
251 Park Ave S, 5th Floor; New York, NY 10010;
(212) 674-9744, FAX 674-9092;
email thefund@artsinternational.org

Open to: performing artists and organizations. **Frequency:** triannual. **Remuneration:** grants of up to $25,000 (most grants $1000-10,000) to cover expenses related to festival participation including travel, lodging, artists' fees and per diem. **Guidelines:** U.S. citizen or permanent resident who has been invited to international festival. **Application procedure:** application; work sample; proposal; bio; copy of invitation from festival; full budget showing all costs of participation in festival and festival's contribution to these costs. **Deadline:** 5 Sep 2000; 16 Jan 2001; 2 May 2001. **Notification:** 2 months. (See Arts International in this section.)

UNITED STATES/JAPAN CREATIVE ARTISTS' FELLOWSHIPS

All applications and inquiries to: Japan/U.S. Friendship Commission;
1120 Vermont Ave NW, Suite 925; Washington, DC 20005;
(202) 418-9800; email artist@jusfc.gov;
Web site http://www.jusfc.gov

Open to: creative, interpretive or traditional artists, including playwrights, translators, composers, librettists and lyricists. **Frequency:** annual. **Remuneration:** monthly stipend to cover housing, living expenses and modest professional support services; round-trip transportation for artist and family members; stipend to study Japanese language in U.S. if necessary. **Guidelines:** U.S. citizen or permanent resident; to enable established artist to pursue discipline in Japan for 6 consecutive months; artist who has spent more than 3 months in Japan ineligible. **Application procedure:** write or call for guidelines and application materials. **Deadline:** 26 Jun 2001. **Notification:** Sep 2001.

NATIONAL ENDOWMENT FOR THE ARTS LITERATURE PROGRAM FELLOWSHIPS FOR TRANSLATORS

1100 Pennsylvania Ave NW, Room 720; Washington, DC 20506;
(202) 682-5428; Web site http://arts.endow.gov
Amy Stolls, *Literature Specialist*

Open to: translators. **Frequency:** annual. **Remuneration:** $20,000 fellowship. **Guidelines:** previously published translators of exceptional talent; guidelines available Jan 2001. **Application procedure:** write for guidelines and application. **Deadline:** Mar 2001; exact date TBA.

NATIONAL ENDOWMENT FOR THE HUMANITIES DIVISION OF PUBLIC PROGRAMS/HUMANITIES PROJECTS IN MEDIA

1100 Pennsylvania Ave NW; Washington, DC 20506;
(202) 606-8269, FAX 606-8557; Web site http://www.neh.gov
James J. Dougherty, *Assistant Director*

Open to: independent radio and television writers and producers. **Frequency:** annual. **Remuneration:** varies. **Guidelines:** support for planning, writing or production of, as well as collaboration on, television and radio projects focused on issues central to the humanities, and aimed at a national adult or broad regional audience; no adaptations of literary works. **Application procedure:** submit draft proposal before making formal application; write or visit Web site for guidelines. **Deadline:** 11 Sep 2000 and 16 Apr 2001 for consultation grants; 1 Nov 2000 for planning grants; 1 Feb 2001 for planning, scripting and production grants. **Notification:** Nov 2000 for Sep deadline; Mar 2001 for Nov deadline; Jul 2001 for Feb and Apr deadlines.

NATIONAL ENDOWMENT FOR THE HUMANITIES DIVISION OF RESEARCH PROGRAMS/COLLABORATIVE RESEARCH

1100 Pennsylvania Ave NW; Washington, DC 20506;
(202) 606–8209; email mbackas@neh.gov;
Web site http://www.neh.gov
Margot Backas, *Senior Academic Advisor*

Open to: translators. **Frequency:** annual. **Remuneration:** amount varies according to project. **Guidelines:** U.S. citizen or resident for 3 years; money to support collaborative projects to translate into English works that provide insight into the history, literature, philosophy and artistic achievements of other cultures and that make available to scholars, students, teachers and the public the thought and learning of those civilizations. **Application procedure:** application and supporting materials; write for guidelines. **Deadline:** 1 Sep 2000. **Notification:** Apr 2001.

NEW PLAY COMMISSIONS IN JEWISH THEATRE

National Foundation for Jewish Culture; 330 Seventh Ave, 21st Floor;
New York, NY 10001; (212) 629–0500, ext 205, FAX 629–0508;
email nfjc@jewishculture.org;
Web site http://www.jewishculture.org
Kim Bistrong, *Grants Administrator*

Open to: North American not-for-profit theatres. **Frequency:** annual. **Remuneration:** grant of $1000–5000. **Guidelines:** approximately 5 awards a year to theatres that have completed at least 2 seasons of public performances and are commissioning either new full-length play, adaptation, work for young audiences, musical or opera dealing substantively with issues of Jewish history, tradition, values or contemporary life; theatre must commit to presenting at least a public workshop production and/or staged reading of work, followed by discussion with audience; funds may be applied to commissioning fee, playwright's residency expenses or workshop costs; write, call or email for guidelines. **Application procedure:** completed proposal, cover sheet and supporting materials, submitted by theatre. **Deadline:** 1 Oct 2000. **Notification:** Dec 2000; exact date TBA.

NEW YORK FOUNDATION FOR THE ARTS (NYFA)
155 Ave of the Americas, 14th Floor; New York, NY 10013-1507;
(212) 366-6900, FAX 366-1778; email nyfaafp@artswire.org;
Web site http://nyfa.org
Penelope Dannenberg, *Director of Programs*

ARTISTS' FELLOWSHIPS

Open to: playwrights, composers, librettists, screenwriters. **Frequency:** award alternates biennially among disciplines. **Remuneration:** $7000 fellowship. **Guidelines:** NY State resident for 2 years prior to deadline; students ineligible. **Application procedure:** application and supporting materials; application seminars held each Sep. **Deadline:** next deadline for playwrights, composers, librettists and screenwriters Oct 2001; exact date TBA.

ARTISTS IN THE SCHOOL COMMUNITY

Open to: schools. **Description:** matching grant to assist schools that bring in artists, including playwrights, composers, librettists and lyricists, for residencies of 12 days-10 months; residency activities include artist-conducted student, teacher or parent workshops, lecture-demonstrations, readings and performances. Financial arrangement: artist is paid by school; recommended minimum fee of $250 a day. **Guidelines:** artist must be NY state resident. **Application procedure:** application from school; individual artist may not apply but is encouraged to write for guidelines and to collaborate with eligible sponsors to set up residencies; artist may also contact program for information and for help in finding sponsors. **Deadline:** 2 Apr 2001; subsidiary deadlines for smaller grants in Oct, Nov, Feb, Jun each year. **Notification:** Jul 2001. **Dates:** Sep 2001-Jun 2002.

NEW YORK THEATRE WORKSHOP PLAYWRITING FELLOWSHIP
New York Theatre Workshop; 79 East 4th St; New York, NY 10003;
(212) 780-9037, FAX 460-8996
Chiori Miyagawa, *Artistic Associate*
Open to: playwrights. **Frequency:** annual. **Remuneration:** commission; amount of award varies. **Guidelines:** writer of color under 30 years of age and resident of New York City; must be available to attend monthly group meetings and 1-week summer retreat. **Application procedure:** script, artistic statement, resume and cover letter. **Deadline:** TBA; contact theatre in Jan 2001 for exact date.

PEW FELLOWSHIPS IN THE ARTS
The University of the Arts; 230 South Broad St, Suite 1003;
    Philadelphia, PA 19102; (215) 875-2285, FAX 875-2276;
    Web site http://www.pewarts.org
Melissa Franklin, *Director*
Open to: playwrights, composers, screenwriters. **Frequency:** annual; award rotates among various disciplines (next award for playwrights, composers, screenwriters will be in 2004). **Remuneration:** up to 12 $50,000 fellowships. **Guidelines:** to give artists living in Southeastern PA the opportunity to dedicate themselves wholly to the development of their work for up to 2 years; students not eligible; call or write for application and guidelines. **Application procedure:** application and work sample. **Deadline:** TBA.

PILGRIM PROJECT
156 Fifth Ave, Suite 400; New York, NY 10010; (212) 627-2288,
    FAX 627-2184
Davida Goldman, *Secretary*
Open to: playwrights, solo performers, individual producers and theatre companies. **Frequency:** ongoing. **Remuneration:** grant of $1000-7000. **Guidelines:** grant toward cost of reading, workshop production or full production of play that deals with questions of moral significance. **Application procedure:** script only; write for further information. **Deadline:** ongoing.

THE PLAYWRIGHTS' CENTER GRANT PROGRAMS
2301 Franklin Ave East; Minneapolis, MN 55406-1099;
    (612) 332-7481; email pwcenter@mtn.org;
    Web site http://www.pwcenter.org
Carlo Cuesta, *Executive Director*

JEROME PLAYWRIGHT-IN-RESIDENCE FELLOWSHIPS

Open to: playwrights, solo performers. **Frequency:** annual. **Remuneration:** 5 1-year fellowships of $7200. **Guidelines:** U.S. citizen or permanent resident; emerging playwright whose work has not received more than 2 professional full productions; fellow must spend year in residence at Center, where fellow has access to developmental workshops, readings and other services; send SASE for guidelines. **Application procedure:** application and supporting materials. **Deadline:** 15 Sep 2000. **Notification:** 15 Jan 2001. **Dates:** 1 Jul 2001-30 Jun 2002.

MANY VOICES MULTICULTURAL COLLABORATION GRANTS

Open to: playwrights, translators, composers, librettists, solo performers, screenwriters. **Frequency:** annual, contingent on funding. **Remuneration:** $200–2000 grant each to 2-4 teams. **Guidelines:** team of 2 or more artists of differing cultural backgrounds with commitment from MN organization to produce proposed collaborative work; team's lead artist must be MN playwright of color. **Application procedure:** send SASE for guidelines. **Deadline:** 31 Jul 2001. **Notification:** 1 Oct 2001. **Dates:** 1 Oct 2001-30 Jun 2002.

MANY VOICES PLAYWRITING RESIDENCY AWARDS

Open to: playwrights, solo performers. **Frequency:** annual, contingent on funding. **Remuneration:** 8 awards: $1250 stipend, playwriting class scholarship, 1-year Playwrights' Center membership, opportunity to participate in playwriting roundtables, dramaturgical assistance, workshop and public reading. **Guidelines:** MN resident of color. **Application procedure:** send SASE for guidelines. **Deadline:** 31 Jul 2001. **Notification:** 1 Oct 2001. **Dates:** 1 Oct 2001-30 Jun 2002.

MCKNIGHT ADVANCEMENT GRANTS

Open to: playwrights, solo performers. **Frequency:** annual. **Remuneration:** 3 grants of $8500; up to $1500 per fellow for workshops and staged readings using Center's developmental program or for allocation to partner organization for joint development and/or production. **Guidelines:** U.S. citizen or permanent resident and legal MN resident since 1 May 1999; playwright of exceptional merit and potential who has had at least 2 plays fully produced by professional theatres; funds intended to significantly advance fellow's art and/or career and may be used to cover a variety of expenses, including writing time, residency at theatre or other arts organization, travel/study, production or presentation; fellow must designate 2 months of grant year during which he or she plans to participate actively in Center's programs, including weekly attendance at and critical participation in readings and workshops of other members' work; send SASE for guidelines after 1 Dec 2000. **Application procedure:** application and supporting materials. **Deadline:** 1 Feb 2001. **Notification:** 1 May 2001. **Dates:** 1 Jul 2001-30 Jun 2002.

MCKNIGHT NATIONAL PLAYWRITING RESIDENCY

Open to: playwrights, solo performers. **Frequency:** annual. **Remuneration:** $20,000 residency to cover commission and travel and housing. **Guidelines:** U.S. citizen or permanent resident whose work has made significant impact on contemporary theatre and who has had at least 2 plays fully produced by professional theatres; playwright must spend 3 months in residence at Center, where playwright has access to developmental workshops, readings and other services; residency is by nomination of MN theatre only; send SASE for list of eligible MN theatres and guidelines. **Application procedure:** nomination by MN theatre professional; application and supporting materials. **Deadline:** 1 Feb 2001. **Notification:** 15 Apr 2001. **Dates:** 1 Jul 2001-30 Jun 2002.

PRINCESS GRACE AWARDS: PLAYWRIGHT FELLOWSHIP

Princess Grace Foundation–USA; 150 East 58th St, 21st Floor;
New York, NY 10155; (212) 317-1470, FAX 317-1473;
email pgfusa@pgfusa.com; Web site http://www.pgfusa.com
(Ms.) Toby Boshak, *Executive Director*

Open to: playwrights. **Frequency:** annual. **Remuneration:** $7500 grant; 10-week residency at New Dramatists (see listing in Membership and Service Organizations), with travel to New York City; inclusion of submitted script in New Dramatists' lending library and in its ScriptShare national script-distribution program for 1 year. **Guidelines:** U.S. citizen or permanent resident; award based primarily on artistic quality of submitted play and potential of fellowship to assist writer's growth; send SASE for guidelines and application. Application procedures: application; unproduced, unpublished play (no adaptations); letter of recommendation and resume. **Deadline:** 31 Mar 2001.

TCG ARTISTIC PROGRAMS

Theatre Communications Group; 355 Lexington Ave;
New York, NY 10017-6603; (212) 697-5230, FAX 983-4847;
email grants@tcg.org; Web site http://www.tcg.org
Emilya Cachapero, *Director of Artistic Programs*

EXTENDED COLLABORATION GRANTS

Open to: not-for-profit theatres, in collaboration with playwrights. **Frequency:** annual, contingent on funding. **Remuneration:** grant of $5000 (6 awarded in 1999-00). **Guidelines:** augments normal development resources of TCG Constituent theatre by enabling playwright to develop work over an extended period of time in collaboration with director, designer, choreographer, composer and/or artist from another discipline; period of collaboration must exceed that which theatre would normally support; funds cover inter-city transportation within the U.S. and Canada and other expenses related to research and meetings among the collaborators. **Application procedure:** playwright may not apply; application submitted by artistic leader of TCG constituent theatre. **Deadline:** late fall 2000, spring 2001 (both contingent on funding; exact dates TBA).

NATIONAL THEATRE ARTIST RESIDENCY PROGRAM

CATEGORY I: RESIDENCY GRANTS

Open to: playwrights, translators, composers, librettists, lyricists and other theatre artists in association with not-for-profit professional theatres. **Frequency:** annual (contingent on funding). **Remuneration:** approximately 10-14 grants of $50,000 or $100,000. **Guidelines:** experienced theatre artists who have created significant body of work and theatres with high artistic standards and organizational capacity to provide substantial support services to artists; funds cover compensation and residency expenses of 1 or 2 resident artists, working singly or in collaboration, during discrete periods used exclusively for residency-related activities that total at least 6 full months over 2-year period; proposals must be developed jointly by artists and institutions; theatres applying for $100,000 grant must have minimum operating budget of $500,000 in most recently completed fiscal year; theatres applying for $50,000 grant must have minimum operating budget of $250,000 in most recently completed fiscal year; write for guidelines. **Application procedure:** 2 copies of application and supporting materials. **Deadline:** 1 Dec 2000 intent to apply; 15 Dec 2000 application. **Notification:** Mar 2001.

CATEGORY II: MATCHING GRANTS

Open to: playwrights, translators, composers, librettists, lyricists and other theatre artists in association with not-for-profit professional theatres. **Frequency:** annual, contingent on funding. **Remuneration:** $25,000 or $50,000 in matching funds. **Guidelines:** matching funds to support the continuation of particularly fruitful partnerships; to be considered, applicant must meet Category I eligibility requirements. **Application procedure:** 2 copies of application and supporting materials. **Deadline:** 1 Dec 2000 intent to apply; 15 Dec 2000 application. **Notification:** Mar 2001.

NEA/TCG THEATRE RESIDENCY PROGRAM FOR PLAYWRIGHTS

Open to: playwrights in association with not-for-profit professional theatres. **Frequency:** annual (contingent on funding). **Remuneration:** grant of $25,000 to playwright and $5000 Seagram/Universal Residency Award to host theatre (12 awarded in 1999). **Guidelines:** playwright must be citizen or permanent resident of U.S. at the time of application and have had at least one play published or produced within the last 5 years; theatre must have history of developing new work, high artistic standards and a minimum operating budget of $150,000 in the most recently completed fiscal year; a total of 6 months (not necessarily consecutive) must be dedicated to the development of a new work with the host theatre; call or write for application and guidelines. **Application procedure:** intent to apply card, followed by application and supporting materials. **Deadline:** write, call or email for 2000 deadlines.

THE THANKS BE TO GRANDMOTHER WINIFRED FOUNDATION
Box 1449; Wainscott, NY 11975-1449; (516) 725-0323

Open to: playwrights, translators, composers, librettists, lyricists, TV and radio writers, solo performers. **Frequency:** biannual. **Remuneration:** grants of $500-5000. **Guidelines:** U.S. citizen; woman 54 years of age or older; grant must be applied to a project designed to enrich or empower the lives of adult women 21 years of age or older only; projects designed for children or adolescents not eligible. **Application procedure:** project description; write or call for guidelines. **Deadline:** 21 Sep 2000; 21 Mar 2001. **Notification:** 1 Nov 2000 for Sep deadline; 1 May 2001 for Mar deadline.

TRAVEL AND STUDY GRANT PROGRAM
c/o Jerome Foundation; 125 Park Square Ct; 400 Sibley St;
St. Paul, MN 55101; (651) 224-9431, FAX 224-3439
Cynthia Gehrig, *President*

Open to: theatre artists and not-for-profit theatre administrators, including playwrights, composers, librettists and lyricists. **Frequency:** annual. **Remuneration:** grant up to $5000 for foreign or domestic travel. **Guidelines:** resident of Minnesota; program funded by Target, General Mills and Jerome foundations to support period of significant professional development through travel and study for independent professional artist or staff member of not-for-profit organization; write for guidelines. **Application procedure:** application, work sample and resume. **Deadline:** Feb 2001; exact date TBA.

U.S. DEPARTMENT OF STATE FULBRIGHT STUDENT PROGRAM AT THE INSTITUTE OF INTERNATIONAL EDUCATION
809 United Nations Plaza; New York, NY 10017-3580;
(212) 984-5330; Web site http://www.iie.org/fulbright

Open to: playwrights, translators, composers, librettists, lyricists. **Frequency:** annual. **Remuneration:** fellowship or grant; amount varies with country of award. **Guidelines:** specific opportunities for study abroad in the arts; write for brochure. **Application procedure:** application and supporting materials. **Deadline:** 25 Oct 2000. **Notification:** Jan 2001.

U.S.-MEXICO FUND FOR CULTURE

Londres 16, 3rd Floor; Col. Juarez México; 06600 Mexico D.F.;
    52-5-592-3586, FAX 52-5-566-8071;
    email usmexcult@fidemexusa.org.mx;
    Web site http://www. fidemexusa.org.mx

Beatriz Nava, *Program Officer*

Open to: playwrights, translators, librettists, lyricists, screenwriters, TV and radio writers, and producing organizations. **Frequency:** annual. **Remuneration:** grants of $2000-25,000. **Guidelines:** Mexican and North American artists and cultural institutions; program sponsored by Bancomer Cultural Foundation, the Rockefeller Foundation and Mexico's National Fund for Culture and the Arts to fund performing arts projects of excellence that reflect artistic and cultural diversity of Mexico and U.S. and encourage mutual collaboration between artists of both countries; media arts, script translation and adaptation of fiction, drama and poetry also considered; for brochure and application materials, send $1.01 postage 8½" x 11" SASE to U.S. Mexico Fund for Culture, c/o Benjamin Franklin Library, Laredo, TX 78044-3087. **Application procedure:** write for guidelines and application or visit Web site. **Deadline:** 31 Mar 2001; no application before 15 Jan 2001. **Notification:** Aug 2001.

THE WALT DISNEY STUDIOS FELLOWSHIP PROGRAM

500 South Buena Vista St; Burbank, CA 91521-0705;
    (818) 560-6894, FAX 557-6702;
    Web site http://www.members.tripod.com/disfel

Troy Nethercott, *Program Director*

Open to: playwrights, screenwriters, television writers. **Frequency:** annual. **Remuneration:** 1-year salary of $33,000 for up to 8 writers; travel and 1 month's housing for fellows from outside Los Angeles area. **Guidelines:** to enable writers to work full-time at developing their craft in Disney Studios features or television division; no previous film or TV writing experience necessary; writer with Writers Guild of America credits eligible but should apply through the Guild's Employment Access at (213) 782-4648; call or visit Web site for guidelines. **Application procedure:** application and notarized standard letter agreement with resume and writing sample (for feature division: screenplay approximately 120 pages long or full-length play; for TV division: 30-minute TV script approximately 45 pages long, full-length play, or one-act more than 24 pages long). **Deadline:** 21 May 2001; no submission before 1 May 2001. **Notification:** finalists notified fall 2001, others winter 2001. **Dates:** fellowship year begins Jan 2001.

WISCONSIN ARTS BOARD ARTIST FELLOWSHIP AWARDS

101 East Wilson St, 1st Floor; Madison, WI 53702; (608) 264-8191,
    FAX 267-0380; email mark.fraire@arts.state.wi.us;
    Web site http://arts.state.wi.us

Mark Fraire, *Grant Programs and Services Specialist*

Open to: playwrights, composers. **Frequency:** biennial. **Remuneration:** $8000 fellowship. **Guidelines:** WI resident for at least 1 year at time of application; artist must produce 1 public presentation of work as part of fellowship; send SASE for guidelines and application. **Application procedure:** application and work sample. **Deadline:** 15 Sep 2000. **Notification:** Jan 2001.

EMERGENCY FUNDS

How do emergency funds differ from other sources of financial aid?

Emergency funds aid writers in severe temporary financial difficulties. Some funds give outright grants, others make interest-free loans. For support for anything other than a genuine emergency, turn to Fellowships and Grants.

THE AUTHOR'S LEAGUE FUND
330 West 42nd St, 29th Floor; New York, NY 10036;
(212) 268-1208, FAX 564-8363
Susan Drury, *Administrator*
Open to: playwrights. **Type of assistance:** interest-free loan; request should be limited to immmediate needs. **Guidelines:** published or produced working professional; must demonstrate real need. **Application procedure:** application and supporting materials. **Notification:** 2-4 weeks.

CARNEGIE FUND FOR AUTHORS
1 Old Country Rd, Suite 113; Carle Place, NY 11514
Open to: playwrights. **Type of assistance:** emergency grant. **Guidelines:** playwright who has had at least 1 play or collection of plays published commercially in book form (anthologies excluded); emergency which has placed applicant in substantial verifiable financial need. **Application procedure:** write for application form.

THE DRAMATISTS GUILD FUND
330 West 42nd St, 29th Floor; New York, NY 10036;
(212) 268-1208, FAX 564-8363
Susan Drury, *Administrator*
Open to: playwrights, composers, librettists, lyricists. **Type of assistance:** interest-free loan; request should be limited to immediate needs. **Guidelines:** published or produced working professional; must demonstrate real need. **Application procedure:** application and supporting materials. **Notification:** 2-4 weeks.

PEN FUND FOR WRITERS & EDITORS WITH AIDS
PEN American Center; 568 Broadway; New York, NY 10012;
(212) 334-1660, FAX 334-2181; email pen@pen.org
Victoria Vinton, *Program Coordinator*
Open to: playwrights, translators, librettists, lyricists, screenwriters, television writers, radio writers. **Type of assistance:** grant or interest-free loan of up to $1000. **Guidelines:** emergency assistance for published and/or produced writer who is HIV-positive and having financial difficulties. **Application procedure:** application, work sample, documentation of financial emergency and resume. **Notification:** 6-8 weeks.

PEN WRITERS FUND

PEN American Center; 568 Broadway; New York, NY 10012;
(212) 334-1660, FAX 334-2181; email pen@pen.org
Victoria Vinton, *Program Coordinator*

Open to: playwrights, translators, librettists, lyricists, screenwriters, television writers, radio writers. **Type of assistance:** grant or interest-free loan of up to $500. **Guidelines:** emergency assistance for published and/or produced writer in financial difficulties. **Application procedure:** application, work sample, documentation of financial emergency and resume. **Notification:** 6-8 weeks.

STATE ARTS AGENCIES

What can my state arts agency do for me?

Possibly quite a bit—ask your agency for guidelines and study them carefully. State programs vary greatly and change frequently. Most have some sort of residency requirement, but eligibility is not always restricted to current residents, and may include people who were born in, raised in, attended school in or had some other association with the state in question.

What if my state doesn't give grants to individual artists?

A number of state arts agencies are restricted in this way. However, those with such restrictions, by and large, are eager to help artists locate not-for-profit organizations that channel funds to individuals. The New York State Council on the Arts, for example, is prohibited from funding individuals directly, and must contract with a sponsoring not-for-profit organization when it awards grants to individual artists. Yet NYSCA has a number of ways of supporting the work of theatre writers. The Literature Program funds translations and writers' residencies in communities. The Individual Artists Program assists not-for-profit organizations in commissioning new theatre works. NYSCA also subgrants funds to the New York Foundation for the Arts (see Fellowships and Grants, and Development), which provides funds and project development assistance for individual artists.

At the least, every state has some kind of Artist-in-Education program; if you are able and willing to function in an educational setting you should certainly investigate this possibility.

ALABAMA STATE COUNCIL ON THE ARTS

201 Monroe St; Montgomery, AL 36130-1800; (334) 242-4076,
FAX 240-3269; email staff@arts.state.al.us;
Web site http://www.arts.state.al.us/
Al Head, *Executive Director*

ALASKA STATE COUNCIL ON THE ARTS

411 West 4th Ave, Suite 1E; Anchorage, AK 99501-2343;
(907) 269-6610, FAX 269-6601; email info@aksca.org;
Web site http://www.aksca.org/
Helen Howarth, *Executive Director*

AMERICAN SAMOA COUNCIL ON CULTURE, ARTS AND HUMANITIES

Box 1540; Office of the Governor; Pago Pago, AS 96799;
011-684-633-4347, FAX 011-684-633-2059;
Web site http://www.nasaa-arts.org/new/nasaa/gateway/AS.html
(Ms.) Le'ala E. Pili, *Executive Director*

ARIZONA COMMISSION ON THE ARTS

417 West Roosevelt St; Phoenix, AZ 85003; (602) 255-5882,
FAX 256-0282; email general@ArizonaArts.org;
Web site http://az.arts.asu.edu/artscomm/
Shelley Cohn, *Executive Director*

ARKANSAS ARTS COUNCIL

1500 Tower Bldg; 323 Center St; Little Rock, AR 72201;
(501) 324-9766, FAX 324-9154; email info@arkansasarts.com;
Web site http://www.arkansasarts.com
Joy Pennington, *Executive Director*

CALIFORNIA ARTS COUNCIL

1300 I St, Suite 930; Sacramento, CA 95814; (916) 322-6555,
FAX 322-6575; email cac@cwo.com;
Web site http://www.cac.ca.gov/
Barry Hessenius, *Executive Director*

COLORADO COUNCIL ON THE ARTS
750 Pennsylvania St; Denver, CO 80203; (303) 894-2617,
FAX 894-2615; email coloarts@artswire.org;
Web site http://www.coloarts.state.co.us
Fran Holden, *Executive Director*

CONNECTICUT COMMISSION ON THE ARTS
755 Main St; 1 Financial Plaza; Hartford, CT 06103;
(860) 566-4770, FAX 566-6462; email kdemeo@ctarts.org;
Web site http://www.ctarts.org
John Ostrout, *Executive Director*

DELAWARE DIVISION OF THE ARTS
Carvel State Office Bldg; 820 North French St, 4th Floor;
Wilmington, DE 19801; (302) 577-8278, FAX 577-6561;
email delarts@artswire.org; Web site http://www.artsdel.org/
Peggy Amsterdam, *Director*

DISTRICT OF COLUMBIA (DC) COMMISSION ON THE ARTS AND HUMANITIES
410 8th St NW, 5th Floor; Washington, DC 20004;
(202) 724-5613, FAX 727-4135; email dccah@erols.com;
Web site http://www.capaccess.org/ane/dccah/
Anthony Gittens, *Executive Director*

FLORIDA DIVISION OF CULTURAL AFFAIRS
Department of State, The Capitol; Tallahassee, FL 32399-0250;
(850) 487-2980, FAX 922-5259;
Web site http://www.dos.state.fl.us/dca/index.html
Peg Richardson, *Director*

GEORGIA COUNCIL FOR THE ARTS
260 14th St NW, Suite 401; Atlanta, GA 30318;
(404) 685-ARTS (2787), FAX 685-2788;
Rick George, *Interim Executive Director*

GUAM COUNCIL ON THE ARTS & HUMANITIES AGENCY
Box 2950; Agana, GU 96910; (671) 475-CAHA (2242/3),
FAX 472-ART1 (2781); Web site http://www.guam.net/gov/kaha
Deborah J. Bordallo, *Executive Director*

STATE FOUNDATION ON CULTURE AND THE ARTS (HAWAII)

44 Merchant St; Honolulu, HI 96813; (808) 586-0300,
FAX 586-0308; email sfca@sfca.state.hi.us;
Web site http://www.state.hi.us/sfca/
Ronald K. Yamakawa, *Interim Executive Director*

IDAHO COMMISSION ON THE ARTS

Box 83720; Boise, ID 83720-0008; (208) 334-2119, FAX 334-2488;
email cconley@ica.state.id.us;
Web site http://www2.state.id.us/arts
Rodger Madsen, *Interim Executive Director*

ILLINOIS ARTS COUNCIL

James R. Thompson Center; 100 West Randolph St, Suite 10-500;
Chicago, IL 60601; (312) 814-6750, FAX 814-1471;
email info@arts.state.il.us;
Web site http://www.state.il.us/agency/iac/
Rhoda A. Pierce, *Executive Director*

INDIANA ARTS COMMISSION

402 West Washington St, Room W072; Indianapolis, IN 46204-2741;
(317) 232-1268, FAX 232-5595; email arts@state.in.us;
Web site http://www.state.in.us/iac/
Dorothy L. Ilgen, *Executive Director*

IOWA ARTS COUNCIL

Capitol Complex; 600 East Locust; Des Moines, IA 50319-0290;
(515) 281-4451, FAX 242-6492; email jhenke@max.state.ia.us;
Web site http://www.culturalaffairs.org/iac/index.html
Roger Johnson, *Acting Chair*
Jodi Chapman-Henke, *Public Information Officer*

KANSAS ARTS COMMISSION

700 Southwest Jackson, Suite 1004; Topeka, KS 66603-3761;
(785) 296-3335, FAX 296-4989; email KAC@arts.state.ks.us;
Web site http://arts.state.ks.us
David Wilson, *Executive Director*

KENTUCKY ARTS COUNCIL
Old Capitol Annex; 300 West Broadway; Frankfort, KY 40601;
(502) 564-3757, FAX 564-2839; email kyarts@mail.state.ky.us;
Web site http://www.kyarts.org
Gerri Combs, *Executive Director*

LOUISIANA DIVISION OF THE ARTS
Box 44247; Baton Rouge, LA 70804; (225) 342-8180,
FAX 342-8173; email arts@crt.state.la.us;
Web site http://www.crt.state.la.us/arts/index.htm
James Borders, *Executive Director*

MAINE ARTS COMMISSION
55 Capitol St; 25 State House Station; Augusta, ME 04333-0025;
(207) 287-2724, FAX 287-2335; email jan.poulin@state.me.us;
Web site http://www.mainearts.com/vendors/meet_vendors/default.asp
Alden C. Wilson, *Executive Director*

MARYLAND STATE ARTS COUNCIL
175 West Ostend St, Suite E; Baltimore, MD 21230; (410) 767-6555,
FAX 333-1062; email moliver@mdbusiness.state.md.us;
Web site http://www.msac.org/
James Backas, *Executive Director*

MASSACHUSETTS CULTURAL COUNCIL
120 Boylston St, 2nd Floor; Boston, MA 02116-4600;
(617) 727-3668, FAX 727-0044; email web@art.state.ma.us;
Web site http://www.massculturalcouncil.org/
Mary Kelley, *Executive Director*

MICHIGAN COUNCIL FOR THE ARTS & CULTURAL AFFAIRS
G. Mennan Williams Bldg, 3rd Floor; Box 30705; 525 West Ottawa;
Lansing, MI 48909-8205; (517) 241-4011, FAX 241-3979;
email artsinfo@cis.state.mi.us;
Web site http://www.commerce.state.mi.us/arts/
Betty Boone, *Director*

MINNESOTA STATE ARTS BOARD
Park Square Court; 400 Sibley St, Suite 200;
St. Paul, MN 55101-1928; (651) 215-1600, FAX 215-1602;
email msab@arts.state.mn.us;
Web site http://www.arts.state.mn.us/
Robert C. Booker, *Executive Director*

MISSISSIPPI ARTS COMMISSION
239 North Lamar St, Suite 207; Jackson, MS 39201;
(601) 359-6030, FAX 359-6008;
email vlindsay@arts.state.ms.us;
Web site http://www.arts.state.ms.us/
Betsy Bradley, *Executive Director*

MISSOURI ARTS COUNCIL
111 North 7th St, Suite 105; St. Louis, MO 63101; (314) 340-6845,
FAX 340-7215; email moarts@mail.state.mo.us;
Web site http://www.missouriartscouncil.org/
Beverly Strohmeyer, *Acting Executive Director*

MONTANA ARTS COUNCIL
Box 202201; Helena, MT 59620-2201; (406) 444-6430,
FAX 444-6548; email mac@state.mt.us;
Web site http://www.arts.state.mt.us/
Arlynn Fishbaugh, *Executive Director*

NEBRASKA ARTS COUNCIL
Joslyn Carriage House; 3838 Davenport St;
Omaha, NE 68131-2329; (402) 595-2122, FAX 595-2334;
email cmalloy@nebraskaartscouncil.org;
Web site http://www.gps.K12.ne.us/nac_web_site/nac.htm
Jennifer A. Severin, *Executive Director*

NEVADA ARTS COUNCIL
602 North Curry St; Carson City, NV 89703;
(775) 687-6680, FAX 687-6688;
Web site http://dmla.clan.lib.nv.us/docs/arts
Susan Boskoff, *Executive Director*

NEW HAMPSHIRE STATE COUNCIL ON THE ARTS
40 North Main St; Concord, NH 03301-4974; (603) 271-2789,
FAX 271-3584; Web site http://www.state.nh.us/nharts/
Rebecca Lawrence, *Director*

NEW JERSEY STATE COUNCIL ON THE ARTS
Box 306; 225 West State St; Trenton, NJ 08625-0306; (609) 292-6130,
FAX 989-1440; email njsca@arts.sos.state.nj.us;
Web site http://www.njartscouncil.org/
Barbara F. Russo, *Executive Director*

NEW MEXICO ARTS
Box 1450; Santa Fe, NM 87504-1450; (505) 827-6490,
FAX 827-6043; Web site http://www.nmarts.org
Margaret Brommelsiek, *Executive Director*

NEW YORK STATE COUNCIL ON THE ARTS
915 Broadway, 8th Floor; New York, NY 10010; (212) 387-7000,
FAX 387-7164; Web site http://www.nysca.org
Nicolette B. Clarke, *Executive Director*

NORTH CAROLINA ARTS COUNCIL
Department of Cultural Resources; Raleigh, NC 27699-4632;
(919) 733-2111, FAX 733-4834; email ncarts@ncmail.net;
Web site http://www.ncarts.org/home.html
Mary B. Regan, *Executive Director*

NORTH DAKOTA COUNCIL ON THE ARTS
418 East Broadway, Suite 70; Bismarck, ND 58501-4086;
(701) 328-3954, FAX 328-3963; email comserv@state.nd.us;
Web site http://www.state.nd.us/arts/
Troyd Geist, *Executive Director*

COMMONWEALTH COUNCIL FOR ARTS AND CULTURE (NORTHERN MARIANA ISLANDS)
Box 5553, CHRB; Saipan, MP 96950; (670) 322-9982, -9983,
FAX 322-9028;
Web site http://www.nasaa-arts.org/new/nasaa/gateway/NorthernM.html
Robert Hunter, *Executive Director*

OHIO ARTS COUNCIL

727 East Main St; Columbus, OH 43205-1796; (614) 466-2613,
FAX 466-4494; Web site http://www.oac.state.oh.us/
Wayne P. Lawson, *Executive Director*

OKLAHOMA ARTS COUNCIL

Box 52001-2001; Oklahoma City, OK 73152-2001; (405) 521-2931,
FAX 521-6418; email okarts@arts.state.ok.us;
Web site http://www.oklaosf.state.ok.us/~arts/
Betty Price, *Executive Director*

OREGON ARTS COMMISSION

775 Summer St, NE, Suite 350; Salem, OR 97301-1284;
(503) 986-0082, FAX 986-0260;
email oregon.artscomm@state.or.us;
Web site http://art.econ.state.or.us/
Christine T. D'Arcy, *Executive Director*

PENNSYLVANIA COUNCIL ON THE ARTS

Finance Bldg, Room 216; Harrisburg, PA 17120; (717) 787-6883,
FAX 783-2538; Web site http://artsnet.org/pca
Philip Horn, *Executive Director*

INSTITUTE OF PUERTO RICAN CULTURE

Box 9024184; San Juan, PR 00902-4184;
(787) 725-5137, FAX 724-8393;
Web site http://www.nasaa-arts.org/new/nasaa/gateway/PR.html
Dr. José Ramon de la Torre, *Executive Director*

RHODE ISLAND STATE COUNCIL ON THE ARTS

95 Cedar St, Suite 103; Providence, RI 02903-1062;
(401) 222-3880, FAX 521-1351; email info@risca.state.ri.us;
Web site http://www.risca.state.ri.us/
Randall Rosenbaum, *Executive Director*

SOUTH CAROLINA ARTS COMMISSION

1800 Gervais St; Columbia, SC 29201; (803) 734-8696,
FAX 734-8526; Web site http://www.state.sc.us/arts/
Suzette M. Surkamer, *Executive Director*

SOUTH DAKOTA ARTS COUNCIL
Office of the Arts; Department of Education and Cultural Affairs;
800 Governors Dr; Pierre, SD 57501-2294;
(605) 773-3131, FAX 773-6962; email sdac@stlib.state.sd.us;
Web site http://www.state.sd.us/state/executive/deca/sdarts/sdarts.htm
Dennis Holub, *Executive Director*

TENNESSEE ARTS COMMISSION
401 Charlotte Ave; Nashville, TN 37243-0780;
(615) 741-1701, FAX 741-8559; email dadkins@mail.state.tn.us;
Web site http://www.arts.state.tn.us/
Rich Boyd, *Executive Director*

TEXAS COMMISSION ON THE ARTS
Box 13406; Austin, TX 78711-3406; (512) 463-5535,
FAX 475-2699; email front.desk@arts.state.tx.us;
Web site http://www.arts.state.tx.us/
John Paul Batiste, *Executive Director*

UTAH ARTS COUNCIL
617 East South Temple; Salt Lake City, UT 84102-1177;
(801) 236-7555, FAX 236-7556;
Web site http://www.dced.state.ut.us/arts
Bonnie H. Stephens, *Director*

VERMONT ARTS COUNCIL
136 State St, Drawer 33; Montpelier, VT 05633-6001;
(802) 828-3291, FAX 828-3363; email info@arts.vca.state.vt.us;
Web site http://www.state.vt.us/vermont-arts
Alexander L. Aldrich, *Executive Director*

VIRGIN ISLANDS COUNCIL ON THE ARTS
41-42 Norre Gade; St. Thomas, VI 00802; (340) 774-5984,
FAX 774-6206; email vicouncil@islands.vi;
Web site http://www.nasaa-arts.org/new/nasaa/gateway/VI.html
John Jowers, *Executive Director*

VIRGINIA COMMISSION FOR THE ARTS
Lewis House, 2nd Floor; 223 Governor St; Richmond, VA 23219-2010;
(804) 225-3132, FAX 225-4327; email vacomm@artswire.org;
Web site http://www.arts.wire.org/~vacomm/
Peggy J. Baggett, *Executive Director*

WASHINGTON STATE ARTS COMMISSION
234 East 8th Ave; Box 42675; Olympia, WA 98504-2675;
(360) 753-3860, FAX 586-5351; email pamm@wsac.wa.gov;
Web site http://www.arts.wa.gov
Kristen Tucker, *Executive Director*

WEST VIRGINIA COMMISSION ON THE ARTS
1900 Kanawha Blvd E; Charleston, WV 25305-0300; (304) 558-0240,
FAX 558-2779; email ressmeyr@wvlc.wvnet.edu;
Web site http://www.wvculture.org/
Richard Ressmeyer, *Director*

WISCONSIN ARTS BOARD
101 East Wilson St, 1st Floor; Madison, WI 53702; (608) 266-0190,
FAX 267-0380; email artsboard@arts.state.wi.us;
Web site http://arts.state.wi.us/static
George Tzougros, *Executive Director*

WYOMING ARTS COUNCIL
2320 Capitol Ave; Cheyenne, WY 82002; (307) 777-7742,
FAX 777-5499;
Web site http://commerce.state.wy.us/cr/arts/index.htm
John G. Coe, *Executive Director*

COLONIES AND RESIDENCIES

What entries make up this section?

Though artist colonies that admit theatre writers constitute the majority of the listings, there are other kinds of residencies, such as artist-in-residence positions at universities, listed here as well. You can also find listings in Development and the Fellowships and Grants sections that could be considered residencies. We have also included some "writers' rooms" where playwrights in need of a quiet place for uninterrupted work are welcome. Of course there are hotels and inns throughout the country that would be desirable for an artist seeking a quiet place to work, but we have chosen to limit our listings to those places set up as retreats for writers or that, in addition to reasonable lodging, provide services to benefit writers.

Note: you should assume that each deadline listed in this section is the date application materials must be *received*, unless stated otherwise.

ALDEN B. DOW CREATIVITY CENTER

Northwood University; 4000 Whiting Dr; Midland, MI 48640;
   (517) 837–4478, FAX 837–4468; email creativity@northwood.edu;
   Web site http://www.northwood.edu/abd

Ron Koenig, *Executive Director*

Open to: playwrights, translators, composers, librettists, lyricists, screenwriters. **Description:** 4 "Creativity Fellowships" each year for individuals working in any field, including the arts; 10-week summer residency at Northwood University, which provides environment for intense independent study; program includes interaction among fellows and formal presentation of work at end of program. **Financial arrangement:** travel, room, board, $750 stipend for project costs. **Guidelines:** projects that are creative, innovative and unique; prefers 1 applicant per project; no accommodation for spouses, children or pets; write for brochure or visit Web site for more information. **Application procedure:** project description, work sample, resume and $10 application fee. **Deadline:** 31 Dec 2000. **Notification:** 1 Apr 2001. **Dates:** Jun–Aug 2001.

ALTOS DE CHAVON

c/o Parsons School of Design; 2 West 13th St, Room 707;
   New York, NY 10011; (212) 229–5370, FAX 229–8988;
   email altos@spacelab.net

Stephen D. Kaplan, *Arts/Education Director*

Open to: playwrights, composers, screenwriters. **Description:** residencies of 3½ months for 15 artists a year, 1–2 of whom may be writers or composers, at not-for-profit arts center located in tropical Caribbean surroundings 8 miles from town of La Romana in the Dominican Republic; efficiency studios or apartments with kitchenettes; small individual studios nearby; small visual-arts-oriented library. **Financial arrangement:** $100 nonreturnable reservation fee; resident pays rent of $350 per month and provides own meals (estimated cost $20 a day). **Guidelines:** prefers Spanish-speaking artists who can use talents to benefit community, and whose work relates to Dominican or Latin American context; residents may teach workshops and are expected to contribute to group exhibition/performance at end of stay; write for further information. **Application procedure:** letter explaining applicant's interest in program, work sample and resume. **Deadline:** 15 Jul 2001. **Notification:** 1 Aug 2001. **Dates:** residencies start 1 Feb 2002, 1 Jun 2002, 1 Sep 2002.

APOSTLE ISLANDS NATIONAL LAKESHORE

Route 1, Box 4; Bayfield, WI 54814; (715) 779-3398, ext 301,
FAX 779-3049
Myra Dec, *Chief, Resources Education*
Open to: playwrights, composers, lyricists, solo performers. **Description:** 1 writer, poet, visual artist or choreographer at a time housed for 2-3 weeks on island in national park; cabin near beach and forest; no running water or electricity; resident must bring 2-3-week supply of food. **Financial arrangement:** free housing. **Guidelines:** artist "with accomplishment, artistic integrity" and ability to relate to park through their work; must donate 1 mutually agreed upon work to park and communicate experience of residency through 1 program for public. **Application procedure:** application, project description, work sample, resume and cover letter. **Deadline:** 15 Jan 2001; no submission before 1 Oct 2000. **Notification:** 1 Mar 2001. **Dates:** Jun-Sep.

ATLANTIC CENTER FOR THE ARTS

1414 Art Center Ave; New Smyrna Beach, FL 32168;
(904) 427-6975, (800) 393-6975, FAX (904) 427-5669;
email program@atlantic-centerarts.org;
Web site http://www.atlantic-centerarts.org
Paul Markunas, *CEO*
Nicholas Conroy, *Program Director*
Open to: playwrights, composers. **Description:** 7 3-week workshops each year offering writers, choreographers, media visual and performing artists opportunity of concentrated study with internationally known Master Artists-in-Residence. **Financial arrangement:** resident pays $100 a week for tuition, $25 a day for private room with bath; scholarships available. **Application procedure:** Master Artist specifies submission materials and selects participants; write or call for brochure. **Deadline:** 3 months before residency. **Notification:** 2 months before residency. **Dates:** exact dates TBA; see brochure or Web site.

BLUE MOUNTAIN CENTER

Box 109; Blue Mountain Lake, NY 12812; (518) 352-7391
Harriet Barlow, *Director*
Open to: playwrights, composers, librettists, lyricists, solo performers. **Description:** 4-week residencies for 14 writers, composers and visual artists at center in Adirondack Mountains. **Financial arrangement:** free room and board. **Guidelines:** artist whose work is aimed at a general audience and reflects social concerns. **Application procedure:** send SASE for information. **Deadline:** 1 Feb 2001. **Notification:** early Apr 2001. **Dates:** mid-Jun-Oct.

BYRDCLIFFE ART COLONY

The Woodstock Guild; 34 Tinker St; Woodstock, NY 12498;
   (914) 679-2079, FAX 679-4529; email wguild@ulster.net;
   Web site http://www.woodstockguild.org
Artists Residency Program
Open to: playwrights, translators, librettists, lyricists, solo performers, screenwriters. **Description:** 4-week residencies for writers, composers and visual artists at historic 300-acre colony in the Catskill Mountains, 1½ miles from Woodstock village center, 90 miles north of New York City; private room and separate individual studio space in Villetta Inn, spacious turn-of-the-century mountain lodge; common dining room and living room; residents provide own meals, using community kitchen. **Financial arrangement:** resident pays fee of $500 per session. **Guidelines:** proof of serious commitment to field of endeavor is major criterion for acceptance; professional recognition helpful but not essential; send SASE for further information. **Application procedure:** application, work sample, project description, resume, reviews and articles if available, contact information for 2 references and $5 fee. **Deadline:** 1 Apr 2001 (applications received after deadline considered for space still available). **Notification:** 15 May 2001. **Dates:** Jun-Sep.

CAMARGO FOUNDATION

125 Park Square Ct; 400 Sibley St; St. Paul, MN 55101
William Reichard, *U.S. Secretariat*
Open to: playwrights, translators, composers. **Description:** 11 concurrent residencies, most for scholars and teachers pursuing projects relative to Francophone culture, but also including 1 for writer, 1 for composer and 1 for visual artist, at estate in ancient Mediterranean fishing port 30 minutes from Marseilles; furnished apartments; music studio available for composer. **Financial arrangement:** free housing; residents provide own meals. **Guidelines:** resident outlines project to fellow colony members during stay and writes final report; families welcome when space available; write for guidelines. **Application procedure:** application, project description, bio and 3 letters of recommendation. **Deadline:** 1 Feb 2001. **Notification:** 5 Apr 2001. **Dates:** Sep-Dec; Jan-May.

CENTRUM CREATIVE RESIDENCIES PROGRAM
Fort Worden State Park; Box 1158; Port Townsend, WA 98368;
(360) 385-3102, FAX 385-2470; Web site http://www.centrum.org
Ted Senecal, *Residency Program Facilitator*
Open to: playwrights, translators, composers, librettists, lyricists, solo performers, screenwriters, television writers. **Description:** creative residencies for writers, composers, poets, visual artists and choreographers at center near Victorian seaport in 440-acre Fort Worden State Park; self-contained cabins near beach and hiking trails; separate studio space. **Financial arrangement:** free; some stipends available. **Guidelines:** artist who has clear direction and some accomplishment in field. **Application procedure:** application, project description, work sample and resume. **Deadline:** 21 Aug 2001. **Notification:** 16 Oct 2001. **Dates:** Jan–May 2001; Sep–Dec 2001.

DJERASSI RESIDENT ARTISTS PROGRAM
2325 Bear Gulch Rd; Woodside, CA 94062-4405; (650) 747-1250,
FAX 747-0105; email drap@djerassi.org;
Web site http:// www.djerassi.org
Dennis O'Leary, *Executive Director*
Judy Freeland, *Residency Coordinator*
Open to: playwrights, translators, composers, librettists, lyricists, solo performers, screenwriters. **Description:** 1-month residencies for writers, choreographers, composers, media, visual and interdisciplinary artists and performers concurrently at 600-acre ranch in Santa Cruz mountains 1 hour south of San Francisco; interdisciplinary projects encouraged; collaborative projects considered. **Financial arrangement:** free room and board. **Guidelines:** emerging or established artist whose work has clear direction; send SASE for application or print from Web site. **Application procedure:** application, sample of published work or work-in-progress, resume and $25 fee. **Deadline:** 15 Feb 2001 for 2002 residencies. **Notification:** 15 Aug 2001. **Dates:** Apr–Nov.

DORLAND MOUNTAIN ARTS COLONY
Box 6; Temecula, CA 92593; (909) 302-3837; email dorland@ez2.net;
Web site http://www.ez2.net/dorland/Admissions
Open to: playwrights, composers, lyricists. **Description:** 1-month residencies for 6 writers, composers and visual artists concurrently in individual studios on 300-acre nature preserve 50 miles northeast of San Diego; no electricity. **Financial arrangement:** $50 nonrefundable processing fee upon scheduling, if accepted; resident pays cabin donation of $300 per month. **Guidelines:** artist must demonstrate clear direction and accomplishment in field. **Application procedure:** send SASE for application and information. **Deadline:** 1 Sep 2000; 1 Mar 2001. **Notification:** 2 months. **Dates:** year-round.

DORSET COLONY FOR WRITERS

Box 519; Dorset, VT 05251; (802) 867-2223, FAX 867-0144;
    email theatre@sover.net; Web site http://www.theatredirectories.com
John Nassivera, *Executive Director*

Open to: playwrights, composers, librettists, lyricists. **Description:** residencies of 1 week-1 month at house located in historic village in southern VT. **Financial arrangement:** resident pays fee for housing according to means (suggested fee $120 a week); meals not provided; large, fully equipped kitchen. **Guidelines:** artist must demonstrate seriousness of purpose and have record of professional achievement (readings or productions of works); collaborative teams may apply; work sample may be requested from less established artist. **Application procedure:** letter of inquiry with description of proposed project and desired length and dates of stay; resume. **Deadline:** ongoing. **Notification:** 2-3 weeks. **Dates:** 10 Sep-30 Nov; 15 Mar-20 May; some winter residencies available in ancillary space.

THE GELL WRITERS CENTER

c/o Writers & Books; 740 University Ave; Rochester, NY 14607;
    (716) 473-2590, FAX 442-9333
Joseph Flaherty, *Executive Director*

Open to: playwrights, translators, librettists, lyricists, solo performers, screenwriters, television writers. **Description:** 2 private bedrooms available in house surrounded by 23 acres of woodlands; workshops on creative writing sometimes available at extra cost; residents provide own meals. **Financial arrangement:** resident pays $35 a day. **Application procedure:** write or call for application and brochure. **Deadline:** ongoing. **Notification:** 1 week. **Dates:** year-round.

THE HAMBIDGE CENTER FOR CREATIVE ARTS AND SCIENCES

Box 339; Rabun Gap, GA 30568; (706) 746-5718, FAX 746-9933;
    email hambidge@rabun.net;
    Web site http://www.rabun.net/~hambidge

Open to: playwrights, translators, composers, librettists, lyricists. **Description:** residencies of 2 weeks-2 months for professionals in all areas of arts and humanities on 600 acres in northeast GA mountains; 8 private cottages with bedroom, kitchen, bathroom and studio/work area; evening meal provided Mon-Fri, May-Oct only; send SASE for guidelines. **Financial arrangement:** resident pays minimum of $125 a week toward total cost; limited financial assistance available. **Application procedure:** application, work sample, resume, reviews, 3 letters of recommendation from professionals in applicant's field and $20 fee. **Deadline:** 1 Nov for spring and summer residencies; 1 May for fall and winter residencies. **Notification:** 2-3 months. **Dates:** year-round.

HAWTHORNDEN CASTLE INTERNATIONAL RETREAT FOR WRITERS

Lasswade, Midlothian; Scotland EH18 1EG; 44-131-440-2180
Administrator

Open to: playwrights. **Description:** residencies of 4 weeks for playwrights, poets and novelists at medieval castle on secluded crag overlooking valley of the River Esk 8 miles south of Edinburgh; 5 writers in residence at any one time; fully furnished study-bedroom; communal breakfast and dinner, lunch brought to writer's room; typewriter rental and use of excellent libraries in Edinburgh can be arranged. **Financial arrangement:** free room and board. **Guidelines:** author of at least 1 published work. **Application procedure:** write for application and further information. **Deadline:** 30 Sep 2000. **Notification:** mid-Jan 2001. **Dates:** Feb–Dec 2001.

HEADLANDS CENTER FOR THE ARTS

944 Fort Barry; Sausalito, CA 94965; (415) 331-2787, FAX 331-3857
Kathryn Reasoner, *Executive Director*

Open to: playwrights, composers, librettists, lyricists, screenwriters, television writers. **Description:** residencies of 1-3 months for artists in all disciplines at center in national park on 13,000 acres of coastal wilderness across the bay from San Francisco; accommodation in 4-bedroom house with communal kitchen; evening meal provided in mess hall Sun–Thur; 11-month "live-out" residencies available for Bay Area artists only, providing studio space, 2 meals a week and access to center's facilities but no housing; all residents encouraged to interact with fellow artists in other media and with the environment. **Financial arrangement:** stipend of $500 a month, travel and free housing for artist from outside Bay Area; $2500 stipend and studio space for Bay Area artist. **Guidelines:** CA, NC, NJ or OH residents only; students ineligible. **Application procedure:** call or write for information (applications available Apr 2001). **Deadline:** 1 Jun 2001. **Dates:** Feb–Dec 2002.

HEDGEBROOK

2197 East Millman Rd; Langley, WA 98260; (360) 321-4786
Linda Bowers, *Director*

Open to: playwrights, librettists. **Description:** residencies of 1 week-2 months for women writers of diverse cultural backgrounds working in all literary genres; 6 individual cottages on 30 wooded acres on Whidbey Island, near Seattle; writer furnishes own computer. **Financial arrangement:** free room and board. **Guidelines:** woman writer of any age, published or unpublished; women of color encouraged to apply. **Application procedure:** application, project description, work sample and $15 fee; send SASE for application. **Deadline:** 1 Oct 2000 for winter–spring 2001; 15 Mar 2001 for summer–fall 2001. **Notification:** 2 months. **Dates:** year-round.

HELENE WURLITZER FOUNDATION OF NEW MEXICO
Box 1891; Taos, NM 87571; (505) 758-2413, FAX 758-2559
Michael Knight, *Director*
Open to: playwrights, composers, screenwriters. **Description:** 11 studio/apartments available to writers, composers and poets; length of residency flexible, usually 3 months; residencies currently booked through 2002. **Financial arrangement:** free housing and utilities; resident provides own meals; no financial aid. **Application procedure:** application, project description, work sample and resume; write or fax for application. **Deadline:** ongoing. **Dates:** 1 Apr-30 Sep; residencies available on limited basis 1 Oct-31 Mar.

ISLE ROYALE NATIONAL PARK ARTIST-IN-RESIDENCE
800 East Lakeshore Dr; Houghton, MI 49931;
(906) 482-0984 (general information), 487-7152 (Greg Blust),
FAX 482-8753; email greg_blust@nps.gov;
Web site http://www.nps.gov/isro/
Open to: playwrights, composers, lyricists, solo performers. **Description:** 1 artist at a time housed for 2-3 weeks in cabin on remote island near Lake Superior; no electricity; resident must bring 2-3-week supply of food. **Financial arrangement:** free housing. **Guidelines:** writer with artistic integrity, ability to live in wilderness environment and to relate to park through their work; must donate 1 work to park and communicate experience of residency through programs for public. **Application procedure:** application, project description, work sample and resume. **Deadline:** 16 Feb 2001. **Notification:** 15 Apr 2001. **Dates:** Jun-Sep.

THE JAMES THURBER WRITER-IN-RESIDENCE
The Thurber House; 77 Jefferson Ave; Columbus, OH 43215;
(614) 464-1032, FAX 228-7445
Michael J. Rosen, *Literary Director*
Open to: playwrights. **Description:** 4 residencies a year, each for 1 academic quarter (2 for journalists, 1 for playwright, 1 for poet or fiction writer); writer teaches course at Ohio State University. **Financial arrangement:** $6000 stipend; furnished apartment provided. **Guidelines:** playwright who has had at least 1 play produced by a major theatre; teaching experience helpful. **Application procedure:** letter of interest and curriculum vitae. **Deadline:** 15 Dec 2000. **Notification:** 2 months. **Dates:** winter or spring 2001.

THE JOHN STEINBECK WRITER'S ROOM

Long Island University–Southampton Campus Library;
    Southampton, NY 11968; (631) 287-8382, FAX 287-4049;
    email library@southampton.liu.edu
Robert Gerbereux, Library Director

Open to: playwrights. **Description:** small room, space for 4 writers; carrel, storage space, access to reference material in room and to library. **Financial arrangement:** free. **Guidelines:** writer working under contract or with specific commitment. **Application procedure:** application. **Notification:** 1 week. **Dates:** year-round.

KALANI OCEANSIDE ECO-RESORT INSTITUTE FOR CULTURE AND WELLNESS,

RR2 Box 4500; Pahoa–Beach Road, HI 96778; (808) 965-7828,
    FAX 965-0527; email kalani@kalani.com;
    Web site http://www.kalani.com
Richard Koob, *Director*

Open to: playwrights, translators, composers, librettists, lyricists, solo performers screenwriters, television writers. **Description:** up to 20 artists share four 500-1000-square-foot studio spaces for 2-week to 2-month residencies at 113-acre coastal resort spa with private rooms, communal kitchen facilities and shared or private baths. **Financial arrangement:** artist eligible for 50% discount on regular daily room rates of $75-135; artist has option of preparing own food or paying an additional $27 per day for resort's meals. **Guidelines:** any artist with demonstrated ability to complete projects. **Application procedure:** application, project description, work sample and resume with $10 fee. **Deadline:** ongoing. **Notification:** within 1 week of receipt of application. **Dates:** ongoing, but discounted rates more available May-Nov.

LEDIG HOUSE INTERNATIONAL WRITERS' COLONY

55 Fifth Ave; 15th Floor; New York, NY 10003; (518) 392-7656,
    FAX 392-2848
David Knowles, *Executive Director*

Open to: playwrights, translators, screenwriters, television writers. **Description:** residencies of 1 week-2 months for up to 10 writers of all genres at 150-acre farm in upstate NY with library and computer access; private sleeping and work space; communal living and dining rooms; all meals provided. **Financial arrangement:** free room and board. **Guidelines:** published and unpublished writers proficient in English. **Application procedure:** project description, work sample, resume and letter of recommendation with SASE for notification; call or fax for guidelines. **Deadline:** 31 Nov 2000. **Notification:** 31 Dec 2000. **Dates:** spring session 1 Apr-26 Jun; fall session 20 Aug-31 Oct.

LEIGHTON STUDIOS FOR INDEPENDENT RESIDENCIES

The Banff Centre for the Arts; Box 1020, Station 28;
107 Tunnel Mountain Dr; Banff, Alberta; Canada T0L 0C0;
(403) 762-6180, (800) 565-9989, FAX (403) 762-6345;
email arts_info@banffcentre.ab.ca;
Web site http://www.banffcentre.ab.ca/leighton_studios/
Office of the Registrar

Open to: playwrights, composers, performance artists, screenwriters, television writers. **Description:** residencies of 1 week-3 months for writers and composers at studios situated in mountains of Banff National Park; 8 furnished studios, each with washroom, kitchenette, CD/cassette player and Internet access; living accommodations (single room with bath) on Centre's main campus; nearby access to all amenities of Centre, including dining room, library and recreation complex. **Financial arrangement:** resident pays approximate daily cost of $105 Canadian (about $70 U.S.) for studio, room and meals; discount on studio cost only available for those who demonstrate need. **Guidelines:** established or emerging artist who demonstrates sustained contribution to own field and shows evidence of significant achievement. **Application procedure:** write, email or visit Web site for application and further information. **Deadline:** open; apply at least 6 months before desired residency. **Notification:** 2 months. **Dates:** year-round.

THE MACDOWELL COLONY

100 High St; Peterborough, NH 03458-2485; (603) 924-3886,
(212) 535-9690, FAX (603) 924-9142;
email info@macdowellcolony.org;
Web site http://www.macdowellcolony.org
Cheryl Young, *Executive Director*

Open to: playwrights, composers, screenwriters, video writers. **Description:** residencies of up to 2 months for writers, composers, visual artists, video/filmmakers, architects and interdisciplinary artists at 450-acre estate; studios and common areas accessible for those with mobility impairments. **Financial arrangement:** voluntary contributions accepted; travel grants available; writers in need of financial assistance are eligible for grants of up to $1000 to relieve financial burdens related to their stay at the Colony. **Guidelines:** admission based on talent. **Application procedure:** application, work samples, names of 2 professional references and $20 fee; collaborating artists must apply separately; send SASE, call or visit Web site for application. **Deadline:** 15 Sep 2000 for Jan-Apr 2001; 15 Jan 2001 for May-Aug 2001; 15 Apr 2001 for Sep-Dec 2001. **Notification:** 2 months. **Dates:** year-round.

MARY ANDERSON CENTER FOR THE ARTS

101 St. Francis Dr; Mount St. Francis, IN 47146; (812) 923-8602,
    FAX 923-0294; email maca@iglou.com
Debra Carmody, *Executive Director*
Open to: playwrights, translators, composers, librettists, lyricists. **Description:** residencies of 1 week-3 months for 7 writers and visual artists concurrently at center on beautiful 400-acre wooded site with lake, 15 minutes from Louisville, KY; private studio/bedroom, communal kitchen and dining room. **Financial arrangement:** resident pays suggested minimum fee of $150 a week for room and board; possibility of funded residencies; write for information. **Guidelines:** formal education and production credits are not requirements but will be taken into consideration when applications are reviewed. **Application procedure:** application, project description, work sample, resume and 2 references. **Deadline:** ongoing. **Notification:** 2-4 weeks. **Dates:** year-round.

THE MILLAY COLONY FOR THE ARTS

444 East Hill Rd; Box 3; Austerlitz, NY 12017-0003;
    (518) 392-3103; email application@millaycolony.org;
    Web site http://www.millaycolony.org
Gail Giles, *Director of Admissions*
Open to: playwrights, composers, screenwriters. **Description:** 1-month residencies for up to 6 writers, composers and visual artists concurrently at 600-acre estate in upstate NY; studio space and separate bedroom; colony accommodates artists with disabilities. **Financial arrangement:** free room, board and studio space. **Application procedure:** application and supporting materials; send SASE or email for application. **Deadline:** 1 Sep for Feb-May; 1 Feb for Jun-Sep; 1 May for Oct-Jan. **Notification:** 12-15 weeks after deadline. **Dates:** year-round.

MONTANA ARTISTS REFUGE

Box 8; Basin, MT 59632; (406) 225-3500;
email mtrefuge@pop.mcn.net
Jennifer Pryor, *Administrative Coordinator*
Open to: playwrights, translators, composers, librettists, lyricists, solo performers, television writers, screenwriters. **Description:** 3-month-1-year residencies for 4-5 artists of all disciplines, located in a former gold camp in the midst of the Rocky Mountains, approximately 12 miles from the Continental Divide; Basin has 250 residents, two restaurant/bars, a production pottery, post office and town park; artists housed in 3 fully equipped apartments and one studio apartment, all with kitchens and private phones. **Financial arrangement:** resident pays $400-600 per month; meals not provided; financial aid available for up to full rent. **Guidelines:** open to all artists. **Application procedure:** application, work sample, project description and resume. **Deadline:** ongoing.

NEW YORK MILLS ARTS RETREAT

24 North Main Ave, Box 246; New York Mills, MN 56567;
(218) 385-3339, FAX 385-3366; email nymills@uslink.net
Kent Scheer, *Coordinator*
Open to: playwrights, composers, librettists, lyricists, solo performers, screenwriters.
Description: 1 artist at a time housed for 2-4 weeks in small farming community in
north central Minnesota; housing in small one-bedroom home; resident provides own
meals. **Financial arrangement:** $750 stipend for 2 weeks, $1500 stipend for 4 weeks.
Guidelines: emerging artist of demonstrated ability; must donate 8 hours per week
during residency to community outreach. **Application procedure:** application, project
description, work sample, resume and 2 letters of recommendation. **Deadline:** 1 Oct
2000; 1 Apr 2001. **Notification:** 8 weeks after deadline. **Dates:** Sep-May.

NORCROFT

Box 218; Lutsen, MN 55612; (800) 770-0058;
Web site http://www.norcroft.org
Kay Grindland, *Managing Director*
Open to: playwrights, translators, librettists, screenwriters, television writers.
Description: 4 concurrent residencies of 1-4 weeks for womenwriters in all genres
at remote lodge on shores of Lake Superior; private bedroom and separate individual
"writing shed." **Financial arrangement:** free housing; groceries provided, resident
does own cooking. **Guidelines:** women only; artist whose work demonstrates an
understanding of and commitment to feminist change. **Application procedure:**
application, 5-page writing sample and description of project to be pursued at
colony. **Deadline:** 1 Oct 2000. **Notification:** 1 Apr 2001. **Dates:** May-Oct.

RAGDALE FOUNDATION

1260 North Green Bay Rd; Lake Forest, IL 60045; (847) 234-1063,
FAX 234-1075; email ragdale1@aol.com
Susan Page Tillett, *Director*
Open to: playwrights, composers, librettists, lyricists. **Description:** residencies
of 2 weeks-2 months for writers, composers and visual artists from the U.S. and
abroad on property situated on edge of prairie, 1 mile from center of town.
Financial arrangement: resident pays $105 a week for room and board; partial
or full fee waivers awarded on basis of financial need. **Guidelines:** admission
based on quality of work submitted. **Application procedure:** application,
description of work-in-progress, work sample, resume, 3 references and $20 fee;
send SASE for application. **Deadline:** 15 Jan for Jun-Dec; 1 Jun for Jan-Apr.
Notification: 15 Apr for Jan deadline; 1 Sep for Jun deadline. **Dates:** year-round
except for May and last 2 weeks in Dec.

SNUG HARBOR CULTURAL CENTER

1000 Richmond Terr; Staten Island, NY 10301-9926;
   (718) 448-2500, FAX 442-8534
Rental Coordinator

Open to: playwrights, composers. **Description:** studio workspace in performing and visual arts center with theatre, art galleries, shops, museum, meeting rooms and banquet hall, located in 80-acre historic park. **Financial arrangement:** current monthly rental approximately $15-18 per sq. ft.; renewable 1-year lease; tenant must carry own insurance. **Guidelines:** professional artist. **Application procedure:** work sample with resume. **Dates:** year-round.

STUDIO FOR CREATIVE INQUIRY

Carnegie Mellon University; College of Fine Arts;
   Pittsburgh, PA 15213-3890; (412) 268-3454, FAX 268-2829;
   email mmbm@andrew.cmu.edu;
   Web site http://www.cmu.edu/studio/
Marge Myers, *Associate Director*

Open to: playwrights, translators, composers, librettists, lyricists, solo performers, screenwriters, television writers. **Description:** residencies of 6 months-3 years concurrently for artists in all disciplines; residency provides studio facility located in Carnegie Mellon's College of Fine Arts building, including office and meeting space, work area, computers, sound and video editing equipment; fellows may also use resources of university, including library. **Financial arrangement:** stipend; assistance in finding housing in community. **Guidelines:** writer able to use science and technology in work, interested in taking leadership role in collaborative projects and able to relate work to larger community. **Application procedure:** concept proposal, work sample and resume; admission based on quality of work, clear statement of intention, experience with collaboration and project feasibility. **Deadline:** ongoing. **Notification:** 2 months. **Dates:** year-round.

THE TYRONE GUTHRIE CENTRE

Annaghmakerrig; Newbliss; County Monaghan; Ireland; 353–47–54003,
    FAX 353–47–54380; email thetgc@indigo.ie
Resident Director

Open to: playwrights, composers, librettists, lyricists, screenwriters, television writers. **Description:** residencies of 1 week–1 year for artists in all disciplines at former country home of Tyrone Guthrie, set amid 450 acres of forested estate overlooking large lake; private apartments; music room, rehearsal/performance space and extensive library. **Financial arrangement:** non-Irish artists pay about Irish £2000 (about $2400) a month for housing and meals; self-catering houses also available at reasonable rents; fees may be negotiable depending on factors such as length of stay, nature of project, involvement with Irish artists or institutions, etc. **Guidelines:** artist must show evidence of sustained dedication and a significant level of achievement; prefers artist with clearly defined project; artist teams (e.g., writer/director, composer/librettist) welcome. **Application procedure:** write for application and further information. **Deadline:** ongoing. **Dates:** year-round.

UCROSS FOUNDATION RESIDENCY PROGRAM

30 Big Red Lane; Clearmont, WY 82835; (307) 737–2291,
    FAX 737–2322
Sharon Dynak, *Executive Director*

Open to: playwrights, translators, composers, librettists, lyricists. **Description:** residency of 2 weeks–2 months at "Big Red," restored historic site in the foothills of the Big Horn Mountains; 8 concurrent residencies for writers, composers and visual artists; opportunity to concentrate on own work without distraction and to present work to local communities, if desired. **Financial arrangement:** free room, board and studio space. **Guidelines:** criteria are quality of work and commitment; send SASE for application and further information. **Application procedure:** application, project description and work sample. **Deadline:** 1 Oct for Feb–Jun; 1 Mar for Aug–Dec. **Notification:** 8 weeks. **Dates:** year-round except Jan and Jul.

THE U.S./JAPAN CREATIVE ARTISTS' PROGRAM

Japan–U.S. Friendship Commission; 1120 Vermont Ave NW, Suite 925;
 Washington, DC 20005; (202) 275-7712, FAX 275-7413;
 email jusfc@jusfc.gov; Web site http://www.jusfc.gov
Eric J. Gangloff, *Executive Director*

Open to: playwrights, composers, librettists, lyricists, solo performers, screenwriters, television writers. **Description:** residencies of 6 continuous months for 3-5 artists each year; residents find own housing in location of their choice in Japan. **Financial arrangement:** monthly stipend of ¥400,000 (about $3700) plus ¥100,000 (about $925) for housing and ¥100,000 (about $925) for professional expenses; free travel and pre-departure Japanese language instruction. **Guidelines:** U.S. citizen or permanent resident; mid-career professional artist with compelling reason to work in Japan and whose work "exemplifies the best in U.S. art"; visit Web site for application and further information. **Application procedure:** application, work sample and resume. **Deadline:** 26 Jun 2001.

VIRGINIA CENTER FOR THE CREATIVE ARTS

Box VCCA, Mt. San Angelo; Sweet Briar, VA 24595; (804) 946-7236,
 FAX 946-7239; email vcca@vcca.com;
 Web site http://www.vcca.com
Director

Open to: playwrights, translators, composers, librettists, lyricists, screenwriters. **Description:** residencies of 2 weeks-2 months for writers, composers, and visual and performance artists at 450-acre estate in Blue Ridge Mountains; separate studios and bedrooms; all meals provided. **Financial arrangement:** resident pays suggested minimum of $30 a day for room and board or as means allow; financial status not a factor in selection process. **Guidelines:** admission based on achievement or promise of achievement. **Application procedure:** application, work sample, resume and 2 recommendations. **Deadline:** 15 Sep for Feb-May; 15 Jan for Jun-Sep; 15 May for Oct-Jan. **Notification:** 3 months. **Dates:** year-round.

WALDEN RESIDENCY PROGRAM

Extended Campus Programs; Southern Oregon University;
    1250 Siskiyou Blvd; Ashland, OR 97520; (541) 552–6901,
    FAX 552–6047; email friendly@sou.edu
Brooke Friendly, *Arts Coordinator*
Open to: playwrights. **Description:** 3 6-week residencies for writers of drama, fiction, poetry and creative nonfiction at farm near Ashland, OR; 1 writer at a time housed in cabin with kitchen facilities, which opens onto meadow surrounded by forest. **Financial arrangement:** free; no meals provided. **Guidelines:** OR resident only; send SASE for full application. **Application procedure:** application, project description, work sample and list of publications or productions. **Deadline:** 30 Nov 2000. **Notification:** mid-Dec 2000. **Dates:** Mar–Jul 2001.

WILLIAM FLANAGAN MEMORIAL CREATIVE PERSONS CENTER

Edward F. Albee Foundation; 14 Harrison St; New York, NY 10013;
    (212) 226–2020
Open to: playwrights, translators, composers, librettists, screenwriters. **Description:** 1-month residencies for up to 5 writers, composers and visual artists concurrently at "The Barn" in Montauk, Long Island. **Financial arrangement:** free housing. **Guidelines:** admission based on talent and need; write for further information. **Application procedure:** application, script (recording for composers) and supporting materials. **Deadline:** 1 Apr 2001; no submission before 1 Jan 2001. **Notification:** May 2001. **Dates:** 1 Jun–1 Oct 2001.

THE WRITERS ROOM

10 Astor Pl, 6th Floor; New York, NY 10003; FAX (212) 533–6059;
    Web site http://www.writersroom.org
Donna Brodie, *Executive Director*
Open to: playwrights, translators, composers, librettists, lyricists. **Description:** large room with 35 desks separated by partitions, space for 300 writers each quarter; open 24 hours a day year-round; kitchen, lounge and bathrooms, storage for files and laptops, small reference library; monthly readings. **Financial arrangement:** $50 application fee; $60 key desposit; $110–185 quarterly fee (3-month period). **Guidelines:** writer, emerging or established, must show seriousness of intent. **Application procedure:** application and references; all inquiries by mail or through Web site (no visits without appointment).

THE WRITERS' STUDIO

The Mercantile Library Association; 17 East 47th St;
   New York, NY 10017; (212) 755-6710, FAX 758-1387;
   email mercantile_library@msn.com;
   Web site http://www.fictionlibrary.org
Harold Augenbraum, *Director*

Open to: playwrights, composers. **Description:** carrel space for 17 writers (3 reserved for writers of children's literature) in not-for-profit, private lending library of 175,000 volumes; storage for personal computers or typewriters, library membership, access to special reference collection and rare collection of 19th-century American and British literature. **Financial arrangement:** $200 fee for 3 months, renewal possible for up to 1 year. **Guidelines:** open to all writers; unpublished writer must submit evidence of serious intent. **Application procedure:** application and work sample or project outline.

YADDO

Box 395; Saratoga Springs, NY 12866-0395; (518) 584-0746,
   FAX 584-1312; email yaddo@yaddo.org
Admissions Committee

Open to: playwrights, composers, performance artists, screenwriters. **Description:** residencies of 2 weeks-2 months for artists in all genres, working individually or as collaborative teams of up to 3 persons, at 19th-century estate on 400 acres; approximate total of 200 residents a year (15 concurrently Sep-May, 35 concurrently May-Labor Day). **Financial arrangement:** free room, board and studio space. **Guidelines:** admission based on review by panels composed of artists in each genre; quality of work submitted is major criterion; send 55¢ SASE for application and further information. **Application procedure:** application, work sample, resume, 2 letters of support, $20 fee and SASP for acknowledgment of receipt. **Deadline:** 15 Jan 2001 for mid-May 2001-Feb 2002; 1 Aug 2001 for 1 Nov 2001-mid-May 2002. **Notification:** 1 Apr 2001 for Jan deadline; 15 Oct 2001 for Aug deadline. **Dates:** year-round except early Sep.

MEMBERSHIP AND SERVICE ORGANIZATIONS

What's included here?

A number of organizations that exist to serve either the American playwright or a wider constituency of writers, composers and arts professionals. Some have a particular regional or special-interest orientation; some provide links to theatres in other countries. Taken together, these organizations represent an enormous range of services available to those who write for the theatre, and it is worth getting to know them.

THE ALLIANCE OF LOS ANGELES PLAYWRIGHTS

7510 Sunset Blvd, Suite 1050; Los Angeles, CA 90046-3418;
(323) 957-4752
Dan Berkowitz and Dick Dotterer, *Co-Chairs*

Founded in 1993, ALAP is a support and service organization dedicated to addressing the professional needs of the Los Angeles playwriting community. ALAP's programs and activities include the Playwrights Expo, which brings together L.A. playwrights and dozens of representatives of local and national theatres; the series In Our Own Voices, in which members read from and share their work; the annual Playreading Festival in which local theatres present rehearsed readings of members' plays; the C. Bernard Jackson Award, given in recognition of individuals and organizations that nurture, develop and support L.A. playwrights; symposia and panel discussions; networking and social events; and a hotline listing upcoming events. ALAP's publications include the bimonthly *NewsFlash*, which keeps members posted on upcoming events; the journal *InterPlay*; and an annual *Membership Directory*. Annual dues are $35.

THE ALLIANCE OF RESIDENT THEATRES/NEW YORK

575 Eighth Ave, Suite 17S; New York, NY 10018; (212) 244-6667,
FAX 714-1918; email artnewyork@aol.com
Virginia P. Louloudes, *Executive Director*
Mary Harpster, *Deputy Director*

The Alliance of Resident Theates (A.R.T./New York) is the trade and service organization for the not-for-profit professional theatre, serving more than 300 New York-based theatre companies and professional affiliates (theatres outside NY, colleges and universities, and organizations providing services to the theatre field). Publications of interest include the *Member Directory*, *Rehearsal and Performance Space Guide*; *Internship Directory*, and *Where to Send Unsolicited Resumes, Manuscripts and Headshots*.

ALTERNATE ROOTS

1083 Austin Ave; Atlanta, GA 30307; (404) 577-1079,
    FAX 577-7991; email altroots1@earthlink.net;
    Web site http://www.home.earthlink.net/~altroots1/
Alice Lovelace, *Managing Director*

Founded in 1976, Alternate ROOTS is a service organization run by and for southeastern artists. Its mission is to support the creation and presentation of original performing art that is rooted in a particular community of place, tradition or spirit. It is committed to social and economic justice and the protection of the natural world, and addresses these concerns through its programs and services. ROOTS now has more than 260 individual members across the 13 states of the Southeast, including playwrights, directors, choreographers, musicians, storytellers, clowns and new vaudevillians—both solo artists and representatives of 65 performing and presenting organizations. ROOTS aims to make artistic resources available to its members through workshops; to create appropriate distribution networks for the new work being generated in the region via touring, publications and liaison activity; and to provide opportunities for enhanced visibility and financial stability via publications and periodic performance festivals. Opportunities for member playwrights include readings and peer critiques of works-in-progress at the organization's annual meeting. Artists who are residents of the Southeast and whose work is consistent with the goals of ROOTS are accepted as new members throughout the year. The organization's meetings and workshops are open to the public and its newsletter is available to the public for a small fee. Annual membership dues are $50.

THE AMERICAN ALLIANCE FOR THEATRE & EDUCATION (AATE)

c/o Department of Theatre; Arizona State University; Box 872002;
    Tempe, AZ 85287-2002; (480) 965-6064, FAX 965-5351;
    email aateinfo@asu.edu; Web site http://www.aate.com
Judith Rethwisch, *President*
Christy M. Taylor, *Administrative Director*

AATE is a membership organization created in 1987 with the merger of the American Association of Theatre for Youth and the American Association for Theatre in Secondary Education. AATE provides a variety of services to support the work of theatre artists and educators who work with young people and to promote theatre and drama/theatre education in elementary and secondary schools. To encourage the development and production of plays for young audiences, the AATE Unpublished Play Reading Project annually selects and publicizes promising new plays in this field. AATE also sponsors annual awards for the best play for young people and the outstanding book relating to any aspect of the field published in the past calendar year; only the play or book's publisher may nominate a candidate for these awards. AATE's publications, which are free to members, include a quarterly on-line newsletter with a Playwright's Page; the yearly *Youth Theatre Journal*; and the quarterly *STAGE of the Art*. Membership is open to all and costs $55 for students, $65 for retirees, $90 for individuals and $120 for organizations; please add $20 (U.S. funds) for foreign members (outside the U.S. and Canada).

AMERICAN INDIAN COMMUNITY HOUSE

708 Broadway, 8th Floor; New York, NY 10003; (212) 598-0100,
    FAX 598-4909; Web site http://www.aich.org
Rosemary Richmond, *Executive Director*
Jim Cyrus, *Director of Performing Arts*

American Indian Community House was founded in 1969 to encourage the interest of all U.S. ethnic groups in the cultural contributions of the American Indian, and to foster intercultural exchanges. The organization now serves the Native American population of the New York City region through a variety of social, economic and educational programs, and through cultural programs which include theatre events, an art gallery and a newsletter. Native Americans in the Arts, the performing arts component of the Community House, is committed to the development and production of works by Indian authors, and presents staged readings, workshops and full productions in The Circle, their in-house performance space. The Community House also sponsors several other performing groups, including Spiderwoman Theatre, Coatlicue Theatre Company, the actors' group Off the Beaten Path, the Thunderbird American Indian Dancers, the Silver Cloud Singers and the jazz-fusion and traditional singing group Ulali. A showcase for Native American artists is presented to agents and casting directors once a year.

AMERICAN MUSIC CENTER (AMC)

30 West 26th St, Suite 1001; New York, NY 10010-2011;
    (212) 366-5260, FAX 366-5265; email center@amc.net;
    Web site http://www.amc.net or www.newmusicbox.org
Richard Kessler, *Executive Director*
Lyn Liston, *New Music Information Specialist*

Founded in 1939, the American Music Center provides numerous programs and services for composers, performers and others interested in contemporary American jazz and classical music. The Jory Copying Assistance Program helps composers pay for copying music and extracting performance materials. The center's library contains more than 60,000 scores and recordings, including a large collection of opera and music-theatre works, available for perusal by interested performers. The AMC provides information on competitions, publishers, performing ensembles, composers and other areas of interest in new music, and its publication *Opportunites in New Music* is updated annually. Members receive the monthly "Opportunity Update" and are eligible for discounts on AMC publications; new members receive a free packet of information and articles of interest to the American composer. All members may vote in the annual board elections and attend the annual meeting. Membership is open to any person or organization wishing to support the center's promotion of the creation, performance and appreciation of American music. Annual dues are $55 for individuals ($35 for students under 25 and senior citizens).

AMERICAN TRANSLATORS ASSOCIATION (ATA)
225 Reinekers Lane, Suite 590; Alexandria, VA 22314-2840;
   (703) 683-6100, FAX 683-6122; email ata@atanet.org;
   Web site http://www.atanet.org
Walter W. Bacak, Jr., *Executive Director*
Founded in 1959, the ATA is a national not-for-profit association which seeks to promote recognition of the translation profession; disseminate information for the benefit of translators and those who use their services; define and maintain professional standards; foster and support the training of translators and interpreters; and provide a medium of cooperation with persons in allied professions. Members receive the monthly *ATA Chronicle* and a membership directory. Other publications include a *Translation Services Directory* containing professional profiles of individual members. ATA holds an annual conference and sponsors several honors and awards (see American Translators Association Awards in Prizes). Active membership is open to U.S. citizens and permanent residents who have professionally engaged in translating or closely related work and have passed an ATA accreditation examination or demonstrated professional attainment by other prescribed means. Those who meet these professional standards but are not U.S. citizens or residents may hold Corresponding membership; other interested persons may be Associate members. Interested persons should contact ATA for a membership application, or visit the ATA Web site. Annual dues are $50 for Associate-Students; $95 for Active, Corresponding and Associate members; $120 for institutions; and $175 for corporations.

ASCAP (AMERICAN SOCIETY OF COMPOSERS, AUTHORS AND PUBLISHERS)

1 Lincoln Plaza; New York, NY 10023; (212) 621-6234,
  FAX 621-6558; Web site http://www.ascap.net
Michael A. Kerker, *Director of Musical Theatre*

ASCAP is a not-for-profit organization whose members are writers and publishers of musical works. It operates as a clearinghouse for performing rights, offering licenses that authorize the public performance of all the music of its composer, lyricist and music publishing members, and collecting license fees for these members. ASCAP also sponsors workshops for member and nonmember theatre writers (see ASCAP Musical Theatre Workshop in Development). Membership in ASCAP is open to any composer or lyricist who has been commercially recorded or regularly published. Annual dues are $10 for individuals.

ASIAN AMERICAN ARTS ALLIANCE

74 Varick St, Suite 302; New York, NY 10013-1914;
  (212) 941-9208, FAX 941-7978;
  email artsalliance@earthlink.net;
  Web site http://www.AAartsAlliance.org
Lillian Cho, *Executive Director*

Asian American Arts Alliance is a not-for-profit arts service organization founded in 1983 to increase the support, recognition and appreciation of Asian-American arts. The Arts Alliance strives to assist Asian-American artists and arts groups and works to raise the awareness of the diversity of Asian-American arts and cultures. The organization provides information resources, networking and advocacy services, and professional assistance through technical aid, public forums and roundtables, and a resource library. Public programs and special projects include Artist Series forums, Nuts & Bolts technical assistance workshops and the Chase SMARTS Regrant Program for New York City Asian American arts groups. Publications include the *Directory of Asian American Arts Organizations and Touring Artists,* a bimonthly Asian American Arts Calendar/Resources and Opportunities and a semiannual art magazine, *Dialogue.* There are 7 membership levels: Starving Artist, $20; Mover & Shaker, $45; Arts Organization, $60; Project Leader, $100; Arts Patron, $250; Philanthropist, $500; and Leadership Council, $1000. Members receive discounts on advertising, special publications and events; additional benefits are provided to major donors.

A.S.K. THEATER PROJECTS

11845 West Olympic Blvd, Suite 1250 W; Los Angeles, CA 90064;
(310) 478-3200, FAX 478-5300; email askplay@primenet.com;
Web site http://www.askplay.org
(Mr.) Mead K. Hunter, *Director of Literary Programs*

Since 1989, A.S.K. Theater Projects has been an arts service organization dedicated to playwrights and new playwriting. Each year A.S.K. develops numerous works, either through public readings or in a private writer's retreat, out of which 2-3 plays are selected for workshop productions (see A.S.K. Theater Projects in Development). Allied programs supported by A.S.K. include: the international playwriting program at London's Royal Court Theatre; playwright exchange programs, with the Playwrights' Center, the Royal Court and New Dramatists; the Audrey Skirball-Kenis Playwrights Program at Lincoln Center; the Mark Taper Forum's New Work Festival; the UCLA Playwriting Award and the UCLA Playwriting Fellowship; the Los Angeles Drama Critics Circle Ted Schmitt Award; the playscript publication in TCG's *American Theatre* magazine; the Playwrights-in-the-Schools program; and the L.A. Weekly Playwriting Award. A.S.K. sponsors symposia, salons and labs, which serve as forums wherein issues may be explored or practical approaches to writing shared. A.S.K.'s publications include the *Playwrights Guide to Los Angeles*; the texts of plays given workshop productions; and *Parabasis*, a news magazine for, by and about playwrights. For information about additional programs and publications, contact A.S.K.

ASSITEJ/USA (INTERNATIONAL ASSOCIATION OF THEATRE FOR CHILDREN AND YOUNG PEOPLE)

724 Second Ave S; Nashville, TN 37210; (615) 254-5719,
FAX 254-3255; email usassitej@aol.com;
Web site http://www.assitej-usa.org
Steve Bianchi, *Membership Director*

Founded in 1965, ASSITEJ/USA is a not-for-profit theatre agency which advocates the development of professional theatre for young audiences in the USA and facilitates interchange among theatre artists and scholars of the 60 member countries of ASSITEJ. ASSITEJ/USA sponsors festivals and seminars, operates an international playscript exchange and, with ASSITEJ/Japan, is founder of the Pacific-Asia Exchange Program. Members are theatres, institutions and individuals concerned about the theatre, young audiences and international goodwill. Members receive *Theatre for Young Audiences Today*, published 2-3 times annually, and priority consideration for participation in national and international events. Membership costs $30 a year for students, $35 for retirees, $50 for libraries, $65 for individuals, $125-375 for organizations (depending on size of budget). Write or call for membership application.

THE ASSOCIATED WRITING PROGRAMS (AWP)

Tallwood House, Mail Stop 1E3; George Mason University;
Fairfax, VA 22030; (703) 993-4301, FAX 993-4302;
email awp@gmu.edu

David Fenza, *Executive Director*

Founded in 1967, AWPis a not-for-profit organization serving the needs of writers, college and university writing programs, and students of writing by providing information services, job placement assistance, publishing opportunities, literary arts advocacy and forums on all aspects of writing and its instruction. Writers' Conferences & Centers (WC&C), an association of 88 nonacademic conferences for writers, is now a division of AWP. Writers not affiliated with colleges and universities but who support collective efforts to improve opportunities are also represented by AWP. The *Writer's Chronicle,* published 6 times annually and available for $20 a year, includes listings of publishing opportunities, grants, awards and fellowships; interviews with writers; and essays on writing technique. The *AWP Official Guide to Writing Programs* (9th edition, $25.95 including shipping) offers a comprehensive listing of writing programs and an expanded section on writing conferences, colonies and centers. Write or call AWP for information on membership requirements.

ASSOCIATION FOR THEATRE IN HIGHER EDUCATION (ATHE)

Box 4537; Boulder, CO 80306-4537; (888) 284-3737,
FAX (303) 440-0852; email nericksn@aol.com;
Web site http://www.hawaii.edu/athe

Nancy Erickson, *Administrative Director*

Founded in 1986, ATHE is an organization composed of individuals and institutions that provides vision and leadership for the profession and promotes excellence in theatre education. Membership services include insurance benefits, scholarships, annual professional awards including the Jane Chambers Playwriting Award (see Prizes) and assistance with issues such as tenure and alternate employment opportunities. The annual conference convenes theatre scholars, educators and professionals from all over the world to participate in workshops, performances, plenary sessions and group meetings. ATHE publishes several periodicals of interest to the theatre professional, including *ATHENEWS*, a quarterly newsletter that includes a list of teaching positions available at member organizations; *Theatre* Topics, a semiannual journal; *Theatre Journal,* a quarterly journal; a membership directory and pamphlets on various topics such as assessment guidelines for higher education theatre programs and tenure. There are 5 annual membership levels: Students, $50; Retirees, $80; Individuals, $105; 2-Person Households, $155; Organizations, $195. Members receive all publications.

THE ASSOCIATION OF HISPANIC ARTS (AHA)

250 West 26th St, 4th Floor; New York, NY 10001; (212) 727-7227,
 FAX 727-0549; email aha96@aol.com

Sandra Perez, *Executive Director*

A not-for-profit organization founded in 1975, AHA promotes the Latin American arts as an integral part of this country's cultural life. It acts as a clearinghouse for information on all the arts, including theatre, and 6 times a year publishes a newsletter, *AHA! Hispanic Arts News*, that provides information on playwriting contests, workshops, forums and other items of interest to Latin American artists. AHA also provides technical assistance to Latin American artists seeking funding.

ASSOCIATION OF INDEPENDENT VIDEO AND FILMMAKERS (AIVF)

304 Hudson St, 6th Floor; New York, NY 10013; (212) 807-1400,
 FAX 463-8519; email info@aivf.org;
 Web site http://www.aivf.org

Elizabeth Peters, *Executive Director*

Founded in 1975, the Association of Independent Video & Filmmakers (AIVF) is the membership organization of the Foundation for Independent Video and Film (FIVF). Its mission is to increase the creative and professional opportunities for independent video and filmmakers and to enhance the growth of independent media by providing services and information such as health and production insurance, networking seminars and events, a resource library and publication of books and directories, as well as *The Independent Film & Video Monthly.* As one of the largest organizations serving and representing independent film and video makers, as well as public television and cable access producers, AIVF's membership consists of media artists working in all genres, including documentary, animation, experimental, narrative, interactive and multimedia.

Austin Script Works (ASW)

Box 9787; Austin, TX 78766; (512) 472-5143, ext 18;
  email info@scriptworks.org;
  Web site http://www.scriptworks.org
John Walch, *Artistic Director*

Founded in 1997, Austin Script Works is a playwright-driven organization which provides support for playwrights at all stages in the writing process. ASW's programs include salon readings, staged readings, workshops, one-act commissions, writing retreats, on-line services, full productions and The Harvest Festival of New American Plays (co-produced with the State Theater Company). Associate Membership ($35 annually) is open to anyone. Benefits of Associate membership include participation in salon readings and the 10-minute playwriting retreat; the opportunity to apply for staged readings, 10-minute play showcase productions and the Harvest Festival; and discounts to all ASW events. Core membership ($50 annually) is open only to playwrights living in the central Texas region. Playwrights are selected based on script submission for a three-year period. Core members receive all benefits of Associate members and are also eligible to apply for small stipends, commissions and full productions.

Black Theatre Network (BTN)

2870 East Corand Blvd, #600; Detroit, MI 48202-3146 or
  2603 Northwest 13th St, Suite 312; Gainesville, FL 32609;
  email ga@plowshares.org; Web site http://www.btnet.org
Eileen Morris, *President*

Black Theatre Network (BTN) is a national network of professional artists, scholars and community groups founded in 1986 to provide an opportunity for the interchange of ideas; to publish information regarding black theatre activity; to provide an annual national forum to view and discuss black theatre; and to encourage and promote black dramatists and the production of plays about the black experience. BTN members are eligible to attend national conferences and workshops and receive complimentary copies of all BTN publications, which include the quarterly *Black Theatre Network News*, listing conferences, contests, BTN business matters and national items of interest; *Black Theatre Directory*, which contains over 800 listings of black theatre artists, scholars, companies, higher education programs and service organizations; *Dissertations Concerning Black Theatre: 1900-1994*, a listing of Ph.D. theses; and *Black Theatre Connections*, a quarterly listing of jobs in educational and professional theatre, and other career development opportunities. *Black Voices*, a catalog of works by black playwrights, is available from BTN for $20. Annual dues are $35 for retirees and students, $75 for individuals, $110 for organizations.

BMI (BROADCAST MUSIC INCORPORATED)

320 West 57th St; New York, NY 10019-3790; (212) 586-2000,
FAX 262-2824

Jean Banks, *Senior Director, Musical Theater and Jazz*

BMI, founded in 1940, is a performing rights organization which acts as steward for the public performance of the music of its writers and publishers, offering licenses to music users. BMI monitors music performances and distributes royalties to those whose music has been used. Any writer whose songs have been published and are likely to be performed can join BMI at no cost. BMI also sponsors a musical theatre workshop (see BMI-Lehman Engel Musical Theatre Workshop in Development).

The BMI Foundation (President, Theodora Zavin) was established in 1984 to provide support for individuals in furthering their musical education and to assist organizations involved in the performance of music and music training.

BROADWAY ON SUNSET

10800 Hesby St; North Hollywood, CA 91601; (818) 508-9270,
FAX 508-1806; email BroadwayonSunset@cs.com;
Web site http://www. BroadwayonSunset.org

Kevin Kaufman, *Executive Director*
Libbe HaLevy, *Literary Director*

Broadway on Sunset, a not-for-profit organization established in 1993, provides an individually structured developmental program for musical theatre writers (composers, lyricists, librettists) of all skill levels. Broadway on Sunset emphasizes a full understanding of the principles and standards of Broadway-level musical theatre craft and provides writers opportunities to test their material at each stage of development. BOS sponsors the First Look Competition of new unproduced musicals; the winner receives a concert reading at their Annual West Coast Musical Theatre Conference. Since its inception, Broadway on Sunset has presented more than 100 original musicals as well as interviews and symposia. There are no membership dues but writers may pay a nominal fee to participate in classes, readings and workshops. Writers and composers need to have access to the Los Angeles area to benefit fully from the workshops.

CENTRE FOR CREATIVE COMMUNITIES

118 Commercial St; London E1 6NF; England; 44-20-7247-5385,
   FAX 44-20-7247-5256;
   email info@creativecommunities.org.uk;
   Web site http://www.creativecommunities.org.uk
Jennifer Williams, *Executive Director*
Founded in 1978, the Centre for Creative Communities is a not-for-profit
organization dedicated to promoting community development through arts
and education. CCC conducts research, organizes conferences, produces a
quarterly newsletter and is part of an international network of arts and
education organizations. CCC's specialized arts and education library houses
information on opportunities for artists and performers both in the U.K. and
abroad. CCC is not a grant-giving organization.

CHICAGO ALLIANCE FOR PLAYWRIGHTS (CAP)

Theatre Building; 1225 West Belmont; Chicago, IL 60657-3205;
   (773) 929-7367, ext 60, FAX 338-3060
Allan Chambers, *Board Member*
The Chicago Alliance for Playwrights is a service organization founded in 1990
to establish a network for Chicago-area playwrights and others committed to the
development of new work for the stage. Members of the coalition include
Chicago Dramatists (see listing below), Columbia College New Musicals Project,
New Tuners Theatre/Workshop (see Production), Studio Z and Writers Bloc. The
alliance sponsors forums of interest to writers and publishes an annual directory
of Chicago-area playwrights and their principal works. Write or call for
membership details; annual dues are $25 for individuals and $100 for groups.

CHICAGO DRAMATISTS
1105 West Chicago Ave; Chicago, IL 60622; (312) 633-0630,
FAX 633-0610; email newplays@aol.com
Russ Tutterow, *Artistic Director*

Founded in 1979, Chicago Dramatists is dedicated to the development of playwrights and new plays. It employs a variety of programs to nurture the artistic and career development of both established and emerging playwrights, including play readings, productions, classes, workshops, symposia, discussions, panels, festivals, talent coordination, marketing services, collaborative projects with other theatres, national playwright exchanges and referrals to producers.

The Resident Playwright program seeks to nurture and promote the work and careers of dramatists who will potentially make significant contributions to the national theatre repertory. At no charge, Resident Playwrights benefit from Chicago Dramatists' fullest and longest-term support (a 3-year, renewable term), with complete access to all programs and services. Admittance to the program is selective, with emphasis on artistic and professional accomplishment or potential. While most Resident Playwrights are from the Chicago area, dramatists from around the country who are able to spend substantial time in Chicago may also apply; however, there are no stipends for travel or housing. Interested playwrights should contact Chicago Dramatists for full information and details of the application procedure, which includes the submission of 2 plays, a resume and letters of recommendation and intent. *deadline:* 1 Apr each year (no submission before 1 Mar).

The Playwrights' Network provides any U.S. playwright the opportunity to form an association with Chicago Dramatists. For an annual fee of $95, Network playwrights receive written script critiques, consideration for all programs and productions, class discounts, free admittance to events and other benefits.

Classes and the quarterly 10-Minute Workshop are open to all playwrights. Quarterly flyers announce events and programs, and include application procedures.

THE CHILDREN'S THEATRE FOUNDATION OF AMERICA (CTFA)

Box 8067; New Orleans, LA 70182; (504) 283-8868,
(FAX) 866-0502

Orlin Corey, *President*

Founded in 1958, The Children's Theatre Foundation of America (CTFA) is a not-for-profit organization which seeks to advance the artistic and professional interests of theatre and theatre education for children and youth by funding proposals of artists and scholars working in those fields. In the past CTFA has funded playwriting grants, scholarships, research, performances and lectures, theatre festivals, conferences, symposia, publications and crisis-management assistance. CTFA also administers the annual Aurand Harris Children's Theatre Grants and Fellowships (see Fellowships and Grants), as well as awarding a Medallion for significant achievement in the field of children's theatre.

CORPORATION FOR PUBLIC BROADCASTING

401 9th St; NW; Washington, DC 20004-2037; (202) 879-9600,
FAX 783-1019; Web site http://www.cpb.org

Vice President, Program Strategies

Founded in 1967, the Corporation for Public Broadcasting, a private not-for-profit organization funded by Congress, promotes and helps finance public television and radio. CPB provides grants to local public television and radio stations; conducts research in audience development, new broadcasting technologies and other areas. The corporation helped establish the Public Broadcasting Service and National Public Radio (see entries in this section). It supports public radio programming through programming grants to stations and other producers, and television programming by funding proposals made by stations and independent producers.

THE DRAMATISTS GUILD OF AMERICA, INC.
1501 Broadway, Suite 701; New York, NY 10036; (212) 398-9366,
FAX 944-0420; email tstratton@dramaguild.com
John Weidman, *President*
Christopher Wilson, *Executive Director*

The Dramatists Guild of America, founded over 75 years ago, is the only professional association governed by and established to advance the rights of playwrights, composers and lyricists. The Guild has more than 6000 members worldwide, from beginning writers to Broadway veterans. Membership benefits include a business affairs toll-free hotline, which offers advice on all theatre-related topics, including options, commissions, copyright procedures and contract reviews; model production contracts, which provide the best protection for the writer at all levels of production; collaboration, commission and licensing agreements; seminars led by experienced professionals concerning pressing topics for today's dramatist; access to a national health insurance program and a group term life insurance plan; free/discounted tickets to Off-Broadway/Broadway performances; and a meeting room that can accommodate more than 50 people for readings and backers auditions, available for a nominal rental fee. The Guild has 4 levels of membership: 1. Active ($125 a year): writers who have been produced on Broadway, Off-Broadway or on the main stage of a LORT theatre; 2. Associate ($75 a year): theatrical writers who have been produced in other venues or who have completed a full script; 3. Student ($35 a year): full-time students enrolled in an accredited writing degree program; 4. Estate ($125 a year): representatives of the estates of deceased authors.

Members receive *The Dramatists Guild Newsletter*, issued 6 times a year with up-to-date business affairs articles and script opportunities; *The Dramatist*, a magazine that contains interviews as well as articles on all aspects of theatre; *The Dramatists Guild Resource Directory*, a biannual collection of contact information on producers, agents, contests, workshops and production companies. The periodicals are available to nonwriters on a subscription basis: Individual Subscribers ($25 a year): individuals receive *The Dramatist* only; Institutional Subscribers ($135 a year): educational institutions, libraries and educational theatres receive all 3 periodicals and have access to audiotapes of Guild seminars; Professional Subscribers ($200 a year): producers and agents receive all 3 periodicals.

THE FIELD

161 Sixth Ave; New York, NY 10013; (212) 691–6969,
   FAX 255-2053; email thefield@aol.com
Katherine Longstreth, *Executive Director*

The Field, founded in 1986, is a not-for-profit organization dedicated to helping independent performing artists develop artistically and professionally through a variety of performance opportunities, workshops, services and publications. The Field does not engage in curatorial activity; all artists are eligible to participate in its programs. Of special interest to New York metropolitan area playwrights wishing to produce their own work are programs such as Fielday, a showcase of 12-minute work and Fieldwork, 10-week workshops for works-in-progress, guided by trained facilitators, culminating in performances. Writers should also note Artward Bound, 6 free 10-day summer residencies at various rural locations on the East Coast for multidisciplinary groups of 6–10 artists with at least 3 years professional experience; transportation, room and board, rehearsal space, workshops and career guidance seminars all provided; send resume and completed application. The Field assists artists with many aspects of producing their work, including grant writing, fund-raising, project management, securing performance and rehearsal space, and cooperative promotional efforts. Publications include a monthly newsletter; the *Self-Production Guide*; *Funding Guide for Independent Artists*; *Space Chase Guide to New and Lesser Known Performance Opportunities*, a listing of local performance spaces throughout New York City as well as out-of-town festivals, residencies and artist colonies; and *Gone with the Field Guide*, a listing of performing possibilities for independent artists in 40 cities across the United States. All programs are available to members and non-members; members receive all publications, discounts on programs and may use the Field as an umbrella organization, falling under its not-for-profit status. Annual membership costs $75; individual programs range in cost from $15–75. Field programs are also offered in Atlanta, Chicago, Dallas, Houston, Miami, Philadelphia, Salt Lake City, San Francisco, Seattle, Tokyo, Toronto and Washington, DC.

FIRST STAGE

Box 38280; Los Angeles, CA 90038; (323) 850-6271,
    FAX 850-6295; email firststge@aol.com
Dennis Safren, *Literary Manager*

Founded in 1983, First Stage is a service organization for playwrights that holds staged readings, which are videotaped for the author's archival purposes; conducts workshops; provides referral services for playwrights; and publishes *First Stage Newsletter*. Services are free to nonmembers, except for workshops, which are available to members only. Membership dues are $45 per quarter or $160 per year; $60 per year for nonlocal members.

THE FOUNDATION CENTER

National Libraries:
1001 Connecticut Ave NW; Washington, DC 20036; (202) 331-1400;
79 Fifth Ave; New York, NY 10003; (212) 620-4230, FAX 807-3677;
    Web site http://www.fdncenter.org
Judith Margolin, *Vice President, Public Services, New York Library*
Field Offices:
312 Sutter St; San Francisco, CA 94108; (415) 397-0902;
Hurt Bldg, Suite 150, Grand Lobby; 50 Hurt Plaza;
    Atlanta, GA 30303; (404) 880-0094;
1422 Euclid, Suite 1356; Cleveland, OH 44115; (216) 861-1934

The Foundation Center is a nationwide service organization established and supported by foundations to provide a single authoritative source of information on foundation giving. It disseminates information on foundations through a public service program and through such publications as *The Foundation Directory* and *The Foundation Grants Index*. Of special interest is *Foundation Grants to Individuals*, which lists scholarships, fellowships, residencies, internships, grants, loans, awards, prizes and other forms of assistance available to individuals from approximately 3800 grantmakers (1999 edition $65). The center maintains 5 libraries and a national network of more than 213 cooperating collections. For the name of the collection nearest you or for more information about the center's programs, call toll free (800) 424-9836 or visit the Web site.

GREENSBORO PLAYWRIGHTS' FORUM

c/o City Arts; 200 North Davie St, Box #2; Greensboro, NC 27401;
   (336) 335-6426, FAX 373-2659;
   email gsoplaywrights@juno.com;
   Web site http://www.ci.greensboro.nc.us/leisure/drama
Stephen D. Hyers, *Director*

GPF was founded in 1993 to facilitate a monthly gathering for playwrights to discuss works in progress, share knowledge and encourage each other's artistic growth. Programs include cold and staged readings of member's plays and the annual North Carolina New Play Project open to NC playwrights; winner receives $100 and workshop production; *deadline:* 10 Oct 2000. GPF also provides members with studio space for play development and publishes *New Play Catalog*, which lists plays written by members. Membership is open to anyone. Annual dues are $25.

THE HARBOR THEATRE WORKSHOP

160 West 71st St, PHA; New York, NY 10023; (212) 787-1945
Stuart Warmflash, *Artistic Director*

The Harbor Theatre Workshop, a not-for-profit organization founded in 1994, is a developmental lab for 8 member theatre writers and a company of 30 actors cast specifically for writers' projects. Membership is available to playwrights, composers and librettists who have a body of work, are committed to rewrites and who work well in a supportive, professional atmosphere. The Workshop meets every Thursday in New York City for 3 hours and provides cold and/or rehearsed readings, followed by a short, playwright-driven critique from Workshop members. Full productions, an annual one-act festival and public readings of developed work are produced by the Harbor Theatre Company at least once during the season. Dues for the 1999-2000 season were $350.

HATCH-BILLOPS COLLECTION

491 Broadway, 7th Floor; New York, NY 10012-4412;
    (212) 966-3231, FAX 966-3231 (call first);
    email hatchbillops@worldnet.att.net
James V. Hatch, *Executive Secretary*

Founded in 1975, the Hatch-Billops Collection is a not-for-profit research library specializing in black American art and theatre history. It collects and preserves primary and secondary resource materials in the black cultural arts; provides tools and access to these materials for artists and scholars, as well as the general public; and develops programs in the arts which use the collection's resources. The library's holdings include 1800 oral-history tapes; theatre programs; approximately 300 unpublished plays by black American writers from 1858 to the present; files of clippings, letters, announcements and brochures on theatre, art and film; slides, photographs and posters; and more than 4000 books and 400 periodicals. The collection also presents a number of salon interviews and films, which are open to the public; and publishes transcriptions of its annual "Artist and Influence" series of salon interviews, many of which feature playwrights. The collection is open to artists, scholars and the public by appointment only at a rate of $5 per hour.

HISPANIC ORGANIZATION OF LATIN ACTORS (HOLA)

Clemente Soto Vélez Cultural Center; 107 Suffolk St, 3rd Floor;
    New York, NY 10002; (212) 253-1015, FAX 253-9651;
    email holagram@aol.com; Web site http://www.hellohola.org
Manuel Alfaro, *Executive Director*

Founded in 1975, HOLA is a not-for-profit arts service organization for Hispanic performers and related artists. HOLA provides information, a 24-hour hotline, casting referral services, professional seminars and workshops. The organization publishes a biennial *Directory of Hispanic Talent: HOLA Pages* (including an on-line version) and a newsletter, *La Nueva Ola*, which lists job opportunities, grants and contests of interest to Hispanic artists. Members pay annual dues of $49.

INDEPENDENT FEATURE PROJECT (IFP)

104 West 29th St, 12th Floor; New York, NY 10001-5310;
   (212) 465-8200, FAX 465-8525; email ifpny@ifp.org;
   Web site http://www.ifp.org
Michelle Byrd, *Executive Director*

The Independent Feature Project (IFP), a not-for-profit membership-supported organization, was founded in 1979 to encourage creativity and diversity in films produced outside the established studio system. The IFP produces the IFP Market, which features 300 American independent features, shorts, works-in-progress, documentaries and feature scripts. The IFP and IFP/West publish *Filmmaker*, a quarterly magazine. IFP also sponsors a series of screenings, professional seminars and industry showcases, including a conference on screenplay development. Group health insurance, production insurance, discounts, a Resource Program, publications and a series of transcripts of previous seminars and workshops are available to members. Membership dues start at $100 a year ($65 for students).

INSTITUTE FOR CONTEMPORARY EAST EUROPEAN DRAMA AND THEATRE

The City University of New York Graduate Center; 365 5th Ave;
   New York, NY 10016-4307; (212) 817-1869;
   email seep@gc.cuny.edu
Daniel C. Gerould, *Director*

The Institute for Contemporary East European Drama and Theatre, under the auspices of the Martin E. Segal Theatre Center, publishes a triquarterly journal, *Slavic and East European Performance: Drama, Theatre, Film,* which is available by subscription ($10 a year, $15 foreign) and includes articles about current events in the East European and Slavic theatre, as well as reviews of productions and interviews with playwrights, directors and other theatre artists. The Institute also has available 2 annotated bibliographies of English translations of Eastern European plays written since 1945: *Soviet Plays in Translation* and *Polish Plays in Translation* ($5 each, $6 foreign). The institute is interested in hearing of published or unpublished translations for possible listing in updated editions of these bibliographies; translators may submit descriptive letters or scripts.

INSTITUTE OF OUTDOOR DRAMA

CB #3240; University of North Carolina; Chapel Hill, NC 27599-3240;
(919) 962-1328, FAX 962-4212; email outdoor@unc.edu;
Web site http://www.unc.edu/depts/outdoor/
Scott J. Parker, *Director*

The Institute of Outdoor Drama, founded in 1963, is a research and advisory agency of the University of North Carolina. It serves as a communications link between producers of existing outdoor dramas and is a resource for groups, agencies or individuals who wish to create new outdoor dramas or who are seeking information on the field. The institute provides professional consultation and conducts feasibility studies; holds annual auditions for summer employment in outdoor drama; sponsors conferences, lectures and symposia; and publishes a quarterly newsletter, as well as information bulletins. Writers should note that the institute maintains a roster of available artists and production personnel, including playwrights and composers. It seeks to interest established playwrights and composers in participating in the creation of new outdoor dramas, and to encourage and advise new playwrights who wish to write for this specialized form of theatre.

INTERNATIONAL THEATRE INSTITUTE—U.S. CENTER (ITI/US)

Theatre Communications Group; 355 Lexington Ave;
New York, NY 10017-6603; (212) 697-5230, FAX 983-4847;
email iti@tcg.org; Web site http://www.tcg.org
Martha W. Coigney, *Director*

Now operating centers in 92 countries, ITI was founded in 1948 by UNESCO "to promote the exchange of knowledge and practice in the theatre arts." The U.S. Center of ITI became part of Theatre Communications Group in November 1999. ITI assists foreign theatre visitors in the U.S. and American theatre representatives traveling abroad. The ITI International Theatre Collection is a reference library which documents theatrical activity in 146 countries and houses over 12,700 plays from 97 countries. American playwrights, as well as other theatre professionals, frequently use the collection to make international connections; to consult foreign theatre directories for names of producers, directors or companies with a view to submitting plays abroad; and to research the programs and policies of theatres or managements. ITI answers numerous requests from abroad about American plays and also provides information on rights to foreign plays to American producers, directors and literary managers. TCG/ITI Travel Grants, funded by the Trust for Mutual Understanding, offer modest support ($1000-$2500) for travel and exchange between U.S. theatres and theatre artists and their colleagues in Russia and Central/Eastern Europe. (See TCG Artistic Programs in Fellowships and Grants. Program guidelines are also available on TCG's Web site.)

THE INTERNATIONAL WOMEN'S WRITING GUILD

Box 810, Gracie Station; New York, NY 10028-0082;
(212) 737-7536, FAX 737-9469; email iwwg@iwwg.com;
Web site http://www.iwwg.com
Hannelore Hahn, *Executive Director*

The International Women's Writing Guild, founded in 1976, is a network of international women writers. Playwrights, television and film writers, songwriters, producers and other women involved in the performing arts are included in its membership. Workshops are offered throughout the U.S. and annually at a week-long writing conference/retreat at Skidmore College in Saratoga Springs, NY. Members may also submit playscripts to theatres who have offered to read, critique and possibly produce IWWG members' works. *Network*, a 32-page newsletter published 6 times a year, provides a forum for members to share views and to learn about playwriting contests and awards, and theatre- and TV-related opportunities. The guild offers contacts with literary agents, group health insurance and other services to its members. Annual dues are $35 ($45 for foreign membership).

LA TELARAÑA

PMB 104; 266 Elmwood Ave; Buffalo, NY 14222;
(716) 645-2943; email td6@acsu.buffalo.edu
tatiana de la tierra, *Director*

La telaraña supports Latina lesbian writers by providing information, referrals, access to resources and a connection to each other through *el telarañazo*, a newsletter that includes current news and information on contests; calls for writing submissions and retreats; and a networking/support list of members for members. (All correspondence must be addressed directly to tatiana de la tierra, not to la telaraña.)

LEAGUE OF CHICAGO THEATRES/LEAGUE OF CHICAGO THEATRES FOUNDATION

228 South Wabash, Suite 300; Chicago, IL 60604; (312) 554-9800,
FAX 922-7202; email theleague@aol.com;
Web site http://www.theaterchicago.org

Founded in 1979, the League of Chicago Theatres/League of Chicago Theatres Foundation is a member organization which advocates for the business and artistic needs of the Chicago theatre community. It operates as an information clearinghouse; offers vendor discounts, including a cooperative advertising program; conducts the Annual Theatre CommUNITY Conference; markets "Play Money" Theater Gift Certificates; coordinates the non-Equity general auditions; implements marketing initiatives such as the award-winning Sears Theater Fever; and sells half-price theatre tickets through its seven Hot Tix locations. Publications include the bimonthly *Theater Guide* in partnership with *Stagebill* magazine. Professional companies incorporated for at least one year are eligible to join.

LEAGUE OF PROFESSIONAL THEATRE WOMEN/NEW YORK

c/o Isobel Robins; 248 East 68th St; New York, NY 10021;
(212) 744-6003, FAX 744-6838;
Web site http://www.theatrewomen.org
Isobel Robins and Harriet Slaughter, *Co-Presidents*

Founded in 1979, the league is a not-for-profit organization of theatre professionals providing programs and services which promote women in all areas of professional theatre; create industry-related opportunities for women; and highlight contributions of theatre women, past and present. Through its salons, seminars, educational programs, social events, awards and festivals, the league links professional theatres with theatre women nationally and internationally and provides an ongoing forum for ideas, methods and issues of concern to the theatrical community and its audiences. Programs include the Lee Reynolds Award, given annually to a woman or women whose work for, in, about or through the medium of theatre has helped to illuminate the possibilities for social, cultural or political change; the Oral History Project, which seeks to chronicle and document the contribution of significant theatre women; a membership directory; and panels discussing topics of interest to women theatre professionals with well-known experts in the field. Regular monthly meetings enable members to network, initiate programs and serve on committees. To be eligible for membership in the league, playwrights, composers, librettists and lyricists must have had a work presented in a First Class production in the U.S. or Canada; or in a New York City theatre under Equity's Basic Minimum Contract, excluding showcases; or at least 2 productions presented in a resident theatre, as defined under Equity's Minimum Basic Contract for Resident Theatres. All other theatre professionals must meet criteria listed in brochure. Annual dues are $100. For further details of membership eligibility and application procedure, write or call for membership information brochure.

LITERARY MANAGERS AND DRAMATURGS OF THE AMERICAS (LMDA)

121 Avenue of the Americas, Suite 505; New York, NY 10013;
    (212) 965-0586, FAX 699-6940; email lmda@lmda.org;
    Web site http://lmda.org

DD Kugler, *President*

LMDA is the professional service organization for American and Canadian literary managers and dramaturgs, founded in 1985 to affirm, examine and develop these professions. Among the programs and services it offers to members are a toll-free telephone job line; discussion and announcement listservs; Early Career Dramaturgs, which identifies and encourages new members of the profession and works to establish them in productive professional affiliations, as well as publishing a guide to internships; the University Caucus, which acts as a liaison between training and liberal arts programs and the profession, in addition to publishing a guide to training programs, sourcebooks for teachers of dramaturgy and an annual bibliography; and the Advocacy Caucus, which examines and reports on current working conditions of dramaturgs and literary managers. Publications include the quarterly *LMDA Review*; the *LMDA Script Exchange*; and the *Production Notebooks Project* that documents the conception, research, planning and realization of oustanding theatre productions. Each June, LMDA holds an annual conference. Voting membership is open to dramaturgs and literary managers only. Associate membership is open to playwrights, artistic directors, literary agents, educators and other theatre professionals interested in dramaturgy. Dues are $25 for students, $45 for associate members, $60 for voting members and $130 for institutional memberships.

LUMINOUS VISIONS

267 West 89th St; New York, NY 10024; (212) 581-7455, 724-7059,
    FAX 581-3964

Carla Pinza, *Co-Founder and Artistic Director*

Founded in 1976, Luminous Visions is a multicultural, not-for-profit organization dedicated to developing the creative skills of film and television writers, directors and actors seeking employment within the English-speaking film and television mainstream. Luminous Visions offers year-round youth workshops to develop acting, writing and musical talent in students ages 6-17. The organization sponsors a weekly workshop for writers, an annual Writers Forum and a spring Staged Reading Festival.

MARY ANDERSON CENTER FOR THE ARTS

101 St. Francis Dr; Mount Saint Francis, IN 47146; (812) 923-8602,
 FAX 923-0294; email maca@iglou.com
Debra Carmody, *Executive Director*

The Mary Anderson Center, founded in 1989, is a not-for-profit organization
dedicated to providing artists with a quiet place where they can concentrate and
work on their craft. Named after the 19th-century actress from Louisville who
rose to become an international celebrity, the center is located on 400 acres in
southern Indiana. The center's goal is to provide retreats and residencies for
artists in many disciplines (see the organization's entry in Colonies and
Residencies). As part of its outreach effort to the Midwest and the nation, the
center sponsors symposia, conferences and other gatherings which explore, in a
multidisciplinary mode, topics of major interest to society and to artists.
Contributors to the center receive a quarterly newsletter featuring center
activities and news of area artists.

MEET THE COMPOSER

2112 Broadway, Suite 505; New York, NY 10023; (212) 787-3601,
 FAX 787-3745
Heather Hitchens, *President*

Meet The Composer, a national service organization, was founded in 1974 to
increase opportunities for composers by fostering the creation, performance and
dissemination of their music. A not-for-profit organization, Meet The Composer
raises money from foundations, corporations, individual patrons and government
sources, and designs programs that support all styles and genres of music—from
folk, ethnic, jazz, electronic, symphonic and chamber to choral, music theatre,
opera and dance. MTC provides artist fees to not-for-profit organizations that
perform, present or commission original works. Its programs include: National
Endowment for the Arts Commissioning Music/USA, American Symphony
Orchestra League Music Alive, New Residencies (see Meet The Composer Grant
Programs in Fellowships and Grants), and the Meet the Composer Fund and
Affiliate Network.

MISSOURI ASSOCIATION OF PLAYWRIGHTS

830 North Spoede Rd; St. Louis, MO 63141; (314) 567-6341,
FAX 647-0945
Jo Lovins, *President*

Missouri Association of Playwrights (MAP) was founded in 1976 to assist playwrights in developing their skills. The association's activities include monthly meetings which are open to the public (Sep-Jun) at which members' scripts are presented as fully staged readings or workshops; guest speakers and seminars on playwriting are offered. Periodically the Association presents a full production of one-act plays. Script submission for full productions and staged readings are limited to works of MAP members only. Membership is open to all playwrights, but most members live in the greater St. Louis area (including southwest IL and out-state MO). Annual dues are $20.

NATIONAL ALLIANCE FOR MUSICAL THEATRE

330 West 45th St, Lobby B; New York, NY 10036-3854;
(212) 265-5376, FAX 582-8730; email namtheatre@aol.com;
Web site http://www.bway.net/namt
Trudi Biggs, *Interim Executive Director*

The National Alliance For Musical Theatre, founded in 1985, is the national service organization for musical theatre. The Alliance's goal is to serve as a champion of the musical and to foster its continued growth, both by providing national networking and collaboration opportunities, and by nurturing the creation, development, production and recognition of new musicals. It has 108 member organizations in 32 states and the United Kingdom, including theatres and light opera companies, and performing arts centers that produce or present musicals. As part of its services, the Alliance organizes two annual conferences, maintains a Web site and publishes newletters and a membership directory. The Alliance also produces an annual Festival of New Musicals in New York City, which aims to encourage further production of the showcased works.

THE NATIONAL AUDIO THEATRE FESTIVALS (NATF)
(Formerly Midwest Radio Theatre)
115 Dikeman St; Hempstead, NY 11550; (516) 483-8321;
    FAX 538-7583; Web site http://www.natf.org
Sue Zizza, Executive Director

Founded in 1979, The National Audio Theatre Festivals is a national resource center for audio theatre. NAFT hosts The Audio Theatre Workshop, a week-long hands-on intensive at William Woods University in Fulton, Missouri. NATF is a membership-based professional and educational not-for-profit arts organization, whose services include providing information and referral services and technical assistance to interested individuals and groups; distributing educational materials; and publishing a newsletter and an on-line *Audio Dramatists Directory*, a guide to current audio artists, producers, programmers and profesional resources. NATF also holds an annual script contest to identify and promote emerging and established audio script writers. Winning scripts may be produced during one of a series of audio theatre workshops held each year (see The Audio Theatre Workshop in Development). Membership fees vary; check Web site for more information.

THE NATIONAL FOUNDATION FOR JEWISH CULTURE
330 Seventh Ave, 21st Floor; New York, NY 10001; (212) 629-0500,
    FAX 629-0508; email nfjc@jewishculture.org;
    Web site http://www.jewishculture.org
Richard A. Siegel, *Executive Director*

Founded in 1960, The National Foundation for Jewish Culture (NFJC) is the central cultural agency of the American Jewish community. The NFJC, dedicated to the enhancement of Jewish life in America through the support and promotion of the arts and humanities, provides programs and services to cultural institutions, local communities and individual artists and scholars in every region of the country. The NJFC serves as advocate and coordinator for the fields of Jewish culture through its Council of American Jewish Museums and Council of Archives and Research Libraries in Jewish Studies; sponsors grants and awards to artists, scholars and major cultural institutions such as YIVO, Leo Baeck Institute, American Jewish Historical Society, Histadrut Ivrit and the Jewish Publication Society of America; promotes an understanding and appreciation of contemporary Jewish life and culture through conferences, symposia, publications, media productions, traveling exhibitions, residencies and performances; and presents the annual Jewish Cultural Achievement Awards recognizing outstanding contributions to Jewish life in America through the arts and scholarship.

THE NATIONAL LEAGUE OF AMERICAN PEN WOMEN, INC.

1300 17th St NW; Washington, DC 20036-1973; (202) 785-1997,
FAX 452-6868; email nlapw1@juno.com;
Web site http://members.aol.com/penwomen/pen.htm
Wanda A. Rider, *National President*

Founded in 1897, NLAPW is a national membership organization for professional women writers, composers and visual artists. It holds local monthly meetings, annual State Association meetings, a National Biennial Convention and a National Art Show, and will sponsor the Mature Woman Scholarship Award in 2002 (see Fellowships and Grants). Members, who receive a bimonthly magazine, *The Pen Woman*, and a National Roster, pay national dues of $30 a year; dues for individual branches are separate and vary.

NATIONAL PUBLIC RADIO

635 Massachusetts Ave NW; Washington, DC 20001-3753;
(202) 414-2399, FAX 414-3032; email atrudeau@npr.org
Web site http://www.npr.org
Andy Trudeau, *Director, Program Acquisition and Production*

Founded in 1970, National Public Radio is a private not-for-profit membership organization which provides a national program service to its more than 500 member noncommercial radio stations. It is funded by its member stations, the Corporation for Public Broadcasting and corporate grants. Among the programs available to member stations is *NPR Playhouse*, which presents 29-minute dramatic programs, series and serials. Writers should note that NPR does not itself read or produce plays. It acquires broadcast rights to produced packages and will consider fully produced programs or works-in-progress on tape only.

THE NATIONAL THEATRE WORKSHOP OF THE HANDICAPPED
354 Broome St, Loft 5-F; New York, NY 10013; (212) 941-9511,
FAX 941-9486; email ntwh@aol.com; Web site http://ntwh.org
Rick Curry S. J., *Founder and Artistic Director*
Founded in 1977, the National Theatre Workshop of the Handicapped (NTWH) is
a not-for-profit organization founded to provide persons with disabilities the
opportunity to learn the communication skills necessary to pursue a life in
professional theatre and to enhance their opportunities in the workplace. NTWH
advocates for persons with physical disabilities in the theatre and offers a forum
for dramatic literature on themes of disability. NTWH runs the Playwrights
Workshop, a 2-week program held each spring for 4 playwrights to develop new
works in residence at NTWH-Crosby, a fully accessible residential facility in
Belfast, ME; selected works are fully produced later. NTWH also offers
professional instruction in acting, singing, voice, movement, playwriting and fine
arts at the NTWH studio in New York City. Persons with disabilities who are
interested in participating in these training programs should contact NTWH for
more information.

NEW DRAMATISTS
424 West 44th St; New York, NY 10036; (212) 757-6960,
FAX 265-4738; email newdram@aol.com;
Web site http://www.newdramatists.org
Joel Ruark, *Executive Director*
Todd London, *Artistic Director*
Founded in 1949, New Dramatists is the nation's oldest playwright development
center, designed to provide member playwrights with the resources they need
to create plays for the American theatre. Rather than producing plays, New
Dramatists aids playwrights in the development of their craft through play
readings and workshops; dramaturgy; a resident director program; musical
theatre development and training; ScriptShare (a national script distribution
program); fellowships, awards and prizes; a free ticket program for Broadway
and Off-Broadway productions; writing spaces and accommodations; and
photocopying. All services are provided free of charge to members.

In addition, New Dramatists hosts several playwright exchanges, including
the Brooks Atkinson Exchange/Max Weitzenhoffer Fellowship to the Royal
National Theatre, England; the Sumner Locke Elliott Exchange to the Australian
National Playwrights Centre; the Danish American National Cultural Exchange;
and a bicoastal exchange with A.S.K. Theater Projects, Los Angeles.

Membership is open to emerging playwrights living in the greater New York
area, and to those living outside the area who demonstrate a willingness to
regularly travel to New York and actively participate in this community of artists.
Playwrights interested in applying for membership should write for guidelines.

NEW ENGLAND THEATRE CONFERENCE (NETC)
Northeastern University; 360 Huntington Ave; Boston, MA 02115;
(617) 424-9275, FAX 424-1057; email netc@world.com;
Web site http://www.nctheatreconference.org
Clinton D. Campbell, *Managing Director*
Founded in 1952, New England Theatre Conference is a membership organization primarily but not exclusively for the New England theatre community, including playwrights, teachers, students and theatre professionals. Services include an annual conference, publication of a member directory and annual summer theatre auditions. NETC also administers both the John Gassner Memorial Playwriting Award and Aurand Harris Memorial Playwriting Award (see Prizes). The organization publishes *New England Theatre Journal* and *NETC News*. Membership dues are $20 for students, $35 for individuals and $80 for groups.

NEW PLAYWRIGHTS FOUNDATION
c/o 608 San Vicente Blvd, #18; Santa Monica, CA 90402;
(310) 393-3682; Web site http://www.newplaywrights.org
Jeffrey Lee Bergquist, *Artistic Director*
Founded in 1968, New Playwrights Foundation is a service organization for writers working in theatre, film, television and video. The foundation runs developmental workshops, holds readings, occasionally coproduces video and film projects and assists members in furthering their careers. Membership in NPF is limited to a maximum of 15 writers who must be able to attend meetings in Santa Monica every other Monday. Candidates for membership attend meetings before submitting materials to be reviewed by the group. Annual membership dues are $25.

THE NEW YORK PUBLIC LIBRARY FOR THE PERFORMING ARTS
Library Annex; 521 West 43rd St; New York, NY 10036;
(212) 870-1639, FAX 870-1868; email rtaylor@nypl.org;
Web site http://www.nypl.org
Bob Taylor, *Curator, The Billy Rose Theatre Collection*
Founded in 1931, The Billy Rose Theatre Collection, a division of the Library for the Performing Arts, is open to the public (aged 18 and over) and contains material on all aspects of theatrical art and the entertainment world, including stage, film, radio, television, circus, vaudeville and burlesque. The Theatre on Film and Tape Project (TOFT) is a special collection of films and videotapes of theatrical productions recorded during performance, as well as informal dialogues with important theatrical personalities. Tapes are available for viewing by appointment (call 212-870-1641) to students, theatre professionals and researchers.

NON-TRADITIONAL CASTING PROJECT

1560 Broadway, Suite 1600; New York, NY 10036;
  (212) 730-4750 (voice), -4913 (TDD), FAX 730-4820;
  email info@ntcp.org; Web site http://www.ntcp.org
Sharon Jensen, *Executive Director*

Founded in 1986, the Non-Traditional Casting Project is a not-for-profit organization which exists to address and seek solutions to the problems of racism and exclusion in the theatre and related media, particularly those which involve creative personnel: including, but not limited to, actors, directors, writers, designers and producers. The project works to advance the creative participation of artists of color and artists with disabilities through both advocacy and specific projects. Key NTCP programs include Artist Files/Artist Files Online, a national talent bank; roundtable discussions with industry leaders; forums; and a national Information and Consulting Program. Writers of color and/or with disabilities, who are citizens or residents of the U.S. or Canada and have had at least one play given a professional production or staged reading should send a resume for inclusion in Artist Files/Artist Files Online, indicating their cultural identification and, in the case of disabled artists, any accommodation they may use; those interested in contacting listed artists will call them or their agents directly.

NORTH CAROLINA WRITER'S NETWORK

Box 954; Carrboro, NC 27510; (919) 967-9540, FAX 929-0535;
  email mail@ncwriters.org; Web site http://www.ncwriters.org
Linda Hobson, Executive Director

Founded in 1985, North Carolina Writer's Network (NCWN) is an independent literary arts service organization serving writers at all stages of development. NCWN provides workshops, an annual conference held every November and the Paul Green Playwrights Prize (see Prizes). NCWN also publishes *Writer's Network News*, a 24-page bimonthly newsletter. Annual membership dues are $40.

NORTHWEST PLAYWRIGHTS GUILD

Box 1728; Portland, OR 97207; (503) 452-4778;
  email bjscript@teleport.com; Web site http://www.nwpg.org
Bill Johnson, *Office Manager*

Founded in 1982, Northwest Playwrights Guild is an information clearinghouse and support group for playwrights. The guild sponsors public readings, holds workshops and produces regional conferences on theatre that include the full production of original scripts. The guild publishes a quarterly, *Script*, that contains articles on theatre in the Northwest, as well as update newsletters that provide information on current script opportunities. Membership dues are $25 a year.

OLLANTAY CENTER FOR THE ARTS

Box 720636; Jackson Heights, NY 11372-0636; (718) 565-6499,
FAX 446-7806

Pedro R. Monge-Rafuls, *Executive and Artistic Director*

Founded as a multidisciplinary Hispanic arts center in 1977, OLLANTAY has developed a Hispanic Heritage Center for the Arts in America which provides the resources needed to pursue research and develop new programs and initiatives in the field. The center maintains a resource bank of video and audio tapes, slides, books, plays and articles, which may be viewed by writing for an appointment. Its unique Playwriting Workshop, an annual intensive course of 2-4 weeks, provides an opportunity for playwrights wishing to write in Spanish to work under the direction of major Latin-American playwrights who reside outside the U.S. *OLLANTAY Theater Magazine* is a biannual journal in English and Spanish which gives local playwrights, critics and scholars the opportunity to share their knowledge and experience of Hispanic theatre within the framework of American and world drama. The magazine, which publishes at least one play in each issue, is available to subscribers. Annual subscription is $20 for individuals, $35 for organizations.

OPERA AMERICA

1156 15th St NW, Suite 810; Washington, DC 20005-3287;
(202) 293-4466, FAX 393-0735; email frontdesk@operaam.org;
Web site http://www.operaamerica.org

Jamie Driver, *Managing Director, Artistic & Audience Initiatives*

Founded in 1970, OPERA America is the not-for-profit service organization for the professional opera field in North America and allied international members. OPERA America provides a variety of informational, technical and financial services to its membership and serves as a resource to the media, funders, government agencies and the general public.

PEN AMERICAN CENTER

568 Broadway; New York, NY 10012; (212) 334-1660,
   FAX 334-2181; email pen@pen.org;
   Web site http://www.pen.org
Michael Roberts, *Executive Director*

Founded in 1921, PEN is an international association of writers; the American Center is the largest of the 130 centers that comprise International PEN. The 2700 members of PEN American Center are established North American writers and translators, and literary editors. PEN activities include the Freedom-to-Write program; monthly symposia, readings and other public events; a prison writing program; and a translator-publisher clearinghouse. Among PEN's annual prizes and awards are The Gregory Kolovakos Award, PEN-Book-of-the-Month Club Translation Prize and the PEN/Laura Pels Foundation Award for Drama (see Prizes); and Writing Awards for Prisoners, awarded to the authors of the best fiction, nonfiction, drama and poetry received from prisoner-writers in the U.S. The PEN Writers Fund and the PEN Fund for Writers & Editors with AIDS assist writers (see Emergency Funds). PEN's publications include *Grants and Awards Available to American Writers*, a biennially updated directory of prizes, grants, fellowships and awards (2000-2001 edition $15 postpaid); *The PEN Prison Writing Information Bulletin*; and *A Handbook for Literary Translators*, available for free on the Web site.

PHILADELPHIA DRAMATISTS CENTER (PDC)

1516 South St; Philadelphia, PA 19146; (215) 735-1441;
   email pdc@libertynet.org;
   Web site http://www.libertynet.org/pdc
Ed Shockley, *Artistic Director*
Jon Dorf, *Managing Director*

Philadelphia Dramatists Center is a service organization for professional playwrights, screenwriters and musical theatre writers. Programs and services include developmental readings, writers' circles, chats with area artistic directors and literary managers, craft development workshops, access to actor/director files, discounted tickets to participating theatres, rehearsal space, a telephone hotline listing upcoming events and publication of the bimonthly newsletter *First Draft*. Annual membership dues are $15 for students and $25 for individuals, which includes a subscription to *First Draft*.

PLAYMARKET

Box 9767; Wellington; New Zealand; 64-4-382-8462,
   FAX 64-4-382-8461; email plymkt@clear.net.nz;
   Web site http://www.playmarket.org.nz
Dilys Grant, *Director*
Susan Wilson, *Script Advisor*

Playmarket is a service organization for New Zealand playwrights, established in 1973 as a result of a growing interest in plays by New Zealand writers and a need to find new writers. The organization runs a script advisory and critiquing service, arranges workshop productions of promising scripts, and serves as the country's principal playwrights' agency, preparing and distributing copies of scripts and negotiating and collecting royalties. Playmarket's publications include *The Playmarket Directory of New Zealand Plays and Playwrights*, and the magazine *Playmarket News*.

THE PLAYWRIGHTS' CENTER

2301 Franklin Ave East; Minneapolis, MN 55406-1099;
   (612) 332-7481; email pwcenter@mtn.org;
   Web site http://www.pwcenter.org
Carlo Cuesta, *Executive Director*

The Playwrights' Center is a service organization for playwrights. Its programs include developmental services (cold readings and workshops using an Equity acting company); fellowships; exchanges with theatres and other developmental programs; a biannual journal; the Jones commissioning program; PlayLabs (see Development); playwriting classes; year-round programs for young writers; and the Many Voices program, designed to provide awards, education and lab services to new and emerging playwrights of color. The Center annually awards 5 Jerome Playwright-in-Residence Fellowships, for which competition is open nationally; 2 McKnight Fellowships, for which competition is open by professional nomination; 3 McKnight Advancement Grants open to Minnesota playwrights; and 3 Many Voices Multicultural Collaboration Grants (see The Playwrights' Center Grant Programs in Fellowships and Grants). A broad-based Center membership is available to any playwright or interested person. Benefits of general membership for playwrights include discounts on classes, applications for all Center programs, eligibility to apply for the Jones commission and script-development readings, and the Center's journal. Core (must be MN resident) and Associate Member Playwrights are selected by a review panel each spring, based on script submission. They have primary access to all Center programs and services, including developmental workshops and public readings. Write for Membership information.

THE PLAYWRIGHTS FOUNDATION
Box 460357; San Francisco, CA 94146; (415) 263-3986;
email bayplays@best.com
Belinda Taylor, *President*
Jayne Wenger, *Artistic Director*
The Playwrights Foundation provides developmental support to playwrights throughout the U.S., with emphasis on the northern CA region. It produces the annual Bay Area Playwrights Festival (see Development) and is developing a new year-round playwright services program, New Play Resources.

PLAYWRIGHTS THEATRE OF NEW JERSEY
33 Green Village Rd; Madison, NJ 07940; (973) 514-1787,
FAX 514-2060
Joseph Megel, *Artistic Director*
Founded in 1986, the Playwrights Theatre of New Jersey is both a service organization for playwrights of all ages and a professional developmental theatre. In addition to its New Play Development Program (see Playwrights Theatre of New Jersey in Development), PTNJ co-sponsors, with the New Jersey Council on the Arts, the New Jersey Writers Project, a statewide program which teaches prose, poetry and dramatic writing in schools. Specialized programs include a playwriting-for-teachers project; adult playwriting classes; children's creative dramatics classes; acting classes; and "special needs" playwriting projects which include work in housing projects and with senior citizens, teenage substance abusers, persons with physical disabilities and court- appointed youth, as well as a playwriting-in-prisons initiative; and a program that teaches Spanish-language prose, poetry and dramatic writing. Young playwrights festivals are held in Madison and Newark, in addition to a statewide festival which is part of the New Jersey Young Playwrights Program. Gifted and talented playwriting symposia, hosted by well-known playwrights, provide intensive 2-day experiences for up to 60 students from various school districts.

PLAZA DE LA RAZA

3540 North Mission Rd; Los Angeles, CA 90031; (323) 223-2475,
FAX 223-1804; email admin@plazaraza.org;
Web site http://www.plazaraza.org
Rose Cano, *Executive Director*

Founded in 1970, Plaza de la Raza is a cultural center for the arts and education, primarily serving the surrounding community of East Los Angeles. Of special interest to playwrights is the center's Nuevo L.A. Chicano TheatreWorks project, designed to discover, develop and present the work of Chicano playwrights. Initiated in 1989 and recurring approximately every 4 years, depending on funding, as part of the Nuevo L.A. Chicano Art Series cycle (Visual Arts, Music, Dance and Theatre), the project develops new one-acts through a 2-week workshop with director and actors, culminating in public readings; some plays are selected for subsequent full production. Latino playwrights who are California residents should contact the center for information on when and how to apply for the next round of the program. Plaza de la Raza also conducts classes in drama, dance, music and the visual arts; provides resources for teachers in the community; and sponsors special events, exhibits and performances.

PROFESSIONAL ASSOCIATION OF CANADIAN THEATRES/ PACT COMMUNICATIONS CENTRE

30 St. Patrick St, 2nd Floor; Toronto, Ontario; Canada; M5T 3A3;
(416) 595-6455, FAX 595-6450; email pactcomm@idirect.com;
Web site http://www.pact.ca
Pat Bradley, *Executive Director*

PACT is the national service and trade association representing professional English-language theatres in Canada. PACT was incorporated in 1976 to work on behalf of its member theatres in the areas of advocacy, labor relations, professional development and communications. The members' newsletter *Impact!* is published quarterly. PACT Communications Centre (PCC) was established in 1985 as the charitable wing of PACT in order to improve and expand communications and information services. PCC publishes *The Theatre Listing*, an annual directory of English-language Canadian theatres, rehearsal and performance spaces, government agencies and arts service organizations; and *Artsboard*, the monthly bulletin of employment opportunities in the arts in Canada.

PUBLIC BROADCASTING SERVICE

1320 Braddock Pl; Alexandria, VA 22314-1698; (703) 739-5000,
FAX 739-0775; email www@pbs.org;
Web site http://www.pbs.org

Founded in 1969, the Public Broadcasting Service is a private not-for-profit corporation that acquires and distributes programs to its 347 member stations. The PBS Program Management Department can advise independent producers about the development of specific projects. Information about the preparation, presentation and funding of projects can be obtained from the PBS Program Management Department or by visiting the Web site.

THE PURPLE CIRCUIT

921 North Naomi St; Burbank, CA 91505; (818) 953-5096, -5072;
email purplecir@aol.com
Bill Kaiser, *Coordinator*

The Purple Circuit is a network of gay, lesbian, queer, bisexual and transsexual theatres, producers, performers and "Kindred Spirits" (theatres which are not exclusively gay or lesbian in orientation but are interested in producing gay or lesbian material on a regular basis). The Purple Circuit Hotline (818-953-5072) provides information on gay and lesbian shows currently playing in California and advises travelers on shows around the U.S. and abroad, as well as providing information for playwrights, journalists and others interested in promoting gay/lesbian/bisexual/transgender theatre and performance. The Purple Circuit publishes news, information and articles of interest to its constituency in its quarterly newsletter, On the Purple Circuit. The Purple Circuit Directory lists theatres and producers around the world that are interested in presenting gay, lesbian, bisexual and transsexual works.

THE SCRIPTWRITERS NETWORK

11684 Ventura Blvd, #508; Studio City, CA 91604; (323) 848-9477;
    Web site http://scriptwritersnetwork.com
Bill Lundy, *Chair*

Though the Scriptwriters Network, founded in 1986, is predominantly an
affiliation of film, television and corporate/industrial writers, playwrights are
welcome. Meetings feature guest speakers; developmental feedback on scripts
is available; and staged readings may be arranged in conjunction with other
groups. The network sponsors members-only contests and publishes a
newsletter. Prospective members submit a professionally formatted script and
a completed application; membership is not based on the quality of the script.
There is a $15 initiation fee, and dues are $50 a year for nonlocal members,
$60 for Southern California residents.

THE SONGWRITERS GUILD OF AMERICA

1560 Broadway, Room 1306; New York, NY 10036; (212) 768-7902,
    FAX 768-9048; email songnews@aol.com;
    Web site http://www.songwriters.org
George Wurzbach, *National Projects Director*
Head Office:
1500 Harbor Blvd; Weehawken, NJ 07087-6732; (201) 867-7603
Los Angeles Office:
6430 Sunset Blvd; Hollywood, CA 90028; (323) 462-1108
Nashville Office:
1222 16th Ave; Nashville, TN 37212; (615) 329-1782

Founded in 1931, the Songwriters Guild is a voluntary national association run
by and for songwriters; all officers and directors are unpaid. Among its many
services to composers and lyricists, the guild provides a standard songwriter's
contract and reviews this and other contracts on request; collects writers'
royalties from music publishers; maintains a copyright renewal service; conducts
songwriting workshops and critique sessions with special rates for members;
issues news bulletins with essential information for writers; and offers a group
medical and life insurance plan. Full members of the guild must be published
songwriters and pay dues on a graduated scale from $70-400. Unpublished
songwriters may become associate members and pay dues of $55 per year. Write
for membership application.

S.T.A.G.E. (SOCIETY FOR THEATRICAL ARTISTS' GUIDANCE AND ENHANCEMENT)

Box 214820; Dallas, TX 75221; (214) 630-7722,
   FAX 630-4468; email stage_tx@swbell.net;
   Web site http://www.stage-online.org
Julia Park, *Operations Manager*

Founded in 1981, S.T.A.G.E. is a not-for-profit membership organization based in Dallas/Fort Worth, which serves as an information clearinghouse and provides training and education for the theatre, broadcast, and film industries in north central Texas. The society maintains a library of plays, theatre texts and resource information; offers counseling on agents, unions, personal marketing and other career-related matters; posts job opportunities; maintains a callboard for regional auditions in theatre and film; and sponsors an actor's showcase, Noon Preview. Members of S.T.A.G.E. receive audition postings via email and a monthly publication, *CENTERSTAGE.* Annual dues are $65; $45 for volunteers.

THEATRE BAY AREA (TBA)

870 Market St, Suite 375; San Francisco, CA 94102;
   (415) 430-1140, FAX 430-1145; email tba@theatrebayarea.org;
   Web site http://www.theatrebayarea.org

Founded in 1976, TBA is a resource organization for San Francisco Bay Area theatre workers. Its membership includes 3200 individuals and more than 325 theatre and dance companies. Its programs include TIX Bay Area, San Francisco's half-price ticket booth; TIX By Mail, a half-price ticket catalog; professional workshops; and communications and networking services. Membership includes a subscription to *Callboard*, a monthly magazine featuring articles, interviews and essays on the Northern California theatre scene, as well as information on play contests and festivals, and listings of production activity, workshops, classes, auditions, jobs and services. TBA also publishes *Theatre Directory of the Bay Area*, which includes entries of local theatre companies; the *Performance and Rehearsal Rental Directory of the Bay Area* with listings of rehearsal and performance spaces; *Sources of Publicity*; and *Management Memo*, a monthly newsletter for theatre administrators and artistic directors. The Web site includes a playbill calendar, ticket information and sample *Callboard* articles. Annual dues are $40 (add $14 to receive *Callboard* 1st-class).

THEATRE COMMUNICATIONS GROUP

355 Lexington Ave; New York, NY 10017-6603; (212) 697-5230,
FAX 983-4847; email tcg@tcg.org; Web site http://www.tcg.org
Ben Cameron, *Executive Director*

Founded in 1961 as the national service organization for the not-for-profit professional theatre, Theatre Communications Group (TCG) offers a wide array of services in line with its mission: to strengthen, nurture and promote the not-for-profit American theatre. TCG's programs and services encompass four primary areas of activity: artistic programs, including grants to artists and theatres; management programs, including conferences and forums, industry research and management training; advocacy, serving as the primary national advocate for the field, in conjunction with the American Arts Alliance; and publications. Each of TCG's programs is designed to address at least one of the following central strategies: increasing the organizational efficiency of TCG's member theatres, cultivating and celebrating the artistic talent and achievements of the field and promoting a larger public understanding of and appreciation for the theatre field.

During 1999-2000, TCG claimed 17,000 individual members, including theatre professionals, educators, students, theatre enthusiasts and a network of more than 360 member theatres in 45 states and the District of Columbia, representing a wide range of institutional sizes, structures and aesthetics. In the belief that the diversity of the theatre field is its greatest strength, TCG's membership criteria embrace a wide range of theatres and practices.

TCG's artistic programs available to playwrights include the National Theatre Artists Residency Program, funded by The Pew Charitable Trusts, which supports extended relationships between theatres and individual artists by providing the resources for long-term residencies; the NEA/TCG Theatre Residency Program for Playwrights, which provides $25,000 grants to help playwrights create new works and strengthen relationships with theatres (which also receive a $5000 Seagram/Universal Residency Award when they host a resident playwright); Extended Collaboration Grants, funded by Metropolitan Life Foundation, which help theatres hire playwrights for extended developmental work with other collaborators; the New Generations Program, funded by the Doris Duke Charitable Foundation and The Andrew W. Mellon Foundation, which offers full-time mentorships in resident professional theatres; and TCG/ITI Travel Grants, funded by the Trust for Mutual Understanding, which support travel to Russia and Central/Eastern Europe. (See TCG Artistic Programs in Fellowships and Grants. Program guidelines are also available on TCG's Web site.)

In addition to *American Theatre* magazine, which provides an up-to-date perspective on theatre throughout the country and includes the full texts of five new plays annually, other TCG publications of interest to theatre writers include *Theatre Directory*, a pocket-sized directory, which provides complete contact information for more than 360 not-for-profit professional theatres and related organizations across the U.S.; *Stage Writers Handbook: A Complete Business Guide for Playwrights, Composers, Lyricists and Librettists*, by Dana Singer; *The Production Notebooks: Theatre in Process, Volume I*, edited by Mark Bly; *Stage Directors Handbook: Opportunities for Directors and Choreographers*, edited by the SDC Foundation; and *ArtSEARCH*, a biweekly bulletin of job opportunities in the arts. TCG also publishes plays and musicals, and books on actors and acting, directors, designers, playwrights, theatre history, criticism and theory, and resource books on the not-for-profit professional theatre. (For further information, see the Publications and Useful Publications chapters of this book. A complete publications catalog is available from TCG and on TCG's Web site.)

Individual members receive a free subscription to *American Theatre* magazine, discounted tickets to performances at more than 220 theatres nationwide and discounts on all TCG books and books from other select theatre publishers distributed by TCG. Other benefits include a no-fee affinity credit card and discounts on car rentals, hotel accommodations and express delivery service. Individual memberships are available for $35 a year, $20 for students. (See the TCG membership application in the back of this book.)

THEATRE LEAGUE ALLIANCE
644 South Figueroa St; Los Angeles, CA 90017; (213) 614-0556,
FAX 614-0561; email info@theatrela.org;
Web site http://www.theatrela.org

A not-for-profit association of more than 160 theatres and producers, Theatre LA was founded in 1975 to unite, represent and promote theatre in Southern California. Theatre LA administers the annual Ovation Awards; produces the *Theatre Times Directory* (a cooperative advertising opportunity in the *Los Angeles Times*), operates WebTix (online half-price ticketing), and provides information and referral services for members. Asssociate membership opportunities are also available to individuals, professionals and businesses interested in supporting theatre.

THE THEATRE MUSEUM

1 E Tavistock St; London WC2E 7PA; England; 44-207-943-4700,
FAX 44-207-943-4777

The Theatre Museum, a branch of the Victoria & Albert Museum, is Britain's national museum of the performing arts. In addition to its regular displays, which feature 400 years of the history, technology, art and craft of theatre, and its special exhibitions, the museum houses the United Kingdom's largest archive of performing arts materials, including play texts, photographic and biographical files, theatre programs and reviews, and books about the theatre. The archive and study room is available by appointment (call during office hours) Wednesday to Friday, 10:30-1:00 p.m. and 2:00-4:30 p.m. The museum's education department runs workshops and study days on theatre practice for children, students and teachers. The museum also runs a program of celebrity play readings, seminars and events to give visitors insight into current theatre productions.

THEATRE PROJECT

(Formerly Baltimore Theatre Project, Inc.)
45 West Preston St; Baltimore, MD 21201; (410) 539-3091,
FAX 539-2137; email bby@earthlink.net
Bobby Mrozek, *Artistic Director*

Founded in 1971, the Theatre Project is committed to offering established and emerging performing artists a supportive environment to develop and present their work. Theatre Project productions provide Baltimore with a professional international center for diverse and exceptional artistic voices. Artists receive visitor housing; technical, promotional and front-of-house support; and opportunities to meet with other artists. Additional services include workshops, roundtables, seminars, open auditions and a shared database of Baltimore-area affiliated artists.

UBU REPERTORY THEATER

95 Wall St, 21st Floor; New York, NY 10005; (212) 509-1455,
    FAX 509-1635; email uburep@spacelab.net;
    Web site http://www.uburep.org.
Françoise Kourilsky, *Founder/Artistic Director*
Ubu Repertory Theater, founded in 1982, is a not-for-profit theatre center dedicated to introducing translations of contemporary French-language plays to the English-speaking audience (see Production). In addition to producing several plays a year, Ubu commissions translations and schedules reading programs, photography exhibits, panel discussions and workshops. Ubu publishes a series of contemporary plays by French-speaking playwrights in English translation, distributed nationally by TCG, and houses a French-English reference library of published plays and manuscripts.

VOLUNTEER LAWYERS FOR THE ARTS

1 East 53rd St, 6th Floor; New York, NY 10022;
    (212) 319-2787 (administrative office and Art Law Hotline),
    FAX 752-6575; email vlany@vlany.org;
    Web site http://www.vlany.org
Amy Schwartzman, *Executive Director*
Founded in 1969, Volunteer Lawyers for the Arts arranges free legal representation and legal education for the arts community. Individual artists and not-for-profit arts organizations unable to afford private counsel are eligible for VLA's services; VLA can be especially useful to playwrights with copyright or contract problems. There is an administrative fee per referral of $50-150 for individuals, $150-500 for not-for-profit organizations and $250 for not-for-profit incorporation and tax exemption. VLA's education program offers biweekly seminars on not-for-profit incorporation and evening seminars held regularly to educate attorneys and artists in specific areas of art law. Publications include *Model Contracts for Independent Contractors: Sample Provisions and Job Descriptions* ($15 plus $2.50 postage and handling); and the *VLA Guide to Copyright for Visual Artists* ($5.95 plus $2.50 postage and handling). For more information about VLA's publications and the 40 VLA affiliates across the country, contact Tina Cheung (ext 12) of the New York office; referrals can be made to volunteer lawyer organizations nationwide.

WOMEN'S THEATRE ALLIANCE (WTA)

407 South Dearborn, Suite 1775; Chicago, IL 60602;
(312) 408-9910; Web site http://www.wtac.org
Ester Lebo, *Outreach*

Founded in 1992, the Women's Theatre Alliance (WTA) is dedicated to the development of dramatic works by, for and about women and to the promotion of women's leadership within the Chicago theatre community. Programs of special interest to playwrights include the Play Development Workshop and New Plays Festival which unites women writers with a director and actors for a development process culminating in a 2-week festival of staged readings; Solo Voices, which facilitates the creation of one-woman shows and performance pieces; and the Salon Series, an informal presentation of new work offering social networking opportunities. WTA also publishes a monthly newsletter. Membership is open to all Chicago-area residents. Annual dues are $40.

W.O.W. CAFÉ, ETP

59-61 East 4th St, 4th Floor; New York, NY 10003; (212) 777-4280;
email sil_1210@hotmail.com;
Web site http://www.geocities.com/probe_wowgrl

Founded in 1980, W.O.W. (Women's One World) Café is a women's theatre collective whose membership is primarily but not exclusively lesbian. W.O.W. produces the work of women playwrights and performers. It has no permanent staff and its members are encouraged to participate in all aspects of the group's operations. In lieu of dues, members volunteer their services backstage on fellow members' productions in exchange for the opportunity to present their own work. Each show is produced by the member who initiates it. W.O.W. hosts cabarets in which members and non-members can perform; the first Friday of every month is the Rivers of Honey cabaret for women performers of color; every third Friday is a W.O.W. cabaret open to all women performers. W.O.W. Café also hosts an annual July 4th weekend retreat and a biannual spring Latina Playwrights Festival. The next festival will take place in spring 2002; call, email or visit the Web site for more information; *deadline:* 1 Dec 2001. Women interested in becoming members of W.O.W. Café may attend one of the collective's regular meetings, which are scheduled every Tuesday at 6:30 p.m.

WRITERS GUILD OF AMERICA, EAST (WGAE), AFL-CIO

555 West 57th St; New York, NY 10019-2967; (212) 767-7800,
    FAX 582-1909

Mona Mangan, *Executive Director*

WGAE is the union for freelance writers in the fields of motion pictures, television and radio who reside east of the Mississippi River (regardless of where they work). The union negotiates collective bargaining agreements for its members and represents them in grievances and arbitrations under those agreements. The guild gives annual awards, and sponsors a foundation which currently teaches film writing to disadvantaged high school students. WGAE participates in reciprocal arrangements with the International Affiliation of Writers Guilds and with its sister union, Writers Guild of America, west. The guild publishes a monthly newsletter, which is available to nonmembers by subscription; and a quarterly journal, *On Writing*. Write for information on WGAE's service for registering literary material, or call (212) 757-4360.

WRITERS GUILD OF AMERICA, WEST (WGAw)

7000 West 3rd St; Los Angeles, CA 90048-4329; (323) 951-4000,
    FAX 782-4800; Web site http://www.wga.org

John McLean, *Executive Director*

WGAw is the union for writers in the fields of motion pictures, television, radio and new media who write both entertainment and news programming. It represents its members in collective bargaining and other labor matters. It publishes a monthly magazine, *Written By*. The Guild registers material, including screen- and teleplays, books, plays, poetry and songs (call 323-782-4500). The library is open to the public Mon-Fri (call 323-782-4544).

YOUNG PLAYWRIGHTS INC.

321 West 44th St, #906; New York, NY 10036; (212) 307-1140,
FAX 307-1454; email writeaplay@aol.com;
Web site http://youngplaywrights.org
Sheri M. Goldhirsch, *Artistic Director*

Young Playwrights Inc. (YPI), founded in 1981 by Stephen Sondheim, introduces young people to the theatre and encourages their self-expression through the art of playwriting. YPI strives to identify, develop and encourage playwrights aged 18 years and younger to develop new works for the theatre and to aid in the creation of the next generation of professional playwrights through the Young Playwrights Festival National Playwriting Contest (see Prizes), the Young Playwrights Spring Conference, and the Urban Retreat; to expose young people to theatre and playwriting through WRITING ON YOUR FEET! in-school playwriting workshops; to train teachers to integrate playwriting into basic curriculum through the TEACHING ON YOUR FEET! Teacher Training Institute; to develop and serve audiences that reflect the complex makeup of our society and to create the next generation of theatregoers through the TAKE A GROWNUP TO THE THEATER! ticket subsidy program, student matinees and a discount voucher program; to bring the vital experience of professional theatre free of charge to neglected inner-city public schools, community organizations and youth centers through the Young Playwrights School Tour; and to serve as an advocate for young writers regardless of ethnicity, physical ability, sexual orientation or economic status, and to ensure that their voices are heard and acknowledged by a diverse community of artists and theatregoers.

PART THREE
RESOURCES

Useful Publications
Online Resources
Submission Calendar
Special Interests Index
Book Index

USEFUL PUBLICATIONS

This is a selective listing of the publications that we think most usefully supplement the information given in the *Sourcebook*. Note that publications of interest to theatre writers are also described throughout this book, particularly in the chapter introductions, in the Membership and Service Organizations listings, and in the Online Resources chapter. We have purposely left out any "how to" books on the art of playwriting because we do not want to promote the concept of "writing-by-recipe." Pricing and ordering information may change after this book goes to press, so it would be wise to confirm details before ordering a publication.

AMERICAN THEATRE

Theatre Communications Group; 355 Lexington Ave; New York, NY
10017–6603; (212) 697–5230, FAX 557–5817;
email custserv@tcg.org; Web site http://www.tcg.org

1-year subscription/TCG membership $35; single issue $4.95. This magazine, published 10 times per year, provides comprehensive coverage of all aspects of theatre. *American Theatre* regularly features articles and interviews dealing with theatre writers and their works, and publishes the complete texts of 5 new plays a year. A special Season Preview issue each October lists schedules for more than 350 theatres nationwide, and monthly schedules for more than 300 theatres are published in each issue.

BACK STAGE

770 Broadway, 5th Floor; New York, NY 10003;
email backstage@backstage.com;
Web site http://www.backstage.com

1-year subscription $89, 2 years $139; single issue $2.75, $5 by mail. This performing arts weekly includes industry news; reports from cities across the country; reviews; and columns, including "Playwrights' Corner." The primary focus is on casting, theatres; other producers sometimes run ads soliciting scripts; workshops and classes for playwrights are also likely to be advertised here.

HOLLYWOOD SCRIPTWRITER

Box 10277; Burbank, CA 91510; (818) 845–5525;
email editor@hollywoodscriptwriter.com;
Web site http://www.hollywoodscriptwriter.com

1-year subscription (12 issues) $35, 6 months $25. This 20-page trade paper contains a "MARKETS for Your Work" section that includes "Plays Wanted" listings, as well as interviews and articles giving advice to playwrights and screenwriters. A list of back issues with a summary of the contents of each issue is available; call for information and a free sample.

Literary Market Place 2000

R. R. Bowker; 121 Chanlon Rd; New Providence, NJ 07974;
(908) 464-6800, (888) BOWKER-2, FAX (908) 771-7704;
email info@bowker.com; Web site http://www.bowker.com

1999. 2079 pp, $189.95 (plus 7% postage and handling and sales tax where applicable) paper. Also available on their Web site (various fee options and subscription rates are given). This directory of the American book publishing industry gives contact information for book publishers and those in related fields, and includes 2 "Names & Numbers" indexes totaling over 600 pages. The 2001 LMP is due out in October 2000.

Market Insight...for Playwrights

Box 12778; San Diego, CA 92112-7778; (800) 895-4720;
email info@MarketInSight.virtualave.net;
Web site http://MarketInSight.virtualave.net

1-year subscription (12 issues) $45, email subscription $35. This monthly newsletter for playwrights provides submission guidelines for theatres, residencies, publishers and contests, as well as updates on personnel changes at theatres, special programs for women writers, and more; contest application forms come with each issue; updates are provided via email; call for free sample.

Music, Dance & Theater Scholarships

Conway Greene Publishing Company; 1414 South Green Rd,
Suite 206; South Euclid, OH 44121; (800) 977-2665;
Web site http://www.conwaygreene.com

2nd edition, 1998. 490 pp, $24.95 (plus $4 postage and handling and sales tax where applicable) paper. This guide provides information on more than 1800 theatre, music and dance conservatory and undergraduate programs, as well as more than 5000 professional and educational scholarship opportunities. It also includes detailed information on audition requirements, decision processes at individual schools, special scholarship stipulations and student profiles.

Playhouse America!

Feedback Theatrebooks; 305 Madison Ave, Suite 1146;
New York, NY 10165; (212) 687-4185, (800) 800-8671,
FAX (207) 359-5532; email feedback@hypernet.com;
Web site http://www.hypernet.com/prospero.html

1991. 300 pp, $16.95 (plus $3 postage and handling and sales tax where applicable) paper. This directory contains the addresses and phone numbers of more than 3500 theatres across the country; it includes a cross-reference to specialty theatres (e.g., Dinner Theatres & Showboats, Military Theatres).

POETS & WRITERS MAGAZINE
Poets & Writers, Inc; 72 Spring St; New York, NY 10012;
 (212) 226-3586
Subscription office: Box 543; Mount Morris, IL 61054;
 (815) 743-1123
1-year subscription (6 issues) $19.95, 2 years $38; single issue $4.95. A bi-monthly magazine delivering profiles of noted authors and publishing professionals, practical how-to articles, a comprehensive listing of grants and awards for writers and special sections on subjects ranging from small presses to writers conferences.

PROFESSIONAL PLAYSCRIPT FORMAT GUIDELINES AND SAMPLE
Feedback Theatrebooks; 305 Madison Ave, Suite 1146;
 New York, NY 10165; (212) 687-4185, (800) 800-8671,
 FAX (207) 359-5532; email feedback@hypernet.com;
 Web site http://www.hypernet.com/prospero.html
1991. 28 pp, $4.95 (plus $1.75 postage and handling and sales tax where applicable) paper. This booklet provides detailed instructions for laying out a script in a professional manner, includes a "Margin and Tab Setting Guide" and sample pages of script.

SONGWRITER'S MARKET, Ian C. Bessler, ed
Writer's Digest Books; 1507 Dana Ave; Cincinnati, OH 45207;
 (513) 531-2690, ext 423, FAX 531-2686;
 email songmarket@fwpubs.com;
 Web site http://www.writersdigest.com
2000. 522 pp, $23.99 (plus $3 shipping and handling and sales tax where applicable) paper. This annually updated directory, which lists contact information for more than 2000 song markets, includes a section on musical theatre. It also lists associations, contests and workshops of interest to songwriters. The 2001 edition is due out in fall 2001.

STAGE DIRECTIONS MAGAZINE
SMW Communications; 250 West 57th St, Suite 420;
 New York, NY 10107; (212) 265-8890, FAX 265-8908;
 email stagedir@aol.com;
 Web site http://www.stage-directions.com
1-year subscription (10 issues) $26, 2 years $48; single issue $3.50. This magazine provides information on royalty issues, play publishing, new play festivals and workshops/seminars for playwrights. A special Season Planner issue each November contains a directory of royalty houses.

STAGE WRITERS HANDBOOK: A COMPLETE BUSINESS GUIDE FOR PLAYWRIGHTS, COMPOSERS, LYRICISTS AND LIBRETTISTS by Dana Singer

Theatre Communications Group; 355 Lexington Ave;
New York, NY 10017-6603; (212) 697-5230, FAX 983-4847;
email custserv@tcg.org; Web site http://www.tcg.org

1997. 328 pp, $18.95 (plus $3 postage and handling for 1 book, $1 for each additional book) paper. This comprehensive guide, written by the former Executive Director of The Dramatists Guild, covers such topics as copyright, collaboration, underlying rights, marketing and self-promotion, production contracts, representation (agents and lawyers), publishers, authors' relationships with directors, and videotaping and electronic rights.

THEATRE DIRECTORY 2000-01

Theatre Communications Group; 355 Lexington Ave; New York, NY
10017-6603; (212) 697-5230, FAX 983-4847;
email custserv@tcg.org; Web site http://www.tcg.org

2000. 190 pp, $9.95 (plus $3 postage and handling for 1 book, $1 for each additional book) paper. TCG's annually updated directory provides complete contact information for more than 350 not-for-profit professional theatres, including new TCG theatres that join after this *Sourcebook* is published, and more than 100 arts resource organizations. Includes special interest, personnel and state-by-state indexes for all theatres.

THEATRE PROFILES 12

Theatre Communications Group; 355 Lexington Ave; New York, NY
10017-6603; (212) 697-5230, FAX 983-4847;
email custserv@tcg.org; Web site http://www.tcg.org

1996. 240 pp, $22.95 (plus $3 postage and handling for 1 book, $1 for each additional book) paper. The 12th volume of this biennial series contains artistic profiles, production photographs, financial information and repertoire information for the 1993-95 seasons of 257 theatres.

U.S. COPYRIGHT OFFICE PUBLICATIONS

Library of Congress; Copyright Office; Publications Section, LM–455;
101 Independence Ave SE; Washington, DC 20559;
(202) 707–3000; Web site http://www.loc.gov/copyright

There are many ways to receive free informational circulars and registration forms: via Web site; call (202) 707-9100 and key in your fax number to receive them by fax; you may also call or write, but these methods take longer.

THE WRITER

c/o Kalmbach Publishing Co; 21027 Crossroads Circle; Box 1612;
Waukesha, WI 53187; (262) 796–8776, FAX 798–6468;
email editor@writermag.com;
Web site http://www.writermag.com

1-year subscription (12 issues) $29, 2 years $55, 3 years $78. This monthly magazine announces contests in a "Prize Offers" column and publishes a special "Where to Sell Manuscripts" section, which includes lists of play publishers in the September issue.

WRITER'S MARKET, Kirsten Holm, ed

Writer's Digest Books; 1507 Dana Ave; Cincinnati, OH 45207;
(513) 531–2690, ext 287, FAX 531–2686;
email writersmarket@fwpubs.com;
Web site http://www.writersmarket.com

2000. 1120 pp, $29.99 (plus $3 postage and handling and sales tax where applicable) paper; it is also available in a book/CD-ROM/online package for $49.99. This annually updated directory lists more than 4000 places where writers may sell their manuscripts. It includes many opportunities for playwrights and screenwriters. The 2001 edition is due out in September 2000.

ONLINE RESOURCES

What's here and what's not.

Now that nearly every organization, theatre and otherwise, has established an Internet presence, our goal in presenting Online Resources in *Dramatists Sourcebook* is to spotlight sites that offer useful information distinct from opportunities already included elsewhere in the book. Many URLs from local playwrights' home pages, community playwrights' forums and college playwriting courses appear in the far reaches of search engine results. In the interest of accuracy and longevity, we have opted to include a select menu of sites which are mainstays of the Internet playwriting community—sites with free content and broad professional appeal.

As you well know, empires are destroyed in a day in the online world. The site you landed on this morning might not exist by the time you check back tomorrow. Or worse yet, it might exist but not have been updated or maintained for the last five years. Take the time to assess the editorial merit and accuracy of the site.

What we present here is a guide to the best that's currently available, which you can also use to measure the quality of new ventures. We urge you to take advantage of this powerful medium. Use it as a research tool, a reference desk, a host of networking opportunities and a creative space.

Note: Help us improve our listings for future editions. On your travels through cyberspace, if you happen upon some "must see" sites for playwrights that we've missed, please let us know: ksova@tcg.org.

For beginners.

If the Internet is new to you, it can be an overwhelming experience, particularly when looking over the shoulder of a ten-year-old whiz kid. In fact, experienced users, of any age, may not be the best teachers. Consider picking up a copy of *The Internet: The Rough Guide 2000* (Angus J. Kennedy, Rough Guides Ltd, London). It explains in jargon-free English what the Internet is and how to use it. It also offers a topical index of worthwhile Web sites. Another place to start is *Yahoo! Internet Life's* "100 Best Web Sites for 2000" at: http://www.zdnet.com/yil/content/mag/0001/100compute.html. Both publications will help you transition from page to screen.

Search Engines.

For experienced users, the better you can define your searches the more exacting the results will be. One of the often-overlooked tools for uprooting difficult or obscure information is your choice of search engine. There are over a hundred options available to you, the most popular of which are Alta Vista, Ask Jeeves, Excite, Go/Infoseek, Google, Hotbot, Looksmart, Lycos, MSN Search, Netscape Search, Snap, Web Crawler and Yahoo. So what's the difference? You have likely had the experience of typing "playwriting" in a search engine only to discover through related links on someone else's Web page that your original search results were incomplete. The reason for this is that each search engine indexes its Web sites in slightly different ways. Some do it by the amount of times a particular word appears on the site's homepage, others rank sites by the number of links on the Web that point to them, and still others rely on humans to compile the listings. For detailed information about search engines, including capsule summaries of the 23 most popular sites, visit: http://searchenginewatch.com.

Once you get a handle on the functionality of search engines, Search Engines Worldwide: http://www.twics.com/~takakuwa/search/search.html offers a directory of hotlinks to international search engines organized by country (includes U.S.).

AFRICAN AMERICAN ONLINE WRITERS GUILD
http://www.blackwriters.org

Description: not-for-profit literary arts organization which uses technology to encourage community, provide content and celebrate the culture of African-American writers. **Site includes:** current issue of their newsletter *Cultured Writer*, information and application for AAOWG Mentor Program; bulletin boards and chat; conference information; links to writers' resources; and membership information.

AISLE SAY
http://www.aislesay.com/index.html

Description: no-frills compilation of reviews of professional and community theatre productions from around the country written by local theatre critics. The writing style and quality of the reviews varies significantly, but the coverage is thorough and fair. **Site includes:** reviews; links to critics' biographies; and an index of additional review sources.

AMERICANTHEATER WEB
http://www.americantheaterweb.com

Description: interactive database where theatres around the country can post their production schedules. The listings are not comprehensive but the collection of theatres is diverse. **Site includes:** theatre headlines; current production listings by region; a small bookstore; and free email access and chat.

ARTS JOURNAL
http://www.artsjournal.com

Description: chronicle of feature articles on arts and culture from more than 180 English-language newspapers, magazines and publications. Direct links to the most interesting or important stories are posted every weekday beginning at 5 a.m. PST on the Arts Journal news pages. Stories from sites that charge for access are excluded, as are sites that require visitors to register, with the exception of the *New York Times*. **Site includes:** articles sorted by discipline and date; newsletter; and related links.

ARTSWIRE

http://www.artswire.org

Description: multi-service Web site designed to help artists and arts organizations take advantage of internet technologies through training, planning and technical support. **Site includes:** *ArtsWire CURRENT*, a weekly chronicle of arts and technology related articles; the *Nonprofit Toolkit*, a monthly magazine exploring technology and its relationship to the arts; Spiderschool, online tutorials and workshops; Web Base, a database of cultural resources that includes indices for playwriting and theatre; and job listings.

ASIAN AMERICAN THEATRE REVIEW

http://www.abcflash.com/a&e/r_tang/AATR.html

Description: hub site for Asian-American theatre. **Site includes:** news; calendar; list of Asian-American playwrights and their plays; directory of Asian-American theatre companies; reviews; library of anthologies, individual authors and critical perspectives; bulletin boards; and related links.

BARTLEBYS.COM

http://www.bartleby.com

Description: online version of Bartleby's bookstore, which provides searchable databases of reference materials free of charge. **Site includes:** unlimited access to *Columbia Encyclopedia, Sixth Edition*; *American Heritage Dictionary, Third Edition*; *Roget's II: The New Thesaurus*; *American Heritage Book of English Usage*; *Simpson's Contemporary Quotations*; *Bartlett's Familiar Quotations*; *Oxford Shakespeare*; and *Gray's Anatomy*.

CAMBRIDGE ONLINE DICTIONARY

http://dictionary.cambridge.org

Description: *Cambridge Dictionary* online. **Site includes:** *Cambridge International Dictionary* of English; American English; international dictionary of idiom; and international dictionary of phrasal verbs.

CITYSEARCH

http://www.citysearch.com

Description: nationwide, city-specific entertainment guide for arts, events, restaurants, etc. by city, date or subject. **Site includes:** database of cities by neighborhood and zip code; and hotlinks to local services.

CULTUREFINDER.COM
http://www.culturefinder.com

Description: database to search for and purchase tickets to arts events nationwide. Listings are searchable by event name, performer or composer, organization date and location. **Site includes:** season schedules for over 3000 arts organizations and listings for over 350,000 events in more than 1500 cities.

THE ENCYCLOPEDIA MYTHICA
http://www.pantheon.org/mythica

Description: capsule definitions and explanations from world mythology, folklore and legend. **Site includes:** lists of over 5700 articles; 300 illustrations, maps and genealogy tables from over 25 cultures.

INDIE PLANET
http://www.indieplanet.com

Description: zone for independent/alternative artists to connect. Site has excellent design, and a lively writing style. **Site includes:** reviews and features on theatre, film and several other culture-oriented topics, including real-time interviews with artists; opportunity to create a free home page in their community space; message boards; and chat.

INKSPOT
http://www.inkspot.com

Description: comprehensive community resource center for writers (soon to merge with Random House's site Xlibris). **Site includes:** chat; forums; market and networking information; online workshops; well-maintained classified ads, including contests; tips for young writers and teachers; and feature articles and columns.

INTERNATIONAL CENTRE FOR WOMEN PLAYWRIGHTS INC.
http://www.cadvision.com/sdempsey/icwphmpg.htm

Description: support site for international women playwrights. **Site includes:** membership list; member play list by genre; list of members' recent awards and productions; newsletter called *Seasons*; related links; membership and conference information; and articles on craft.

INTERNET MOVIE DATABASE

http://www.imdb.com

Description: comprehensive searchable database containing information about film, video and made-for-TV movies. **Site includes:** current selections; movie and TV news; U.S. movie show times searchable by date, city, state and zip code; photo galleries; IMDB staff recommendations; independent film index; new releases; box office hits; and user favorites.

JOGLE'S FAVORITE THEATRE RELATED RESOURCES

http://www.on-broadway.com/links/index.asp

Description: searchable database of theatre-related links. Webmasters may add their sites to the database by submitting online form. **Site includes:** listings of awards, news and information; education; media and shopping; professional resources; stagecraft; communities and discussion; tickets and reviews; people; shows; and theatres and companies.

KMC A BRIEF GUIDE TO INTERNET RESOURCES IN THEATRE AND PERFORMANCE STUDIES

http://www.stetson.edu/departments/csata/thr_guid.html

Description: selected list of theatre resources compiled by Ken McCoy, Assistant Professor of Communication Studies and Theatre Arts at Stetson College. **Site includes:** description of selection criteria; list of McCoy's most used sites; resources by theatre subject; primary source materials; listservs and newsgroups; and other guides.

NATIVE AMERICAN WOMEN PLAYWRIGHT'S ARCHIVE

http://staff.lib.muohio.edu/nawpa/NAWPA.html

Description: catalog of the writing of Native American Women Playwrights. **Site includes:** playwright's directory; online exhibit of Spiderwoman Theater; bibliography of Native American Women's Theater; author's roundtable; archive of *NAWPA* newsletters; listings of recent programs and productions; and related links.

NEW YORK THEATRE WIRE

http://www.nytheatre-wire.com

Description: source for what's playing on New York City stages. **Site includes:** articles; publication information; Broadway and Off-Broadway listings; reviews; a museum directory; and classifieds.

THE OFF-OFF BROADWAY REVIEW
http://www.oobr.com
Description: no-frills publication detailing the Off-Off-Broadway scene. **Site includes:** reviews; listings; archives; and information about the Midtown International Theatre Festival.

PLAYBILL ONLINE
http://www.playbill.com
Description: expanded version of *Playbill*'s print publication, including information about both Broadway and Off-Broadway theatre. **Site includes:** news from the U.S., Canada and international theatre communities; Broadway and Off-Broadway listings; online ticket sales; feature articles; jobs bank; and links to the Drama Bookshop and Theatre Central, among others.

THE PLAYWRIGHTING SEMINARS
http://www.vcu.edu/artweb/playwriting/seminar.html
Description: online textbook by playwright Richard Toscan which covers both the craft and the business of playwriting. **Site includes:** seminar topics such as content, film, structure, writing life, script format and business; quotes from established playwrights; and a reading list.

PLAYWRIGHTS ON THE WEB
http://www.stageplays.com/writers.htm
Description: international database of playwrights and their Web sites. **Site includes:** plays listed alphabetically by author and genre; playwrights' discussion forum; callboard; and a link to The Internet Theatre Bookshop.

STAGEBILL ONLINE
http://www.stagebill.com/index.html
Description: performance locator for theatre, dance, opera, jazz and classical music. **Site includes:** searchable database by city, art form, performer, key word and date or date range; in-depth articles and profiles; and chat.

THEATRE CENTRAL
http://www.playbill.com/cgi-bin/plb/central?cmd=start
Description: one of the first theatre portal sites; maintained less vigorously than it used to be. **Site includes:** related links; and hotlinks to wired theatre professionals who submitted themselves to the database.

THEATRE.COM
http://www.theatre.com

Description: Broadway portal site. **Site includes:** theatre news; listings and ticket information; theatre merchandise; links to official Broadway show Web sites; membership information, including eligibility for discount tickets; and the "theatre district" composed of bulletin boards and chat.

THEATRE-LINK.COM
http://www.theatre-link.com

Description: well-organized and -maintained index of theatre-related Web sites. **Site includes:** database searchable by academic programs; Broadway and West End shows; casting and contact services; goods and services; news and information; Shakespeare; shows and performances; theatres and venues; theatre-related resources; groups and organizations; and other indices. Discussion boards are soon to come.

THEATREMANIA
http://theatermania.com

Description: theatre portal site featuring theatre news and information from major cities around the country including select international locations. **Site includes:** theatre tickets and listings organized by city; feature and news articles; links to theatre festivals and awards; theatre store; and membership information.

THE U.S. COPYRIGHT OFFICE
http://lcweb.loc.gov/copyright

Description: branch of the Library of Congress. **Site includes:** what's new section; office information; general copyright information; copyright records; announcements; publications, including forms in downloadable format; legislation; international; and copyright links.

WOMEN OF COLOR WOMEN OF WORDS
http://www.scils.rutgers.edu/~cybers/home.html

Description: features accomplished women playwrights of color with a focus on African-Americans. **Site includes:** writers' bios; list of completed works; links to Amazon.com; directory of libraries and research centers with an African-American focus; list of critical/biographical resources; hotlinks to wired theatres that produce multicultural work; directory of dissertations on featured playwrights; recommended books on African-American theatre history; and related links.

WriteExpress Online Rhyming Dictionary
http://www.writeexpress.com/online2.html

Description: online rhyming dictionary. **Site includes:** searchable database by end, last, double, beginning and first syllable rhymes.

Writersdigest.com
The 101 Best Web Sites for Writers
http://www.writersdigest.com/101sites_2000

Description: well-indexed list of Web resources for writers. **Site includes:** links to search engines; general reference; specialized reference; media, news and reference; job sites; the writing life; genre; poetry; screenwriting; zines; writers' organizations; and more.

WWW Virtual Library Theatre and Drama
http://www.vl-theatre.com

Description: library of international theatre resources updated daily. **Site includes:** links to academic/training institutions; book dealers; conferences for theatre scholars; electronic text archives and plays online; general resources; online journals; monologues in print; plays in print; scholarly books; theatre books in print; theatre companies; theatre image bank; and theatre syllabus bank, among others.

WWW.YOURDICTIONARY.COM
http://www.yourdictionary.com

Description: index of online dictionaries. **Site includes:** dictionaries (of varying completion and quality) in 221 languages; multilingual dictionaries; specialty English dictionaries; thesauri and other vocabulary aids; language identifiers and guessers; index of dictionary indices; web of online grammar; and web of linguistic fun.

Yahoo Theatre Index
http://dir.yahoo.com/Arts/Performing_Arts/Theater

Description: index of theatre-related sites. **Site includes:** thirty-eight different subjects, including playwrights and plays.

SUBMISSION CALENDAR

September 2000–August 2001

Included here are all *specified* deadlines contained in Production, Prizes, Publication, Development, Fellowships and Grants, Colonies and Residencies, and Membership and Service Organizations. Please note that suggested submission dates for theatres listed in Production are not included. There are always important deadlines that are not available at press time and so cannot be included here.

SEPTEMBER 2000

Contact for exact deadline during this month:

OCTOBER 2000

Contact for exact deadline during this month:

NOVEMBER 2000

Contact for exact deadline during this month:

DECEMBER 2000

JANUARY 2001

Contact for exact deadline during this month:

FEBRUARY 2001

Contact for exact deadline during this month:

MARCH 2001

APRIL 2001

MAY 2001

JUNE 2001

Contact for exact deadline during this month:

JULY 2001

Contact for exact deadline during this month:

AUGUST 2001

SPECIAL INTERESTS INDEX

Here is a guide to entries which indicate a particular or exclusive interest in certain types of material, or which contain an element of special interest to writers in certain categories. Under Young Audiences, Media, Multimedia, Performance Art and Solo Performance, we list every entry of interest to writers in these fields. In the cases of Adaptations, Musicals, One-acts and Translations, there are numerous theatres willing to consider these types of material; we list here only those theatres and other organizations that give major focus to them. The Multicultural category is for those organizations expressing general interest in muticultural works. Under African-American, Asian-American, Hispanic/Latin-American and Native American Theatre, we have included only those organizations specifically seeking work by or about people from these ethnic groups. The Student/College Submission category refers to college writing students or students in an affiliated writing program. Young Playwrights is a special interest category only for playwrights 18 or under.

ADAPTATION

A Noise Within, 6
Arden Theatre Company, 15
Asolo Theatre Company, 18
Bailiwick Repertory, 21
California Shakespeare Festival, 26
California Theatre Center, 27
Children's Theatre Company, The, 30
Classic Stage Company, 33
Cornerstone Theater Company, 36
Coterie Theatre, The, 36
Court Theatre, 36
Dallas Children's Theater, 37
Fountain Theatre, The, 48
Germinal Stage Denver, 51
Guthrie Theater, The, 53
Honolulu Theatre for Youth, 56
Human Race Theatre
  Company, The, 57

COMEDY

Adobe Theatre Company, 9
American Theater Company, 14
B Street Theatre, The, 20
BoarsHead Theater, 25
Center Theater Ensemble, 29
Colony Theatre Company, The, 34
Contemporary Drama Service, 177
Dell'Arte Players Company, 38
Dudley Riggs Instant Theatre
   Company, 42
Eldridge Publishing Company, 178
Eureka Theatre Company, 45
Fountain Theatre, The, 48
George Street Playhouse, 50
Gretna Theatre, 53
Hedgerow Theatre, 54
Horizon Theatre Company, 56
John Drew Theater, 62
Kavinoky Theatre, The, 63
McLaren Memorial Comedy
   Playwriting Competition, 152
Midwest Theatre Network Original
   Play Competition/Rochester
   Playwright Festival, 153
Mixed Blood Theatre Company, 75
New American Comedy (NAC)
   Festival, 157
Pegasus Theatre, 87
Rockford Review, 185
Round House Theatre, 97
Signature Theatre, 102
Society Hill Playhouse, 102
State Theater Company, 106
Strawdog Theatre Company, 107
Totem Pole Playhouse, 117
Trustus Theatre, 118
Virginia Stage Company, 121
Walnut Street Theatre Company, The,
   122
Watertower Theatre, Inc, 122

We Don't Need No Stinkin' Dramas,
   170
Willows Theatre Company, 124

DISABILITIES: Theatre for and by People with Disabilities

Arena Stage, 15
Bailiwick Repertory, 21
City Theatre Company, 32
Jean Kennedy Smith Playwriting
   Award, The, 147
Milwaukee Public Theatre, 74
National Theatre of the Deaf, 76
National Theatre Workshop of the
   Handicapped, The, 312
Non-Traditional Casting Project, 314
Other Voices Project, 201
Playwrights Theatre of New Jersey,
   318
Theater by the Blind, 110
Victory Gardens Theater, 120
VSA Arts Playwright Discovery
   Award, 169

EXPERIMENTAL THEATRE

Actors' Gang Theater, 8
Actors Theatre of Louisville, 9
Axis Theatre, 20
Barter Theatre, 22
BoarsHead Theater, 25
Bristol Riverside Theatre, 26
Childsplay, 31
City Theatre Company, 32
Cleveland Public Theatre, 33
Collages & Bricolages, 176
Crossroads Theatre Company, 37
Dixon Place, 39
Hidden Theatre, 55
Intiman Theatre, 61
La Jolla Playhouse, 65

GAY AND LESBIAN THEATRE

HISPANIC/LATIN-AMERICAN THEATRE

MULTICULTURAL THEATRE

MULTIMEDIA

MUSICAL THEATRE

NATIVE AMERICAN THEATRE

ONE-ACTS AND SHORT PLAYS

PERFORMANCE ART
(see also Experimental Theatre)

RELIGIOUS/SPIRITUAL THEATRE

SOLO PERFORMANCE

STUDENT/COLLEGE SUBMISSIONS

TRANSLATION

WOMEN'S THEATRE

YOUNG PLAYWRIGHTS PROGRAMS

BOOK INDEX

Remember the two alphabetizing principles used throughout the book: First, entries beginning with a person's name are alphabetized by the first name rather than the surname. However, you can find these entries indexed by both names. Hence you will find the Robert J. Pickering Award for Excellence under R and P. Second, we alphabetize this book word-by-word, e.g., "A. D. Players" would be listed before "Academy Theatre." Regardless of which way "theatre" is spelled in an organization's title, it is alphabetized as if it were spelled "re," not "er."

CIES, 235
Cincinnati Playhouse in the Park, 31, 151
Cintas Fellowships, 234
City "In Sight", 211
City Theatre Company, 32
Citysearch, 342
Clarence Brown Theatre Company, 32
Clark Publications, I. E., 180
Classic Stage Company, 33
Clauder Competition for Excellence in Playwriting, 136
Cleveland Play House, The, 33, 205
Cleveland Play House Playwrights' Unit, 40
Cleveland Public Theatre, 33
Coconut Grove Playhouse, 34
COLAB New Play Program, 103
Coldwater Community Theater, 161
Collaborative Research, 245
Collages & Bricolages, 176
Colonial Players, Inc, 135
Colony Studio Theatre, The, 34
Colony Theatre Company, The, 34
Colorado Council on the Arts, 259
Colorado Shakespeare Festival, 219
Columbia College Chicago Theater/Music Center, 167
Columbia Entertainment Company Children's Theatre School, 144
Columbus Screenplay Discovery Awards, 136
Columbus Society, Christopher, 136
Commissioning Music/USA, 308
Commonweal New Play Workshop, 34
Commonweal Theatre Company, 34
Commonwealth Council For Arts And Culture (Northern Mariana Islands), 263
Company of Fools, 35
Coney Island, USA, 35
Confrontation, 176

Conneticut Commission on the Arts, 259
Contemporary American Theater Festival, 35
Contemporary Arts Center, 193
Contemporary Drama Service, 177
Contemporary Theatre, A, 5
Conway Greene Publishing Company, 335
Copyright Office, 338
Cornerstone Dramaturgy and Development Project, 194
Cornerstone Theater Company, 36
Coronet Theatre, 209
Corporation for Public Broadcasting, 297
Coterie Theatre, The, 36
Council for International Exchange of Scholars (CIES), 235
Court Theatre, 36
CPB, 297
Cross Cultural Institute of Theater Art Studies (C.C.I.T.A.S), 65
Crossroads Theatre Company, 37
CSC, 33
CTFA (The Children's Theatre Founcation of America), 297
Cultured Writer, 341
Culturefinder.com, 343
Cumberland County Playhouse, 37
Cunningham Prize for Playwriting, The, 136
Curtis Associates, Harden, 225
C.W. Post College of Long Island University, 176

D

Dallas Children's Theater, 37
Dallas Theater Center, 38
Danish American National Cultural Exchange, 312
David Henry Hwang Writers Institute, 194

Klein Playwriting Award, Marc A., 152

KMC A Brief Guide to Internet Resources in Theatre and Performance Studies, 344

Kolovakos Award, The Gregory, 142

Kopaloff Company, The, 226

Kumu Kahua Theatre, 64, 149

Kumu Kahua Theatre/UHM Department of Theatre & Dance Playwriting Contest, 149

L

L.A. Black Playwrights, 199

L.A. Theatre Works, 64

L. Arnold Weissberger Award, 150

La Jolla Playhouse, 65

La MaMa Experimental Theater Club, 65

La MaMa Umbria, 65

La Nueva Ola, 302

la telaraña, 305

Lamb's Players Theatre, 66

Lamia Ink!, 181

Lamia Ink! International One-Page Play Competition, 150

Landon Translation Award, Harold Morton, 142

Lantz Agency, 226

Lark Theatre Company, The, 211

Larry L. King Outstanding Texas Playwright Award, 143

Latina Playwrights Festival, 327

Latino Playwrights' Division, 214

Latino Theatre Initiative (LTI), 201

League of Chicago Theatres/League of Chicago Theatres Foundation, 306

League of Professional Theatre Women/New York, 306

Ledig House International Writers' Colony, 275

Lee Reynolds Award, 306

Lehman Engel Musical Theatre Workshop, The, 200

Leighton Studios for Independent Residencies, 276

Lewis Galantiere Literary Translation Prize, 131

Library of Congress, 338, 346

Lifeline Theatre, 66

Lillenas Drama Resources, 181

Lincoln Center Theater, 66

Literary Managers and Dramaturgs of the Americas (LMDA), 307

Literary Market Place 2000, 335

Little Theatre of Alexandria, 150

Little Theatre of Alexandria National One-Act Playwriting Competition, The, 150

Littleway's Juneteenth Jamboree of New Plays, Lorna, 200

Live Bait Theatrical Company, 67

LMDA (Literary Managers and Dramaturgs of the Americas), 307

LMDA Review, 307

LMDA Script Exchange, 307

LMP, 335

Locke Elliott Exchange, Sumner, 312

Lois and Richard Rosenthal New Play Prize, 151

Long Beach Playhouse, 67

Long Island University, 275

Long Play Contest, 137

Long Wharf Theatre, 68

Lorna Littleway's Juneteenth Jamboree of New Plays, 200

Lorraine Hansberry Playwriting Award, The, 148

Los Angeles Designers' Theatre Commissions, 151

Los Angeles Theatre Center, 75

Louisiana Division of the Arts, 261

Love Creek Annual Short Play Festival, 151

Love Creek Productions, 151, 206

About Theatre Communications Group

Theatre Communications Group (TCG), the national organization for the American theatre, offers a wide array of services in line with our mission: to strengthen, nurture and promote the not-for-profit American theatre. Artistic Programs supports theatres and theatre artists by awarding $6.1 million in grants annually, and offers career development programs for artists. Management Programs provides professional development opportunities for theatre leaders through workshops, conferences, forums and publications, as well as industry research on the finances and practices of the American not-for-profit theatre. Advocacy, conducted in conjunction with the dance, symphony, opera and museum fields, includes guiding lobbying efforts and providing theatres with timely alerts about legislative developments. The country's leading independent press specializing in dramatic literature, TCG's Publications publishes *American Theatre* magazine, the *ArtSEARCH* employment bulletin, plays, translations and theatre-reference books. Through these programs, TCG seeks to increase the organizational efficiency of our member theatres, cultivate and celebrate the artistic talent and achievements of the field, and promote a larger public understanding of and appreciation for the theatre field. TCG serves over 360 member theatres and 17,000 individual members.

THEATRE COMMUNICATIONS GROUP

Ben Cameron, *Executive Director*

2000–2001 BOARD OF DIRECTORS

Kent Thompson, *President*
Alabama Shakespeare Festival

David Henry Hwang, *Vice President*
Playwright

Judith O. Rubin, *Vice President*
Playwrights Horizons

Paula Tomei, *Treasurer*
South Coast Repertory

Abel López, *Secretary*
GALA Hispanic Theatre

Gary Anderson
Plowshares Theatre Company

Jessica L. Andrews
Arizona Theatre Company

Judson Bemis, Jr.
Outsell, LLC

Kathleen Chalfant
Actor

Dudley Cocke
Roadside Theater

Chris Coleman
Portland Center Stage

Walter Dallas
Freedom Repertory Theatre

Gordon Davidson
Mark Taper Forum

Peter Donnelly
Corporate Council for the Arts

Oskar Eustis
Trinity Repertory Company

Michael Fields
Dell'Arte Players Company

Marian A. Godfrey
The Pew Charitable Trusts

Charles F. (OyamO) Gordon
Playwright, University of Michigan

Todd Haimes
Roundabout Theatre Company

Linda Hartzell
Seattle Children's Theatre

David Hawkanson
Guthrie Theater

Michael Maso
Huntington Theatre Company

Susan Medak
Berkeley Repertory Theatre

Charles Newell
Court Theatre

Jo Allen Patton
Paul G. Allen Foundations

José Rivera
Playwright

Suzanne M. Sato
AT&T Foundation

Regina Taylor
Actor, Playwright

Susan Tsu
Costume Designer, University of Texas

Jack Viertel
Jujamcyn Theaters

TCG is proud to publish the following authors:

Jon Robin Baitz
Eric Bogosian
Peter Brook
Caryl Churchill
Pearl Cleage
Constance Congdon
Culture Clash
The Five Lesbian
   Brothers
Dario Fo
Richard Foreman
Athol Fugard

Peter Hall
Tina Howe
David Henry Hwang
Adrienne Kennedy
Harry Kondoleon
Tony Kushner
Craig Lucas
Charles Ludlam
Eduardo Machado
Emily Mann
Donald Margulies
Conor McPherson

Robert O'Hara
Suzan-Lori Parks
José Rivera
Nicky Silver
Stephen Sondheim
Alfred Uhry
Paula Vogel
Naomi Wallace
Thornton Wilder
George C. Wolfe

To order books, visit our Web site: http://www.tcg.org
Catalog available upon request

TCG INDIVIDUAL MEMBERSHIP

As a *Sourcebook* user, you're invited to become an Individual Member of **Theatre Communications Group** — the national organization for the American theatre and the publisher of ***American Theatre*** magazine.

As an Individual Member of TCG, you'll get inside information about theatre performances around the country, as well as substantial discounts on tickets to performances and publications about the theatre. Plus, as the primary advocate for not-for-profit professional theatre in America, TCG will ensure that your voice is heard in Washington. We invite you to join us today and receive all of TCG's benefits!

MEMBERS RECEIVE A FREE SUBSCRIPTION TO *AMERICAN THEATRE* AND THESE SPECIAL BENEFITS

- A FREE subscription to *American Theatre*—10 issues...5 complete playscripts... artist profiles...in-depth coverage of contemporary, classical and avant-garde performances...3 special issues—including *Season Preview* (October), *Summer Festival Preview* (May) and *Theatre Training* (January).
- Discounts on tickets to performances at more than 160 participating theatres nationwide.
- 15% discount on resource materials including *Theatre Directory, ArtSEARCH, Stage Writers Handbook, Stage Directors Handbook* and *Dramatists Sourcebook*— all musts for the theatre professional or the serious theatergoer.
- A FREE catalog of TCG publications.
- 10% discount on all books from TCG and other select theatre publishers.
- Your personalized Individual Membership card.
- Access to members-only areas of the TCG Web site.
- Opportunity to apply for a no fee TCG Credit Card.
- Special discounts for Hertz Rent-A-Car, Airborne Express and Hotel Reservations Network.

JOIN NOW AND SAVE

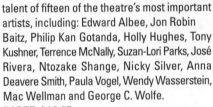
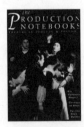

Take Advantage NOW and SAVE!
Become a **TCG INDIVIDUAL MEMBER** and
Receive Extraordinary Benefits

☐ **YES**, I would like a one-year Individual Membership to TCG, which includes a subscription to *American Theatre.*
- ☐ Individual Membership ~~$35.00~~ $28.00
- ☐ Student Membership (enclose copy of ID) $20.00

☐ I prefer a two-year membership.
- ☐ Individual Membership ~~$70.00~~ $50.00

Not only would I like to become a member,
but I would like to take advantage of my discounts right now!
(Discount prices are only good if you are a member. If you are not a member, please use the full price for your order.)

☐ Please begin my one-year subscription to *ArtSEARCH.*
Individual ☐ with E-mail ~~$64.00~~ $54.40 ☐ without E-mail ~~$54.00~~ $45.90
Institutional ☐ with E-mail ~~$90.00~~ $76.50 ☐ without E-mail ~~$75.00~~ $63.75

☐ **TOTAL ORDER** _____

To order, you may: Send this form to: TCG Order Dept., 355 Lexington Ave., NY, NY 10017-6603 or Call (212) 697-5230, ext. 260; Fax (212) 983-4847; or send E-mail to: custserv@tcg.org; or visit our Web site at www.tcg.org. Credit card orders: please include your billing address if it is different than your mailing address.

☐ Check is enclosed. ☐ Please charge my credit card: ☐ VISA ☐ MC ☐ AMEX

NAME _____

OCCUPATION/DATE _____

ADDRESS _____

CITY _____ STATE _____ ZIP _____

*PHONE/FAX/E-MAIL _____

CARD# _____ EXP. DATE _____

SIGNATURE _____

* All orders must have telephone number

For Individual Membership outside the U.S., please add $12 per year (U.S. currency only, drawn from a U.S. bank).
Allow 6-8 weeks from receipt of order.

[Mkt. code: DDSB0